How Fathers Care for the Next Generation

How Fathers Care for the Next Generation

A Four-Decade Study

John R. Snarey

Harvard University Press
Cambridge, Massachusetts
London, England
1993

Copyright © 1993 by the President and Fellows of Harvard College
Printed in the United States of America
10 9 8 7 6 5 4 3 2 1

Library of Congress Cataloging-in-Publication Data

Snarey, John R., 1948–
    How fathers care for the next generation : a four-decade study / John Snarey.
      p.   cm.
    Includes bibliographical references and index.
    ISBN 0-674-40940-X (alk. paper)
    1. Fathers—United States—Longitudinal studies. 2. Father and child—United
States—Longitudinal studies. 3. First-born children—United States—Longitudinal
studies. I. Title.
HQ756.S547 1993
306.874'2—dc20   92-23597
                 CIP

To Carol, Johnny, and Elizabeth, for intellectual inspiration, emotional comic relief, and acts of charity which made this book possible

> In youth you find out what you *care to do* and who you *care to be*—even in changing roles. In young adulthood you learn whom you *care to be with*—at work and in private life, not only exchanging intimacies, but sharing intimacy. In adulthood, however, you learn to know what and whom you can *take care of*.
>
> Erik H. Erikson
> *Dimensions of a New Identity*

Acknowledgments

I take this welcome opportunity to thank several people who have contributed to the completion of this book. Sheldon (1896–1980) and Eleanor (1898–1972) Glueck of the Harvard Law School began the longitudinal study of the men presented here over four decades ago, when the fathers were still boys. The Gluecks also supervised the reinterviewing of the men during their early adulthood years. George E. Vaillant of the Harvard University Health Services then gave the study new life by initiating and supervising the reinterviewing of the men at midlife; he also guided my postdoctoral research training in the study of adult development. The book would not have been possible without Vaillant's exemplary dedication to longitudinal research. The Gluecks, Vaillant, and myself are all, in turn, indebted to the immense loyalty of the men who have given of themselves to the study for over four decades.

The psychosocial and ethical foundations of the study are located in the theoretical work of Erik H. Erikson, particularly his sociomoral conception of generative care as the hallmark of adult maturity. The original proposal for the present investigation was enriched through discussions with Joseph H. Pleck, an unusually generative colleague, who also advanced the preparation of Chapter 4. Anthony Maier collaborated in the preparation of Chapter 6, and Carol Snarey assisted with the preparation of Chapter 10. Chapter 8, revised with the assistance of Linda Son, is a substantially modified and updated report of a study which was originally published as J. Snarey, L. Son, V. Kuehne, S. Hauser, and G. E. Vaillant, "The Role of Parenting in Men's Psychosocial Development," *Developmental Psychology*, 23(4).

Expert research assistance was provided by Eva Milofsky, Anthony Maier, Valerie Kuehne, Kurt Keljo, Jennifer Kogos, and especially Linda Son and Merry Porter. Several colleagues provided helpful comments and suggestions on drafts of various chapters. I wish to thank Robert Agnew, Nancy Ammerman, Jay Belsky, Marvin Berkowitz, Henry Biller, Pamela Del Couture, Eugene Emory, George Engelhard, Harriet Heath, Thomas Lickona, Tracy MacNab, Norma Radin, Harriet F. Simons, Stephen J. Thoma, Steve Tipton, Terry Tivnan, and Philip Zodhiates. In addition, several students who provided helpful comments deserve special mention: Jerry Belloit, Ashley Bryant, Susan L. Curry, Julie Earles, Leanne Embry, Amy Fleece, Amiee Handfinger, Charles Kendall, Jennifer Kogos, Tracy Nunley, and Gary Whetstone. Skillful editorial assistance was provided by Karen DeNicola, Susan Latimer, and especially Carol Snarey and Anita Safran. Finally, I must thank Angela von der Lippe, Editor for the Behavioral Sciences at Harvard University Press, for encouraging this book while it was still in gestation.

The research was supported in part by a research award from the National Institute of Mental Health and a faculty grant from Northwestern University. Completion of the manuscript was advanced by Emory University's sabbatical program.

Contents

Tables

Foreword

George E. Vaillant

Today, even the most highly motivated and best intentioned fathers often feel unsure of how to do their jobs, perhaps in part because their own fathers were not highly involved in rearing their children. Nevertheless, few men today expect their wives to do all of the work of parenting. *How Fathers Care for the Next Generation* is the story of these contemporary fathers.

Snarey's research structure for his book provides a model of how the great longitudinal studies of the past should be used and harvested by the intellectual grandsons and granddaughters of the progenitors. In the late 1930s, Sheldon and Eleanor Glueck of the Harvard Law School began what started out as a cross-sectional study of 500 delinquent boys and 500 comparison nondelinquent boys. Trained as she was in clinical social work, Eleanor Glueck made sure that the life histories of the parents and, within limits, those of the grandparents were included. The Gluecks followed their subjects for twenty-five years—a full generation. Over these years, at different points in time, social workers, internists, criminologists, psychoanalysts, and social psychologists all recorded their contrasting views of the inner-city youth selected by the Gluecks.

Over the same quarter of a century the Gluecks grew older and retired. I was lucky enough to become their intellectual child and heir. As director of the Study of Adult Development, I, in turn, have followed these men (the original comparison subjects) for a second generation. During this time the Gluecks' men continued to parent their children, and, more recently, their children have become parents. In 1982, John Snarey, young enough to have been the Gluecks' grandson, joined the Study. Snarey has capitalized on the fact that the Gluecks' subjects, as boys, had discussed their parents and, as parents, have discussed their children. And since the Gluecks' subjects' children have grown up, Snarey has listened to these daughters and sons talking about their fathers. By including the grown children of the adolescents studied by the Gluecks, he has added a fourth generation to the Study. His subjects also tell him of their thoughts about the fifth generation. Thus the reader is treated to an extraordinary continuum of children and fathers.

Having studied closely the literature on social-psychological influences on development, Snarey has cast his analysis firmly in Eriksonian terms. Erik Erikson's "ethical rule of adulthood is to do to others what will help them, even as it helps you to grow." But Erikson provides no data to support his position. In bringing to bear a modern battery of empirical tests upon Erikson's optimistic view of adult development, Snarey provides evidence that the responsive participation of fathers in their children's lives, both when they were young and when they were adolescents, not only had a significant impact on these children's lives, but also was of significant influence on the fathers. In other words, generativity is a two-way street. As one son told Snarey, "I believe a father should really show his love to his children a lot. To be around and loving, I think, would be the most important thing. Because I think it gives them a feeling of wanting to find it in themselves, to pass it on to the next generation. You know, to emulate that with their own children, to be loving and thoughtful and to raise them well, to be with them when they need it." Snarey goes on to document that fathers who participate more in childrearing are also more likely to become societally generative at midlife. Serious social scientists will appreciate Snarey's methodological care to see that illustrative anecdote is always balanced with quantitative data, that rich case studies counterbalance rigorous analytic chapters. In these ways, *How Fathers Care* is the finest empirical test of Erikson's theories in existence.

Finally, Snarey provides a message of inspiration to young fathers. For his evidence suggests that when children themselves become parents, they do not usually replicate the negative aspects of childrearing practices of their fathers. Instead, it is the good that fathers do that most often lives on. The last sentences in this book are perhaps the sentences with which readers should also begin. "Good fathering, it seems, really does matter. It matters over a long time, over a lifetime, and even over generations."

The same can be said for the Gluecks' original parenting of the longitudinal study on which this book is based. Were they still alive, I am sure that they would have felt proud of their intellectual grandson's book and its exceptional contribution to understanding how fathers care for the next generation. I am.

1

Generations and Generativity

This book is about good fathers. By good, I mean "generative" fathers: men who contribute to and renew the ongoing cycle of the generations through the *care* they provide as birth fathers (biological generativity), childrearing fathers (parental generativity), and cultural fathers (societal generativity). It is also about the family members with whom fathers' lives are complexly nested: fathers' own fathers and mothers, their wives, embryos and infants, daughters and sons. Most centrally, this book aims to understand fathers' childrearing or parental generativity: the ways good fathers constructively care for their daughters and sons in childhood and adolescence and promote their children's social-emotional, intellectual-academic, and physical-athletic development.

In contrast with earlier neglect, research and interest in the topic of fatherhood are now thriving. In the new studies the father appears as a central and primary caregiver rather than as an inconsequential figure in childrearing or a background variable in research. This reevaluation, however, makes the shortcomings of the existing literature all the more conspicuous. Researchers have not had the opportunity to conduct *longitudinal* studies of the precursors of fathers' behavior toward their children, *and* the subsequent consequences of this behavior for the fathers' own lives *and* for their children's adulthood outcomes. Researchers have also found it difficult to integrate the findings from the various studies because of the absence of a unifying theoretical perspective. In contrast, this book is able to address all of these issues because it is based on a distinctive data set that extends over four decades and three generations. All segments of the study are unified by their common grounding in Erik H. Erikson's lifespan model of psychosocial development.

True to its Eriksonian heritage, this book is inherently interdisciplinary, addressing issues of ongoing concern to professionals and students in the fields of human development, family studies, and the helping professions. Through the use of measures and memories—studies and stories—this investigation begins in the present and moves *back in time* through four decades in the lives of over 200 fathers. First, I explore how fathers' childrearing participation helps to predict differences in their own *middle adulthood* life outcomes. These include their midlife work success, marital success, and their demonstrated ability to care for the success and succession of the generations beyond the family sphere. Second, I investigate the contribution of fathers' childrearing support to the subsequent *early adulthood* educational and occupational success of the children. Third, I inquire whether some fathers' own *early adulthood* experience of coping with a specific type of threat to biological generativity—infertility—contributes to the fathers' later ability to care for the succession of the generations within as well as beyond the family sphere. Fourth, I search out the precursors—the initial building blocks—of the fathers' parental generativity in their own *boyhood* families of origin, as well as in their early adulthood families of procreation. To what extent do boyhood and adulthood experiences predict the fathers' involvement in rearing their children? Finally, I will reflect on the wisdom these generative lives offer to men who want to be good (not perfect) fathers today.

The Generations Studied: Fathers and Children of the Baby Boom

This investigation includes 240 fathers who are part of a four-decade longitudinal study that was begun in the 1940s in Boston. The sample was first interviewed under the direction of Sheldon and Eleanor Glueck of the Harvard Law School; the subjects served as a control group of boys for a second group of delinquent (but otherwise similar) boys in their larger study. All of the subjects were originally born into lower- and working-class families, as defined by Hollingshead's (1959, 1975) Index of Social Status. In the first phase the Gluecks conducted interviews with the boys (average age 14), as well as with the boys' parents and teachers. In the second and third phases of the study, the boys (but not their parents) were reinterviewed when they were young adults (age 25 and again at age 31). During a fourth phase of the study, conducted under the direction of George E. Vaillant at the Harvard University Health Services, the men in the control group (the fathers in this study) were again interviewed at midlife (average age 47). Subsequently, the men have completed periodic questionnaires.

The study's sample and longitudinal procedure will be described in more detail in Chapter 2. While each father's "individual life has its longitudinal logic," however, "all lives lived interdependently within a given historical period share a kind of historical logic" (Erikson, 1964, p. 207). To understand the historical events that had a unique impact upon the lives of these fathers and their offspring, it is important to first identify and describe the birth cohorts to which these fathers and their children belong. In this discussion, as well as throughout the book, the terms "fathers" and "study fathers" will be reserved for the 240 actual Glueck subjects who originally entered the investigation as boys. All other family titles will be used *from the point of view of these fathers*: "sons" or "daughters" will refer to the offspring of the subjects; "wives" to the spouses of the subjects; and "their own mothers" or "their own fathers" to the parents of the original subjects.

The Fathers and the Silent Generation

The study's 240 men were born during the 1920s and 1930s. Most belong to a cohort of North Americans that a number of writers have called the "silent generation" because, as a cohort, they seemed remarkably unremarkable—discreet, conforming, cautious, conventional, silent (see Strauss & Howe, 1991). The silent generation is generally understood to include persons born between 1925 and 1942. It thus includes the average and most common year of birth of the study fathers, 1929—the year after Herbert Hoover was elected President of the United States, the year that the stock market crashed, and the year before the last Allied troops departed from the Rhineland, leaving Germany's Nazi Party to grow in strength.

The fathers' families of origin were ethnically diverse, although the sample unfortunately did not include African-Americans. They all grew up in the core neighborhoods of Boston and attended the local public schools. Poverty characterized most (79%) of their boyhood homes (Glueck & Glueck, 1968). During the Great Depression of the 1930s, when they were children, approximately 33% of the entire nation's work force was unemployed. From 1929 to 1933, the average yearly income for American families dropped by nearly 40% (Elder, 1974, pp. 19–20). Most of the men in the study vividly recall observing their parents' struggle to provide for the family's economic survival. Their own fathers often endured long work hours, and they as children silently endured their fathers' long absences. As Gordon, one of the Glueck subjects, recalls, "My dad always worked so hard. There were three boys, and those were tough days, tough days, for him. Right after the Depression, times were tough for everybody." Maxwell, another one of the study fathers, also described his own father as "a hard-working man." He continued, "I can't ever remember him being sick or anything until before he passed away. He worked very hard, and he was never around; he'd leave early in the morning, come back in the evening, and then work late at night preparing for the next day . . . He had a tough life. "

As these children grew older, their own economic contributions went into the pool necessary to maintain the household. Maxwell explained that his father "peddled fruit and candy" to make a living. "He used a huge laundry basket with a big handle on it, and he used to stuff his fruits and candies and everything in there and put it on his shoulder and carry it." Maxwell started "working" by helping his father carry his wares; "then, when I was 12 or 13 years old, I got another job [after school] delivering papers at a downtown office building, which was right around the corner from where my father peddled fruit and candy. So I had my paper route and was also helping my father carry stuff at the same time." Maxwell, typical of most of the fathers as boys, turned his earnings over to his parents "so we could eat."

The economic realities also limited their educational opportunities and subsequent life chances. Maxwell managed to graduate from high school, for example, but Gordon did not. As he recalls, "I think [my father] was kind of disappointed that I quit high school." The Gluecks (1968) observed that more than half of the boys in the comparison sample quit school, usually to help their families. Their parents struggled to balance their need to have their children start earning money, and their desire to promote their children's future life opportunities. Approximately 38% of the 240 study fathers graduated from high school, as had approximately 38% of all youth before World War II (see Jones, 1980; Bureau of the Census, Aug., 1984). The most common class year among the high school graduates was 1947—the year after Boston lost to St. Louis in the seventh game of the World Series, the same year that Jackie Robinson became the first African-American to be signed as a major league baseball player, and the year before Harry Truman was elected President of the United States.

As they came to the end of their teenage years, three-quarters of the subjects could also say along with Gordon, "then I went into the service." Most had missed World War II (1939–1945) and even fewer ever "saw action" in the war. Yet several were still involved in other overseas military assignments—the postwar occupation of West Germany and Japan, the Greek conflict (1947), and the Korean War (1950–1953).

The economic recovery begun during World War II continued after the war, but the members of the silent generation did not usually share in these benefits as full equals with the somewhat older GI war veterans. As Harry, one of the study fathers, explained, he and his peers often were left to stand by unobtrusively:

> Our generation was kind of lost in the shuffle because when we were born . . . we were just coming out of the Depression, and then along came the war, and we were kind of shoved aside for that. With the guys coming home after the war, there was again nothing for us. Everybody was geared toward the veterans for any jobs. They would get up to $9.20 an hour, and we would get $20.00 a week as a stipend for unemployment. There were no jobs to be had, and there was no money around for encouragement, and everybody missed the younger generation. So, I felt that we were lost. We were shuffled

They were quietly ignored, but, nevertheless, they were resilient. This "in between" generation eventually took great advantage of the rising postwar economy, which particularly benefited their adulthood families of procreation. According to Strauss and Howe (1991), from age 20 to 40, households of this cohort showed the steepest rise in real per capita income and per household wealth. Among the study fathers, for instance, one quarter became solid members of the middle class and three quarters were able to purchase their own homes. As Gordon commented on his upward occupational mobility, "I had dropped out of school, but I still accomplished these things." This does not mean that the study fathers did not go through an economic struggle—

Gordon and most of the other men did—but even when it was necessary for the men to work at several jobs to provide for their families,
jobs were at least available.

Members of the silent generation married at younger ages than did
their recent predecessors. The average age of marriage among both
the study fathers, as well as in the general population of men at that
time, was 23 years. Their wives were even younger, of course, with
an average age of 20 at the time of marriage (Strauss & Howe,
1991, p. 286). Their generation also had more children than other
generations in this century. Of course, from day one of fatherhood,
the men's participation in childcare was circumscribed by the expectations of the larger society. Gordon vividly recalls the day he became
a father:

> Oh, I felt great! Oh, God, yeah! Of course, I wasn't in the room when
> he was born, not in those days, but I was pretty proud! I was working
> on a house out in Wellesley, we were sand-blasting it, and the boss
> came around, and he said, "Gordy, Bernice went to the hospital, you
> got a baby son!" I says, "What! I got to get out of here, I got to go
> home!" He says, "No, no, no, no! You got to work, you need the money!"
> You know, because he wouldn't pay me if I went home. So we finished
> cleaning up, and he took me home.
>
> I was in a hurry so I just washed my hands real quick like and then
> my wife's uncle, who had a car, took me over to the hospital. Before I
> went into the hospital, I turned around and looked, and my arms from
> here up were all black—it looked like I had a pair of white gloves on.
> He says, "Here, put on my jacket before they have you arrested." But
> I just wanted to get into the hospital and see how my wife was and see
> my newborn baby.
>
> When I first saw him, he was real pinkish-like, and had a lot of black
> hair, and it looked like his forehead was kind of flat (laughs). So I went
> in and my wife asks, "Did you see the baby?" I say, "Yeah." She says
> "He's beautiful, huh?" I say, "Yeah . . . but how come he looks pink and
> his head is flat?" So she's all panicky and everything. She couldn't wait
> for the nurse, so I left to get the nurse to get the baby, and the nurse
> goes, "Oh, you fool, that's how babies look."

His joy was bounded by some thorny facts about becoming a father
in the 1950s: Gordon's employer expected that he would not leave
work to join his wife and newborn son until it was convenient for the
employer; their hospital did not permit him or any fathers to be in

the delivery room, and the nurse poked fun at his lack of knowledge about babies. Such scenarios were repeated many thousands of times as Gordon's silent-generation peers, along with the slightly older World War II veterans, together produced the "baby boom."

The Fathers' Children and the Baby Boom Generation

Virtually all of the fathers' children included in this study (99%) are members of the North American baby boom generation, which is generally understood to include persons born between 1946 and 1964 (Jones, 1980; Russell, 1987). The study fathers' offspring tend to be the middle members of the cohort; over 80% of the study's 240 children were born during the 1950s. Their average and most common year of birth was 1954—the year after Eisenhower was inaugurated as President of the United States, the same year that Vietnamese Communists occupied Hanoi, and the year before Rosa Parks refused to give up her seat near the front of a bus to a white passenger in Montgomery, Alabama. As was true for their parents, their individual life histories and the history of their cohort are intricately intertwined.

Born into the placid, prosperous 1950s, these children lived in a country at peace, although the Cold War and the threat of nuclear annihilation were definite anxiety-producing undercurrents. Many of these children experienced material advantages that were literally remarkable compared with their parents' economic experiences. The study fathers, in fact, often took great pleasure in giving their children what they never had themselves as boys. Maxwell always tried to make sure that Cindy, his daughter, "never wanted for nothing." During early childhood, he made sure she had "all the toys," during later childhood he made sure she had a new "two-wheeler bike," and during adolescence, "as soon as she got her license, she had a car right away." Cindy also recalled that, even after she had graduated from college, he liked to slip some money unobtrusively into her hand: "I'd be so touched, because that was the way he was saying 'I love you, and I think you're doing a good job, but here's a little help.'" Similarly, Gordon commented about his son, Gordon Jr., "I bought him things that I never had when I was a kid, growing up . . . When new things would come out, we'd always make sure they had them." Of course, the study fathers were not consistently well off throughout their childrearing years. Labor strikes aimed at securing more adequate long-term contracts sometimes meant that the men and their children experienced short-term but unforgettable poverty. Seasonal variations were also a part of the breadwinning experience for many of the men. Gordon, who worked in a construction trade, was often out of work during part of the winter. He recalls that, at Christmas time, "I'd be wondering where I'm going to get money for gifts. Every year it was like, 'What are we going to do?' My kids were afraid to look out the window and say, 'Yippie! It's snowing out!' because that meant I couldn't work!"

Despite seasonal and contract-negotiation cycles, the generally strong economy made it possible for many of the study fathers' children to make important educational advances relative to their parents. Among the new generation, 91% graduated from high school (compared to 38% of the Glueck subjects, and approximately 85% among the baby boom cohort in general) (Glueck & Glueck, 1968; Longman, 1985, p. 79). The most common year of high school graduation among the study fathers' children was 1973—the year after the landslide victory of Richard Nixon over George McGovern in the Presidential election, the same year that the Vietnam War cease-fire agreement was signed (although fighting continued), and the year before Nixon resigned as a result of the Watergate scandal. Having witnessed the beginning of the end of a despised war and the exile of a despised president, they had great expectations for their future beyond high school.

More of the children of the Glueck subjects went to college than joined the military. Almost half attended college for at least one year, but half of these had their educational dreams diverted, often by the false promises of vocationalized community colleges which they attended (cf. Brint & Karabel, 1989). Almost a quarter of the study fathers' children actually graduated from college, and about one out of every five of these graduates went on to receive master's degrees. These figures are similar for the whole of the baby boom cohort, although the level of education is even higher among males born between 1947 and 1951 who had the added incentive of avoiding the draft during the Vietnam War (Bureau of Census, Aug., 1984). The children's success is again striking when contrasted with their parents' educational experiences.

The study fathers, like other baby boom parents, were usually very supportive and proud of their children's educational achievements.

For instance, Gordon Jr.'s father "was very excited" because his son "was the first person in the family to get a high school diploma" and attend college. Gordon Sr. also viewed his son's achievements from a multigenerational family perspective: "He has accomplished a tremendous amount. Oh, my father would have been so proud of him." Maxwell's daughter, Cindy, also went to college. She completed her bachelor's degree and then earned a master's degree. She recalls that her father felt quite honored when she graduated from college: "He said, 'You're the first one in my family to graduate from college.' That made me feel real special. I was touched by that."

As this cohort came of age during the 1960s and 1970s, however, many also came to question the values and actions of their parents' generation (for example, the emphasis on acquiring material goods, the development of a huge defense industry, rigid conformity to society's values, and particularly the call to fight in Vietnam). This generation's countercultural orientation, as Tipton's (1982) analysis has shown, emphasized different ethical principles: (a) nonviolence and (b) sexual freedom ("make love not war"), (c) expressive autonomy ("do your own thing"), (d) spiritual awareness (LSD, the "Jesus movement"), (e) self-knowledge ("get in touch with yourself"), (f) respect for the integrity of the situation ("go with the flow"), and (g) tolerance for others ("different strokes for different folks"). This compact summary does not capture the detailed elegance of Tipton's description, but it is sufficient to illustrate his (1982) thesis that the baby boom cohort's countercultural ethic replaced traditional ideals of virtue and duty with "impulsivity" and "self-expression" as the essential "motives of human action" (pp. 15–16).

Erik Erikson (1967), like Tipton, has described the youth of the 1960s as characterized by a "skepticism of all authority," including "paternal" authority, and by "a cast of mind which is essentially anti-institutional" (p. 861). Particularly with regard to the anti-establishment cast of mind, Erikson also distinguished overlapping subgroups. He suggested that a majority of the youth seemed to actually be morally conventional—"all too needy for, trusting in, and conforming to present institutions, organizations, parties, [and] industrial complexes," while a second contrasting minority of ideological youth seemed "to plead with existing institutions for permission to rebel—just as in private they often seem to plead with their parents to love them doubly for rejecting them" (p. 861). Especially within the minority, but to some degree also within the majority, Erikson also identified a third unusually mature subgroup of youth who were "deeply interested in and responsive to a more concerted critique of institutions from a newer and more adequate ethical point of view" (p. 862).

The Glueck men's children were influenced by the countercultural values of the 1960s, but also reflect the diversity described by Erikson. This can be seen, for instance, in the contrasting experiences of the children of Gordon, Maxwell, and Bart.

Gordon Jr. explained that he became "a little more trouble" to his parents when he was in high school. Gordon Sr. felt that this was hardly surprising because, in his words, "the 60s were the teenage years for him." Gordon Jr. also referred to the historical setting when he reviewed the difficulties between himself and his father:

> I think my father was more involved with us than most fathers just because he got a lot of enjoyment out of seeing us having fun. It was his way of relaxing. He was always ready to have a good time with his kids . . . .
>
> Still, we had a separation period, in my later teens, during the late 60s. I was going through a thing where I had long hair, and I was taking drugs. We never really were distant, but there was a time when we didn't see eye to eye.
>
> I remember signing up for the military, because my best friend was joining the Navy. Dad did not want to see me go, of course; not in those years. This was the Vietnam era, things were really getting hot. I went down to the recruiting station . . . and enlisted for two years' active duty in the Navy, which meant a year and a half in Vietnam and six months' training . . . . I took the written exam, and I scored at the top of my class. (But that doesn't say much, because I think half the other kids flunked it on purpose. This was the age of the "draft dodgers" and whatnot.) I remember being in line, and I was all excited, going up to the medical doctors for the examination. The kid standing in front of me had really long hair; he said, "What are you so excited about?" I said, "Well, I'm excited. I want to join." He looked at me, "You want to join? What are you, nuts?" He went on and on, but I was still all excited. I got up to the doctor, who was a lieutenant; he listened to my heart and says, "Do you know you have a heart problem?" . . . .
>
> Boy, was I bent out of shape. I mean, I had come right down to signing the papers, and we were probably maybe a month or so away

from going . . . . I look back at it now, and I see how many relatives and friends that I lost over there. I have come to think that it is positive that I didn't get in. But at the time I thought it was devastating. All my buddies were going, and I was still here. I really didn't know what I wanted to do. You know, 18 years old. I was mixed up.

Gordon's story, clearly that of a working-class 1960s kid, underscores that there are significant social class differences within the baby boom cohort. The subgroups Erikson describes, that is, can be seen intersecting with variations that go along with social class.

Cindy also mingled conformity and rebellion in her approach to the countercultural values of her cohort, but in a qualitatively different style. Her mother worked 3:00 to 11:00 and her father worked midnight to 7:00; this shift work meant that Maxwell was literally almost "always home" with his children when they were home and awake. During her childhood, therefore, Cindy experienced him as "always there." But during her high school years, Cindy came to view his presence as authoritarian and simplistic.

I remember getting into more fights with my dad . . . . If I saw something differently than he saw it, I was going to make sure that my opinion was heard. I definitely liked to express my opinion. So I would force it until he would end up feeling exasperated . . . Then I'd get the thing, "This is my house, and if I say the sky's black and it's really blue but I say it's black, then it's black to you." He realized that I wasn't going to think the way he thought. Teenagers tend to have their own ideas about things, and I was making it known to him. I think that was a shock to him. But, [even though I was becoming more independent], I still saw things as black and white as my father did.

Cindy's ability to maintain almost perfect straight-A grades in high school contributed to her self-confidence and growing independence from her parents, although, as she admits, she was just as dogmatic as her father. That didn't work for her in college.

I'd see people, and they were not necessarily believing or doing the things that I was taught were, you know, right. And yet, I saw a lot of good in these people, and I didn't really feel that I had a right to judge them. Yet, there was a part of me from my upbringing with religion that did . . . I learned that I want to let go and just let people be. People are basically good, even if they may think differently. Who am I to judge?

Cindy came to believe that gray, not black or white, was the most common color. Thus she did not become involved in student protests. Yet she used her encounters with the countercultural lifestyles and alternative religions that populated her campus to establish her own, more mellow value orientation.

Bart came from a family background similar to those of Gordon Jr. and Cindy, and his father, Harry, was also highly involved in childrearing. He also recalled how the historical events of his teenage years affected his father. "I think he felt very frustrated. He was very conservative, but it was the sixties—Vietnam, drugs. He worried a lot about these things. I think . . . he pictured himself being like Archie Bunker. Back then, when I was in high school, I think that was my perception of him sometimes too. We argued a lot." Bart, in college, developed a complex ethical appraisal of social institutions and acted on his critique. Yet he continued to see concerns within the context of his cohort's concerns: "I got some really poor grades. It was— I want to say the sixties, but actually it was the beginning of the seventies. So I spent a lot of time down in Washington; it didn't matter if there was an exam coming up or not. I guess I got caught up in the times, and my grades suffered." Bart later turned his grades around and went on to complete a graduate degree. He was unusual in his anti-war attitude, however; most working class youth who were the first in their family to go to college did not wish to risk their course grades and educational gains for the sake of solidarity with "rich kids" who were protesting the war.

Despite significant differences among Gordon Jr., Cindy, Bart, and other members of the baby boom generation, their cohort's collective values and ethical critiques had a massive influence on the society they inherited from their parents. Their generally anti-establishment energies fueled the anti-war movement, alternative religious movements, and the sexual revolution of the 1960s. The trend also led to other human rights movements that stressed, for example, the rights of women, children, and of racial and cultural minorities. Their influence was promoted by the baby boomers' sheer numbers—76 million of them. The number of people aged 14 to 24, in fact, increased 52% from 1960 to 1970 (Elder, 1975).

In contrast to their social reform successes, however, most of the middle members' personal occupational successes were slowed by the size of their cohort. Accustomed to experiencing the world as revolving around them, they felt adrift when they graduated from college into a stagnating economy and a flooded job market. Younger and middle members of the cohort have also experienced intense competition from earlier-born members for most resources. In contrast to the study fathers' smaller cohort, which began in poverty and entered adulthood at a time when the economy was expanding, their offspring enjoyed relative affluence in childhood but came of age at a time when the country's economy no longer could sustain the same standard of living for so many people. In this regard, Gordon Jr., Cindy, and Bart have all been reasonably fortunate. Gordon Jr., today, owns an unusually prosperous business; Cindy is a specialized public school teacher; and Bart has found ways to combine his commitment to understanding and protecting the natural ecology with his need to support his own children. Like their fathers, however, they and other, younger members of the baby boom have had to contend with the fact that the older members of their cohort had "gotten there first," just as many of their fathers had to contend with the fact that the older GI war veterans often "got first dibs."

Many baby boomers, including many of the children of the fathers in this study, became first-time parents starting in the late 1970s through the 1980s, and their families have attempted to adapt to the unfavorable economic conditions of these years. From 1960 to 1988 the participation of married women with children in the labor force increased from 29% to 60% (Select Committee on Children, Youth, and Families, 1989; Hayghe, 1986). During this period, average household net income declined by 6% (Levy, 1987). Mortgage payments, for example, took 14% of the average homeowner's gross income in 1950, 21% in 1973, and 44% ten years later (Will, 1991; C. Russell, 1987). Two-earner baby-boom couples today are finding it difficult to maintain the same standard of living as that provided by a single breadwinner in the early 1960s. In a further attempt to adapt to rising economic constraints, these young couples are having smaller families. Gordon Jr. has two children under his roof, for instance, and Cindy, although she has many children under her care as a special educator, has no children by birth as yet. In this regard they, and the other children of the study fathers, are like their cohort peers; busy maintaining their careers and raising, on average, their 1.8 children in the 1990s (Barringer, 1991; Select Committee on Children, Youth, and Families, 1990).

Generativity:
The Theoretical Perspective

Erik H. Erikson, the first professor of human development at Harvard University, provides the central theoretical tools used in this study. Erikson's creative work also illustrates the core theoretical concept of this book, "psychosocial generativity," meaning an adult's caring activities which create or contribute to the life of the next generation. He views generativity as the primary developmental task of adulthood. Erikson's contention that personality development continues throughout the adult years is one of his most far-reaching contributions to the study of human development. In this study I will use Erikson's concept of generativity as a developmental aim or endpoint to illuminate the journey of fathers across the years from boyhood and early adulthood through late middle adulthood.

Overview of Erikson's Theory

Generativity versus stagnation is the seventh in a sequence of eight stages in Erikson's model of ego or personality development. Erikson (1964) uses the term "ego" to refer to the organizing structure of personality that has cognitive functions and establishes contact with the outside world, but he also uses it to recall the "age-old term which in the scholastics stood for the *unity* of body and soul, and in philosophy for the *permanency* of conscious experience." That is, a person's "feelings, thoughts and acts" are highly interrelated within each stage of development (p. 147; compare Maier, 1976). Erikson uses the term "stage" in a functional, metaphorical sense to refer to one of the eight psychosocial crises in lifetime ego development (Snarey, Kohlberg, & Noam, 1983). The term "crisis" is used simply to indicate that, at every stage, the person comes to "a turning point" or "a crucial period of increased vulnerability and heightened potential" (Erikson, 1976, p. 5). Each of these crises marks the intersection of cognitive, emotional, and psychomotor changes which together challenge the ego in its interaction with its socializing environment.

In this scheme the person experiences the psychosocial crises of (1) trust versus mistrust and (2) autonomy versus doubt, during the first two years of life; (3) initiative versus guilt, during the early childhood years; (4) industry versus inferiority, during later childhood; (5) identity versus identity confusion, during adolescence; and (6) intimacy versus isolation, during the early adult years. Following the psychosocial task of generativity versus stagnation (7), which a person generally faces during the middle adulthood years, is (8), the crisis of integrity versus despair, which is central during late adulthood. Each of the eight psychosocial crises, if successfully resolved, gives rise to a corresponding ego "strength": (1) hope, (2) will, (3) purpose, (4) competence, (5) fidelity, (6) love, (7) care, and (8) wisdom. These ego strengths (originally called "virtues" by Erikson) can be understood as stages of moral will or moral courage (E. Erikson & J. Erikson, 1981).

When Erikson brought together the eight stages of life and their corresponding virtues, he gave us the first psychosocial stage model of human development that encompassed the entire life span (Snarey, 1991). Each of the stages has a biological base in physical maturation and cognitive development and a sociological base in the role expectations of the society. Erikson portrays the synchronization of these structures as a kind of cogwheeling across the course of human development: "The very processes of growth provide new energy even as a society offers new and specific opportunities according to its dominant conception of the phases of life" (1968, p. 163). "It is the joint development of cognitive and emotional powers paired with appropriate social learning which enables the individual to realize the potentialities" of each stage of development (Erikson, 1964, p. 225). Biopsychological and sociological processes interact throughout the life cycle and give rise to a series of vital psychosocial tasks that intensify to a crisis or turning point in an ordered sequence (E. Erikson, J. Erikson, & Kivnick, 1986; Snarey, 1987). The resolution of each crisis results in growth.

To illustrate this process and review the stages of Erikson's model as well, we ought to consider briefly each of the psychosocial stages that precede generativity. It is important to understand that, although these stages are associated with chronological ages, Erikson emphasizes that age does not define a stage (1975; E. Erikson, J. Erikson, & Kivnick, 1986). Each of the eight tasks is present in some form throughout the entire life cycle. Furthermore, during the course of development, "earlier stages are not replaced" but rather "are absorbed into a hierarchic system of increasing differentiation" (1975, p. 206).

1. Trust. Erikson relates psychosocial development during the first year of life to the infant's task of developing a favorable balance of basic trust over mistrust. The question "Can I trust?" builds upon the infant's biological preoccupation with "Will I be fed again?" Consistent, trustworthy parental care enables infants to attain a favorable balance of trust over mistrust, which, in turn, helps ensure that the strength of "hope" will become a fundamental quality of the person in all later stages of the life cycle. Thus from the very beginning of the life cycle Erikson sees a dialogue "between the child's developmental readiness and the pattern of [parental] care readied for the child by the community" (1980a, p. 16). Fathers who relate to their infants and children in a consistent and trustworthy manner may thus promote their offspring's sense of faith in life itself. Such fathers may also help protect their children, as adults, from neurotic mistrust.

2. Autonomy. Beginning around the second year of life, the child becomes preoccupied with autonomy versus shame and doubt. This tension is engendered by the toddler's growing motor control and developing cognitive differentiation of self and others, combined with parental toilet training or other social concerns with cleanliness and self-control. Achieving a reasonably favorable balance of autonomy over shame at this stage enables the child to develop the strength that Erikson (1964) calls "will," as in willpower or free will. Will, that is, refers to "the unbroken determination to exercise free choice as well as self-restraint, in spite of the unavoidable experience of shame and doubt" (p. 119). Fathers who protect their children from overwhelming defeat and promote their freedom of self-expression may have helped protect their children, as adults, from experiencing excessive doubt and undue concern with shame or loss of face.

3. Initiative. In Stage 3 of Erikson's scheme, initiative versus guilt, new levels of physical and intellectual maturation allow play-age children to broaden their social world beyond the family and to increase their curiosity and ability to explore this new world (for example, running fast, asking questions about how things work). If the child completes this stage with a sense of initiative outweighing his or her sense of guilt, purposefulness will be an enduring ego strength. Purposefulness, moderated but not inhibited by guilt or fear, is the ability to envision and strive for "valued goals" (Erikson, 1964, p. 122). Fathers who are not overly critical and who do not make excessive use of guilt may help protect their children from overcompensatory

showing-off behavior, excessive feelings of guilt, and inordinate moralistic reasoning during adulthood.

4. Industry. Around ages 5 to 7, children generally join up with society. "Whether the school is field or jungle or classroom," Erikson (1950) explains, "children receive some systematic instruction" during this time of life (pp. 258–259). At this time children also typically enter a new stage of cognitive development, concrete operations, which enables them to apply logical thought processes to solve concrete problems (Piaget, 1967). Thus the child's biocognitive readiness to learn to work is synchronized with society's definition of the beginning of the schooling-age period (compare Demos, 1970). In general, this synchronization of social instruction and psychological development functions to help activate and then satisfy the fourth task of psychosocial development—industry. The result of achieving a reasonably favorable balance of industry over inferiority is competence—the enduring belief that one can begin a project and also complete it at an acceptable level of quality. The mentorship of a good father during these years may give children a subsequent advantage in their ability to work hard, to think of themselves as industrious, and to feel generally productive. In contrast, childhood experiences of perceiving oneself as not measuring up to expected standards may lead to feelings of inferiority or incompetence in adulthood.

5. Identity. Maturing youths, Erikson observes, are confronted with a "physiological revolution within them and with tangible adult tasks ahead of them" (1950, p. 261). As adolescents develop the cognitive ability to think of infinite hypothetical possibilities, society requires that they learn to fill specific adult roles. These two changes are synchronized in adolescents' psychosocial task of achieving a sense of identity and working out what they should do with their lives. Identity formation often takes the social form of a search for a political, religious, or moral ideology that can function to provide a durable set of values on which an inner coherence can be based. Achieving a favorable balance of identity over identity confusion, according to Erikson (1964), leads to the strength of fidelity—a sense of commitment to a self-chosen value system and "the ability to sustain loyalties freely pledged in spite of the inevitable contradictions of value systems" (p. 125). Fathers who provide their children with supportive freedom and guard their growing intellectual, emotional, and physical autonomy may also help their children to learn from other parent-

like teachers and to construct a stable sense of their own ego identity. In this way, fathers also help buffer their children from role confusion or the nonreflective, premature acceptance of an identity which belongs more to parents and peers than to themselves (cf. Erikson, 1958; Snarey, Friedman, & Blasi, 1986).

6. Intimacy. The psychosocial task of achieving intimacy is to establish a close, intimate, long-term relationship with another person. In our society, this task parallels the social expectation of marriage or equivalent forms of commitment. This requires "the capacity to commit [oneself] to concrete affiliations and partnerships and to develop the ethical strength to abide by such commitments, even though they may call for significant sacrifices and compromises" (Erikson, 1950, p. 263). Mature intimacy may logically presuppose the prior attainment of a reasonably stable identity, because intimacy involves the "mutual verification through an experience of finding oneself, as one loses oneself, in another" (Erikson, 1964, p. 128). Identity confusion, that is, limits the "ability to fuse your identity with somebody else's without fear that you're going to lose something yourself" (Evans, 1969, p. 48). In addition to the achievement of personal identity, the crisis of intimacy is likely made possible and necessary by the synchronization or cogwheeling of the cognitive ability to see the limits of an adolescent logical mode of introspecting endlessly, and the intensifying biosocial need to survive through the culturally defined roles of spouse and parent. It seems likely that parents who provide a loving model of marital intimacy promote their adult children's successful attainment of a favorable balance of intimacy over isolation. Such intimacy gives rise to the ego strength of love, but the possible consequence of intimacy failure is isolation.

7. Generativity and 8. Integrity. Maturing forms of trust, autonomy, initiative, industry, identity, and intimacy are subsequently integrated into a more comprehensive concern with generativity (Stage 7) and integrity (Stage 8). We will now consider generativity in greater depth.

Erikson on Generativity

The psychosocial task of middle adulthood, Stage 7, is the attainment of a favorable balance of generativity over stagnation and self-absorption. Generativity can only be lived in dynamic tension with self-care; the challenge is to achieve a reasonable surplus of procreativity, productivity, and creativity over a pervading mood of personal depletion or self-absorption. Most broadly, Erikson (1975) considers generativity to mean any caring activity that contributes to the spirit of future generations, such as the generation of new or more mature persons, products, ideas, or works of art. Most centrally, Erikson bases adult generativity on a "procreative drive" (1980b, p. 215) and the "need to be needed" (1964, p. 130). Regardless of the angle of vision, however, generativity's psychosocial challenge to adults is to create, care for, and promote the development of others, from nurturing the growth of another person to shepherding the development of a broader community.

The vice that results from generativity failure is "rejectivity," a kind of indifference which Erikson (1982) defines as "the unwillingness to include specified persons or groups in one's generative concern—one does not care for them" (p. 69). Erikson views rejectivity as a foundation for the universal social problem of "pseudospeciation," which he defines as the distorted belief and corresponding behaviors "that another type or group of persons are, by nature, history, or divine will, a species different from one's own—and dangerous to mankind itself" (p. 69). In contrast, the adult virtue that results from the successful resolution of the crisis of generativity versus self-absorption is *care*—"the widening concern for what has been generated by love, necessity, or accident; it overcomes the ambivalence adhering to irreversible obligation" (E. Erikson, J. Erikson, & Kivnick, 1986, p. 37). Thus generative care aims to be inclusively attentive to all that has been created.

Generativity is more complex, multifaceted, and differentiated than any other stage in Erikson's model, in part because it spans a greater number of years. When Erikson wrote about generativity as "establishing and guiding the next generation," for instance, he was clearly painting in broad strokes that cover genes, practices, products, and ideas. It is therefore especially helpful to articulate Erikson's implicit distinctions among various types of generativity related to biological procreation, parenthood, and productivity or creativity. This task of theory development was taken up by John Kotre (1975; 1984; Kotre & Hall, 1990; for review, see Tipton, 1985).

Types of Generativity

Kotre has for some time been concerned with some men's apparent difficulty with "caring for offspring" (1975, p. 434). He describes

Types of gen. [margin handwriting]

Erikson's stage of generativity, most broadly, as including "the desire to invest one's energy in forms of life and work that will outlive the self" (Kotre & Hall, 1990, p. 310). In *Outliving the Self,* Kotre (1984) distinguishes four types of generative care: First is biological generativity, which refers to "the begetting, bearing, and nursing" of offspring. Here, the infant is the "generative object" (p. 11). Second is parental generativity, which involves childrearing activities that care for and promote offspring, "initiating them into a family system." Here, the child is the generative object (p. 12). Third is technical generativity, which involves "teaching" a myriad of skills "to successors, implicitly passing on the symbol system in which the skills are embedded." Now, the apprentice and the skill are the generative objects (p.13). Fourth is cultural generativity, which involves "mentoring"—"creating, renovating, and conserving a symbol system, explicitly passing it on to successors." The disciple or mentee and the culture are thus the final generative objects (p. 14).

Many of the rich details of Kotre's typology are not captured by a brief summary. It must be noted, nevertheless, that the first two types of generativity in his scheme parallel the two initial types of generativity (birth parenthood and childrearing parenthood) that Erikson tentatively theorized may prepare us for the realization of genuine midlife generativity. Kotre's last two types, in contrast, reflect different but overlapping dimensions of the unified core characteristics that Erikson attributes to the stage of midlife generativity. It is likely that the distinction between "teaching technical skills" and "mentoring cultural symbols" illustrates social class differences rather than genuine developmental differences, however. Therefore, and more in keeping with Erikson's original theorizing, this present study of fathers systematically distinguishes and empirically measures three types of generativity: (1) biological (that is, *birth fathers*), (2) parental (that is, *childrearing fathers*), and (3) societal (that is, *cultural fathers*).

Biological generativity. A person's biological generativity is most directly indicated by the birth of his or her child. Having waited for this moment for several months, men, like women, feel a great sense of achievement that in part has to do with their linking the generations. Biological generativity, according to Kotre (1984, p. 12), also involves the initial nursing and nurturing of the infant. An infant's physical viability is its parents' primary concern during the early months of the infant's life and, even with the relatively low infant mortality rates for the middle class in the United States, biological generativity is incomplete without the initial care necessary to ensure the child's biological survival. Obviously, then, even literal biological generativity is not strictly limited to the biological facts of conception and birth since, for example, adoptive parents of infants also provide a portion of the care necessary to assure the infant's initial biological life (Weiss, 1990, p. 166). In terms of Erikson's formulation, then, biological generativity means the birth and care of the child during its first year of life; this, of course, also supports the infant in the task of developing a favorable ratio of trust over mistrust (Stage 1).

Biological generativity can potentially occur over a period of several decades but, especially for women, it is most likely to occur successfully in the period from the late teens to the early thirties. This biological foundation places time limits on a couple's procreativity and, furthermore, promotes socially defined expectations for achieving biological procreation "on schedule." The opposite of biological generativity is the experience of infertility, first intimated by a couple's being "behind schedule," despite their efforts to achieve a pregnancy. Reproductive difficulty, of course, is a direct threat to biological generativity and an indirect threat to parental generativity. Furthermore, even though Erikson acknowledged that "generativity can find expression in productivity or creativity as well as procreativity" (E. Erikson & J. Erikson, 1981, p. 255), infertility may also be an indirect threat to societal generativity because it can weaken the psychosocial preparation for it. This last possibility is one of the ideas that will be investigated in this book.

Parental generativity. The hinge which links biological and societal generativity is parental generativity. Paternal and maternal generativity involve carrying out childrearing activities that promote children's ability to develop their full potential in terms of realizing a favorable balance of autonomy (Stage 2), initiative (Stage 3), industry (Stage 4), and identity (Stage 5). Under these criteria, it is obvious that not all parenting is necessarily generative parenting, even though parenthood may be "the prime generative encounter" in the lives of many people (Erikson, 1964, p. 130).

Describing the ego strength of successful generativity, "care," Erikson (1964) notes that this virtue is able to overwhelm the hesitancy that is inevitable when considering life-long responsibilities and commitments. Childrearing fathers, as much as birth or cultural fathers, are obligated to make such an irreversible commitment. Parental generativity, that is, requires the "significant sacrifices" of love and the generative "commitment to take care of [what] one has learned to care for" (Erikson, 1982, p. 67). These requirements underscore that parenting is a moral endeavor. As ethicist William Everett (1977) has observed, for instance, asking oneself the question "Am I a good parent?" represents one of the most widespread acts of ethical self-reflection among adults (p. 91). In this sense, parental generativity may promote the moral character of adults as they become centered on and centered by the generative ego strength of "care."

It is also noteworthy that parental generativity provides one of the most basic and beautiful examples of synchronization between life cycles. On the one hand, children provide opportunities for parents to satisfy their own developmental need to be generative. On the other hand, through their generativity, parents provide support for their child's development, whether the crisis at hand involves their school-age son's striving for industry in the face of inferiority fears, or their teenage daughter's striving to construct an independent identity in the face of the risks of identity confusion or premature identity fore-closure.

Societal generativity. Societal generativity principally involves caring for other younger *adults:* serving as a mentor, providing leadership, and generally contributing to the strength and continuity of subsequent generations. Midlife men who are cultural fathers have demonstrated a capacity for establishing and guiding the next generation, beyond raising their own children, through their actual sustained responsibility for the growth, well-being, and leadership of other adults. Depending on the opportunities available to a particular man, this could mean serving as a master in a master-apprentice work role, serving as a labor union leader, coaching an athletic team, founding a neighborhood improvement committee, serving on a local social service or school board, or exercising responsibility for other adults through an administrative work role.

The biosocial foundations of societal generativity are found, in part, in the new awareness of death that characterizes middle age. Standing in the middle of one's life, knowing that the years remaining are probably fewer than the years lived and facing the finitude and limit-edness of our existence, can be a suddenly sobering experience. Such midlife existential anxiety about death, however, can stimulate midlife questions about life, such as: Why live? How will the planet be a better home for the next generation because I have lived? (Kotre, 1984, pp. 112–116; Kohlberg & Ryncarz, 1990). Societal generativity, therefore, is more broadly socially inclusive than the other types of generativity. While biological generativity focuses on continuing one's personal genetic inheritance, and parental generativity focuses on parenting one's present children, societal generativity can encompass the future of *all* children-becoming-adults and promote an ethically inclusive cycle of the generations. Erikson's concept of stagnation most directly applies to the failure to become societally generative. The absence of productivity and care threatens the entire future of the society's corporate life history, because generativity "is the link between the life cycle and the generational cycle" (E. Erikson & J. Erikson, 1981, p. 258).

Generativity Chill

The absence of generativity is a threat to society's corporate life, as noted above, but it is even more precisely a threat to an adult's psychosocial life. I will call the anxiety resulting from threats to an adult's generativity a "generativity chill." More specifically, the concept of generativity chill is intended to refer to a type of anxiety (awareness of the self as finite, limited, bounded) that results from a specific type of existential imperilment (the threatened loss of one's child, creation, or creativity).

In introducing the concept of generativity chill I intend to extend Erikson's work in ways that are consistent with the spirit of his ideas. In his book *Young Man Luther,* Erikson (1958) refers to a type of anxiety "which is like an ego-chill—a shudder which comes from the sudden awareness that our own nonexistence is entirely possible. Ordinarily we feel this shudder only when a shock forces us to step back from ourselves" (p. 111). Generativity chill, in this sense, is a specific type of ego chill arising from the moments when an adult faces the possibility of losing the child he or she has helped to create, whether the threat comes in the form of a reproductive difficulty that hinders the child who is still only a fantasy in his father's mind or in the form of a near-death accident or illness that threatens the living being to whom he already says, "I am your father."

It seems likely that brief or extended threats to generativity will have a significant impact upon a father's selfhood: a man's sense of biological generativity is initially embedded in the reality of a birth; his sense of parental generativity, in the reality of parenting practices. A threat to the very foundations of a man's generative self, therefore, may also function to challenge his sense of generative selfhood with the threat of stagnation and death. There is, I believe, a circularity between generativity and death: awareness of death progressively prompts biological, parental, and societal generativity and in turn, all three types of generativity progressively assuage the fear of death through a maturing love of life. Thus a major threat to generativity may reactivate the fear of death.

Relationships between Types of Generativity

The three types of generativity, while distinct and differentiated, are also interrelated and interdependent. It is important to clarify the theoretical relationships between biological, parental, and societal generativity.

Biological generativity overlaps with and also prepares the way for parental generativity, just as parental generativity overlaps with and prepares the way for a more inclusive societal generativity. Biological generativity usually occurs during early adulthood in our society, but the "mere fact of having or even wanting children . . . does not 'achieve' generativity" in the broader parental or societal senses (Erikson, 1950, p. 267). Parental generativity begins with the arrival of a child, which usually occurs during the parents' early adulthood, and continues throughout the parents' life, while societal generativity usually begins around midlife and remains predominant until late adulthood. Even during the mature years, however, not all parenting is genuine generative parenting (Erikson, 1982; Kotre, 1984).

Just as biological generativity is prior to the socially broader concept of parental generativity, parental generativity is prior to the broader concept of societal generativity. Each type prepares the way for a more inclusive form. Erikson (1950, 1969a), for instance, has suggested that achieving societal generativity is more difficult without the prior experience of parenting children. In fact, parenthood functions as a moral metaphor and model for good citizenry in most domains of adult life. Erikson is careful to acknowledge in a discussion of parenting, however, that "there are people who, from misfortune or because of special and genuine gifts in other directions, do not apply this drive to offspring but to other forms of altruistic concern and of creativity, which may absorb their kind of parental responsibility" (Erikson, 1959, p. 103). "Serving as a parent may cultivate generativity," as Kotre and Hall (1990) state, "but childlessness does not necessarily thwart its development" (p. 312). Erikson, however, also argues that parent-like forms of altruism themselves then become necessary for adult development, because "the only way to counteract the possible effects of a necessary deprivation is a kind of sublimation" (E. Erikson & J. Erikson, 1981, p. 263; Erikson, 1980b).

The interrelations between types of generativity can be seen in the biological-social life history of the family. In the developmental transition from intimacy to generativity, for instance, there is a biologically based urgency for intimacy to lead to procreation. Biological generativity, in turn, functions to link intimacy to parental generativity which, for the couple, represents "a vigorous expansion of mutual interests" and an "investment in that which is being generated and cared for together" (Erikson, 1982, p. 67). In the process of intensive parenting, fathers as well as mothers usually develop important competencies for care. And while parenting continues in some sense throughout the entire adult life cycle (Bozett, 1985; Cath, 1986), young adult children are usually eventually launched from the nest, and the ability or proclivity to generate new children wanes. Concurrently, the larger society needs mature adults to help establish the next generation of adults and ideas. This synchronization, according to Erikson (1975), provides an opportunity for adults to "apply the energies saved from" their abated parental commitments "to wider communal responsibilities" (p. 243). In sum, in the language of Erikson's embryonic analogy, intimacy is an epigenetic predecessor of biological generativity which, in turn, is an epigenetic predecessor of parental generativity which, in turn, prepares the way for societal generativity.

Even though this is a study of men, the role of father is obviously complexly interrelated with women's roles of wife and mother. Thus it is important to acknowledge that Erikson's model has been criticized by Gilligan (1982) as being defined by the experience and perspective of men (compare Miller-McLemore, 1989; see Erikson, 1975, pp. 225–247). Equally important, however, is that Erikson was the first to advocate an ethic of "care" as the hallmark of midlife psychosocial maturity for both women and men. Moreover, the empirical evidence demonstrates that the stage of generativity reflects the experience of women as well as of men (Peterson & Stewart, 1990; Pita, 1986; Ryff & Heincke, 1983; Ryff & Migdal, 1984). The gender-inclusive and culturally universal nature of Stage 7 is well captured in Joan Erikson's (1988) description of psychosocial generativity: "The overriding burden of the generative years in every culture is the generational future: the maintaining and vitalizing of the basic strengths in the not yet mature segment of the community, and the passing on of such tradition and culture that life may have meaning and value" (pp. 102–103).

Perhaps what is most important to recognize, however, is an underlying unity: Gilligan implicitly and Erikson explicitly both portray the origins of care in adulthood experiences of parenting and caregiving as well as in the childhood experiences of being parented. As Gilligan (1982) states, "maturity" is "realized by interdependence and taking care" (p. 172); an understanding of this, Gilligan concludes, can lead to "a more *generative* view of human life" (p. 174, italics added). Baier's (1987) insightful commentary on Gilligan's work is even more explicit: "And how will men ever develop an understanding of the 'ethic of care' if they continue to be shielded or kept from that experience of caring for a dependent child . . . ?" (p. 52). In this sense, gender differences in the scheduling and expression of generativity may exist (Messina, 1984). Perhaps it would be surprising if it were otherwise, Erikson acknowledged, given the different institutional roles which route the lives of fathers and mothers in our society. Erik and Joan Erikson (1981; Erikson, 1974) suggest that institutional changes are necessary to free women to develop careers more easily in addition to bringing up families. Of course, the primary change would be for fathers to invest more of their energies in childrearing and to be valued for doing so. The ability of the Erikson model of generativity to make sense of these issues also testifies to its power to provide a sensitive psychosocial perspective on the experience of fathering in our time.

Erikson on Integrity and Ethics

Following the psychosocial task of generativity is the eighth stage, integrity versus despair. Integrity, according to Erikson, is a post-narcissistic "love" of the human life cycle as a process which imparts "a sense of coherence and *wholeness*" to life and the world (1982, p. 65). "It is the acceptance of one's one and only life cycle as something that had to be and that, by necessity, permitted no substitutions" (1950, p. 268). In contrast, "Despair expresses that feeling that time is now short, too short to attempt to start another life and to try out alternative roads to integrity" (1950, p. 269). The attainment of a favorable ratio of integrity over despair gives rise to the ego virtue of wisdom. This final ego virtue "entails the ability to use experience in grasping fundamental principles that integrate and give substance to all that one knows" (Power, Power, & Snarey, 1988, p. 137).

While the last stage of integrity is generally beyond the focus of this book, looking back on the life cycle from the vantage point of this quite explicitly ethical stage reminds us that all of the stages potentially give rise to ego strengths or virtues. These ego strengths or virtues can be understood as types of moral will or moral courage, although not as specific moral values (compare Capps, 1983, 1984). As such, the sequence of virtues also provides a model of the course of ethical development. Furthermore, when one stands back and takes in the entirety of this sequence of virtues, one can observe with Erikson (1975) that "the individual proceeds developmentally from the moralism of childhood through the ideology of adolescence to some [more universal] adult ethics" (p. 206).

It is this "ethical orientation," according to Erikson (1975), "which makes the difference between adulthood and adolescence" (p. 207). As he states in a discussion of identity, for instance, "adolescence is the period when the moral precepts absorbed in childhood must be superseded by an ideological orientation on which a future commitment to ethical behavior can be based" (Erikson, 1969c, p. 686). Especially at the higher stages, therefore, Erikson's psychosocial theory is also a theory of ethical development. Adolescent "fidelity," young adulthood "love," and adulthood "caring" represent increasingly sophisticated capacities for sociomoral commitments that are freely made, but ethically binding (Snarey, Kohlberg, & Noam, 1983; compare Browning, 1973; Côté & Levine, 1988; Piediscalzi, 1973). Thus it is not surprising that Erikson's stage model has been used as a theoretical tool for interpreting the empirical relationships between ego and moral development stages (Lee & Snarey, 1988). For example, the maturity and general-stage equality of ego and moral development that were found to characterize middle adulthood, parallel generativity in Erikson's model; it is when the individual's personal development becomes more stable and his or her attention shifts to concerns for the development and care of others. As Erikson (1980a) previously speculated, "there is good reason to allocate to adulthood" a more universal ethical orientation that is "consonant with the generative engagements of that stage" (p. 56; compare Erikson, 1968, p. 260).

Consistent with the logic of his stage model, Erikson (1980a) views the course of ethical development, which leads to the generative virtue of care, as representing a hierarchical process of reintegration. Childhood morality and adolescent ideology are reintegrated into a more complex adulthood ethic of generative care. Erikson (1974) recounts these developmental processes by noting that after you have learned "what you care to do and who you care to be" (identity), and "whom you care to be with" (intimacy), you are ready to learn "what and whom you can take care of" (generativity) (p. 124). The strengths of generativity, in turn, may finally be integrated into an even more encompassing sense of integrity and wisdom. Thus generativity and care are constant themes, even though it is during middle adulthood that they become the overwhelming preoccupation and ethical virtue.

How the Book Is Organized

The text consists of five quantitative—statistically reported—empirical studies, alternating in sequence with four qualitative—descriptively reported—life stories.

Quantitative Studies

Chapter 2 presents the study's general research method and an initial report of the varieties of paternal generativity. The study's research method is described and terms are defined. The chapter also reports on the patterns that characterized the fathers' parental generativity.

Chapters 4, 6, 8, and 10 take the reader *back in time*, beginning with the men's status at midlife and eventually moving back to the men's boyhood experiences.

In Chapter 4 I consider the questions, What are the longitudinal consequences of variations in fathers' childrearing participation for the fathers themselves at midlife? How well can fathers' parental generativity predict their own subsequent midlife outcomes in terms of success at love (marital happiness), work (occupational mobility), and societal generativity (care for the next generation)?

In Chapter 6 I ask, What are the consequences of the fathers' childrearing for their children as young adults? Focusing on the children's early adulthood accomplishments, I consider whether, and to what extent, fathers' parental generativity can predict their sons' and daughters' educational and occupational mobility as adults. I report the results of an investigation on the specific impact of fathers' generativity on their children's subsequent life chances and outcomes.

In Chapter 8 I focus on men who experienced infertility in early adulthood. How do the ways the men coped with this threat to their biological generativity predict their subsequent work, love, and societal generativity at midlife? I examine whether infertility, as a threat to biological generativity among some men, can broaden our understanding of parental and societal generativity in most men.

In Chapter 10 I explore the early boyhood experiences that are precursors of later variations in the men's parental generativity. A focus of this chapter is the boyhood family of origin, including the boyhood characteristics of the men's own fathers and the nature of the men's boyhood relationships with their own fathers. I also investigate to what extent the characteristics of their ongoing family life predict their level of parental generativity. In sum, why do some men become especially involved in rearing their children?

Together, these empirical studies trace the precursors and consequences of childrearing fathers across three generations, four decades, and four periods of the life cycle.

Qualitative Stories

Between each of the five empirical chapters I present the life story of one of four particular father-child relationships. Each story is actually a "self-portrait" because a father and his son or daughter give their perspective in their own words. Beyond providing a vivid portrait of their relationship in review, therefore, the joint conversation is also an example of their style of interaction. Each self-portrait is based on the verbatim transcript of two supplementary tape-recorded interview sessions, which took a total of four to six hours with each Glueck father and his son or daughter. The aim of this life-story research method, which builds on the anthropological approach of Oscar Lewis (1959, 1964, 1969), is to provide rich details, put human faces on the statistical findings, and personalize the scientific study of fathering.

To protect the reader from the difficulties and redundancies that characterize any interview transcript, the self-portraits have been shortened and edited. I deleted probe questions and some redundancies, streamlined the flow of some sentences and paragraphs, and occasionally reorganized the sequence of some stories into chronological order or collected scattered comments on the same topic. All of the case study participants reviewed the transcript of their story and supplied or approved the addition of missing information. To protect confidentiality, proper names and background details have been changed. Aside from disguising identities, however, nothing has been fictionalized.

The father-child interviews were chosen from interviews with a subgroup of men who served as the childrearing rating reliability sample, which will be discussed in the next chapter. The four cases were selected for inclusion because they, as a group, provided the most balanced sampling of the different childrearing participation styles among successful fathers—men whose children were upwardly mobile by early adulthood and who themselves were societally generative at midlife. Otherwise, these four portraits of generative successes are reasonably representative of the 240 fathers' general backgrounds. The original sample included a broad ethnic mix, for example, and the paternal ancestors of the four self-portrait fathers similarly represent different ethnic backgrounds—Russian, English, Irish, and Italian.

At the beginning of each story, a brief introductory section describes the general background of the father and his son or daughter. Each story then follows the same three-part format, corresponding to the original three-part interview, which will now be outlined so that it might serve as a road map for each self-portrait.

1. Early Memories. The father and his adult son or daughter were first interviewed separately and privately about their earliest memories of each other. The father's interviewer also asked him to share his early memories of his own father.

2. Joint Life Review. In the second part of the interview the father and his adult son or daughter were interviewed together. They were told that this was "story-telling time"—a time for the two of them to review the stories that make up their joint story. Each was encouraged

to jog the other's memory and to contribute his or her own perspective as they shared stories illustrating how they had spent time together. The only chronology that was required was that they were to begin with stories from the son's or daughter's first ten years of life, and then to tell stories about themselves from the years when the son or daughter was in the second decade of life. In each self-portrait, therefore, the joint-interview section is subdivided into "The First Decade" and "The Second Decade." Many vignettes are conventional but quite revealing, others are hilarious tales of high-spirited misadventure, and a few have the power to evoke tears.

3. Current Reflections. The third section of each self-portrait presents each father's and his adult child's private current reflections regarding the most significant ways the father had influenced his son's or daughter's success. The son or daughter was also questioned about his or her current or anticipatory reflections on parenting the next generation.

Commentary footnotes alongside each self-portrait provide an ongoing sense of how I interpret each story. My comments focus on how a story illustrates the primary themes and variables that were the focus of the preceding empirical chapter, as well as how it illustrates the general themes of biological, parental, or societal generativity. These footnotes, obviously, are not intended to replace the reader's own interpretation of the lives of the fathers and their children. Finally, at the very end of each self-portrait, a brief concluding query is raised concerning how the self-portrait may foreshadow the findings to be reported in the forthcoming chapter.

After the last story and the last study, the book's concluding Chapter 11 summarizes the study's limitations and presents a life-span overview of men's generativity. The overview weaves the quantitative and qualitative findings together and draws out the study's tentative conclusions regarding men's spoken or unspoken question, "What does it mean to be a good father today?"

2

Varieties of Fathers' Parental Generativity

Fatherhood is a common experience of adult men—more than 90% of all adult males in the United States eventually marry, and over 90% of these married couples eventually have one or more children in the home (Carter & Glick, 1970; Hogan, 1987). But the ways that fathers care for and promote their children's development vary considerably. What are the basic varieties of parental generativity among the fathers in this study? The study fathers and their childrearing patterns during their children's first and second decades of life are described in this chapter.

What We Know from Prior Research

An initial lesson offered by prior studies of paternal childcare is that there are many different ways to define it. One of the earliest methods was a simple dichotomy—absence versus presence. In fact the largest body of relevant prior studies involves the impact of a father's absence, not his presence, upon his children. This extensive line of research, from the early post-World War II studies of the impact of fathers' war absence upon their children, to ongoing studies of single-mother families, has generally been interpreted as indicating that fathers' absence predicts children's antisocial behavior, cognitive immaturity, poor academic achievement, sex-identity conflict, and low self-esteem. The findings are difficult to interpret, however, and several critical reviews take a cautious stance toward these conclusions (Block, Block, & Gjerde, 1986; Pedersen, 1976; Pleck, 1981; Radin, 1981b). At any rate, they simply do not tell us a great deal about the many positive ways fathers spend time with their children.

Common Indices of Paternal Presence

Russell and Radin (1983) have suggested five categories of research on paternal involvement in childcare. These include: (1) the father's presence at birth, (2) general availability, (3) time spent in childcare, (4) time spent in play, and (5) degree of responsibility for childcare. The following brief review of prior research is organized according to these categories. More comprehensive or wider ranging reviews are available elsewhere (Lamb, Pleck, Charnov, & Levine, 1987; Lamb & Sagi, 1983; Parke & Tinsley, 1981; Ross & Taylor, 1989).

Presence at Birth

Is a father present at the birth of his child? Attendance at birth has been used as an initial measure of paternal care, since fathers are not always or necessarily present. It is essentially an application of the father-present versus father-absent research approach to one specific situation. Four decades ago, almost no fathers in the United States were present in the delivery room during their child's birth. Increasingly, however, the current expectation among all social classes is that the father will attend childbirth classes and the delivery (Gallup, 1983; Hanson & Bozett, 1987). Today well over three out of every four fathers are present and usually provide support for their spouses during the delivery (Gallup, 1983; Hanson & Bozett, 1987). Of course, this particular trend is also testimony to the effects of changing policies which had functioned as barriers to fathering. Four decades ago, few hospitals in the United States permitted fathers to be present in the delivery room, and "not until 1974 did the American College of Obstetricians and Gynecologists endorse the father's presence during labor. And yet by 1980, fathers were admitted to delivery rooms in approximately 90% of American hospitals" (Parke, 1981, p. 20).

General Availability

How many hours a week are fathers typically at home and potentially available to their children when their children are awake? One pioneering study reported that fathers were generally available approximately 25 hours each week by this criterion, compared with approximately 63 hours each week for mothers (Kotelchuck, 1976; cf. Robinson, 1977). This large difference, of course, shows the allocation of time in the daily schedules of full-time housewives versus

breadwinning fathers. In this sense, available time is negatively correlated with the time a parent spends working outside of the home.
More recent surveys have shown that this time differential between
fathers and mothers has been reduced, although not eliminated, as
mothers have increased the hours that they work outside of the home
(Easterbrooks & Goldberg, 1985; Lamb, Pleck, Charnov, & Levine,
1987).

Time Spent in Childcare

How many hours a week do fathers typically spend in actual specific
childcare tasks? This criterion is more precise because it only "counts"
the actual time spent on a specific type of care. One small but now
classic study, for instance, introduced the 37-seconds-a-day father,
based on the observations of one sample of 10 babies and their fathers
engaging in one specific type of interaction (Rebelsky & Hanks, 1971).
These new fathers spent an average of only 37.7 seconds each day in
"verbal interaction" with their infants during their infants' first three
months of life (range = 0 seconds to 10 1/2 minutes).

   With different criteria, the results have been somewhat more encouraging. One review of a half-dozen studies noted that all reported
estimates of the average amount of time that fathers spend specifically
on childcare tasks (for example, feeding, changing clothing) ranged
from 1.6 and 2.8 hours a week. In contrast, estimates of hours spent in
the same specific childcare tasks by mothers who were not employed
outside of the home have ranged from approximately 9 to 18 hours
per week (Russell & Radin, 1983).

   Currently, however, the amount of time that fathers spend in specific childcare tasks is increasing (Gallup, 1991; McDermott, 1990;
Pleck, 1985). For instance, a study of somewhat less traditional families reported that fathers' participation in more diverse childcare
functions (feeding, helping to bathe, reading to them, taking on trips)
averaged 2.25 hours of childcare per *day* rather than the similar
figure noted above per *week* (Grossman, Pollack, & Golding, 1988).
Comparisons among studies, of course, are fraught with difficulties.

Time Spent in Play

How many hours a week do fathers typically spend in play with their
children? Numerous studies have consistently found that a greater

percentage of the time fathers spend with their children is devoted to play activities rather than to other childcare tasks. The time that typical fathers spend playing with their children has been estimated at approximately 9 hours per week (Russell & Radin, 1983). Full-time mothers, of course, might conceivably devote twice as many hours to playing with their children, although several studies report no significant differences between fathers and mothers on several measures of duration of play (Pedersen, 1980).

Within the category of "play activities," qualitative differences mark fathers' and mothers' interactions with children. In particular, although nearly all men and women play with their infants, fathers' play involves more physical-athletic interaction. Fathers' play, that is, consists of more limb movement, active arousal, initiative, and is generally more rough-and-tumble (Ricks, 1985). In contrast, mothers' play more typically involves visual attention. This pattern is consistent with the reports that mothers are more likely than fathers to spend time in "verbal interaction" with their infants. Field (1978) has also shown, however, that this difference between fathers and mothers is less clear when primary, as opposed to secondary, caretaker fathers are compared to primary caretaker mothers. As she reported, "primary caretaker fathers and mothers engaged in more smiling, imitative grimaces and high-pitched vocalizations than did secondary caretaker fathers" (p. 183). Perhaps this was because primary caretaker parents were more familiar with their babies.

Fathers' preferences for physically stimulating and exciting activities are not restricted to young infants (MacDonald & Parke, 1986). Fathers of school children often participate in activities beyond the family sphere, such as scouting, Little League, and similar physically oriented organized activities (Bradley, 1985). They use more verbal joking and rough physical play in their interactions with their older children (Maccoby, 1990). Likewise, fathers of adolescents spend a greater proportion of the time they are together with their children in leisure rather than in work activities, and they tend to promote assertiveness rather than politeness (Montemayor & Brownlee, 1987; Power & Shanks, 1989). From birth through adolescence, in effect, a working-hard-at-playing quality distinguishes paternal from maternal childrearing participation.

This style of rough-and-tumble play with physical contact models socially acceptable assertion but not necessarily aggression. Children who roughhouse with their fathers, for instance, usually quickly learn that biting, kicking, and other forms of physical violence are not acceptable. It is also important to note that one of the most common types of physical contact between fathers and their children is nurturant and supportive physical touching. Two studies by Salt (1982, 1991), for instance, have shown that preadolescent children "perceive" that their "fathers do more affectionate and nurturing types of touch than they do playful types of touch" (1991, p. 553).

Degree of Responsibility

Finally, how often do fathers assume full responsibility for their children? Having the sole responsibility for a child's care during some portion of a day is far more demanding than sharing or being available to help with childcare. A caretaker with full responsibility, for instance, must be cognizant of all aspects of a child's needs and development—physical, intellectual, and emotional.

One often-cited study estimated that fathers spend an average of only 1 hour per week taking sole responsibility, compared with mothers who report that they have the sole responsibility an average of 40 hours per week (Kotelchuck, 1976). Subsequent studies reported that, while some fathers "help out" with specific tasks, few assume the regular and full "responsibility" for one or more specific childcare tasks (for review, see Lamb, Pleck, Charnov, & Levine, 1987).

These findings are historically dated and culturally limited. It should not be assumed that fathers today still shoulder a trivial amount of childcare responsibility. A U.S. Census Bureau survey, for instance, indicates that fathers now provide the primary childcare for 25% of preschool-age children and 11% of school-age children whose mothers work part time, and for 10% of preschool-age children and 5% of school-age children whose mothers work full time (1987 data; Bureau of the Census, 1990, July). (Fathers' childcare time is higher when their wives work part time rather than full time because couples are more able to use a shift-work system when mothers work part time, but they often need a more highly structured system of outside care when mother and father both work full time.) A Gallup Poll also found that 10% of men report taking "all or most" of the responsibility for childcare when their children are sick and home from school, and 28% of men report taking "all or most" of the responsibility for disciplining their children. Not unimportantly, the estimates offered by women are consistent with the percentages provided by men (1990 data; Gallup, 1991, pp. 14–15). Within the increasing number of dual-earner families, in particular, the amount of time fathers have the sole responsibility for childcare is more than double that of single-earner families (Crouter, Perry-Jenkins, Huston, & McHale, 1987).

The idea that fathers seldom assume sole or significant responsibility for any childcare tasks is "culturally limited": cross-cultural research has shown that men often have a significant degree of responsibility for children (Whiting & Whiting, 1975; Mackey, 1985). For instance, Mackey (1985) and his colleagues unobtrusively observed children associated with adult groups in public settings during daylight hours in 18 different cultural groups scattered across five continents. The percentage of observed children who were with adult "men only" groups ranged from 8.3% in Brazil (rural Karaja) to 32% in Israel (kibbutzim). In the United States (132 sites in Virginia) children were observed in public settings to be exclusively with adult men 17.5% of the time, with groups of adult men and women 39% of the time, and with groups of adult women only 43.5% of the time. In other words, even though women-children groups were the most common, children were in the company of men in about three-fifths of the observed cases, and men had the sole responsibility for children in almost one-fifth of the observed cases. Mackey's cross-cultural findings also indicated that the quality of men's behavior toward their children was similar to that of women's, and that men's treatment of boys and girls was surprisingly "gender neutral" (p. 169).

Conclusions

The above review of five categories of parent-child involvement suggests that the fundamental importance of the father-child relationship is not less than that of the mother-child relationship, and that children and adolescents can be as satisfied with the time they spend with their fathers as with their mothers (Hanson, 1986; Montemayor & Brownlee, 1987). Nevertheless, differences between father-child and mother-child relationships suggest at least two additional conclusions, one quite hopeful and one somewhat critical.

Most positive is the finding that, since the mid-1960s in the United States, the number of fathers who are becoming more highly involved in rearing their children is growing, and the amount of time fathers spend in childcare is increasing (Juster, 1985; Juster et al., 1978; Pleck, 1985, 1990). It appears that these trends will continue. The national Gallup Poll shows that a clear majority of men today derive "a greater sense of satisfaction from caring for their family than from a job well done at work" (59%), and these same men (75%) and their wives (80%) also believe that fathers "who stay home and care for children rather than work are just as capable as women of being good parents" (Gallup, 1991, p. 15). Other polls predict that fathers will be even more involved with their families in the year 2000—by the end of this decade (Chapman, 1987; McDermott, January 1990). Of course, the research also shows that the so-called "new fathers" —the ones who have received much attention in the popular media—are still uncommon (LaRossa, 1988). Nevertheless, the childrearing involvement of so-called "old fathers" exhibits so much variation that it still make sense to distinguish the growing number of "good fathers" from the less significantly involved fathers.

The review of prior surveys shows, however, that global measures of time spent in general childcare are not adequate as the sole measure of paternal participation in childrearing. Summary measures of time spent in general childcare activities, for instance, probably miss the unique contributions of men to their children and mask important differences between various types of paternal childrearing participation. The definitions of childcare in various studies, for instance, often reflect strikingly different but implicit assumptions about what childcare is and how it should be measured. Fathers' childcare is fairly consistently distinguished from housework and paid work. It is sometimes mistakenly distinguished from fathers' play activities with their children. Nevertheless, it is otherwise often defined in undifferentiated terms that are of little help in understanding fathers' psychological involvement with their children. Perhaps most unfortunately, the measurement of childcare typically does not employ a developmental perspective. Most measures make it difficult to consider that different types of fathers' childcare might vary in their relevance to aspects of development during different age periods of children's lives.

Beyond measuring the specific quantity of men's general childcare activity, it is important to measure fathers' participation in various specific types of childrearing activities (Zaslow, Pedersen, Suwalsky, Rabinovich, & Cain, 1986). In particular, men's parental generativity must be defined in more developmentally "sensitive" ways to make it possible to predict the origins and impact of variations in fathers' childcare practices. In sum, assessing the quantity of participation in specific types of activities and responsibilities is likely to be a more effective and helpful approach to assessing fathers' parental generativity. This chapter will introduce the types of paternal childrearing participation measured in the present study to operationalize the Eriksonian concept of parental generativity.

Research Questions

The key variables throughout this book are the types of fathers' parental generativity—forms of childrearing participation which provide developmental support or renew their children's physical, social, and intellectual capacities during the children's first and second decades of life. In this first brief empirical chapter, I seek the answers to two questions about fathers' childrearing activities.

Question 1: What is the frequency of men's participation in different types of childrearing?

How frequently do fathers' childrearing activities provide support for their offspring's social-emotional, intellectual-academic, and physical-athletic development during childhood and adolescence? The aim here is to establish the assessment of different types of parental generativity, which will make it possible to paint a more finely detailed portrait of childrearing fathers' activities. Such a multidimensional picture will be of significant benefit in later chapters, when the origins and consequences of fathers' generativity are explored.

Question 2: How are different types of childrearing participation related?

The relations between different types of fathers' childrearing activities begin to reveal the ways fathers' childrearing participation is patterned. If, for instance, fathers are highly involved in all types of activities with their young children but randomly participate in only a few activities of any type with their adolescents, then different types of participation will be significantly correlated within a childrearing decade but not across childrearing decades. In contrast, if men tend to focus on a particular type of participation consistently, regardless of their offspring's age, then that particular type of participation during the childhood decade will be significantly correlated with the same type during the adolescent decade. Many patterns are theoretically possible, of course, but my aim here is to clarify the empirical reality of childrearing participation among the Glueck subjects, the origins and consequences of which will then be addressed in subsequent chapters.

How the Study Was Conducted

Subjects

The 240 fathers in this study were originally part of the Gluecks' larger control group. This "Glueck sample" initially included 500 nondelinquent school boys (ages 14 +/– 2) from the Boston area who served as the control group for a sample of 500 delinquent boys; both groups were extensively studied during the 1940s. The control group (our sample) and the delinquents had been carefully matched for IQ, ethnicity, age, and residence in high crime neighborhoods. While the control group had been chosen for absence of obvious delinquency, it is important to note that eventually 19% of the control subjects spent some time in jail, a datum suggesting that the sample is only modestly biased toward good behavior.

Over 90% of the nondelinquent men (N = 456) were reinterviewed at age 25 and again at age 31 (Glueck, 1966; Glueck & Glueck, 1962, 1964, 1968). George Vaillant and his colleagues later followed 392 of these 456 men into middle age. This data gathering involved a 2-hour semiclinical interview at age 47 +/– 2 years, a questionnaire at age 52 +/– 2 years that assessed the educational and occupational attainments of the Glueck subjects' adult children who were 25 years of age or older, and subsequent semiannual questionnaires (Snarey & Vaillant, 1985).

The "father sample" in this study was affected by attrition and by the requirements of the investigation. Not all men had children when interviewed during early adulthood; among those who did, only the files that included complete and thorough data could be rated on fathers' participation in childrearing at two points in time. In addition, complete and thorough midlife interviews were required to rate subjects on the midlife outcomes (marital enjoyment, occupational mobility, and societal generativity). These restrictions reduced the sample from 456 to 240: the study's core sample of fathers.

When these 240 subjects were compared with the 216 excluded, besides the expected differences in fertility and mortality, significant bias was found in only one general area. Attrition was more common among men from multiproblem families, who in youth and adult life were the most antisocial and in adult life were the most severely mentally ill. These men, nonetheless, did not differ from the others in terms of IQ, ethnicity, childhood emotional problems, or childhood environmental strengths. Because the conclusions of the research presented in this book are based on comparisons among the individuals remaining in the study, however, these limitations should not seriously prejudice the findings.

Rating Parental Generativity

The three types of generativity defined earlier—biological (birth fatherhood), parental (childrearing fatherhood), and societal (cultural fatherhood)—must be operationalized in terms of measurable behavior before they can be studied. How parental generativity was measured is described below; how other types of generativity were rated will be described in later chapters, when they become a focus of the investigation.

Parental generativity is the keystone of the biological-parental-societal generativity arch that spans the gap between the generations and, of course, parental generativity is also the key variable in this study. In practical terms, parental generativity was defined as constructive care for a child's personal course of development. Empirically, it was operationalized as the tabulated instances of the men's actual childrearing participation which cared for one or more of three areas of their offspring's development, based on the traditional analytical tripartite breakdown of social-emotional, intellectual-cognitive, and physical-behavioral domains of human functioning (Chapter 1; Gedo & Goldberg, 1973). Each of these three types was tabulated for the childhood decade and for the adolescent decade of childrearing.

Interview Rating Procedure

The men's longitudinal interviews at ages 25, 31, and 47 cohere into a description of their childrearing participation culled from their responses to several sets of open-ended questions regarding their (a) relationship to wife and children, (b) personal interests and activities, (c) social-recreational activities, (d) religious activities, and (e) their children's activities and accomplishments. These data were technically collected blind in the sense that the interviewers did not know that the men's activities with their children would eventually be evaluated in relation to their children's outcomes or to the men's own midlife outcomes.

The frequency with which each father reported participating in rearing his first-born child was tabulated for the child's first decade of life (childhood, ages 0 to 10) and for the child's second decade of life (adolescence, ages 11 to 21). The first-decade participation rating was based either on the father's first or second early adulthood interview. The second-decade rating was based either on the father's second or third adulthood interview, depending on the year of his first child's birth. The division of the childrearing years into two decades was chosen because the interview data did not provide sufficient information to permit reliable tabulations for more narrowly defined periods of time. Prior research has also suggested, however, that fathers' influence upon their offspring differs when their offspring are children aged 10 or younger compared to when their offspring are older than 10 years of age (Landy, Rosenberg, & Sutton-Smith, 1969). The ratings were also limited to the fathers' first-born children, because the interview data did not provide sufficient information to permit reliable ratings for second-born or younger children.

Rating Guidelines for Varieties of Childrearing Participation

Each father's set of longitudinal interviews was culled for all instances of childrearing participation. Each example was classified according to six varieties of childrearing, as defined by the combination of the three types of childrearing participation and two parenting decades. Each father was thus rated on each of the following six categories of childrearing participation:

1. childhood social-emotional development
2. childhood intellectual-academic development
3. childhood physical-athletic development
4. adolescent social-emotional development

5. adolescent intellectual-academic development
6. adolescent physical-athletic development

The raters assigned childrearing activities to these six categories, on the basis of the following scoring rules. First, an activity was classified, according to the father's intent, in terms of an activity's primary function rather than simply according to content. Teaching a child how to pitch a baseball counted as a form of parental generativity that primarily promoted the child's physical development, for instance, but teaching a child how to understand baseball strategy or baseball statistics counted as promoting intellectual development, and accompanying a child to a baseball game for the sake of companionship counted as promoting social-emotional development. Second, without information regarding the intended function of a particular father-participation activity, the activity was assigned to the primary or most obvious category. Action-skill lessons and medical care activities, for instance, were counted as promoting physical-athletic competence; intellectual-skill lessons and cognitive activities were counted as promoting intellectual-academic competence; and companion activities were counted as promoting social-emotional competence.

Rating Reliability and Validity

Many studies of "parents" are really studies of "mothers" only, suggesting that mothers are thought to be better informants about family practices. In contrast, this study is obviously based on fathers' self-reports about family practices. Thus it is important to note that research comparing parents' perceptions with independently observed behavior in their families has shown that fathers "provide relatively objective" and "valid" information about family interaction patterns (Feldman, Wentzel, & Gehring, 1988, p. 33). Fathers' self-reports, in fact, showed the most convergence with observed behavior.

In the present study, each father's childrearing activities, as drawn from their longitudinal interviews, were rated by one of two expert judges uninformed about other aspects of the fathers' lives. To assess directly the validity as well as the reliability of the fathers' childrearing ratings, three issues were examined. These included interrater reliability, activity weighting, and activity sampling representativeness.

First, to estimate the level of interrater reliability, the longitudinal interviews for 35 of the fathers were randomly selected and independently rated by two blinded raters. Comparing the independently assigned ratings, the interrater reliability correlation coefficients for parental generativity during the childhood decade were .77 for care of social-emotional development, .78 for care of intellectual-academic development, and .97 for care of physical-athletic development. Regarding the adolescent decade, the interrater reliability coefficients were .83 for care of social-emotional development, .77 for care of intellectual development, and .95 for care of physical-athletic development. In sum, interrater reliability was fully adequate for research purposes.

Second, the agendas of the original interviews provided interviewees with three times as many opportunities to discuss their children's social-emotional development as to talk about their intellectual or physical development. Weighting was used to make the mean childrearing ratings comparable across the different types of childrearing being assessed. Specifically, each father received three points for each example related to intellectual or physical development and one point for each example related to social-emotional development.

Third and finally, it was important to estimate the reliability of the six childrearing ratings, because the interviews had gathered a sample of each father's parental generativity activities, rather than producing a comprehensive inventory of their childrearing activities. To evaluate the adequacy of this procedure, the Glueck fathers were stratified by their children's social mobility. A subgroup of ten father-child dyads was then selected (by the criterion of convenience) for an extended interview during restricted periods of time when the interviews could be conducted. Each adult child and his or her father were asked to recall together, in a joint tape-recorded interview, the diverse ways the father had been involved in the child's first decade of life and in adolescence. (One of the ten interviews was conducted with only the adult child of a deceased father.) Each of the ten interview transcripts was rated for types of parental generativity by two blinded raters. Overall interrater reliability for the ten cases was estimated to be .86; differences between the two ratings were resolved by averaging.

The childrearing ratings based on the recall interviews were compared with their longitudinally assessed ratings. The findings showed that, on average, the subjects recalled approximately 9 times as many childrearing activities as were noted in the fathers' own previous two longitudinal assessments (that is, a mean of 82.3 activities in the recall interview, compared with a mean of 9.2 activities in the combined set of longitudinal interviews). When the mean frequencies for the six different categories of childrearing participation were ranked from most common to least common, however, the rank order of the six childrearing activities based on the comprehensive recall inventory was identical to the rank order based on the longitudinal interview ratings, except that the two least frequently used varieties were reversed. (The ranked recalled childrearing activities, from most frequent to least frequent, were as follows: (1) childhood social development, (2) adolescent social development, (3) adolescent intellectual development, (4) childhood physical development, (5) adolescent physical development, and (6) childhood intellectual development.)

The correlations between the longitudinal and recall assessments were also examined. The correlations were positive, strong, and statistically significant for the total quantity of all childrearing activities during the childhood decade ($r = .78$, $p < .01$), the adolescent decade ($r = .74$, $p < .05$), and both decades combined ($r = .76$, $p < .05$). Similarly, the correlations between the longitudinal and recall assessments for the six individual ratings were all positive and reasonably strong. Despite the small size of the reliability sample, four of these six individual correlation coefficients were also statistically significant (intellectual activities during childhood, $r = .67$, $p < .05$; physical activities during childhood, $r = .70$, $p < .05$; social-emotional activities during childhood, $r = .45$, $.05 < p < .20$; intellectual activities during adolescence, $r = .69$, $p < .05$; physical activities during adolescence, $r = .51$, $.05 < p < .15$; and social-emotional activities during adolescence, $r = .84$, $p < .01$).

The above analyses show that the longitudinal ratings of fathers' childrearing used in this study provide a reasonably reliable and valid assessment of the fathers' childrearing activities that is adequate for research purposes.

What We Found: Patterns of Fathers' Parental Generativity

Examples of actual childrearing activities that were assigned to each of the six varieties of fathers' childrearing participation are summarized in Table 2.1. The basic patterns that characterize the frequency

Table 2.1   Childrearing rating categories: examples of fathers' parental generativity

Support of social-emotional development	Support of intellectual-academic development	Support of physical-athletic development
	During the childhood decade	
Rocks to sleep	Provides educational toys	Takes to doctor
Comforts child when afraid of the dark	Plays with and responds to baby's sounds	Gives bottle, feeds
Takes to visit relatives	Reads to child	Plays exercise games
Plays social games like peek-a-boo	Plays word games	Changes diaper
Takes trick-or-treating	Takes to children's museum	Teaches how to swim
Gives birthday party	Takes to library, bookstore	Takes shopping for first baseball glove
Spends special time with child before bedtime	Consults with teacher	Makes child's breakfast
Takes around with him during evening routine	Monitors homework	Monitors immunizations
Accompanies to church	Changes residence so child will be in better school	Demonstrates and encourages use of an erector set
Takes on Sunday drives	Provides music lessons	Takes to skating lessons, gymnastic lessons, others
Encourages child to invite friends home	Gives child a magazine subscription	Teaches how to ride a bike
Supports joining Scouts	Teaches how to identify different bird species, star constellations, and so on	Teaches how to dribble a basketball
	During the adolescent decade	
Takes on duo camping trip	Takes to science museum	Monitors personal hygiene
Monitors character of child's friends	Teaches baseball statistics	Teaches how to pitch a curve ball
Accompanies to church	Enrolls child in a nature study field trip	Provides sex education
Buys new house to provide nondelinquent peers	Takes to art gallery	Gives boxing lessons
Accompanies to ball game	Enrolls child in special courses	Teaches how to fish
Spends special time with child on weekend	Provides religious education	Takes shopping to buy new corrective shoes
Talks about emotionally charged issues	Takes on trip to visit other cultural groups	Takes to dentist
Chaperons a dance	Takes to library, bookstore	Monitors possible drug or alcohol abuse
Allows slumber party	Discusses school courses	Monitors nutrition
Provides guidance on dating problems	Discusses books or newspaper articles with child	Teaches how to improve hockey game
Gives advice on resolving a social conflict	Gives feedback on term paper	Teaches how to drive an automobile
Encourages to invite friends to the house	Solicits and discusses political opinions	Takes for physical exam

of interaction and relations among the fathers' six basic varieties of childrearing participation are described below. These findings set the stage for subsequent chapters, which will report on the men's boyhood or adulthood background characteristics that predict their childrearing practices and the consequences of their participation for their own outcomes at midlife, and for their children's subsequent outcomes in adulthood.

Level of Fathers' Parental Generativity

On average, 9.3 childrearing activities were noted in the fathers' two combined childrearing assessments. Some fathers, of course, were less involved than others: the men's records indicate that 35% participated in 0 to 6 childrearing activities; given that there were three types of parental generativity assessed at two points in time, this meant that, on average, these 85 men were not very active in their children's lives. Another 41% of the fathers had 7 to 12 activities noted in their two interviews; because the reliability study also indicated that the actual childrearing activities were probably about 9 times higher than the estimated childrearing ratings, the ratings for these 98 fathers suggest that, on average, they were substantially involved with their children. Finally, 24% of the men were involved in 13 to more than two dozen childrearing activities; this meant that these 57 fathers were highly involved in their children's lives.

Total participation among all of the fathers was, on average, higher at the time of the interview during the childhood decade ($M = 5.04$) than at the time of the interview during the adolescent decade ($M = 4.24$). During both decades, fathers provided more support for their children's social-emotional development relative to other types of childrearing participation, although the total decreased from the childhood decade ($M = 3.49$) to the adolescent decade ($M = 2.28$). The second most common type of fathers' childrearing participation during the childhood decade was support of physical-athletic development ($M = .85$); that contribution decreased and was ranked third during the adolescent decade ($M = .53$). Fathers provided the least amount of care during the childhood decade for their children's intellectual-academic development ($M = .70$), but intellectual-academic childrearing support subsequently increased and became the second most common form of childrearing participation during the adolescent decade ($M = 1.44$).

To consolidate these variations in childrearing participation levels, and to also consider possible gender differences and interaction effects, a repeated-measures analysis of variance was conducted. (The design included two within-subjects factors: childrearing decade—childhood or adolescence, and type of development—physical-athletic, intellectual-academic, or social-emotional; it also included one between-subjects factor, gender.) The results showed that there was not a significant main effect for gender [F (1, 238) = 1.24, p = N.S.]; that is, fathers give their daughters and sons similar levels of overall childrearing support. There was a significant main effect for childrearing decade [F (1, 238) = 25.66, $p < .005$], but there was not a significant gender-by-decade interaction; this finding indicated that fathers offer a significantly higher level of overall childrearing support during the childhood than during the adolescent decade to daughters and sons alike. There was also a significant interaction between type of parental generativity and the decade of childrearing [F (2, 476) = 44.80, $p < .001$], but no significant gender-by-decade or gender-by-type interaction. Post hoc analyses indicated that fathers' support of social-emotional development was significantly greater during childhood than during adolescence [t (239) = 9.50, $p < .001$], support of physical-athletic development was also significantly greater during childhood than adolescence [t (239) = 2.34, $p < .05$], but support of intellectual-academic development was greater during adolescence than childhood [t (239) = −4.08, $p < .001$].

Relationships Between Types of Parental Generativity

The correlation matrix reported in Table 2.2 summarizes the patterns of association between the ratings for the three types of parental generativity during the childhood decade, during the adolescent decade, and between the childhood and adolescent decades.

Within the childhood decade, as shown in Table 2.2, there are no significant correlations between the three types of parental generativity. Fathers who give especially strong childrearing support in one area are not more likely also to engage in other types of childrearing support. For instance, fathers who offer their children much care for their physical-athletic development are *not* therefore significantly more likely to provide strong social-emotional or intellectual-academic support.

Table 2.2 Associations between types of parental generativity: correlation matrix

	Fathers' childrearing support of:					
	Childhood development			Adolescent development		
Fathers' childrearing support of:	Social	Intellectual	Physical	Social	Intellectual	Physical
Childhood development						
Social-emotional	—					
Intellectual-academic	.062	—				
Physical-athletic	.096	.077	—			
Adolescent development						
Social-emotional	.299***	.002	.020	—		
Intellectual-academic	.045	.168**	.220***	.214***	—	
Physical-athletic	.012	.032	.304***	.237***	.137*	—

Note: *$p \leq .05$, **$p \leq .01$, ***$p \leq .001$; N = 240.

Within the adolescent decade, in contrast, all three types of parental generativity are significantly and positively correlated. Fathers who are active in one type of childrearing tend to be quite active in all three types of childrearing. For instance, fathers who give their adolescents a great deal of intellectual-academic support are more likely also to provide support for social-emotional and physical-athletic development.

It is notable that ratings for the *same* type of parental generativity were always significantly and positively correlated between the childhood and adolescent decades. For instance, fathers who were highly involved in caring for their offspring's social-emotional development during the first decade also tended to be highly supportive of social-emotional development during the adolescent decade. This was also true for physical-athletic and intellectual-academic childrearing support.

It is also notable that between the childhood and adolescent decades, with only one exception, the ratings for *different* types of parental generativity were not significantly correlated; fathers who were highly supportive of their children's social-emotional participation during the childhood decade, for instance, were not more likely to be especially supportive of their children's intellectual-academic or physical-athletic development during the adolescent decade. The one exception was that fathers who were highly supportive of their offspring's physical-athletic development during the childhood decade were also likely to be highly supportive of their offspring's intellectual-academic development during the adolescent decade. This finding is consistent with the previously noted finding that support of physical-athletic development was the second most frequent type of participation during the childhood decade, but it was replaced by support of intellectual-academic development as the second most frequent type of care provided during the adolescent decade.

Discussion of the Findings

The level of childrearing participation during the two combined decades was relatively low for 3.5 out of every 10 fathers; 4 out of 10 fathers were substantially involved with their children; and 2.4 out of every 10 were very highly involved. Total participation among all of the fathers was, on average, higher during the childhood decade than during the second decade, supporting the common observation that children's involvement with their parents tends to decline when adolescents' psychosocial attention turns to issues of separation and identity achievement.

The approach used to classify different types of childrearing activities turned out to have intuitive validity as well as being psychometrically valid and reliable. It proved reasonable, for instance, to count companion activities as promoting social-emotional competence, intellectual skill lessons and cognitive activities as promoting intellectual-academic competence, and action skill lessons or medical care activities as promoting physical-athletic development. The classification of childrearing activities according to their function rather than simply content was also possible within similar settings. For instance, a father who took his daughter to the beach could receive credit for promoting all types of development: talking with her about her concerns during a father-daughter walk on the beach would be rated as promoting social-emotional development; teaching her how to identify different kinds of seaweed or shore birds on the beach would be rated as promoting intellectual-academic development; and challenging her to a 50-yard dash up the shore line would be rated as promoting physical-athletic development. Of course, although an event, such as a visit to the beach, might potentially provide opportunities to care for all three types of development, fathers' actual choices were usually more limited, apparently reflecting personal preferences to support particular types of development during particular age-periods.

It is noteworthy that the fathers' treatment of sons and daughters was much the same. There were no significant gender differences, that is, in the quantity or types of childrearing that fathers provided for their offspring. The influence of the child's sex upon a father's childrearing involvement has been investigated in several studies, but the results have been inconsistent. Some studies report that fathers prefer to interact with sons (Barnett & Baruch, 1987; Belsky, 1979a; Bloom-Feshbach, 1979; Bronstein, 1988a; Lamb, 1977). Other studies report that fathers are more involved with daughters (Lamb, Hwang, Broberg, Brookstein, et al., 1988). Finally, several studies show no significant paternal preference for sons or daughters (Belsky, Giltrap, & Rovine, 1984; Feldman & Gehring, 1988; Grossman, Pollack, & Golding, 1988; Russell & Russell, 1987). The age of the children involved in these investigations appears to explain some of the different findings. Among studies of fathers of infants, the evidence fairly consistently indicates that fathers show more interest in sons than in daughters (Bronstein, 1988a). Among studies of fathers of older children, however, important associations between fathers' childrearing and their children's gender are less common. Crouter and Crowley (1990) considered the possibility of a difference in the apparent "preference" of fathers in single-earner versus dual-earner families (see Volling & Belsky, 1991). The results of their study revealed that fathers in single-breadwinner families spent more time in one-on-one activities with their sons than with their daughters, but that fathers in two-breadwinner families spent equivalent amounts of time with their sons and daughters.

Continuities as well as discontinuities were seen in the relative frequency of childrearing support that fathers provided to their daughters and sons across the three types and two decades of childrearing. Continuity was indicated by the finding that support of social-emotional development was the most prevalent type of care during both the childhood decade and the adolescent decade. Fathers, for instance, continued to be in the audience for their children's athletic games during both childrearing decades. Continuity was also notable in the finding that ratings for the same type of childrearing participation were always significantly correlated between the childhood and adolescent decades. Fathers' high involvement in their children's physical-athletic development during the childhood decade carried over to their adolescent decade. The findings also showed that the three different types of childrearing were always significantly correlated during the adolescent decade. This may suggest that, by adolescence, fathers have developed a more comprehensive understanding and integrated approach to promoting their children's development.

The discontinuities, however, are equally interesting. The three different types of childrearing within the childhood decade were not correlated, suggesting that fathers of younger children may tend to focus on one isolated area of their child's development in a way that may not integrate into a comprehensive approach to their child's growth. In contrast to the ongoing continuity of care for social-emotional development across both decades, discontinuity characterizes the other two types of parental generativity. Support of physical-athletic development ranked second and was much higher during childhood compared to adolescence. This finding is generally consistent with the research of MacDonald and Parke (1986), which indicates that fathers' physical play with their offspring peaks in childhood and declines thereafter. In contrast, care for intellectual-academic development moved up to second place and assumed more importance during adolescence than during childhood. The correlation coefficients also indicate that fathers who provided more physical-athletic childrearing support during childhood later tended to increase their support for intellectual-academic development during adolescence. This shift in fathers' childrearing practices in relation to their children's age is difficult to interpret, but it suggests that fathers' ongoing childrearing participation is invested in different areas of development according to their awareness of their children's changing capacities and developmental tasks. Effective fathering, from this perspective, can be understood as an interactional process of adjusting to the child's different levels of competence and experience (Lee, 1991). During infancy, for instance, father-infant interaction is between two people of drastically disparate levels of experience. As this balance gradually shifts during childhood and adolescence, psychologists from Anna Freud (1952) to Jay Belsky (1984) have suggested that effective childcare givers, both parental and nonparental, must also reorient their childrearing participation accordingly. Even during later life, when the experiential contrast between father and child becomes less striking and the balance of competence gradually shifts in favor of the adult child, the relationship must again change if it is to be effectively maintained.

From the perspective of adult development, continuities and discontinuities in fathers' parental generativity may also indicate that the men were attuned to their own personal needs and predispositions, as well as to their children's developmentally based capacities and tasks. The increase in intellectually oriented activities during the second decade of childrearing, for instance, may reflect an adjustment to their adolescents' new intellectual abilities, but it may also express the fathers' own desire to launch their adolescents successfully into college and careers. Similarly, the change in physical-athletic attention may reflect the adolescents' decreased physical vulnerability and increased intellectual stamina, but it may also reflect the men's own decreased physical stamina (MacDonald & Parke, 1986). The origins of continuities are also likely found both in the fathers' and their children's lives. Tendencies to support intellectual-academic development across both decades, for instance, may reflect the men's perception of their children's innate and ongoing strengths, the men's own ongoing personal character preferences, psychological vulnerabilities, or broader societal expectations. Untangling the historical origins and long-term consequences of these childrearing activities, however, is the task of subsequent chapters.

Placing the Findings in Context

It is important to acknowledge that the historical and personal context of the men's childrearing activities gave each specific childrearing activity a distinctiveness that could not be fully contained by any number of rating categories. (The limits of the data and other related caveats, such as the lack of childrearing participation ratings for the fathers' wives, will be discussed at length in the final chapter.)

The first self-portrait of a father-son relationship, presented in the next chapter, begins to illustrate the distinctiveness of each father's varieties of childrearing participation. It also begins to unveil the common features of many paternal generativity success stories. Statistically-oriented readers may be tempted to skip or skim the qualitative stories, just as narrative-oriented readers may be tempted to skip or skim the quantitative studies. It would be unfortunate to follow this inclination. The self-portrait stories allow one to draw near to the historical context of the lives under study; putting them together with the statistical studies makes it possible to draw out insights that would otherwise be unobtainable.

3

Bill and Bill Jr.: Father–Son Harmony

This self-portrait of a father-son relationship is, in part, the story of how a father's parental generativity contributed to his son's physical-athletic, social-emotional, and intellectual-academic development. It is also the story of an unusually strong father-son bond that was engendered during the son's infancy, became more complex during the course of his childhood and adolescent years, and was further strengthened when the son himself experienced fatherhood.

The father, Bill Sr., is a cordial, well-groomed man in his late fifties. His father, Richard, was a skilled worker, and Bill too is a highly skilled factory worker—a precision mechanical inspector. He has been married for over 35 years, and he and his wife, Betty, have six children.

The son, Bill Jr., is warm and cordial like his father. He is a college graduate, with advanced graduate training in personnel management. Currently, he is a major administrator for the same company where his father works. Bill Jr. has been married for about 15 years; he and his wife, Debbie, have three children.

Father and son gave their stories while seated around the kitchen table in the house in which Bill Sr. and Betty had raised Bill Jr. and their other children.

Early Memories

The Father Looks Back a Generation

My father was a freight brakeman on the railroad. He went back and forth on the trains between Boston and Connecticut and Rhode Island. They'd bring the boxcars to their destination and put them on different sidings, separate the different boxcars, and then pick up another set to bring back again.

I recall him taking us down to his caboose; we always had a lot of fun down there, my young sister and I, climbing up on the bunks and everything. He worked different hours, so we didn't get to do that too much, actually. Maybe that's why we enjoyed it so much, when he did take us down there.

Every now and then, my father would also take us on an outing someplace. I remember he used to get free passes for the family and take us on a trip to New York by train; we used to have some pretty good times there. Those are about the only memories I can really recall. He was pretty well tied up most of the time with his work. He was working quite a bit. He'd even be gone weekends sometimes.

He was a quiet man. (Well, I'm not really sure, because I didn't get to enjoy him that much in the short time I had him. But it seemed to me that he was kind of quiet.) He was also the kind of man who enjoyed life. When there was music around, he'd start dancing. He loved to dance, he loved to have a good time. He liked to polka and waltz, and the family, we were all brought up dancing. We all enjoyed a good time. (My wife, Betty, and I still go dancing on Saturday nights. We go down to a place where they still have a big band, one of the last places with a swing band. It's terrific.)

We used to just have good times at home, just being a family, I guess. I remember my father played the accordion, and we had some enjoyable times at home just enjoying his music. I've always been a music lover, maybe because of that. I like anything from classics to rock—you can see the collection I have in the other room, and get an idea. I have CDs, LPs, of Bach, Beethoven, Mozart, right up to the Moody Blues. I'm a great Moody Blues fan. I have about 13 of their albums. I like any kind of music, except real heavy jazz. When I think of my father, I remember enjoyable music, mainly.

My father got involved in disciplining me sometimes. I remember one time, I was down the street hanging out with a bunch of kids, and my father came down, he was mad because I hadn't come home early enough, and he pulled me up the street by the ear, I remember. Right by the ear, led me right up the street, and I was embarrassed as heck (laughs). But he disciplined me sometimes, and my mother did, too.[1]

I lost my father when I was, ah, fifteen. Things were tougher after

---

1. Bill's longitudinal records confirm that both parents provided firm but kindly supervision, and that his father also used physical punishment to discipline him when he was a young teenager. His boyhood records do not indicate that his mother used physical punishment.

he died. There were eight of us, to begin with, and I was number six (laughs). Everything we on the bottom got was hand-me-down. The older boys got things like ice skates and everything, and we were down at the bottom, and we wore the ice skates that they wore years before that. That's the way it went in those days. The firemen would come down to the park in the winter and flood it; it would harden into ice, solidify, and that's where we did our skating, too. Most of the time I'd be skating on my ankles, because the skates never really fit. We'd stuff them with paper, lace them up the best we could. But, we were happy. Still, I regret that we were never really involved in anything; we didn't have Little League or anything like that in those days.[2]

After he died, it was pretty bad. Having him for so few years, I had a long time of grief. I remember I didn't cry or anything, but I was eaten up inside. I didn't let it out. (My wife has helped me over the years to get things out.)[3]

I think after my father died, I kind of lost interest in school, to tell you the truth. Because it seemed like after that, I wanted to quit. So I have a feeling that might have affected me somehow. I was 15 when he died, and I quit when I was 16.

My mother complained about money quite a bit, not having enough money, and right after my father died, three members of my family got married the same year. My oldest brother, my second oldest brother, and my oldest sister all got married in that same year, all in the latter part of the year he died. So maybe I used that as an excuse to quit school so I could go to work and make money and help my family and help my mother out. She was hard-pressed for money at the time, because she had lost so many children that paid. See, the way we were brought up, when we got our pay, we gave our whole pay to my mother and she gave us in return what we needed for the

2. As we know that Bill Sr. was highly involved in childrearing, this specific regret raises our expectation that he will rework or compensate for his past by making sure that Bill Jr. has lots of father-son baseball memories.

3. Previous research suggests that a supportive relationship between husband and wife can help to resolve and prevent the intergenerational transmission of suffering from father to child (see Quinton & Rutter, 1985). The positive quality of Bill's marital relationship, juxtaposed with the death of his father when Bill was 15 years old, is also consistent with the findings of an exploratory study by Jacobson and Ryder (1969). They reported that the death of a father before the boy was 12 years old was predictive of subsequent marital difficulties during adulthood, but that when the death of a father occurred after the boy was 12 years old, that event predicted a positive marital relationship.

week. I was a paperboy, I had a route on the paper before school and after school. I gave the whole pay, and she gave me so much for spending money. Then later on, when I started to work full time, I still gave her my whole pay but we split my overtime when I'd work on Saturday.

I guess I was influenced by my parents to start my own family. As you're growing up, you see how your mother and father have grown up and met each other and fallen in love and got married, and it just seemed like the thing that was going to happen, just seemed like a normal thing. I met my wife where I worked when I was about 18, and we fell in love, and I guess we went together for about a year, we finally got engaged and a year later, in 1952, we got married.

My father was a good provider for the family. Sometimes he worked 50–60 hours a week, I'd say. There were periods, days at a time, when I wouldn't see him at all, because he'd be down in Hartford or New Haven. I've always tried to be a good provider for my family, too. I think we have that in common. I saw that in him, and I try to emulate that by treating my children the same way in making sure they had food and clothes, their toys, and everything. I think every one of them had bikes and everything when they were growing up. I tried to always let them, make them, have more than I had.[4]

The Father's Earliest Memories of His Son

Well (sighs), one of the earliest things I can remember vividly was when Bill got sick. He was about a year old, going on two, and we thought we might lose him. We were really worried. He had gotten pneumonia down in his intestine, and we thought he had appendicitis. We took him to the children's hospital, and after a couple of days, they did a job on that. They knocked the pneumonia right out of him, and he was okay after that.[5]

I also remember that as a child he was very allergic. We couldn't

4. Bill Sr.'s reaction at age 15 to the death of his father was to drop out of school and, understandably, to feel "eaten up inside." By age 18, however, he had met his future wife and had begun to discover a way of restoring life. By creating his own family and becoming a father to his own son, he was able to "emulate" his own father and apparently to rework his loss. In this three-generational context, the "first" memory he offers us of his son takes on added significance.

5. In Eriksonian terminology, the first memory Bill shares concerning his son was an experience of generativity chill.

give him regular formula; we had to give him a soybean formula. We had to watch what he ate. I remember when he was broken out from head to foot with rash. He was all red in the scalp, between his legs, everywhere. It must have really been sore. But finally we took him to this doctor in Bradford, Dr. Sims, who was a pediatrician, and he found out the problems that we had. He changed his diet and everything, and Bill got over that.

As a little boy, he always enjoyed playing. He got along well with others. He had his little fights with the kids in the block and everything, but they all had that. He seemed to be a happy child most of the time. I think we raised him halfway decent. I think we always gave him love and affection. We always went to his things he had in school: plays and things like that, and then in sports. I'd always go to his baseball games. One time he was picked for the Allstar team in Youth Baseball. He was on the Pirates, I remember. I was proud of him that time. He was never much of a hitter, but he was a great fielder. A great defensive player.

The Son's Earliest Memories of His Father

My earliest memory of my father goes back to having pneumonia and being in the hospital. I remember him coming in, and my being very upset at being there, and him having brought several things that were really important to me—a toy airplane and some books. I can vividly see him and my mother coming into the room at that point.[6]

When I was a young boy, he was a companion. He was someone that I was with all the time. I remember, when I was about age 4, him practicing baseball with me. My memories of him were that he wanted to do a lot of things with me, that he was very friendly.[7]

I can recall, when I was 9 years old, him taking me outside in the middle of the night, at 2:00 in the morning, to show me when the Telstar had made its first pass. He talked about his interest in science—I remember his interests because they were shared interests.

6. It would not be unreasonable to speculate that this early "memory" is partly a reconstructed or internalized family story (Fivush et al., 1986; Neisser, 1967). In the context of this and the other self-portraits, however, the significance of "first" memories resides primarily in their metaphorical power.

7. Both of Bill Jr.'s earliest childhood memories of his father's childrearing activities would be coded as promoting both physical-athletic and social-emotional support.

He was very much interested in the stars, and we got a little telescope and we'd look at the stars. He was very interested in nature. He would watch—even in the city—we would watch the birds that were there. Star gazing, bird watching, this type of things.[8]

Joint Reflections on the First Decade
Life Threatened

BILL SENIOR: Well, in the beginning, we took him to the doctors a lot. Over to Bradford, to Dr. Sims, with your rash and everything. You were pretty young then, do you remember your rash?

BILL JUNIOR: No. My first memory of illness was when I had pneumonia.

BILL SENIOR: Oh, yeah, we had to take you to the children's hospital. We were going crazy outside because they wouldn't let us come in, and we heard him moaning and groaning in there. They were trying to find out what was wrong with him. We thought he had appendicitis. It turned out he had pneumonia down in his intestine. Oh, that was a big worry.

BILL JUNIOR: I remember that I was very insulted because the hospital was real crowded, and they put me into a crib. I remember thinking I was too big for a crib, because I slept in a bed at home (laughs).[9]

Family Vacations

BILL JUNIOR: I also have recollections of going up to New Hampshire from when I was very young, until I was, say, 8 or so. It was about the time we bought the house, so I'm going to guess that we could no longer afford to go on vacations up there.

---

8. Bill Jr.'s other early memories of his father also include childrearing activities that primarily promoted his sense of intellectual-academic industry and excitement. It seems appropriate, for a son who was being prepared to leave the working class, that all of the noted activities literally encouraged Bill Jr. to look beyond his small backyard.

9. Generativity chill has a prominent position in their joint reflections, just as it did in Bill Sr.'s privately shared earliest memory of his son and Bill Jr's privately shared earliest memory of his father.

BILL SENIOR: That's right. We used to go up to New Hampshire before we moved here. We started that when you were two years old, did that for several years, then we eventually got away from it for a while. Up to a place in Lake Winnipesaukee where my wife and I had gone on our honeymoon. (Pauses, as if to savor the memory.) Then we just kept going back there, because it was a family place. They had a nice beach, the water was shallow, it was safe for the kids, and they had housekeeping cabins, so we could supply our own food and cook our own food. It was kind of nice. We had a lot of good times up there.[10]

BILL JUNIOR: I remember having a lot of fun up there. We didn't have a lot of money, so our family vacations were here on the beach. My father would be here with us on the weekends, at the public beach just across the street.

BILL SENIOR: We had a lot of fun. We have the beach right across the street from us, and so we lived on the sea shore. When they were kids, they were like fish. They were in the water all the time. They loved the water. We enjoyed a lot of days over there, before it became polluted like it is now. Can't swim over there any more. It's a shame, because we got such a nice beach over there, but the way the water's gotten polluted, you don't dare go swimming. I just go over there and walk, that's about all. It's a shame the way manufacturing goes against the environment. I love the water so much, I really miss it.[11]

BILL JUNIOR: The whole family feels that way. I can recall my father buying me my first diving mask; I was very young, probably five years old. Remember the double snorkel mask?

BILL SENIOR: I got you that when we were up at Lake Winnipesaukee.

BILL JUNIOR: You remember it, sure. I was proud of it. (I am into scuba diving now.)

BILL SENIOR: He loves to scuba dive. He showed me a picture a little while ago; he had a lobster in front of him, a 9-pound lobster.

10. In the absence of other information, family vacations were coded as providing support for a child's social-emotional development.

11. The life history of an individual and the life history of a community are always intertwined. In the present-day Boston community only 4% of the sewage is adequately treated before discharge into Boston Harbor (Linden, 1988); hence fathers raising their children in the same neighborhoods of Boston today obviously cannot get them to enjoy the ocean by taking them for a swim at city beaches.

He goes down and catches them by hand (laughs). He goes down and pulls them out of the rocks.[12]

Father's Advice and Intuition

BILL SENIOR: I remember a time when you were a kid, you came crying to me, up in Old Street. You said, "Joey Allen hit me!" I said, "Go kill him!" He went running down the street and he beat him up (laughs). He came back.

BILL JUNIOR: I was probably about 12 or 13. There was also a place up the street here that served ice cream in the summer and it closed during the winter. Three of us kids had broken into the basement, the cellar, and had our clubhouse in there. We thought this was pretty serious stuff—to have a secret club and to smoke cigarettes down there. Well, the police came one day, banged on the door, said "We know you're in there" and they took the two other kids and I ran out the back way. I came home, and I was distraught because I really felt there was this major crime I had committed, and later on I found out they had just yelled at the two kids and took them home. But I really thought I was ready to be dragged off in handcuffs. I can recall my father coming up to me—thinking that no one knew my deep dark secret, sitting in my room, sitting at my desk reading, him coming in to me and saying, "I know something's bothering you. What's going on?" It was probably all over my face, but that stands out. Me pouring out the whole story, and him saying, "Well, you know . . ." I don't know what he said, I don't remember the words he said, but calming me down and reassuring me that things would work out okay.[13]

Encouragement of Athletic Participation

BILL JUNIOR: On the positive side, I guess my memories predominantly are real sports oriented. Growing up, baseball dominated my life: first Farm League, then Little League from 7 to 12, and then

12. The gift of his first snorkel mask supported Bill Jr.'s physical-athletic development, and possibly his intellectual-academic interests, in a way that has endured to the present.

13. Bill provided social-emotional support rather than emulating his own father's use of physical discipline.

Babe Ruth League from 13 on up. I started Farm League in Boston where I was born. My father was a coach.

BILL SENIOR: Bill has always been very good at sports. I coached one of the teams there, and I enjoyed my involvement with him in that. Then we moved here. I didn't coach but I took him to his games. If I had to work overtime, my wife would drop him off and I'd go down after I finished work, and if he was in the middle of a game, I'd see the rest of the game. I enjoyed being in it myself and so, sometimes, I also used to do a little assistant coaching. You know, "help out the coach."

BILL JUNIOR: We moved here when I was about 7 and, as small as our yard was, my father and I stretched the parameters of that, playing catch and doing everything we could. I recall making a decision when I made my first communion: Did I want to go to a baseball game or did I want to get a religious statue? The baseball game won out! Sports was very much a big part of my upbringing. All baseball. Until my teens, I didn't know that there were other sports outside of baseball.

I remember one year, around the 6th or 7th grade, they selected the best players from both Allstar teams and combined them to make one team. I played shortstop. We were a traveling team that went around the area. I was always a pretty good player, so I was always proud to have my parents in the stands. Remember that?

BILL SENIOR: Oh, yeah! I remember he was proud to see me show up, at his games or other things like that. You could just see the smile on his face; it was something that you knew. When I'd show up at any of the kids' games or something, they always looked up and saw me, and the look in their eyes—you knew that they were happy you were there, to watch them play.

BILL JUNIOR: My recollection was of me playing the sport, my father practicing with me, and then coming to the games. I didn't feel like it was an adult and a kid. He would play the catcher and I would play the pitcher, and he would treat me like I was a real pitcher: "Okay, I'm giving you a signal for a curve now." I felt that we were on an equal level in terms of my being a baseball player with him being a baseball player. I felt that he treated me, thinking back now, as a grown-up player. Someone who is not "I'm practicing with you so you can be a better pitcher." I didn't feel that way in practice.

BILL SENIOR: I felt the same. I always tried to help him as much as I could. I felt like I was playing when I was practicing with him, about like we were teammates in the sense that we both got a lot of enjoyment out of that. Anytime we had a minute, we'd be throwing the ball back and forth.

BILL JUNIOR: Very much. Practice time was almost all the time. It was ongoing. Anytime you could get the time you were out in the back yard throwing. I lived baseball.

BILL SENIOR: He always excelled in sports. I always felt proud of him in sports because I never saw anyone who tried harder at sports than he did. He was so aggressive. He always gave the extra effort. It wasn't any specific game; it seemed to be every game. That was his trait—to try hard at everything he did. Like, I'd take him out—just batting balls out to him—and I'd hit up a fly ball, nowhere in this world did I think he was going to make that catch, but he'd make a diving, unbelievable catch, because he gave that extra effort and went full tilt at it. I always really thought so much of him for that, for the try. Even if he didn't make the catch, but the effort he gave was fantastic.[14]

He's always been very aggressive. I remember when we got him a bike. He was still a little boy, so in order to ride the bike, he had to get up on the front step and get on the two-wheeler and ride down the street. He'd go boom! crash! but he'd get up, bring the bike back, get up on the step, get on it again. He did it and did it until he mastered it. He was cut, bruised, and everything, but he didn't give up. Bill's always been that way. Always worked hard at everything he did and managed to master just about everything he went after too.

Father's Concern for Neighborhood Children

BILL JUNIOR: I remember there were three boys who visited their grandparents, who lived down the street, during the summer. I can remember my father being on vacation and being home and saying, "Come on, let's go for a walk," and one of the other boys came along,

14. Throughout this joint account of baseball, the father's participation merges support for physical-athletic and social-emotional development. Bill helped his son to practice the physical skills of the game, and their emotional bonding was also deepened by their physical-athletic interaction. He attended the games and made his presence felt from the stands by making eye-contact with his son on the field. He encouraged the development of both physical skills and emotional confidence to help the son give his best effort.

and these boys didn't have their father—their father had passed away. My father invited them along. I was about 12, and I remember thinking to myself, "Gee, I really didn't want them to come," because I wanted him to myself, and then thinking afterwards that he would be a pretty nice guy, because these kids didn't have any father.[15]

That was kind of indicative of that period of time where he was working so much, there wasn't a lot of time. We did get the weekends, but even then with six kids, that was pretty full time.

BILL SENIOR: That's for sure. The main things I remember are going on picnics, and going to the park or the drive-in or the beach. Local stuff; the carnival, when it came into town.

BILL JUNIOR: I can remember you spending a fortune trying to win a stuffed animal for Barbara—our one sister. Things like that.

Developing Shared Interests

BILL JUNIOR: I can recall from early on—from 5 years old and up through my teens and on—the music was always there. What I was always proud of was that my father's musical interests equalled or bettered that of my contemporaries. I could always talk with him about music. When the Beatles came out, I was the only kid who had a parent who thought the Beatles were a good band and who was interested.[16]

I was learning classical interests from him and sharing contemporary interests with him. There was a lot of, "Here's the latest stereo equipment. Here's the latest recording that's out. . . ."[17]

BILL SENIOR: I remember that, because I've always been able to enjoy all kinds of music, and just like he says, when the Beatles came along, I thought they were great. Anything from rock to classical.

BILL JUNIOR: To be in fourth grade and have your father liking the Beatles, you know, was something significant. I never had hassles

15. Bill Sr.'s sensitivity to and mentorship of fatherless boys may reflect an altruistic style of coping with the fact that he had lost his own father at an early age; in the process, he also provided his own son with a model of social-emotional concern for others.

16. Bill Sr.'s openness to contemporary rock music communicated his availability to his son. This message, like the Beatles' rule over rock music, was ongoing throughout Bill Jr.'s second decade of life.

17. Their joint conversations regarding music also provided intellectual-academic support.

about, "Shut that off." (Both laugh.) No. If anything, my mother was the one—she'd be telling him as well as me. One other thing that comes to mind is my father was working out at a shipyard in Shoreline. He worked on the tracking ships that they were building to electronically track the first space capsules. And I remember having a lot of dialogue with him about those space capsules—the Vanguard, the Mercury—and the Redstone rocket.[18]

I remember that he took me down there, when they had opening ceremonies, and I got tours. I was proud that he was a part of what was actually going into the ships. Then I remember seeing them later on TV, when the ships were recovering the capsules out of the ocean. I was proud that my father had a piece of that.[19]

Joint Reflections on the Second Decade

Replicating the Father's Work-Roles

BILL JUNIOR: He started working two jobs about the time I became a teenager. They had the fifth child when I was 10 and then the last when I was 16 and he had to work even harder. I can recall him getting up in the middle of the night one night and punching a hole in the wall, releasing his frustration that way.

He still came to see my games, and we also started to go to a lot of professional football games together, but he was less involved with actual athletic participation. He wasn't actively a full coach.[20]

18. Bill Sr. encouraged Bill Jr.'s intellectual-academic interests in space exploration throughout most of Bill Jr.'s childhood: Vanguard, the earliest space program Bill Jr. mentioned, launched satellites into orbit in 1957 and 1958, when he was 4 or 5 years old. In 1961, when Bill Jr. was 7 years old, a Redstone rocket carried a Mercury capsule into space with the first U.S. astronaut, Alan Shepard, on board for a 15-minute suborbital flight. In 1962, when Bill Jr. was 9 years old, another Mercury flight carried the first U.S. astronaut to orbit the Earth, John Glenn, into a three-orbit flight of the planet. (Telstar, which Bill Jr. mentioned earlier, was also launched later in 1962.) Mercury, the most recent of the space programs he referred to, ended in 1963 when Bill Jr. was 10 years old (Lewis, 1990; Oberg, 1990).

19. It makes sense that a father who was preparing to launch his son into upward social mobility would give him rockets and soaring astronauts as symbols of success. The idea that his father's societal generativity at work had contributed something to the success of these symbols also may have diminished Bill Jr.'s ambivalence about leaving his family's working-class background.

20. This shift in roles from coaching to observing his son's physical-athletic development illustrates a common change in fathers' childrearing activities during the transition from the childhood decade to the adolescent decade.

BILL SENIOR: That's right. It was hard to spend as much time with him. I had to get the house payment and everything, so I had to make extra money at the time. Although I believe the mortgage was something like $98 a month, it was a lot of money.

BILL JUNIOR: I also started working when I was 13. A paper route, that was my first job. So I also had less time.

BILL SENIOR: Right, Bill was a paperboy, and he helped with bringing money in then.[21]

After that, when you were about 14, you started working at Tremont Street Jewelers.

He was a hard worker and a hard player. He had a paper route and then, when he was in high school over at University High, he had a job after school at a jeweler's. He used to be, like a courier for them, delivering parcels and packages.

Even when he went to University High School, he paid for most of his tuition. He worked at a jewelry store in town after school and helped raise money for his tuition.

BILL JUNIOR: I started doing both. I maintained the paper route and the jeweler's during high school.

BILL SENIOR: Oh? That's right, you were doing both.

BILL JUNIOR: Yeah, I had two jobs, too.

BILL SENIOR: Yeah, I can see it now.

Essay Contest Encouragement

BILL JUNIOR: My recollection is that I was pretty independent on homework.

BILL SENIOR: He was usually a straight A student. He seemed to retain what he learned in class, and he didn't need to be pushed at homework or anything.

BILL JUNIOR: I do recall one time your pushing me to do my best. When I was in eighth grade, I went to parochial school. The nuns could be very, very controlling. This particular nun, in the eighth grade, certainly was. Anyway, they had asked both sets of eighth graders (about 30 or 40 children) to enter a contest, a greater New England area writing contest, to write an essay on the president as a

21. Parallels between generations are sometimes indicators of successful parental generativity. Here it is noteworthy that the son's boyhood work experience replicates what the father himself had done as a boy.

leader, and you picked the president of your choice. I wrote an essay, and I didn't get along with this particular nun, and she critiqued my essay and was very negative on it, and I decided I wasn't going to enter the contest. Somewhat, probably, vindictive toward her, I was going to show her a lesson. The day before the entries were due, my father said to me, "Well, how's your essay coming along?" I told him, "I'm not going to enter that contest, so-and-so, she just hates me," and I wasn't going to pay attention to her. Then my recollection is that you kind of forced me to go upstairs and write it—"Well, you really should write another one." So I went up and I wrote another one, and submitted it to her. She said, "Well, I'm not going to have time before I submit this to look this over, so it'll have to go in as is." Well, it was a contest winner. So I remember having that encouragement from him.[22]

BILL SENIOR: He wrote a terrific essay on President John F. Kennedy, and he won a trip to Washington because of it. We saw him off on the bus that time. My wife and I were both so very proud of him. We still have a copy of it somewhere.

BILL JUNIOR: I was one of something like 50 students throughout New England that won a trip to Washington. They xeroxed copies of my paper and passed it around the neighborhood!

Private School Opportunity

BILL JUNIOR: When I got older, I wanted to go to University High, which is one of the more prestigious schools around here, and I passed the entrance examination, but financially, it was a burden. When I entered that in '67, the tuition was already a lot of money. And, quite frankly, my parents didn't have it, and my father went up to the local parish and talked to the monsignor of the parish about (this is my recollection of it), how could we get some assistance here, and the monsignor subsequently went to the school and through his connections at the school, got me some scholarship monies.

BILL SENIOR: Well, I remember going to the monsignor, and he did work something out at the time. I thought the church was giving something towards it, but I found out later, when a new pastor took

22. In terms of the coding system, encouraging his son to write an essay for the contest was coded as supporting adolescent intellectual-academic development.

over, that the monsignor must have been giving that out of his own money.

BILL JUNIOR: Oh, I didn't know that . . .

BILL SENIOR: Because the new pastor didn't know anything about continuing it. So (laughs) . . . he must have been giving that out of his own pocket. I don't believe it was that much money, but still.

BILL JUNIOR: It was $200, but it was much money to us. I lost it in my sophomore year (laughs) by virtue of having a real attitude. I had a real high grade average, but, um, I had a real attitude problem, too. I was a real wiseguy in class and they felt that, attitudinally, I needed some improvement so they dropped my scholarship. I remember coming home with that; that wasn't fun. My parents said to me, "If you want to continue, it's your responsibility, you're footing the bill. You lost it, you go from there." See, by that time, I was working. My sophomore year I was delivering papers in the morning, and I was a messenger boy downtown after school. So I came up with the money on my own.

BILL SENIOR: He didn't change his wiseguy attitude, but he could keep it, since he was paying for it.

BILL JUNIOR: Yeah. I maintained it for a few more years, anyway.

Son's Inner Drive

BILL JUNIOR: I also have a lot of good baseball memories from my teens. I loved playing baseball; my father encouraged me. I was a pretty good player, and I got the awards to go along with that type of thing. But, still, I wasn't outstanding, either. You know, I'm not on the Red Sox today (laughs).

BILL SENIOR: His style of really playing hard also continued through his teenage years. He was always zealous at everything he did in sports. He always tried hard. He played heads up at everything. He tried, strived, at everything he did. He was always a hard-nosed baseball player—that's just the way he is. That's how he got to get better at it, by trying hard. He just had that *drive* in him. That is how he is now in his work and everything.

I got to admit, I've always been proud of that trait about him. That's one thing I've always admired about him, that drive he has. I wish I could have been that way, but I was never that way, myself. I've never been an aggressive person. I've always been sort of laid back. Well, I had the drive that I had to have to raise the family; that's about all. The one thing I've been aggressive at, I guess, is raising a family.[23]

Following His Father's Model

BILL JUNIOR: I can remember, when I was around 14 or 15, that I was very proud because my father was an usher, the head usher, at church. I became one of the ushers with him, as did my brother later, and I thought that was a big honor. Ushering with my dad was something that was pretty special.

BILL SENIOR: I recall the ushering. It was the 7:00 service every Sunday. My two oldest boys used to help me out, making the collection. We enjoyed doing it together. I remember that the boys seemed to be proud of it. I felt proud of them, too, because they were doing something to help me in the church. I remember the first time Bill ushered with me, it made me feel good.

BILL JUNIOR: It was also special because, during my late teen years, we actually started seeing less of each other since I started working then and he was working.

BILL SENIOR: Yeah, that's true.

BILL JUNIOR: I used to get up and leave the house at 5:30 in the morning for my paper route; in fact, he would drop me off at my papers on his way to work. I'd do my paper route, then I'd catch the bus to school from my grandfather's house, then I'd go into Boston afterwards, to do my job after school. I didn't really have any extracurricular activities after school because of that, and . . . you probably didn't get home until late.

BILL SENIOR: I was working more then, too. I don't think we did get together too much during his late teen years.

BILL JUNIOR: There were weekends. We spent more time together on weekends. Friday nights were the school dances. (You would drop

---

23. Bill Sr.'s comment underscores the continuities and discontinuities across three generations. Richard, his own father, worked especially hard at breadwinning and died when Bill Sr. was 15. Bill Sr. reworked his background by working especially hard at childrearing. His childrearing support, in turn, promoted Bill Jr.'s ability to work hard. During the childhood decade, Bill Sr. focused on his son's physical-athletic development, and during the adolescent decade he gave more encouragement to his son's social-emotional "drive" and determination.

us off at the dance, before I got my license, and then you picked us up.)[24]

Saturdays I was still playing baseball, the first year in high school, and he came to my games. But I didn't play high school baseball after my sophomore year, when I started my job in Boston.

BILL SENIOR: Yeah, he got away from it, when he had to start to work. So I really wasn't going to any games, except for the younger boys. I was going to their games, because they were coming up in baseball then.

BILL JUNIOR: When we went to a baseball game, or other event—we still went together all through that time—but there'd always be all my other friends, and I'm sure we were all talking a mile a minute. I don't recall individual conversations, or things like that, at that time.

You know, it sounds as we retell it that there was no interaction when I was a teenager, or we didn't see each other at all, but that's not true. There were many conversations about sports, dialogues about readings—shorter swappings of things, but there was no regularly scheduled events where I did this or that with him. I mean, he came when there were parent nights at school, and he was there at things of that nature, but nothing that really stands out on a regular basis.

BILL SENIOR: Except for music.

Common Interests: Music, Reading, Sports

BILL JUNIOR: Oh yeah, music. Our favorites range from contemporary to classical.

BILL SENIOR: I've been a Moody Blues fan for years. The Moody Blues are my favorite group. I still like the Beatles music. I even got a Paul McCartney CD just recently; he had a lot of his old things, called "All the Best." I still liked him. Now I'm thinking of getting a new CD the BeeGees got out. I like Queen, Dire Straits. I'm not as big on Stevie Ray Vaughan as John, my younger son, is, but I like him.

24. The family's love of dancing is an example of intergenerational continuity—it was an interest passed down from the grandfather, to the father, to the son.

On the classical side, Mozart is my big one. Mozart is my favorite composer. Most of my music is by him. I like Tchaikovsky, Beethoven; I like a lot of the baroque, like Vivaldi and Bach, Handel, and then I like into the early classical period with Haydn. He must have written, I think it was, 104 symphonies. And I think Mozart sort of followed in his footsteps. Some of Mozart's style is similar to Haydn. And I like Schubert—I have 10 of his symphonies. There's very few that I don't like. I'm not too crazy about Stravinsky—I like a little of his music. And the modern Russian composers. My favorite Russian is Tchaikovsky, and I like Rimsky-Korsakov, also.

Baroque is my favorite relaxation music. Because I think that's a kind of music that you don't really listen to, but it's there. And when you're trying to do something, it relaxes your mind so that you can think straight.[25]

BILL JUNIOR: The classical element was always there, growing up, but I didn't pay as much attention to it at the time. I knew that he had that element—he would trot out things and play it. I can recall my father explaining pieces to me, saying "I bought this because I really liked this piece" and listening to Vivaldi's *Four Seasons* and having discussions about it. I never was able to attain, for instance, his love of opera, but I can remember him trying to convince me that opera was a good thing. You know, "Listen to this!" "Listen to the music, you're not listening, if you listen to it, maybe you'll get it." I never got it. But I always gave it a chance, and I can remember having more dialogue about music and the aspects of music.

As a kid, rock music was what I was more interested in, popular things. The fact that he was up-to-date with what I was liking, with popular things, got my attention. He is very open-minded to music, just like he's open-minded to new ideas in general. That's always something that I have had a lot of respect for.

We don't all love the same music, but music is pretty much a predominant theme through our family.

BILL SENIOR: Yeah, everyone likes music. As a matter of fact, I'm

25. The father's knowledge of classical music, untypical of his working-class background, may have helped his son, in turn, to interact more easily with people from more advantaged backgrounds. Researchers have found that the apparent effect of such "cultural capital" on social status mobility is "particularly strong for the sons of the least educated fathers" such as Bill Sr. (DiMaggio & Mohr, 1985, p. 1245).

the only one who doesn't play an instrument. Bill has played guitar before, and John's a very good electric guitarist, he's a lead guitarist, and Jim has played drums, he still has drums upstairs. He hasn't played lately. My sons Tom and Sam are good on harmonica. So they all seem to be musically inclined. It goes back to my grandfather. My grandfather had an accordion, and then my father also played it. I picked it up, but I guess I was too lazy to put the work into it.

BILL JUNIOR: Unfortunately, the one thing that none of us got from him was his voice, because he is a good singer. All of us are terrible.

BILL SENIOR: My wife always wanted me to go up and sing in the church choir, but I always bowed out and said, "Nah, I haven't got the time to go up and practice and everything else," so I never did. I thought I'd probably get a little stage fright.

BILL JUNIOR: On the other hand, I did sing in the church choir, and I wasn't shy, and I had a terrible voice, and I thought because I was good and loud, that I was good!

We also shared the same reading interests. We both are really avid readers, and as a kid, I remember I tried to read a lot of my father's books that were beyond my age, growing up. For pleasure reading, he had a very strong interest in science fiction, and I subsequently developed that and read a lot of science fiction.

BILL SENIOR: It was a swap: "Gee, I've just read this, and this is what I think of it, and I think you ought to read this, and let me know what you think." We still do that today.

BILL JUNIOR: Yeah, we still do that today. We both still like science fiction. One might say, "I didn't think as much of that as you did," yeah. We're still very open, I mean, today, he'll say, "I really think it's great," and I'll say, "Gee, I don't agree with that." We have that conversation a lot of times.

BILL SENIOR: Yeah, and I'll say, "Okay" (laughs).

BILL JUNIOR: We both share some favorite authors that write around certain types of themes. Thrillers, for instance, the Tom Clancey series.

BILL SENIOR: Yeah, the *Colonel of the Kremlin* and *The Patriot Games*.

BILL JUNIOR: One thing I don't share with him is horror.

BILL SENIOR: Yeah, I like horror stories, too. Stephen King and (laughs) books like that.

BILL JUNIOR: I don't like to be scared, but, otherwise, we have a lot of the same reading interests.[26]

BILL SENIOR: A lot, yeah, and we also shared the same love of sports. We've always been Patriots fans, Red Sox fans, Bruins fans, Celtics fans.

BILL JUNIOR: That's a different father-son story. As a teenager, I grew up where football was a big thing, but there wasn't a local football team. Then a local football team got started, and we started going out to the games, and then we got season's tickets together. That became a regular event, that we would get out to the games together. Only thing is, when it comes to spectator sports, he's too emotional. When a team loses, he's depressed. They're no good, and they're bums, and that's it. That doesn't happen to me.

BILL SENIOR: No, he takes it more in stride. He's more of a good sport than I am. I've always been kind of a poor sport. I take things personal. I remember one time, I got so mad at a Dallas Cowboys game, when the Patriots were losing, I pounded my fist and broke my watchband. I pounded the bench in front of me and the watch went flying off—. It cost me $40 for a new watchband; they had to send to Seiko in Japan to get the same one. I mellowed a little after that (laughs). I'm not as bad as I was.[27]

BILL JUNIOR: He's learned to shut off the TV before he gets mad!

BILL SENIOR: I walk away, sometimes, rather than get too upset. Like in a Patriots' game, when they're making stupid plays, I'll switch to another channel and watch that for awhile. I always wind up going back to the game again, but after I've calmed down.

BILL JUNIOR: Yeah, I can't recall him being one of those parents in the stands who is yelling and making a fool of himself. I recall him showing up, being in the stands, cheering for me. I can hear his voice saying, "Come on, get a hit" and that type of thing, but I can't recall him being emotional about something that happened in the game.

BILL SENIOR: Sometimes I'd yell at the umpire if I thought he made a bad call: "Put on your glasses," or something like that. But I

26. In terms of the coding system, sharing reading was coded as promoting his son's intellectual-academic development.

27. This is the second mention of the father's expression of anger. Bill Sr., like the other effective childrearing fathers, was not a saint. Childrearing fathers, like all fathers, had to deal with frustrations and conflicts in themselves and in their children.

never pressed him in a game, or anything like that. I always let him do his own thing. I didn't believe in badgering a kid. Because if the kid was doing badly, he knew he was doing badly, why multiply it and mushroom the situation by making him feel even worse by yelling at him? I always told him that, hey, you try the best you can, you're out there to have fun, that's all.

BILL JUNIOR: I recall that being a theme. As long as you give your best, that was okay. All the sports I was involved with were always fun. I never felt pressured to be a success or to reach to attain some level; we're just out there to have some fun.

Son's Young Adult Identity Struggle

BILL JUNIOR: I would say that those years, from junior year of high school on, were the years that I probably struggled more with my identity and what I wanted to be. I started rebelling against more things, my grades dropped off, I went off to college, and they were very proud that I went to college—I was the first one on either side of their family to go to college. After a year and a half, I decided I didn't want to be there. There were things going on in high school that they didn't like: sometimes they didn't like the people that I was associating with, didn't like some of my girlfriends, didn't like when my grades started dropping off in high school at the end, because I just didn't really care. Same thing in college, because I didn't really want to be there.

BILL SENIOR: I'll have to rely on his memory, if he can think of anything more about that time.[28]

BILL JUNIOR: If you look at that period of time, 1969–1970, the Vietnam War was a very predominant theme. I thought I was very much a radical, and my views on what was going on and things of that nature drifted that way. I was into rebellion: I wanted to grow my hair long, and I had the idea my parents didn't like that. I wanted to wear a particular style of clothes; we had arguments about that. So during those years there were more arguments; a one-on-one argument tended to be more with my mother. She would be the one to say, "You can't do that."

28. The father's sensitive, caring attitude is apparent in his encouragement of Bill to tell the rest of the story, not telling it himself.

He was more easygoing about that sort of thing. When I moved (I moved out of the house when I was 18 or 19 and got my own apartment), my mother was very upset about that. I'm sure my father was too, but he didn't show that he was upset; he came down to talk to me at my apartment. My mother said, "I won't talk to you for the next couple of years." She was angry, as if I had done something terrible. But my father came down and met my (pause) "roommate," and then talked to me about [her]. He was always just a lot more easygoing. So, during those years as I was striving to be different, I still could have a conversation with him. I don't recall it being different. I did what I did, and I argued with my mother about it.[29]

BILL SENIOR: She was the more restricting of the two of us, and she voiced her opinion more than I did. I was more laid back, I guess. I didn't like his appearance; he sort of went what you call "hippie style." He grew his hair long, and he had this Van Dyke beard, he wore this Buffalo Bill buckskin jacket all the time, and he just didn't know what he wanted to do. He lived with a . . . he had a roommate down there. But I try to be liberal, I guess, and go along with it. His mother was just against it completely. I was against it, but I didn't voice it that way. I thought if I was patient he'd get over it eventually. Which he did, but his mother went through hell in the process.

BILL JUNIOR: I guess I have to comment on it from this perspective. I think that I was probably, at times, a difficult teen to manage—I was very headstrong, I was very, very outspoken in the things I felt very strongly about. My father, obviously, weathered through those things; we both weathered through those things together.

BILL SENIOR: I imagine we all go through a rebellious time. In my day you basically just did what your parents said and that was it, but you still had your moments of rebellion. Times have changed since then, though. Things have gotten more progressive and liberal. I try to adapt to the times. It's not always easy.

He quit that hippie life, you might say, and he seemed to put himself back on his feet again. Anyway, I felt so proud of him when

---

29. Bill Jr.'s rebellion demonstrates a common adolescent usage of clothing, hair style, and peer relations to separate from his family and to state who he is not, well before he is ready to say who he is. Throughout his identity conflict, however, he still enjoyed his father's social-emotional support. Bill Sr., who had lost his own father during adolescence, was determined that Bill Jr. would not have the same experience.

he went to college at night. It took him a long time, because you can't do it like you can at full time. I was so proud when he got that degree. I've always been proud of him for finishing college.

Father Enforces Family Curfew

BILL JUNIOR: I can recall one thing you did to me when I was dating Debbie—the girl who is now my wife. We worked together at a bank, and we'd get out at midnight. I was a freshman in college. I was going to school full time during the day, then I'd work second shift, from 4 to midnight. I met Debbie and we were dating. My parents were getting upset because I was coming in at 4 or 5 o'clock in the morning. My father laid down some rules and said, "You have to be in by 1 o'clock," or whatever it was. So the first night that rule was in effect, he said, "I want you to be in by 1 o'clock or the door's going to be bolted." Well, we pulled into the driveway at 5 minutes to 1 here, and we sat talking in the driveway for another 15 minutes, and I realized it was 10 minutes after 1, and I ran up the stairs, and the door was bolted. I turned around—my girlfriend lived a couple miles from here, and I could see her taillights going up the street, so I decided I'd jump the back fence and chase her car so I'd catch her. I didn't—I ended up walking all the way to her house. Well, he was standing behind the door, ready to open up the door and say, "See, I was going to lock you out," but I ran so fast, he never caught me. I ended up jumping over the back fence and running up the street and ended up sleeping in her basement that particular night.

BILL SENIOR: I was just going to try to teach him a lesson, then let him in. But he took off too fast, so I couldn't let him in. I was right there, though. As it turned out, by me not being able to get him before he took off, he did get a lesson out of it.

BILL JUNIOR: Yeah, I had a long walk, in a blizzard, so I walked two miles to sleep somewhere I didn't want to sleep.

Current Reflections

The Father's Perspective

Looking back, at the minimum, I just wanted him to just be able to have his family and provide for them like I did. But he's far surpassed that (laughs). I get a lot of pleasure from what he's done. Because I've been just a plain working Joe, myself, and I've always hoped that he would be more than what I was. That's why I went along with my wife with the parochial school because I was able in that way to help him achieve that. (My wife was raised through parochial school, and she wanted that for the kids.)

Bill went ahead and did his own thing; then pushed himself and got his education. See, when he first went to college (he was there about a year and a half), he didn't know what direction he was going in. So he dropped out of school. We were very disappointed at the time. And he went off and got his own apartment, and he was working at the city hospital as a porter. I'm proud that he eventually got his act together. I got him a job in Westinghouse, the plant where I work. He went on the tuition program there, and he got his education—he got his diploma from college. And now he's going for his master's degree. And I couldn't be more proud of the way he did that turn-around. So many people have dropped out and never go back. I'm so proud of the way he put himself together and did it. And he's really brought himself up through the company: now he's manager of the personnel department at Westinghouse. His hope, I think, is to be a vice-president of the company some day.

I think his success is due to just what he has inside him. His ambition. He's a very ambitious person; he has a lot of drive in him. That's why I say I wish I had his drive. Because I never pushed myself to go back to school or anything. I quit school (although my wife did talk me into going back to Shoreline High School here to get my high school equivalency certificate, which I did).

I just tried to be a decent father and to provide for him as he grew up. Maybe he's seen my life and didn't want to have to work so many hours like I do, to make the amount of money I do. Maybe he saw that he could be a professional person and get a higher rate of pay and have a decent schedule so that he could get to take care of his children—instead of being away more than he prefers, like I have been. Maybe that might be what he has in mind, not being what I was. By being better, I mean I want them to be better off than what I was.

I believe a father should really show his love to his children a lot. To be around and loving, I think, would be the most important thing. Because I think it gives them a feeling of wanting to find it in themselves to pass it on to the next generation. You know, to emulate that with their own children, to be loving and thoughtful and raise them well, to be with them when they need it.[30]

The Son's Perspective

Probably the most significant influence was that my father was always looking at making himself better: developing himself intellectually, reading, looking at different pieces of music. I was always impressed with that. I thought he was a real smart guy, something that I should be like too. So those things, those readings and music and things like that—I *think* I got involved with them because they were important to him to better himself, and they became important to me. Maybe I wasn't trying consciously to better myself, but I wanted to do that, too. He had dropped out of high school but I can recall at an early age that he studied. He had a series of books on math. I can remember trying to read those at an early age because my father read them: *Algebra for the Practical Man, Trigonometry for the Practical Man.*[31]

I tried to do the things that he did. That was all before he went back to get his GED, when I was a teenager. So, even from early on, he influenced me to be very academically oriented.

You also have to understand that my parents were the first ones in their family to purchase a house. The first ones in their family to purchase a car. To do things like that. I knew those things, I was proud of those things.[32]

My father is a precision-measurement mechanical inspector.[33]

30. The eloquence of Bill's description of parental generativity recalls the eloquence of Erik Erikson's (1950) and Joan Erikson's (1988) writings on generativity.

31. These two books were part of a popular mathematics self-study series originally introduced in 1931, which continued to be published until the 1960s. The underlying values of the series are expressed in the preface to the first volume: "In olden days" mathematics was available only to the elite but today "all of us are free to study any part of the subject." Today, "the practical [that is, the working-class] man must have a knowledge of the basic principles of mathematics in order that he may fully understand their application in his work" (Thompson, 1931/1946, p. v; Thompson, 1947).

32. Just as his parents were "the first ones in the family" to purchase a house and car, Bill Jr. was the first in his family to go to college, and his father also took a special pride in his son's achievement.

33. Bill Sr.'s generativity beyond the family sphere is not immediately evident from his job title. As an inspector, however, he often makes decisions that influence the lives of others, and he uses one-to-one encounters as opportunities for care. As he has grown older, he has come to take a special pleasure in providing

He basically made his own career. The way he became an inspector was by gradually taking on additional responsibilities. Then one day, someone said, "Gee, we need someone who can do that," and he had the bravado to say, "I can do that," when he had never done this thing before. I, again, remember him as a self-made man. Someone who just pushed himself to get ahead. I guess that initiative was the singular thing about him that stood out to me.[34]

In general, there were times when recognizing my father's self-madeness (if that's a word) and hearing about those events in his life, I became very proud of him. For instance, it was very difficult for him to get the job of inspector in Westinghouse that he got. It was 1968 (I was fifteen at the time). It was hard to get into it, but he got into it. Now, being in the company myself, I know how very seldom we hire at his skill level, which is a high skill level. So I even further understand that accomplishment. But, back then, I remember being very proud that he got that.

I know this is very simplistic in nature, but I think part of my success is due to reading. I had such a strong interest in so many things, just from reading—I was a voracious reader—that when it came to doing things, academic or professional, I had learned about a lot of different subjects, taken them in, grown intellectually, and was able to transfer that into some of the things that I wanted to do. It goes back to the things I said earlier: My father influenced me with his reading, his curiosity and openness, and his desire and ability to stretch himself intellectually.[35]

There was always a questioning on his part: Why does this work? What about this music? What about this type of thing? That was fundamental. Perhaps surprisingly, there weren't things like, where he said, "You should get an education," or "You should do that." Those type of things didn't really occur. It was more fundamental in nature. It was more of a way of life that he modeled.

As I grew older, I saw that he continued the same involvement with

---

guidance to new employees, explaining things to young workers, and encouraging his colleagues' new ideas. He has also has given some of his time to community activities.

34. Bill Jr.'s admiration for his father is clear. Similarly, Bill Sr. expressed admiration for his son's boyhood industry and adulthood ambition.

35. Bill Jr. has also volunteered his time as a tutor and mentor in two reading-oriented educational programs for nonadvantaged youth.

my younger brothers. He has always had a real interest in what we were doing, and a desire to do things with us. I have my own children now and so, looking back, I also find it amazing that my father spent so much time with me. The other thing was that, on some of our joint activities, it was not a father and son in terms of an "authority figure." It became more friends in that arena. And I saw that with my other younger brothers. In the music. Sitting down to discuss that with them. It's more adult to adult, even when one of us, myself, was actually at a child level. He really just enjoyed it. He got very caught up in us. Of course, when you stepped out of that arena (baseball or whatever), you still had the authority relationship in other places. Let me see if I can explain how that worked? All right, you were in the backyard pitching, and you're sort of like chums. Then you come into the house, and he might tell me to go upstairs and do my homework. There were those times he stepped in and, of course, there were those times that I resented it and resisted it. Sure.

A father's most important concern, broadly, should be the children's development. I'm shaping my own philosophies now about the development of my own three children. I've always been involved in a lot of different things, from working in Head Start programs when I was in college to working with different sports teams and coaching youth leagues and all that. I am concerned about parenting that I see; a lot of people (friends and local town people) push their children. Making them do things. The issue in my mind is, trying to identify what a child is both good at and enjoys doing and wants to do, and adding the support and encouragement there, and drawing that fine line between giving direction and pushing them. To be honest, that's a situational model. I think about that a lot.

The Son Looks Ahead a Generation

The way my father raised me has influenced the way I am raising my own children in a number of different ways. What I talked about earlier, the sports analogy. I was encouraged, I was supported. Baseball was made to be fun, it was made to be of interest. I was never pushed, I was never pressured. That incorporates into my own parenting philosophy— I'm doing that with my own children now. I thought of it recently as I played with my son, Billy. After about two or three hours of practice, he said, "I think I've had enough baseball for today,

Dad," and I remembered that I literally would go the entire day playing baseball. Just hours and hours and hours of games. So, we're just breaking him in![36]

The growing intellectually, the reading, that's very important to me, with my kids personally. The music is also filtering in there. In terms of my dealing with issues with my children, I guess I want to utilize some of my father's technique and add certain things. I would like to utilize the fact that there was not the easy touch, but the flexibility, the openness, the open-mindedness, the understanding. I do some things differently, though. My own personal style incorporates more seeking out. When my children bring an issue to me, O.K., I do more probing. I don't like to tell them the answers. I like them to find those things for themselves . . . . I also don't think we had the dialogue about feelings when I was growing up. I have that with my children now. We talk about their feelings about things.[37]

The main thing is that I want my children to be true to themselves. If they're true to themselves and they accomplish what they want to accomplish, whatever that might be, I would be very happy and pleased. I want my relationship with them to allow them to be true and honest to what's important to them, to the principles and values they hold in life and, hopefully, I will be proud of that and realize that they have become good people.

Because I made a very conscious decision when I decided to have children, that it was a very important thing to do, and it wasn't something that you take lightly; you basically had the responsibility for some lives. I was married for 7 years before we had our first child, and that was a conscious decision. To be honest, I felt that I was too immature to have a child. I really was. I was constantly questioning myself and saying, "Can I make a good father?" When I looked around at the models I saw around me, unfortunately, I felt that I was seeing more negative models than positive models. And I was concerned, "Did I have the ability?" But I did have one very positive model, my own father. So that's why my children's development is so important to me. His overall priority was to do the best for us. If you broadly say that's development, I think his priority was the same.

36. Bill Jr.'s passing on his athletic skills by coaching youth and adult athletic teams also illustrates his own societal generativity.

37. Note that Bill Jr.'s parental generativity is explicitly understood in relation to his father's parental generativity.

The basic question I tried to answer is, "Why do we have children?" If it's not a conscious effort, then we have children because it's the act of having children, but if it's a conscious effort, we have children to further the interests of society and the world and our own personal interests as well. And, therefore, I as a parent—again, I gave both perspectives when I gave that answer—we look for my child to develop. If my child develops, the child will be giving something back to me by giving me the satisfaction. Not the satisfaction in that they achieved this certain goal that I set for them, but rather the satisfaction that they became people of value.

My father is very proud of my children. He's very proud of the fact that he's a grandfather. If I can interject a personal feeling on that, I'm very proud of having children, and I feel that my children are a continuation of me, of sorts. I think that when I have grandchildren, maybe I'll feel that even further. I think maybe that's how my father feels.

We have discussions about my kids, now. So it's gone from music and sports and reading. I'm not totally certain whether it's a condition of parenthood or a condition of age, but there is now even a greater closeness.

Concluding Query

Bill and Bill Jr.'s story also foreshadows the themes of the next chapter—fathers' own work, love, and societal generativity at midlife. For instance, although Bill Sr. worked for the same factory all of his life, he educated himself and rose within that system. Did the fact that he worked at parenting so hard influence his job advancement and occupational mobility? Bill Sr. also acknowledged that his wife's support helped him to resolve issues related to his own father and apparently also promoted his ability to be a good father to his own children. Is it possible, however, that Bill Sr.'s childrearing participation also reciprocally contributed to the positive quality of his marital relationship? Bill Sr. was obviously more highly involved in childrearing than many fathers, and he showed clear evidence of being societally generative at work. Is it likely that his parental generativity made an important contribution to his ability to become societally generative?

4

Midlife Consequences
of Paternal Generativity for Fathers
Themselves

with Joseph H. Pleck

By the time fathers reach midlife they will have given of themselves
in various ways and amounts of time. Is it reasonable to expect
that differences in fathers' parental generativity will predict differences in how they themselves will turn out at midlife? One of the
most interesting questions in the study of human development is how
children and childrearing affect the very core areas of the parents'
own existence—work life, marital life, the life of the self. This chapter
reports on the significance of fathering for fathers themselves, focusing on how their childrearing involvement may contribute to predicting their work success, marital success, and attainment of Eriksonian societal generativity.

What We Know from Prior Research

The small body of prior research suggests that childrearing brings
both benefits and costs to fathers. The review of prior research that
follows focuses on the significance of parental generativity in terms
of the father's own occupational and marital outcomes and personal
development. More comprehensive and wider-ranging reviews are
available elsewhere (Bronfenbrenner & Crouter, 1982; Cath, Gurwitt, & Gunsberg, 1989; Cowan, 1988; Hoffman, 1984; Huston-
Stein & Higgins-Trenk, 1978; Kanter, 1977; Lamb & Sagi, 1983;
Lamb, Pleck, & Levine, 1985; LaRossa & LaRossa, 1981; J. Osofsky &
H. Osofsky, 1984; Rapoport & Rapoport, 1965; Russell, 1986; Zedeck & Mosier, 1990).

Occupational Outcomes

The capacity to work, according to Sigmund Freud, is one of the two primary indices of adult health and maturity (Erikson, 1950, pp. 264–265). Men's work roles and other roles are interconnected, of course, but the degree to which they mutually influence each other is complex and unclear. Our society, furthermore, often places work and family in opposition. The objective structure of work and family roles that most American fathers face includes an extensive occupational sex segregation with men traditionally dominating higher paid jobs. The general expectation of most fathers' colleagues and employers is that men's participation in childrearing and family work will *not* take precedence over their paid work, but that women's family roles *will* assume priority (see Pleck, 1988).

In support of a high degree of mutual influence between work and family roles, some studies focus on the dilemmas stemming from apparently inconsistent demands of men's work and men's families. For instance, men are often expected to put in extra time at the workplace during the early adulthood era, although this is when they are more likely to have young children (Levinson, 1978, 1986). A study by Greenberger and O'Neil (1990) showed that fathers' concerns about their children (that is, beliefs about the consequences of maternal employment for children; worry on account of the perceived quality of child care; children's problem behaviors) contributed an additional 20% to the explained variance in the men's role strain (spillover of pressures and conflicts from job to family and vice versa) beyond that accounted for by demographic variables. Child-related concerns, which are associated with a less positive orientation to work, also contributed an additional 10% to the explained variance in fathers' commitment to the workplace. Other studies have found that fathers who report greater work satisfaction and involvement spend less time at home, and those who report greater family satisfaction and participation were less involved at the workplace, especially in work "extras"—discretionary committees, business meetings before or after work hours, and employment-related social gatherings (Elder, 1974; Grossman, Pollack, & Golding, 1988; Russell, 1982a).

The mutually negative influence of work and family involvement among fathers is also suggested by Bailyn's (1977, 1978) cross-sectional survey of male managers. It showed that family-oriented

accommodators, compared with men who were less willing to accommodate their careers to the needs of their families, held lower status
positions within organizations and placed lower value on the worth of
demanding career tracks. They were also more loyal to their employer,
perhaps because their employment contributed to their family's security. It is not possible to know, however, if their work involvement
was an accommodation to the priority they gave to family life, or if
their family involvement was an accommodation for work positions
not attained, or if other mediating variables came into play, such as
socioeconomic status. The finding by Radin and Sagi (1982) that
socioeconomic status has a negative correlation with some measures
of father participation is consistent with the possibility of mediating
incentives. Nevertheless, the above studies suggest that most fathers
experience some degree of direct conflict between their work and
family life.

In contrast with what the above studies suggest and common sense
would expect, longitudinal and some cross-sectional studies support
the view that a negative relationship between paid work and childcare
time is neither straightforward nor inevitable. Some studies report
that men who have performed well at work are also men who have
done well at home (Weiss, 1990). A cross-sectional study conducted
by Baruch and Barnett (1986), for instance, found that socioeconomic
characteristics had little relation to levels of childcare. Pleck (1985)
explored the relationship between paid work and childcare time (as
distinct from housework time) in more detail in analyses of two
national surveys, one based on time diaries and the other based on
time estimates. His findings showed that, after controlling for family
life-cycle stage, education, and sex-role attitudes, the effects of paid
work on childcare among fathers were weak and not always significant: $r = -.164$ $(p < .01)$ in the time estimate survey, and $r = -.008$
$(p = \text{N.S.})$ in the time diary survey. The significant regression coefficient in the time estimate survey was interpreted as showing that an
increase of 1 hour in a father's paid work time is, on average, associated with a 10-minute decrease in his childcare time.

Tentative longitudinal evidence is also provided by three additional
studies. Russell (1982a), 2 years after the original study, reinterviewed
18 families in which fathers were highly involved. The results were
inconclusive: although in half of the families the level of fathers'
involvement had diminished, most of them reported that they had to

change for employment or economic reasons. Similar evidence is available from Vaillant's (1977) three-decade longitudinal investigation known as the Grant Study. While the Grant sample did not permit an actual longitudinal assessment of the relationship between a man's social mobility and childrearing participation, Vaillant's analyses did not indicate any significant association between a man's upward or downward social mobility and the quality of his fathering. Finally, Grossman and her colleagues conducted a longitudinal study in which the men were assessed before the birth of their first child (Grossman, Eichler, & Winickoff, 1980) and again when their child was age 5 (Grossman, Pollack, & Golding, 1988). Concurrent rather than longitudinal variables were the strongest predictors of fathers' job satisfaction. The authors reported that the quantity of time the fathers spent with their children was negatively associated with the men's job satisfaction at the same point in time, but the quality of fathers' interactions with their children and their play time were positively associated with their job satisfaction at the same point in time. These findings show that "men who enjoyed their work also had sensitive and responsive interactions with their 5-year-old children," but also suggest that satisfying careers "leave relatively little time for such family interactions" (1988, p. 87).

Conflicts between breadwinning and childrearing obligations raise numerous practical moral dilemmas for most fathers. For childrearing fathers, in fact, these strains may be felt on an almost daily basis. Nevertheless, as the above review indicates, the data are insufficient to justify linking men's childrearing involvement with their socioeconomic outcomes in a causal way. In particular, the common sense notion that childrearing interferes with breadwinning is far from straightforward.

Marital Outcomes

The capacity to love is the other half of Freud's definition of adult maturity (Erikson, 1950, pp. 264–265). Men's marital success may reflect in part their ability to love. A number of studies, most cross-sectional, have explored the possible impact of fathers' shared childrearing upon their relationships with their wives.

It would be surprising if the arrival of a family's first child did not influence marital enjoyment. Couples making the transition to parenthood must adjust to (a) the physical strain of childcare, (b) the emotional strain of new familial responsibilities, and (c) the psychological strain of personal confinement (Belsky & Isabella, 1985). Many studies, of course, do report an *initial* decline in various marital qualities after the birth of the first child (for reviews, see Belsky & Pensky, 1988; Worthington & Buston, 1986). Both quantitative and qualitative studies have shown that parenthood produces substantial stress in marriages (Hoffman, 1983; Miller & Sollie, 1980; Sollie & Miller, 1980). It is possible, however, that the disruptions in marital intimacy and satisfaction reflect, in part, initial temporary changes following a child's arrival, as well as more significant changes that would have taken place over time in most marriages regardless of the arrival of a child (White & Booth, 1985). Some studies, moreover, report very mixed findings regarding the impact of a first child upon the marital relationship. For instance, a well-designed longitudinal study by Belsky and Rovine (1990) examined marital relations in 128 middle- and working-class families. The data were collected from the last trimester of a couple's first pregnancy through their first child's third birthday. The findings showed that during the transition to parenthood, marital quality declined in some families, but it actually improved in other families (more than 30% of the husbands and wives had fewer disagreements and arguments), and still other families showed no change (40% of the husbands and wives experienced no meaningful change in feelings of love for each other).

Other studies continue to report a mixed or more random picture of a first child's impact upon marriages after the transition to parenthood has passed (Russell, 1982a, 1986; MacDermid, Huston, & McHale, 1990). Parents in Russell's (1982a, 1986) study of families with slightly older children (ages 2.9 to 5.7 years) were questioned about the effect of a nontraditional lifestyle, which involved shared childcare responsibilities, upon their marital relationship. About 45% of the couples thought their marital relationship had improved, and about 45% thought it had deteriorated. Russell noted that it was likely that a portion of the increased marital tension was due to work overload, since both the husband and wife worked full time in over half of the couples. Russell has also noted, however, that tension increases when the mother judges the quality of the father's childcare performance to be unsatisfactory (compare DeFrain, 1979; Lein, 1979).

Subsequent studies support Russell's suggestion that the variations in the positive and negative effects of childcare upon marital outcomes, while mixed, are not necessarily random. Several correlational studies have suggested that the quality of marital relationships is linked more closely to parent-child relationships for men than it is for women (Dickstein & Parke, 1988; Elder, Liker, & Cross, 1984; Lamb & Elster, 1985; Liker & Elder, 1983), although not all findings are consistent on this point (see Lorenz, Conger, Simons, Whitbeck, & Elder, 1991). Fathers' childrearing participation, more than mothers' parenting, appears to be contingent on a supportive marital relationship. It is not possible in these studies, however, to determine whether or not poor marital relations impinge on fathers' childrearing participation or whether particular father-child relationships interfere with marital happiness.

A longitudinal study by MacDermid, Huston, and McHale (1990) indicated that the negative link between parenting and marital satisfaction was far from inevitable. The authors found that couples were at risk for marital difficulties when there was incongruity between spouses' sex-role attitudes and the actual division of household and childcare tasks. Fathers who held traditional sex-role attitudes but were very involved in childcare tasks, for instance, reported lower levels of marital happiness one to two years after the birth of their first child (McBride, 1989; Steffensmeir, 1982). In another study, fathers' increased involvement in childrearing was shown to have a more negative effect on marital relations in dual-earner than in single-earner families (Crouter, Perry-Jenkins, Huston, & McHale, 1987). Crouter and her colleagues suggest that this negativity may actually be an antecedent of father involvement, "resulting from mothers 'pushing' fathers to become involved" (p. 439). Such antecedent negativity, of course, could also result from fathers or a changing economy "pushing" traditional mothers to work outside of the home. The possible long-term consequences remain unexplored in all of these studies.

Several studies have also reported that shared childcare has a fairly consistent positive effect on marital relationships in some particular situations. Gronseth (1978), for instance, studied dual-earner couples in which both parents shared both childcare and paid work. An important qualification is that neither parent was employed full time. This small but innovative pilot study ($N = 16$ families) showed that marital equality and marital satisfaction increased after the couples implemented a work-sharing pattern. In a 3-year longitudinal study of men's transitions to fatherhood, H. Osofsky and Culp (1989) similarly found that fathers who report satisfaction with the division of family tasks and decisions also report good marital adjustment and sexual satisfaction. These findings suggest that marital difficulties reported by studies of the initial period of parenthood cannot be generalized, for instance, to two or three decades later at midlife. As Cowan (1988) concluded, "Our findings suggest that later assessments may provide a more accurate gauge of both positive and negative outcomes of men's transition to parenthood" (p. 20).

One of the few studies to address these "later assessments" is the Heaths' (Heath, 1976, 1989; Heath & Heath, 1991) quantitative and qualitative analysis of marital happiness among a longitudinally studied sample of college men born during the 1930s and matriculated during the 1950s. Heath (1976) found that during the men's early thirties "increasing paternal competence" was "significantly related to a host of marital characteristics," including a marital happiness index based on several measures (p. 36). Heath and Heath (1991) similarly reported that during the men's mid-forties "competent and satisfied" fathers also tended to be happily married husbands (p. 126). Being a happily married man, they observed, was also predicted by psychological maturity (being, for example, psychologically less defensive, ethically more sensitive). Overall, the Heaths (1991) found that paternal competence, marital competence, and psychological maturity were highly correlated. They also note, however, that the "small sample" and "type of data secured" did not permit them to test statistically for alternative interpretations of the relationships between paternal, marital, and personal maturity (1991, p. 384). It may be that childrearing promotes both marital well-being and psychological maturity, or it may be that "success in one role predicts success in others" because psychologically mature persons are able to replicate their successes in different roles (p. 170).

In sum, the literature on the short-term impact of parenting upon marital happiness is substantial but still somewhat controversial, and the literature on the long-term impact is meager. Overall, the prior research literature is inconclusive.

Eriksonian Developmental Outcomes

Freud's designated two major spheres of adult functioning, *"lieben und arbeiten,"* "to love and to work," are united in Erikson's model of the seventh stage in the life cycle (Erikson, 1950, pp. 264–265; Erikson, 1968, p. 136; Hazan & Shaver, 1990; MacKinnon, 1991; Smelser & Erikson, 1980). The degree to which a man's external life is characterized by mature love (caring for others) and mature work (creativity, productivity) tends to be critically correlated with the maturity level of his psychosocial development.

Parental generativity (rearing one's children) contributes to but is not synonymous with societal generativity (Chapter 1). Parenting research has demonstrated that adults who are effective, responsive parents are also more likely to score well on measures of psychosocial maturity. These studies suggest but do not establish patterns of causality between parenting and adult psychological growth (Cox, Owen, Lewis, & Henderson, 1989; Frank, Hole, Jacobson, Justkowski, & Huyck, 1986; Gurwitt, 1982; Gutmann, 1975; Lewis & Rosenblum, 1974; Russell, 1989). Eriksonian researchers, in particular, have suggested that parenting may be a critical (although not sufficient) condition for the later achievement of generativity (Anthony & Benedek, 1970; Doyle, 1985; Farrell & Rosenberg, 1981; Heath, 1978; Mac-Nab, 1985). Eriksonian theory's emphasis upon developmental crises is particularly suited to address the possibly dual nature of fathering as a source of stressful crises and developmental opportunities (Cowan, 1988).

The reasonableness of an Eriksonian perspective is suggested by Cowan and Cowan's (1987, 1988) longitudinal study of men's first two years of fatherhood, which demonstrated that the first child contributed new dimensions to men's self-concepts. Prior to fatherhood, the men's identities centered on independence, aggressiveness, and self-concerns. Following fatherhood, their identities were more differentiated and included an understanding of themselves as caring, empathetic, and aware of others. Similarly, Speicher-Dubin's (1982) cross-sectional investigation of sociomoral development in the Oakland Growth Study found that fathers who had the primary responsibility for the care of their children also scored significantly higher in their moral development than did fathers whose wives were primarily responsible for childcare.

One of the first longitudinal studies of men to draw explicitly upon an Eriksonian perspective was conducted by Heath (1976, 1977, 1978, 1989; Heath & Heath, 1991). Beginning in the 1950s, he followed up a group of men from their entrance into college ($N = 85$)

through the onset of their midlife ($N = 65$). One of the many aims of this pioneering study was to test the Eriksonian idea that parenting contributes to generativity by investigating the specific impact that fathering had, in the men's own evaluations, on the way they had changed since leaving college. Heath's (1976, 1977) findings showed that the men's composite assessment of being a good father (high parental competence) was significantly related to almost a quarter of the assessed characteristics of the men's adult personalities as well as to a composite index of general competence in different roles.

In a subsequent report, Heath (1978) clarified the impact of fatherhood upon his subjects' psychological development. Using a multidimensional model of maturity, Heath found that fatherhood apparently promoted men's abilities to understand themselves, to understand others sympathetically, and to integrate their own feelings. Curiously, the fathers themselves rated fatherhood as having had only a moderate impact upon their maturity, compared to the effect their occupations and spouses had on their development. Nevertheless, more than two-thirds of the men were able to claim that fatherhood had increased "his awareness of himself, his values, and familial relationships, the allocentric [reality-oriented] quality of his values and familial relationships, and the acceptance and integration of his emotional needs" (1978, p. 276). Most recently, Heath and Heath (1991) report that the men who enjoyed being fathers (high parental satisfaction) were also more likely to have "volunteered to serve others or been elected to a leadership position in their communities or professions within the preceding ten years" (p. 227). As the Heaths (1991) commented, "Enjoying being a parent—one of the more demanding and selfless roles an adult assumes—reflects and nurtures an other-centered and giving character. With such a character, it is not that big a step to want to give to our larger family—our community" (p. 227). In our Eriksonian terminology, of course, this finding supports the proposition that men's parental generativity contributes to their successful attainment of societal generativity.

Vaillant's 35-year study of college men also found that parental adaptation was related to other forms of psychosocial adaptation beyond the family sphere. More specifically, Vaillant (1977, 1978) investigated the level of men's personal and career adjustment and related it to several outcomes for the men and their children over age 15. Only 3 of the 23 men who were found to have the highest degree of social adjustment reported greater psychological distance from their children than they desired, while 3 of the 6 men with the lowest social adjustment scores reported such distance. "Men who, in Erikson's terms, had become most generative (that is, were most truly responsible for other adults, enjoyed their work, and helped others to grow) were also the men who had best mastered intimacy at an earlier period and maintained stable first marriages. Indeed, contrary to popular prejudice, career success (career consolidation) and closeness to children [as rated by the men themselves] were significantly correlated ($r = .45$)" (p. 658). In contrast, a high proportion of the 30 men with the lowest overall adjustment ratings had little work responsibility beyond themselves and had failed to show societally generative traits. Vaillant also found that men who reported warm relationships with their own fathers were more likely to have young adult children with positive outcomes, such as low drop-out rates and high attendance rates at competitive colleges.

Sachs (1983) conducted a small but interestingly designed study of the effect that the transition to parenthood had on first-time fathers' generative development. Fifteen first-time fathers were tested and personally interviewed before the child's birth and again 4 or more months after the child's birth. A comparison group of 15 men, married but not fathers, was also interviewed and tested. Test results indicated that the psychosocial generativity of fathers and controls was not significantly different in a statistical sense. This is not surprising, given that the men were fairly young (aged 25 to 40), their experience of fatherhood was as yet quite brief, the sample was quite small, and the measure had not been previously validated. For many of these same reasons, however, the trends shown in the interview results were quite striking. All 14 categories of change in generative identity addressed in the interviews indicated that new fathers tended to work on their identities as generative males to a greater extent than did their nonfather counterparts. In sum, the interviews documented that fathers were more likely than nonfathers to redefine themselves in terms of generative themes.

Pruett's (1989) combined longitudinal and retrospective investigation of 17 "nurturing fathers" and their families provides several insights that build on the work of Vaillant and Sachs. Pruett, like Vaillant (1977), did not note any association between occupational class and good fathering. He also observed, consistent with Vaillant and Sachs, that fathering had or was having a profound impact upon the men's psychosocial development: "For the majority of the [child-rearing] men in the study, becoming a father in such a devoted and focused manner seemed to provide a secure anchorage for the whole of their adult development. It was, or became, a choice and commitment of such great depth that it served as an ongoing, growth-promoting experience, encouraging personal flexibility and empathy" (p. 400). For each of these men, their identity as a father was central to their lives. Their experiences as fathers appeared to have promoted a generative self-confidence that they were "generous and capable" men who were capable of being responsible for "the very survival of another human being" (p. 400). The sample and research design, of course, do not rule out other interpretations. It is possible, for instance, that some of the 17 fathers originally became more involved in childrearing because those very character traits that were thought to be the result were really the cause of their involvement.

Finally, Grossman's (1987) study of 42 men's transitions to parent-hood is relevant because of the close correspondence between Grossman's dual focus on the men's growing autonomy and affiliation and Erikson's (1982) conception of identity (work) and intimacy (love) as the dual developmental foundation of psychosocial generativity. Grossman reports that, as theorized, first-time fathers "who were more affiliative at year 1 were also feeling better about themselves" as shown by their higher scores on a measure of emotional well-being. The findings suggest that fathers may become less stereotypically masculine to provide for their children's nurturance needs, and that this affiliative nurturance is important for the fathers' own personal development (compare Gutmann, 1975).

Despite the common patterns found in these studies, it is important to note that parental generativity has no doubt received varying emphases by different cohorts (Logan, 1987). At different times in history, as Erikson has more generally observed, levels of interest in different stages of life have varied (E. Erikson & J. Erikson, 1981). For instance, men who came of age and entered the major professions prior to the value revisions of the feminist movement and in a time that provided few rewards for men's participation in childrearing were more likely to regard their occupation as relatively more important than fatherhood for their psychosocial development (compare Heath, 1978). In contrast, the new cohort of postfeminist era fathers may express and promote their personal development just as well via parenting (see Deutschman, 1991; Kotre, 1984; Logan, 1987). These contrasts underscore the importance of not overgeneralizing the story of a particular cohort. Of course, it is also important to note that Erikson's model provides for these historical variations by revealing different ways in which the universal psychosocial tasks of generativity can be attained in different historical times and sociocultural settings. The suggested ages he gives for the generative years, for instance, are always intended to serve as a crude pedagogical device and not rigid stage-defining criteria for all contexts.

In summary, the above review of fathers' occupational outcomes, marital outcomes, and personal development has shown that parental generativity may have both benefits and costs for fathers. Some studies focusing on the costs suggest that occupational demands not only prevent fathers from increasing their participation but penalize their careers if they do. Other studies show no such negative effects. Research focusing on the benefits of fathering to fathers themselves tentatively suggests that childrearing participation may be instrumental in promoting the men's marital enjoyment and psychological development, although some studies suggest that marital well-being can be negatively affected. Because occupational, marital, and psychological consequences are interrelated, many of the findings are virtually impossible to interpret, as few studies have looked at more than one of the outcomes in the same population of men, and most of the studies have been cross-sectional and correlational.

Research Questions

"The father-child relationship is a two-way process, and children influence their fathers just as fathers alter their children's development" (Parke, 1981, p. 9). The research presented in this chapter considers three areas of fathers' mid-lives that may be influenced by their children: occupational mobility (work), marital success (love), and societal generativity (cultural fatherhood). Each question about the effects of childrearing is presented below, together with hypothesized answers which build on the findings of prior research. The general expectation regarding childrearing fathers is that they will experience occupational costs as well as marital and psychosocial developmental gains.

Question 1: Does fathers' parental generativity predict the state of their occupational careers at midlife?

This question calls for the exploration of the possible occupational cost to fathers for their involvement in childrearing. It is expected that fathers who are highly involved in childrearing will be less likely to show upward occupational mobility at midlife, compared with fathers who were less involved in childrearing. This assumption is based on the literature review, which, while far from straightforward, indicated that some trade-offs take place in the amount of time and energy that men invest in their work versus their families.

Question 2: Does fathers' parental generativity predict the state of their marriages at midlife?

No adequate long-term longitudinal studies exist to guide us in anticipating the condition of the men's marriages years later at midlife. On the basis of the research literature so far, however, it is a tenable hypothesis that men who were more involved with their children during earlier adulthood will be on better terms with their spouses at midlife.

Question 3: Does fathers' parental generativity predict their psychosocial development at midlife?

This question explores the possible contribution of fathers' childrearing participation to their subsequent midlife attainment of societal generativity. It is theorized that fathers who are more highly involved in childrearing will be significantly more likely to become cultural fathers during midlife. The Eriksonian rationale for this thesis is that the experiences and skills of parental generativity function in a hierarchical fashion as quasi-prerequisites for societal generativity.

How the Study Was Conducted
Rating Scales

The analyses reported in this chapter were based on the entire core sample of 240 fathers. The fathers were rated on three outcomes at midlife (love, work, and societal generativity). Predictor variables included the background characteristics of their boyhood family of origin and their adulthood family of procreation, and, of course, the fathers' childrearing participation ratings. All ratings were made by judges who were blind to other aspects of the fathers' lives, including the ratings made by other judges. The interrater reliability reported for each variable, unless indicated otherwise, is the correlation coefficient based on a comparison of the ratings assigned by the original rater with the ratings assigned by a second rater to the same randomly selected subgroup of cases (see Tinsley & Weiss, 1975).

Father's Midlife Outcome Variables

Each man was assessed at midlife for occupational mobility, marital success, and societal generativity. These ratings were based on his interview at age 47.

Father's occupational mobility by midlife. The fathers' occupations were assigned ratings from the occupational subscale of Hollingshead's Index of Social Status (1959, 1975; see Haug, 1972; Myers & Straus, 1989). The scale was reversed so that it ranged from 1 (low) to 7 (high). Interrater reliability was estimated to be .92. The degree of occupational mobility among the fathers was then estimated by subtracting their parents' mean occupational rating (described below) from their own occupational rating and adding 7 to the difference to create a scale ranging from 1 (extreme downward occupational mobility) to 7 (perfect stability) to 13 (high upward occupational mobility).

Father's marital success at midlife. The fathers were rated on the long-term midlife outcome of their first marriage in terms of whether they had remained happily married, become dissatisfied with their marriage, or actually divorced. The rating ranged from (1) divorced, to (2) married but unsure about marital enjoyment, to (3) married with clear marital enjoyment. The Glueck subjects were interviewed at age 47; the men's children-oriented activities were excluded from consideration when marital enjoyment was being assessed. There was 90% exact agreement between the raters; interrater agreement was estimated to be .85, using Cohen's kappa which corrects for chance agreement.

Father's societal generativity at midlife. Each man's societal generativity at midlife was assessed by means of the Societal Generativity Index, which is a rating system adapted for this study from Vaillant's previous Adult Life Stage Eriksonian rating system (Vaillant & Milofsky, 1980). The Societal Generativity Index ranges from (1) generativity failed or clearly absent, to (2) generativity unclear or ambiguous, to (3) generativity clearly achieved. A man was rated as exhibiting societal generativity at midlife if he demonstrated a clear capacity for establishing, guiding, or caring for the next generation through sustained responsibility for the growth, well-being, or leadership of younger adults or of the larger society. A man's care for his own children, that is, was not relevant to the rating of societal generativity. What was important was actual service as a consultant, guide, teacher, coach, manager, or mentor to younger adults or to the larger society. In essence, the criterion that differentiated the cultural fathers from the other fathers was their assumption of responsibility for other adults beyond the sphere of their nuclear families. Therefore, to ensure that the ratings of societal generativity were not influenced by knowledge of the achievement of biological or parental generativity, information about a subject's nuclear family and his possible child-rearing activities was excluded from consideration by the raters. There was 85% exact agreement between the raters; interrater agreement was estimated to be .76, using Cohen's kappa.

The Societal Generativity Index's advantages for this study are twofold. First, the measure is based on a subject's actual activities; tangible, externally observable actions provide objective evidence of what is otherwise one of the more subjective stages of psychosocial development. In contrast, previous Eriksonian measures of generativity have usually been in the form of a pencil-and-paper assessment of attitudes and concerns associated with generativity. Second, the measure can be flexibly applied to assess generativity from clinical interview transcripts and personal history records of a subject's activities.

Indirect evidence for the construct validity of the Societal Generativity Index comes from its source prototype: the rating system is a modified item from Vaillant's Adult Life Stage rating system, scores on which have been shown to be significantly associated with ratings of ego-coping mechanisms ($r = .50, p < .01$) and with several behavior-based reports of psychosocial maturity ($r = .25$ to $.46, p < .01$) (Vaillant & Milofsky, 1980, Table 9). *Direct evidence* for the construct validity of the Societal Generativity Index as used in this study was obtained by assessing 18 subjects for level of generativity with both the Societal Generativity Index (based on blinded interview transcripts and questionnaires) and four written Eriksonian measures of generativity, the reliability and validity of which had previously been established. The criterion measures included the generativity subscale from the Developmental Personality Scales (DPS, 11 positive items; Ryff & Heincke, 1983), the Self-Description Questionnaire (SDQ, 10 positive items; Boyd, 1966, 1974), the Jackson Personality Inventory (JPI, 10 items; Ryff & Migdal, 1984), and the generativity subscales from the Measure of Psychosocial Development (MPD, 7 positive items; Hawley, 1984, 1988). The analyses showed that scores on the Societal Generativity Index had a strong positive correlation with the generativity scores from three of the four criterion measures (Hawley's MPD, $r = .57$, $p < .01$; Ryff and Heincke's DPS, $r = .54$, $p < .05$; Ryff and Migdal's version of the JPI, $r = .54$, $p < .05$; and Boyd's SDQ, $r = .31$, $p = .10$). Overall, the analyses support the claim that the Societal Generativity Index's construct validity is adequate for research purposes.

Father's Boyhood Family of Origin

Three variables served to control for variations in the men's boyhood families.

First-generation's occupational levels. To control for social class differences in the men's families of origin, their fathers and mothers were rated on the occupational subscale from Hollingshead's Index of Social Status (1959, 1975; Haug, 1972, Hollingshead & Redlich, 1958; Landecker, 1960). The scale was reversed so that it ranged from 1 (low) to 7 (high). Mothers' premarital occupations were used for those who never worked outside of the home after marriage. The interrater reliability coefficient was .80 for the men's fathers' occupations, and .82 for the men's mothers' occupations.

Father's boyhood Eriksonian industry. To control for variations in men's psychosocial development before the experience of parenting, each man was assessed for boyhood achievement of industry, Erikson's fourth stage of development. On a 9-point index of boyhood industry, boys received points for doing regular chores, adjusting well to school socially and academically (controlling for IQ), participating in after-school jobs, and coping with difficulties in their inner-city homes. The rating was based on the subjects' original interviews at age 14. Multiple raters were used; interrater reliability coefficients were always greater than or equal to .78 (see Vaillant & Vaillant, 1981).

Father's boyhood IQ. Each of the Glueck subjects was given the Wechsler-Bellevue Full-Scale Intelligence Test when he entered the study (Glueck & Glueck, 1950).

Father's Adulthood Family of Procreation

Four variables were used to control for variations in the men's adulthood families of procreation.

His child's gender. The gender of the children was controlled for, using a constructed variable (coded 0 = female, 1 = male).

His child's age. Because the men began their families at different times, the ages of their children varied at the time the men were assessed for their participation in childrearing during the first decade of their child's life and during the second decade of their child's life. The ages of their children at each longitudinal assessment were thus included as a control variable.

Number of children. The men's childrearing participation with their first child and the impact of that childrearing may have been influenced by the total number of children for whom they were responsible. Thus the number of each father's children was also monitored at each longitudinal assessment in order to control statistically for this variation.

Wife's employment outside of the home. Glueck subjects' wives' previous Hollingshead occupational ratings were often based on the women's employment prior to marriage or the birth of their first child. Only a minority of the wives worked outside of the home during their first child's childhood decade (15%), adolescent decade (15%), or either or both decades (25%). Each wife was rated at each longitudinal assessment as follows: (0) wife not working outside of the home, (1) wife employed part-time outside of the home (minimum of 1 day or 7 hours per week), and (2) wife employed full-time outside of the home (35 or more hours per week).

Father's Parental Generativity Variables

The analysis will use the ratings of three types of paternal generativity (support of social-emotional development, support of intellectual-academic development, and support of physical-athletic development) during two decades (childhood and adolescence) to assess the ability of the six varieties of fathers' childrearing participation to predict the fathers' own outcomes.

Statistical Procedures

The statistical analyses reported in this and subsequent chapters rely primarily on multiple regression analysis, which is a method of examining the ability of each predictor variable, while controlling for the effects of all other variables, to predict or account for a percentage of the variance in the outcome variable.

Multiple Regression

It is reasonable to question whether the men's boyhood emotional health, their parents' occupations, wife's education, children's age and sex, and their adulthood participation in six different domains of childrearing are all associated with or predict the men's generativity at midlife. Multiple regression is used here to predict or explain a percentage of the variation in an outcome or dependent variable, such as "fathers' societal generativity at midlife," in terms of the variation in each of a large number of predictor or independent variables, such as the list at the beginning of this paragraph.[1] One advantage of using multiple regression in this investigation is that it provides a more comprehensive account of a life outcome under consideration. Not only does it indicate the individual effect of each independent variable, but it also indicates the cumulative effects of all independent

1. Many precedents exist for parametric analysis of similar outcome measures that may not always be strictly interval scales (Colby, Kohlberg, Gibbs, & Lieberman, 1983; Jencks et al., 1972; Laub & Sampson, 1988). Similarly, our use of regression analysis as the main analytic tool is justifiable on several statistical grounds: (1) The measures are at least ordinal, thus falling in the gray area where there is considerable debate over the appropriate pairing between type of scale and type of statistic (Baker, Hardyck, & Petrinovich, 1966; Gardner, 1975). (2) The F-test has been shown to be a robust statistic, capable of valid inference even with moderate violation of normality assumptions (Cohen, 1965, 1977; Kerlinger & Pedhazur, 1973). (3) With more precise equal interval scales of psychosocial development and social mobility, multiple regression would be an even more powerful method, but the present measures bias against, not in favor of, the hypotheses (Kleinbaum & Kupper, 1978). (4) Finally, analyses using logistic regression or other alternatives yielded results in agreement with those reported.

variables together. This is important, since the variations that occur in most of life's outcomes can seldom be accounted for by a single variable.

Common Misunderstandings

It is important to understand correctly the amount of variance in an outcome that one can reasonably expect to be explained by an independent variable. In absolute terms, the amount of variance that can be accounted for in any particular outcome (such as upward educational mobility) by a set of predictor variables (such as childhood experiences) ranges from 0% to 100%. An independent or predictor variable that is unrelated to the dependent or outcome variable will explain 0% of the variance, and one which is perfectly related will explain 100% of the variance. Should one therefore conclude that a variable that accounts for perhaps 9% of the variance in students' upward educational mobility makes no important contribution to predicting upward mobility (since the model leaves 91% of the variance unexplained)? No. The reason is that the proportion of variance accounted for is relative, calling for a personal judgment, in two senses. It is relative to the other variables the researcher included in the equation. It is also relative to the researcher's subjective judgment of the amount of variance that is ever and can ever be realistically accounted for in the type of research being conducted. Jacob Cohen (1977), one of the most respected authorities on these issues, has provided researchers with realistic "operational definitions of 'small,' 'medium,' and 'large' effect sizes," expressed in terms of r (p. 79). Cohen's (1977) rule-of-thumb definitions are as follows (pp. 79-81, 412-414):

Small. A "small" but statistically significant effect corresponds to an r of .10, for which the implied proportion of variance is $r^2 = .01$, such that 1% of the variance in the dependent variable is attributable to the independent variable. When several independent variables are involved, a combined small effect is one that accounts for 2% of the variance ($r = .14$, $r^2 = .019$).

Medium. A "medium" effect is an r of .30, such that the proportion of variance is $r^2 = .09$, which indicates that 9% of the variance in the dependent variable is accounted for by the independent variable. When several independent variables are involved, a medium effect is one that accounts for 13% of the variance ($r = .36$, $r^2 = .129$). Thus, when a new background variable brought into a stepwise regression equation explains about 10% of the variance in the outcome (r^2 change $= .10$), this is generally to be considered a healthy medium effect.

Large. Finally, a "large" effect is $r = .50$, for which $r^2 = .25$ or 25% of the variance accounted for. When several independent variables are involved, however, a large effect might still be one that accounts for about 26% of the variance ($r = .51$, $r^2 = .26$), given that this is usually as high as one can hope to achieve. The amount of variance that should be defined as large, therefore, is also a function of the ceiling investigators have learned to anticipate as being "about as high as they come" in their field (Cohen, 1977, p. 81). The above figure for a large effect, for instance, might be too large in clinical psychology and too small in economics.

Cohen also notes, emphasizing the relative nature of effect sizes, that a "moderate theoretical effect size may easily, in a 'noisy' research project, be no larger than what is defined here as small" (1977, p. 413). This present study abundantly qualifies as "noisy," given that it involves making predictions over periods of time that range up to 4 *decades*— not, as in a few studies, over a period of 4 years or, as in most studies, over a period of 4 months, or 4 days, or, as in some controlled experiments, even 4 minutes.[2]

Hierarchical Models

In the hierarchical model of multiple regression used in this study, the researcher determines the order in which the predictor variables are entered into the equation. Given that this is a longitudinal study, a hierarchical model has the advantage of being able to take known

2. Another procedure for understanding the real-world importance of a particular correlation is Rosenthal and Rubin's Binomial Effect Size Display (BESD). For example, while an r of .32 between paternal childrearing and children's educational mobility would indicate that childrearing accounts for 10% of the variance in children's educational success ($r^2 = .10$), the BESD procedure demonstrates that an r of .32 is also equivalent to an increase of 32% in the correct prediction of any particular success rate. The BESD estimates that changes in a success rate range from $.50 + r/2$ to $.50 - r/2$. Applying this procedure to the present example ($r = .32$), the children's success rate would be reduced from approximately 66% to approximately 34% if they had not benefited from paternal childcare. (See Rosenthal, 1990; Rosenthal & Rubin, 1979, 1982; Rosenthal & Rosnow, 1984; Rosnow & Rosenthal, 1988, 1989.)

historical-developmental sequences into consideration. In other words, the variables are temporally ordered in the subjects' lives, and hierarchical regression allows the variables to be entered into the model in the same historically determined order: the childhood characteristic can be entered before the adolescent characteristic when predicting an adulthood outcome. This also allows the researcher, in effect, to control for prior background variables (for example, boyhood IQ) before testing the ability of various domains of childrearing participation (for example, support of intellectual development during adolescence) to predict or account for variance in an adulthood outcome (for example, educational achievement).

Variables can be entered as a group, in addition to being entered individually, in a hierarchical model. In the present study, this allows variables from a similar point in chronological time during the subjects' lives to be grouped together in a "block," and the blocks then placed in a temporal hierarchy for entry into the equation. While the longitudinal logic for entering blocks of variables in a predetermined sequence is clear, there are no temporal criteria by which to assign priority among the variables within each block. In this study, two conventional alternative methods of entering the variables within each block are used—forced and stepwise.

Forced variable entry. In forced entry, *all* variables within each block are entered into the equation in order of *decreasing* tolerance.[3] Because all variables in each block enter the equation, the relevant statistics regarding changes in the equation are computed for each single block as a whole, rather than for each individual variable within each block. The final beta (that is, standardized regression coefficient) reported for each variable, in effect, controls for all other variables in the block, as well as for all prior variables in the equation.

Stepwise variable entry. In stepwise entry, a predetermined set of statistical rules is used to *select* which and in what order the different independent variables within a block will be entered into the prediction equation.[4] The relevant statistics regarding changes in the equa-

3. Tolerance is the percentage of a variable's variance that is not redundant with the variance accounted for by the other independent variables in the equation.

4. First, the independent variable that has the strongest correlation with the dependent variable is entered. If the probability of F is smaller than .05, then the variable with the next strongest correlation or the smallest probability of F is entered, and so forth. At every step, however, the variables already incorporated in the equation in previous steps are reexamined for possible removal, and if the

tion are computed for each individual variable within each block that enters the equation. An essentially atheoretical and ahistorical method, stepwise entry tells us which variable or variables within a larger group of independent variables will account for the greatest amount of variance in the outcome variable. This approach is especially useful within the general hierarchical approach when there is no compelling reason to order or control for variables within a particular block or subgroup of variables.

What We Found:
Significance of Childrearing for the Fathers

We sought to determine the ability of fathers' parental generativity to predict three of the fathers' midlife outcomes—occupational mobility, marital success, and societal generativity. The analyses control for each of the men's own parents' occupational levels (father $M =$ 2.46, mother $M = 2.65$), the men's boyhood psychosocial development in terms of Eriksonian industry ($M = 4.41$), and their boyhood IQ ($M = 96$). Control variables also include the child's gender, the wife's employment outside the home during the childhood decade (15.8%) or during the adolescent decade (15.3%), the men's total number of offspring at the time of the childhood rating ($M = 2.2$) and the time of the adolescent rating ($M = 3.6$), and the age of the child in the study at the time of the childhood rating ($M = 5.1$ years) and the adolescent rating ($M = 17.1$ years). The predictor variables are the indices of parental generativity, that is, childrearing participation whereby the fathers further their children's social-emotional, intellectual-academic, or physical-athletic development at two separate age periods.

Predicting Fathers' Occupational Mobility at Midlife

The study fathers, on average, were upwardly mobile by one occupational level above that of their parents (M gain = 1.08). This meant, for example, that men whose parents were semiskilled or skilled blue-

---

probability of F is no longer smaller than .05, the variable is removed. The process continues until no variable from the same group of variables in the equation needs to be removed, and no variable that is not in the equation is eligible for entry.

collar workers became skilled blue-collar workers or white-collar technicians and small-business operators.

Table 4.1 shows the amount of the variance in the fathers' occupational mobility that can be accounted for by their participation in childrearing and whether the contribution is negative or positive. The hierarchical regression model explains a total of 34% of the variance in the fathers' occupational mobility [$R = .582$, $F(17, 222) = 6.67$, $p < .001$].

The contribution of general background variables to the explained variance in occupational mobility is substantial. The men's boyhood IQ, their parents' occupations, and their attainment of boyhood industry, together, account for 26% of the variance in their occupational mobility, and the contribution is significant ($R = .513$, $F = 21.04$, $p < .001$). The contribution of the parents' occupations to the subjects' occupational mobility is negative because occupational mobility was estimated by subtracting the parents' mean occupational rating from the men's own subsequent occupational rating. Thus, for instance, those who started their life in lower-class families and then entered upper-middle class professions were more upwardly mobile than those who started life in middle-class families and then also entered upper-middle-class professions.

Fathers' childrearing during the first decade contributes an additional 3% to the explained variance, after all background variables are controlled for, and the contribution is significant (F change = 2.68, $p < .05$). Secondary analysis, using a stepwise procedure to enter the block of childhood childrearing variables, confirmed that no one variable was individually significant.

Fathers' childrearing during the adolescent decade contributes still another 3% to the explained variance, after controlling for all prior childrearing and background variables, and the contribution is significant (F change = 2.83, $p < .05$). Secondary analysis of the adolescent block of childrearing variables, using a stepwise entry procedure, indicated that the sole significant contributor among the three types of parental generativity was the fathers' support of their adolescents' social-emotional development (R^2 change = .03, F change = 9.40, $p < .01$).

In sum, the total contribution made by childrearing to fathers' occupational mobility is 6% beyond that explained by all background variables, and the contribution is both positive and significant. Only one specific domain of childrearing participation—father's care for his teen's social-emotional development, made a significant individual contribution to the explained variance in the father's own upward mobility at work. Most notably, however, the contribution was positive.

Predicting Fathers' Marital Success at Midlife

Twenty-eight percent of the fathers were happily married at midlife. An additional 53% of the men remained in marriages in which they experienced little or no marital enjoyment by midlife. Nearly one-fifth, or 18% of the fathers' marriages had ended in divorce. Does paternal generativity predict a significant measure of the variation in marital success? If yes, is the contribution to the explained variance positive, that is, do childrearing fathers tend to be more satisfied or happier in their marriages?

The results of the hierarchical regression analysis, with all control variables entered into the equation prior to the childrearing variables, are presented in Table 4.2. The total model accounts for 26% of the variance in the fathers' marital outcomes [$R = .508$, $F (17, 222) = 4.55$, $p < .001$].

The contribution of background variables to the explained variance in midlife marital success is not significant, but fathers' childrearing during the first decade contributes 12% to the explained variance after controlling for background variables (F change $= 10.27$, $p < .001$). The individual contribution of fathers' support of social-emotional development during childhood is also significant, and secondary analysis, using a stepwise procedure to enter the block of childhood childrearing variables, likewise confirmed this finding (R^2 change $= .10$, F change $= 26.05$, $p < .001$).

Fathers' childrearing during the adolescent decade contributes an additional 9% to the explained variance after controlling for prior childrearing and for background variables (F change $= 8.40$, $p < .001$). The individual contributions of supporting intellectual-academic and social-emotional development are also significant, and secondary analysis, using a stepwise procedure to enter the adolescent childrearing variables, confirmed these findings for social-emotional development (R^2 change $= .07$, F change $= 18.77$, $p < .001$) and intellectual-academic development (R^2 change $= .03$, F change $= 8.60$, $p < .01$)

Table 4.1 Predicting fathers' midlife occupational mobility: regression analysis

Independent variables, listed in order of entry[a]	Beta[b]	R	Cumulative variance explained[c]	New variance explained[d]	F change
Block 1. Father's general background:					
His IQ	.257***				
His mother's occupation	-.326***				
His father's occupation	-.228***				
Eriksonian boyhood industry	.197***	.513	.26	.26	21.04***
Block 2. Family context, childhood decade:					
Wife's outside employment	-.017				
His child's gender (male)	.089				
Number of children	-.065				
Child's age	-.081	.533	.28	.02	1.66
Block 3. Father's childrearing, childhood decade:					
Physical development support	-.096				
Social development support	.108				
Intellectual development support	.085	.555	.31	.03	2.68*

Block 4. Family context, adolescent decade:					
Wife's outside employment	.047				
Child's age	−.007				
Number of children	.068	.559	.31	.00	.44
Block 5. Father's childrearing, adolescent decade:					
Intellectual development support	.043				
Physical development support	−.063				
Social development support	.188**	.582	.34	.03	2.83*

a. Hierarchical regression model; blocks are entered in historical order, while individual variables within each block are entered in order of decreasing tolerance.

b. Final standardized regression coefficient and significance level of t for each variable.

c. R^2 statistic.

d. R^2 change statistic.

$*p \leq .05$, $**p \leq .01$, $***p \leq .001$; $N = 240$.

Table 4.2 Predicting fathers' midlife marital success: regression analysis

Independent variables, listed in order of entry[a]	Beta[b]	R	Cumulative variance explained[c]	New variance explained[d]	F change
Block 1. Father's general background:					
Eriksonian boyhood industry	.102				
His father's occupation	−.040				
His mother's occupation	.039				
His IQ	.075	.147	.02	.02	1.30
Block 2. Family context, childhood decade:					
Wife's outside employment	−.007				
His child's gender (male)	.103				
Number of children	.129				
Child's age	−.046	.212	.04	.02	1.42
Block 3. Father's childrearing, childhood decade:					
Physical development support	.088				
Social development support	.309***				
Intellectual development support	.094	.398	.16	.12	10.27***
Block 4. Family context, adolescent decade:					
Wife's outside employment	−.037				
Child's age	.119				
Number of children	−.042	.417	.17	.01	1.37
Block 5. Father's childrearing, adolescent decade:					
Intellectual development support	.154*				
Physical development support	.035				
Social development support	.274***	.508	.26	.09	8.40***

a. Hierarchical regression model; blocks are entered in historical order, while individual variables within each block are entered in order of decreasing tolerance. (A logistic regression model also yields results in agreement with those obtained in this analysis.)
b. Final standardized regression coefficient and significance level of t for each variable within the block.
c. R^2 statistic.   d. R^2 change statistic. $*p \leq .05$, $**p \leq .01$, $***p \leq .001$; N = 240.

In sum, a total contribution of 21% is made by fathers' childrearing during the childhood and adolescent decades to the explained variance in fathers' midlife marital outcomes, after controlling for background variables. Fathers who provided high levels of childhood social-emotional support during the childhood decade and high levels of intellectual-academic and social-emotional support during the adolescent decade were themselves, as men at midlife, more likely to be happily married.

Predicting Fathers' Societal Generativity at Midlife

A total of 41% of the fathers were rated as having achieved some degree of societal generativity, while 59% failed to show any societal generativity by midlife ($M = 1.60$, $SD = .80$) To what extent, if any, can differences in the men's attainment of societal generativity be predicted by the care and support they gave to their children's development?

The results of the hierarchical regression analysis, with all control variables first entered in the equation, is presented in Table 4.3. The total model accounts for 22% of the variance in societal generativity [$R = .471$, $F (17, 222) = 3.72$, $p < .001$].

A 4% contribution of the background variables to the explained variance in societal generativity approaches significance ($R = .19$, $F = 2.25$, $p = .06$). Secondary analysis confirmed that the attainment of boyhood industry, Erikson's fourth stage of psychosocial development, was able to predict significantly the attainment of Erikson's seventh stage of generativity (R^2 change = .03, F change = 6.15, $p < .05$).

Fathers' care during the first decade of their children's lives contributes an additional 7% to the explained variance in the men's midlife societal generativity. This contribution is positive, significant, and beyond that explained by background variables. Secondary analysis, using stepwise entry for the block of childrearing variables, confirmed that the primary contribution was made by the fathers' support of their children's social-emotional development (R^2 change = .06, F change = 16.08, $p < .001$).

Fathers' childrearing during the adolescent decade contributes another 7% to the explained variance in societal generativity, beyond the contribution made by all prior childrearing and background vari-

Table 4.3 Predicting fathers' midlife societal generativity: regression analysis

Independent variables, listed in order of entry[a]	Beta[b]	R	Cumulative variance explained[c]	New variance explained[d]	F change
Block 1. Father's general background:					
His IQ	.065				
His mother's occupation	–.022				
His father's occupation	.014				
Eriksonian boyhood industry	.164*	.192	.04	.04	2.25
Block 2. Family context, childhood decade:					
Wife's outside employment	–.063				
His child's gender (male)	.125				
Number of children	–.009				
Child's age	–.005	.238	.06	.02	1.21
Block 3. Father's childrearing, childhood decade:					
Physical development support	.102				
Social development support	.244***				
Intellectual development support	.080	.367	.13	.07	6.88***

	b	R²			F
Block 4. Family context, adolescent decade:					
Wife's outside employment	-.060				
Child's age	.085				
Number of children	.040	.383	.15	.02	1.06
Block 5. Father's childrearing, adolescent decade:					
Intellectual development support	.124[e]				
Physical development support	-.003				
Social development support	.268***	.471	.22	.07	7.07***

a. Hierarchical regression model; blocks are entered in historical order, while individual variables within each block are entered in order of decreasing tolerance.

b. Final standardized regression coefficient and significance level of t for each variable.

c. R^2 statistic.

d. R^2 change statistic.

e. Approached significance (.05 < p < .10) under forced entry of the block as a whole, *and* attained significance ($p \leq .05$) under stepwise entry of the individual variables within the block.

*$p \leq .05$, **$p \leq .01$, ***$p \leq .001$; $N = 240$.

ables, and the contribution is significant (F change = 7.07, $p < .001$). The individual contribution of social-emotional childrearing is also individually significant. Secondary analysis, using a stepwise procedure to enter the adolescent childrearing variables, confirmed that it was a major contributor (R^2 change = .06, F change = 17.45, $p < .001$). Additionally, however, fathers' support of their adolescents' intellectual-academic development also entered the equation when the weak negative contribution of supporting physical-athletic development was removed as a control variable by the stepwise entry procedure. The additional contribution made by childrearing support of intellectual-academic development was significant and positive (R^2 change = .02, F change = 6.04, $p < .05$).

In sum, a total of 14% of the variance in the fathers' societal generativity at midlife is explained by the fathers' earlier childrearing participation, after the imposition of all control variables. Fathers who cared for their children's social-emotional development during the first decade and also cared for both social-emotional and intellectual-academic development during the second decade were, as fathers at midlife, notably more likely to have become generative beyond the family sphere.

For all regression analyses reported, it is theoretically possible that there is an additional interaction effect at work in which the strength of one domain of childrearing participation is increased when other types of participation or background characteristics are present. However, no tested interactions were statistically significant.

Discussion of the Findings

What can we conclude about the contribution of parental generativity to subsequent midlife outcomes?

Work Success

Parental generativity does not appear to restrain fathers' overall occupational mobility. Our findings were generally consistent with prior research that has shown the primary predictors of men's occupational mobility are their boyhood IQ (McCall, 1977b), occupational levels of parents in boyhood (Jencks, et al., 1972), and boyhood psychological competence (Kohlberg, Ricks, & Snarey, 1984). The findings also show that none of the childrearing participation variables makes a significant negative contribution to the fathers' occupational mobility. In fact, contrary to the speculation that family participation may negatively predict men's career success, fathers' care for their children's intellectual development and their adolescents' social development made a positive and significant contribution to the explained variance in the fathers' occupational mobility.

The positive correlation between childrearing participation and occupational mobility does not eliminate tensions between work life and family life. In fact, a number of surveys conducted across various regions of the country confirm that significant conflicts arise: 65% of fathers responding to a poll conducted by the *Oregonian* (McDermott, January, 1990) and 57% of the fathers in a poll conducted by the *Los Angeles Times* (Smith & Sipchen, 1990) believe that they are being asked to sacrifice too much family time for the workplace, while 55% of fathers with children under 12 surveyed for *Fortune Magazine* (Chapman, 1987) said that they feared that children of working parents suffer because they have too little time with their parents, and 30% said that they had personally turned down a job promotion or transfer because it would have reduced the time they spend with their families. Probably, all good fathers must reframe their career goals and, in some sense, become less ambitious. Despite some work tradeoffs and role conflicts, however, childrearing does not appear to have a measurable long-term negative impact upon work success at the global level of occupational mobility. Just the opposite—childrearing participation predicts career mobility.

It is also important to emphasize that the association between parental generativity and occupational mobility does not necessarily indicate that the former caused the latter. Although a growing body of literature suggests that economic changes in parental work status do influence the quality of parent-child relationships, negative economic changes have been the primary predictors studied. Loss of economic status, for instance, predicts that fathers will become more irritable and hostile, and their childrearing practices will, in turn, become more unstable and tense (Conger, et al., 1990; Elder, Liker, & Cross, 1984; Flanagan, 1990a, 1990b; Ray & McLoyd, 1986). Similarly, the constructive role of positive economic changes (of which occupational mobility would be an example) is also likely (Voydanoff, 1990). Unemployment negatively affects father-child relations, in part because it increases stress and lowers economic security. Occupational mobility may positively affect father-child relations, in part because it increases economic security and self-esteem, which counterbalance possible increases in stress. We would also expect that the impact of economic changes would vary by family. Studies of working class families, for instance, have shown that family cohesiveness and affection greatly moderate the negative impact of economic loss on a father's relations with his wife and children (Cavan & Ranck, 1938; Komarovsky, 1940; Moen, Kain, & Elder, 1983). In sum, it is possible that childrearing participation and occupational success are reciprocally related over time, although our longitudinal findings suggest that these reciprocal relations are modest.

Marital Success

The fathers' parental generativity in earlier adulthood appears to be related to the men's successful midlife attainment of an enjoyable, stable marriage. Fathers' care for their children's social-emotional development during childhood and adolescence, and intellectual-academic development during adolescence were all effective predictors of the fathers' own subsequent marital outcome. Together, these three childrearing participation variables account for one-fifth of the variance in the fathers' midlife marital success.

The interpretation of the significance of parental generativity for marital success is complicated by the possible relation of both to a third variable. For instance, the positive contribution of childrearing participation in this study may reflect, in part, that most of the fathers were heads of single-earner families, and that their involvement was therefore more likely to be the result of personal choice rather than of pressure from their spouses. Refuting this particular interpretation are two facts: the analyses controlled for the wives' employment status, and wives' employment status had no significant main effect. The more important caveat, however, is simply that both parental generativity and marital outcomes may be forms of success that are promoted by a prior set of social and psychological characteristics.

A further complication is introduced by the possibility that parenting and marital dynamics are reciprocally related across the adult years because both are subsystems within the same family system. For instance, improved parental practices and father-child relations could promote improved marital practices and husband-wife relations, but improved marital practices and husband-wife relations could also promote improved parental practices and father-child relations. If the quality of marital relations during the same childrearing assessment times were controlled for, the amount of variance in the midlife marital outcome accounted for by fathers' childrearing would be expected to diminish. Such multiple longitudinal assessments of marital relations were not available, but even if the hierarchical regression analysis was repeated after controlling for marital relations at each childrearing assessment, interpreting the findings would still confront the reverse proposition: marital relations were a function, in part, of the fathers' childrearing participation.

Societal Generativity

The major finding reported in this chapter is that fathers' participation in childrearing contributes to their realization of societal generativity years later during midlife. Fathers' care for their children's and adolescents' social-emotional development, and their adolescents' intellectual-academic development all contributed to the explained variance in societal generativity. Childrearing, overall, accounted for 14% of the variance in psychosocial generativity beyond the family sphere. This finding is fully consistent with the Eriksonian idea that the experience of parenting serves as a foundation, although it is not necessarily a sufficient condition, for the subsequent achievement of societal generativity at midlife. The general finding that men who gave more care to their children's and adolescents' social-emotional development were themselves more likely to exhibit greater psychosocial maturity is also remarkably congruent with the prior longitudinal findings of Heath (1978; Heath & Heath, 1991) and Vaillant (1977, 1978) on parenting and psychosocial generativity.

The actual dynamics by which parental generativity may promote fathers' personal maturity are, of course, very complex and not fully understood. Part of the process, however, seems to hinge on a father becoming bonded, committed to a child who periodically makes demands upon him which he is simply not prepared to meet. The resulting disequilibrium promotes the development of increased complexity in the father's cognitive, emotional, and behavioral repertoire in order to meet the basic needs of this one for whom he would willingly sacrifice all. This commitment beyond the self, in turn, prepares the way for societal generativity which involves a commitment beyond the family. Consistent with this interpretation, Atchley's (1989) vivid speculations further suggest how childrearing provides significant impetus for men's personal development.

> Being a parent challenges one's conception of self, taxes coping ability, and alters just about every aspect of the structure of everyday life. Being a parent can be quite a humbling experience. By the time child rearing is complete, those parents who see it through usually have relatively few illusions about the perfectibility of humankind. They may be more likely than others to be nurturing and sympathetic to younger generations. On the other hand, those who never have children may be more able to preserve their illusions.   (p. 22)

The fathers in this study, having faced the challenges of promoting their children's development, may have had few illusions about life, but they did have clearer ideals, and they were able to pass them on to younger adults outside of their families. For these men, fathering was a lifelong activity.

Other interpretations of the relation between fathering and societal generativity are also helpful. From the perspective of a psychology of trait stability, an early predisposition toward generativity predicts high parental involvement throughout, and clear societal generativity at midlife. For instance, promoting social-emotional development during the childhood decade of childrearing and promoting social-emotional development during the adolescent decade of childrearing were significantly correlated with each other, and both, in turn, were significantly associated with the fathers' societal generativity at midlife. Higher levels of social-emotional childrearing support may be interpreted as an early sign of, or predisposition toward, societal generativity. But parental generativity does not occur in a social vacuum. Fathering functions to bond an adult and child, but it also functions to bond a father to the larger community. For instance, several cross-sectional studies have suggested that when men enter the childrearing years, they also become more involved in neighborhood activities and community organizations through their children (for brief review, see Rossi, 1984). This sociological phenomenon may also contribute to the transition from parental to societal generativity.

In summary, the significant contribution that parental generativity makes to fathers' psychosocial development at midlife is suggested by the apparent contribution that their care for their children's social-emotional and intellectual-academic development make to their mid-life ability to be happy in their marriages and to nurture other adults. Furthermore, there is no evidence that parental generativity has a significant negative influence on men's own occupational mobility. On the contrary, childrearing makes a measurably positive contribution to their work success. Men who are parentally generative during early adulthood usually turn out to be good spouses, workers, and citizens at midlife.

Placing the Findings in Context

It is worth emphasizing that our findings are consistent with the general findings from two previous longitudinal studies of male graduates of elite colleges—Harvard and Haverford (Heath & Heath, 1991; Vaillant, 1974, 1978; Vaillant & Vaillant, 1981). It appears that, regardless of some significant variations in social class backgrounds, "fathering . . . may be good for men as well as for children" (Parke, 1981, p. 11).

It is also essential to emphasize, that longitudinal patterns are subject to other forces. Historical changes, in particular, place limits on the confident generalization of the impact of childrearing upon fathers' midlife outcomes today and in the future. For instance, conditions today are quite different from the expanding labor market and possibilities for occupational mobility the Glueck men experienced. So are the marital norms. Between 1950 and 1989, the divorce rate doubled among the general population. Among the study fathers, about 2 out of 10 first marriages ended in divorce, but among today's fathers, it is estimated that approximately half of all marriages will end in divorce (National Center for Health Statistics, 1990b, 1990c, 1990d).

The Glueck findings, nevertheless, also anticipate recent changes in men's roles. Recent surveys suggest changed attitudes among men in that a majority of husbands now experience fathering as more psychologically rewarding (satisfying, creative, confidence-building) than are their occupations (cf. Gallup, 1991; McDermott, 1990). It has also been found that greater satisfaction in family roles than at work has a stronger predictive effect on men's overall well-being (Pleck, 1985).

5

Joseph and Patricia: Father–Daughter Camaraderie

This self-portrait is, in part, the story of how a father's care for his daughter's development may have, years later, contributed to his own midlife work success, marital happiness, and societal generativity. It is also the story of a father's and daughter's fondness for each other that profoundly mixes humor and care.

Joseph is an outgoing middle-aged man who looks comfortable in his white shirt and tie. His own father, Patrick, was a blue-collar worker, and Joe himself, with a high school education, was a salesman and minor supervisor during his childrearing years. Joe has been married for over 40 years, and he and his wife, Connie, raised five children.

His oldest daughter, Patricia, is just as animated as her father. She is a little taller than Joe and looks even more at ease in her attractive business suit. After graduating from high school, she went to college and earned a degree in nursing and a certificate for advanced study in nursing administration. She is currently a major administrator for a state health agency. Pat has been married for over 5 years and has no children.

Their joint conversation occurred at the kitchen table around which Joe and Connie had raised Pat and her siblings. Major portions of their individual interviews, however, were held in the privacy of their offices.

Early Memories

The Father Looks Back a Generation

My first memory of my dad is a Christmas when I was a very young child. I couldn't even tell you how old I was. I remember decorating the tree with him. It was a party kind of thing, because the holiday vacation was when we got to spend some time with him.

My dad was a fireman. I guess he got one day off every two weeks. We used to go to the station and visit him; that was probably the only way you got to see your father on a regular basis. He worked a lot; he put in a lot of time. In those days you were lucky if you were making 28 bucks a week, if you had a steady job. He's worked hard for everything. I don't think anybody has ever given him anything. He was a self-made guy.

It's very difficult to recall how my father was involved in my life when I was growing up (pause). I was very athletic, even as a small child, but we never participated in any sports together. He was better at using his hands, he'd build an erector set, do electrical work, fix things; he enjoyed doing things like that. Whereas I'm not very good with machines, he's the type of guy who can sit down and take things apart and enjoy doing it. As kids we'd sit there and watch. Bored stiff but we survived. It was what he liked doing. I never had a problem with my dad. He never bothered us, and I never bothered him.[1]

By age 9 or 10, I was a street brat. I was out running around all the time: an athlete in the streets. But Mother was always there, so anything I ever needed I had.

My father was busy scratching for a living, which he did very well, and my running around never bothered him. We all got along pretty good; we were a pretty close family. Josh, my older brother, and I were probably closest. My father was never a disciplinarian; just my mother. I don't think he ever hit me, even if I did something wrong and I probably deserved it. I don't even remember being disciplined, for any reason, though I'm sure there were many occasions when I probably should have at a certain point.[2]

I went to summer camp from age 11 to 19. I was a camper at Boy Scout camps in the early years, 11 or 12, then a paid counselor and then the athletic director. A great life! (There were a lot of problem kids—runaways, broken homes, stuff like that.) Anyway, my

1. Joe's boyhood frustration with the fathering he received immediately raises the question of how he might compensate to ensure that his own children would not struggle with the same memory.

2. Joe's longitudinal records confirm that neither parent used physical punishment during his adolescent years and that he had a distant relationship with his father. His relationship with his mother was apparently average.

father and mother came to visit me at camp at least once a week. Like they were passing by. They didn't have to do it, but it was something they enjoyed doing. Sometimes I didn't even know they were there.

I don't think there was a day at Boston High School that went by when I wasn't doing something athletic. Football—All Boston. Baseball—second team All Scholastic. Basketball—city champs a couple of times. Golf—I dabbled. Track—I had a couple of high school records in the fifty-yard dash, the hundred yard dash. And relays, we had a record in the relay. We went up to Amherst and beat all the suburbanites, kids who were supposed to be good. We had a record there.[3]

My mother never wanted to watch me because most of the time I'd get hurt; she'd actually watch, but if you asked her she would say, "Oh, I wouldn't go and watch him," you know. My father and Josh used to go to all my activities. I was a great competitor. As we got older, my father had more time, and he started to go to all my matches with me. I think he took a very special interest in my activities. He saved all my newspaper clippings.

When my father retired from the fire department, at age 55, he immediately went to work as a master electrician for about three years, and at the same time he was gathering up lumber, so that he could build a cottage in New Hampshire. He'd take so much lumber up to New Hampshire every week and store it, and eventually he got enough, and he started to put in the foundation, mixing concrete in 5-gallon cans. Between my father, aunts, uncles, and my mother, we built the cottage from scratch. A "cottage in New Hampshire." This was something he always wanted to build. Pat probably remembers that; she was about seven years old then.

I see some similarities between my father and myself as a father. He is also very conservative; and I'd say I'm very conservative. My lifestyle, in some ways, is probably similar to his. He was hit by the Depression and I was a Depression baby, so we're both probably conservative in the way that we do things. My children are completely

---

3. Joe's boyhood records confirm that he exhibited high levels of industry during late childhood and early adolescence. In addition to being a hard-working athlete and competent student, he also worked on the high school yearbook and at a local store. Joe's father had set an example of industriousness by setting goals for himself and accomplishing them.

the opposite of both of us. Of course, they are all doing well, so they can afford to be less conservative.

But basically my father and I are different, opposites, as fathers. I would say that I was more interested in being involved in activities that they were in. I usually let them make their own mistakes, but I was here to guide them, I was here if they needed questions answered. We're talking just day-to-day stuff, just being around. We were always around; we tried to be available.

My father probably would have been the same way, but he just didn't have the time. Trying to make it. But I'd say my own father is, in some things, also just more reserved. Generally he talks less than I do. I think he's more of a listener. Stays more in the background. He was the type of guy that could sit down at the table, open a book, and start reading. We'd be just sitting there eating.

He might describe me as athletic and lazy. (I'd just as soon go out and play racquetball, instead of picking up a brush and paint, getting a hammer and a nail, like him.) But I think he's proud of me, the family, and of his grandchildren, great-grandchildren. He still collects newspaper stories about me, you know. When I was involved in Little League (I was a coach, and then held a number of different positions), he always clipped the stories or pictures. In my job now, I still get my picture in the local paper, and he still cuts them out.

Last year he had a heart attack, and he had a clot. This was Sunday after Thanksgiving, and he was down here, and he collapsed on the floor. My beeper went off, they called me, and so I ran home, and the EMTs were there. He didn't want to go to the hospital. My mother said, "He won't go, he won't go." I said, "Look, he's going." Because that clot was going to go somewhere, and they had to watch it, and they told him that he should go. So I said, "Look, if you don't go, after they leave, ten minutes from now you could have this thing, and be dead, gone. So why don't you let them strap you in their chair, like this, and then get the thing taken care of." And I'm strapping him in as I talked and he's looking at me, so he says, "All right." But he was crying. I felt kind of bad for the guy because he's always been independent, all his life. He wouldn't ask you for the right time, unless he had to. And it was pretty sad. He went to the hospital and, about three o'clock in the morning, he had the stroke. And he lost the full use of his hearing, and his leg, and he had a slur. But (laughs), he didn't want to stay in there. He was still being independent. (Pat said, "That's great." I said, "Oh, that's great, but he won't take the medicine.") He'd spit the medicine out. But, that was his only way that he could fight back. Until finally we promised to take him home for Christmas.[4]

So he started to eat, because we promised to take him home. And we did. Now he can eat, and he can talk (although he still has a little bit of a slur), and he can walk (although he still hasn't got full use of his leg). He isn't allowed to drive, of course, but the car is at the end of the driveway (laughs) ready to go. He's a gutsy fighter (just like his granddaughter).

The Father's Earliest Memories of His Daughter

I first saw her through the glass at the hospital. In those days, you couldn't walk in like you can today. They'd scream if you went beyond the desk without having them sterilize you or whatever. You could never go into the nursery and pick up your baby. You couldn't even go in the ward when they were feeding them. Now, people walk all over the joint.

I remember that then they brought her out and let me hold her. I had to have a mask on. Oh, I thought she was great! (Laughs). She had long fingernails, and a dimple in her chin, and you couldn't tell if she had blue eyes, but they looked like they were blue. She had very little hair, but it was light. And, quiet, you know (pauses). Yeah, I thought she was very nice.

I was very pleased with the whole thing, and I didn't have to be there, like today (laughter).

She was a good child. I'd say that she was a very happy child. She was very active; she liked to be moving, and doing things all the time. She was very caring for those around her, and she tried to please.

Then, before she was five years old, she was hit with this problem—pseudarthrosis. The bone marrow didn't grow properly, and the tibia bone curved. She had to wear these special shoes at night to try to

---

4. Many men, like Joe, must integrate the way they previously came to terms with "the caring and the lack of caring experienced as a child" from their own fathers, and, as older adults themselves, with now having to be "responsible for" their fathers in their old age (Erikson, Erikson, & Kivnick, 1986, p. 73).

bring that curve in, and a special brace, and all that. But her leg didn't seem to hold her down at all.[5]

Then it broke and, you know, we went through the treatments, and everything, which I wasn't too pleased with. I think there was a better way to handle it but, in those days, you didn't have many choices. As a matter of fact, at the Children's Hospital, they told me that I "shouldn't be there," that I "should be going to the City Hospital." I said, "Why?" and he said, "Well, that's where you people belong." He meant people that didn't have much money and had to pay on a budget. I was told, flat out, to go to the City Hospital. I said, "Well, I really take exception to that. We want her to have the best that we can possibly give her. My financial status shouldn't have any bearing on this." Oh, we had an ongoing battle.

Taking Pat to the doctor and hospital, the responsibility, the appointments, the waiting, the overwhelming medical bills—it all affected me. I had to pay those bills. We didn't have the coverage you have today. I was with the newspaper at the time, the *Boston Daily Journal*. So we had a little insurance coverage, but it only took care of like $13 a day, and no extras. I owed them, at one given time, about ten grand. In those days, that was a lot of money. But I was working three jobs. Of course, I got on a budget system. I had three or four bills with them. Separate bills. Eventually, I would say, they got every dime they were entitled to. The director and the administrative people—they were bastards. But the doctors were usually great, and the nurses were really great.

I think everything that she did made us proud, because she was an exceptional child, because of her situation, her leg. And it didn't seem to bother her. She was so active. I was especially proud of the fact that she could swim a little in her condition, and go out in the boat alone, and not be scared. A lot of kids would be scared of that.

I also remember her catching her first fish, picking a turtle out of the water. The first time going to the store alone for a paper or some candy, and her not knowing I was behind her while she was walking

5. *Pseudarthrosis* literally means "false joint." In this condition, a segment of the inner shaft of the lower leg bone, between the knee and ankle, loses calcium and is replaced by a softer fibrous tissue which gives the appearance of a false joint. A break then occurs at the frail section (*Dorland's Medical Dictionary*, 1988; Turek, 1977).

on the street. Little accomplishments that maybe somebody else may not think were big, but they are big.

The Daughter's Earliest Memories of Her Father

About as far back as I can go is to an early Christmas. I was probably around 3 years old. My mother sews, and she used to make a lot of our clothes when we were little. I can remember she made me, and my brother Billy (who was real little), new pajamas for Christmas Eve. I can remember sitting with my father, posing with him, for a picture.[6]

Then I can remember being real young in the hospital and him being there. He did whatever he had to do to support and take care of his family. I was always proud of my father. Always! Just about everything the man ever did tickled me. I just thought everything he did was great. I was always glad when he was around.

Joint Reflections on the First Decade
Father's Care

JOE: I remember cuddling and rocking her to sleep. (All my kids liked to be rocked.) I was never much for changing diapers.

PAT: I don't remember him changing my diapers but I remember when he changed Billy's! (Turns to her father.)

Remember the time you changed his diaper, then you picked him up, and the diaper was still on the bed? You said, "This is okay. No problem" (laughter).

JOE: Oh, God (groans and pauses).

She knew I was around; I taught that to all of my kids at an early age. I could go and sit in the back of their room, and they wouldn't know I was there until I made my presence known. They'd turn around

6. The importance of Christmas as a family holiday is one of the many examples of intergenerational continuity evident in their story. Joe's own father, Patrick, worked unceasingly, but he always made sure that he stayed home with his children for Christmas Day. Joe and his daughter, Pat, each shared their earliest memories of their fathers during private interviews, and for both, childhood Christmases were the context of their earliest memories of their fathers. And when Patrick was ill, he demanded that Joe promise to take him home from the hospital in time for Christmas.

and see me; that's the way I was. They knew I was around, they knew I was available.[7]

PAT: He was always there, and he was always very patient. Both of them were. I guess I didn't realize how much patience he had until I was older, and I watched the other younger ones, after me, in the way he dealt with them. I often wondered, "Could I do this?" "Could I sit there and keep answering like this?" He was very patient.

JOE: Oh, I enjoyed it, I enjoyed it. I liked being involved with kids, being involved in all their activities, and I felt that they enjoyed me there.

PAT: I don't ever remember him being a disciplinarian. I can't believe that we were perfect children, but I don't remember anyone getting hit or yelled at.[8]

I think the strongest he ever came down on me was sitting down very quietly and just telling me that he was very disappointed in something I did. Well, that was enough to bring me to my knees in tears; it was horrible. Then he'd usually say something like, "I think that you owe me an apology for what you did," and you'd stand there crying and say "I'm so sorry." That was the end of it; that was literally the end of it. It was never brought up again. A lot of times he would use distraction, but I only know that because I watched him when I was older with the other kids. If you were getting into mischief, he'd say, "Why don't you put the TV set on?" Rather than "Don't touch that, don't do this." It wasn't his style.

Father's Support Through Health Problems

PAT: I was in the hospital for long stretches, and what kid wants to go? I mean, I liked it here (laughs). Going there was no fun, but he was always *my* friend. Just like now. When he'd come to visit me at each hospitalization, he'd bring me a roll of dimes, and he'd say, "Anyone wants to do anything, and you don't want that going on, you

7. As Joe had remarked, when his father and mother came to visit him at camp every week, "sometimes I didn't even know they were there." In contrast, Joe made sure he was seen in a way that suggested he was always there. Most simply, he revised the original pattern, from one in which his parents were seldom there to one in which he was "always there" for his children.

8. Similarly, Joe said that his own father "was never a disciplinarian." Joe was involved in dealing with childrearing problems, however, while his own father was more distant.

just holler. Tell them you have to make a phone call." He would say, "Anyone comes in here, you're not satisfied with their reason, just tell them, 'Time Out.' Tell them they need to get you a pay phone, you just need to talk to your father and discuss it, you're not satisfied with their explanation, and you'll be back." That was it. I was young, I was in a wheelchair, I couldn't reach the phone. But I had my dimes! I think I only had to use them once or twice, and I had somebody dial the number. These were the things he would do that would make me feel like, "I have my dimes, so Dad's right there, so I can handle this." It was great. The way he did it was very effective. There was probably only once or twice when you'd have some nurse that was probably running out of patience, and the whole shift was going crazy. I mean, I can see that now—I am a nurse. But she just maybe didn't go the extra distance to explain what she was going to do, so I called time out. I had to make a phone call. He'd write his work telephone number on the roll of dimes, and the home phone number, and I was all set.

When I did call, I just explained the situation, and we'd talk. He'd tell me how to handle it, and I'd go back and negotiate. He'd say, "I want you to call me back and report back to me and tell me how it worked out. Don't let them do anything till you're satisfied. You tell them, 'Don't touch me.'" I was saying what he said. It gave me some extra power.

JOE: She had a lot of courage. She swam herself! She stuck her leg up in the air with the cast and swam around in the water.

PAT: He had a fiberglass water cast made for me, and I'd swim with that.

JOE: Oh, she swam good. Rowed the boat, too!

PAT: My pseudarthrosis really didn't *seem* to interfere when I was a child. It was never made to feel like a handicap to me.

Daughter's First Job

PAT: When we were young, he gave me and my brother our first job. We accompanied him in the dark of the morning, every morning, to Shoreline because he was opening a new area to deliver papers. On the way over, we were supposed to fold them and put an elastic around them. But it was a tossup, a contest, which one of us would get carsick first (laughs). So you'd hear, "Dad? Pat's going to throw up." "No, no, everything's fine, everything's great." "Dad, Pat just threw up and it's making me sick. Pull over." We'd both throw up, and he'd say, "It's okay, it's a company car" (laughs). Then we'd both get sick, he'd have us lie down in the car; he'd deliver the whole route.

He did the whole job, and then he'd take us home and give us each a buck. When we got back, my mother would say, "How were the kids?" "Great" (laughter). "How did it go?" "Terrific! Get them up tomorrow!" (Laughter.) We would do that every morning! That was our first job, I must have been about 7 years old when we started.[9]

Father Selects the Perfect Story

JOE: What else?

PAT: You used to do a Jack in the Beanstalk rendition. That was your favorite, yeah.

JOE: Yeah, Jack in the Beanstalk.

PAT: Yeah. That was his story. Jack and the Beanstalk was the only story, though (laughs). If you pushed him for a story; that was it. He told it a lot.

JOE: They knew that by heart.

PAT: We knew that by heart, yeah.[10]

Opportunity to Visit the Cardinal

PAT: I remember when you took me over to see the Cardinal. *Just* him and me. That was great. That was my first introduction to imported butterscotch candy. I *still* eat it today.

JOE: He was a riot. Cardinal Cushing. He gave out candy.

PAT: His place was loaded with them! He just had it all over the place. He was a candy lover, a real sweet tooth.

JOE: Cardinal Cushing was a special man. I had met him down in New York. I was working for the newspaper then. We provided a plane to fly him up to Camp Drummond to visit the troops and say Mass.

9. Joe also helped his children replicate his own boyhood attainment of industry by encouraging them to feel they could carry out a real job. His care for their social-emotional development promoted their realization of a sense of industry and prevented a sense of inferiority.

10. "Jack," it is important to remember, is a little person who climbs a tall beanstalk and successfully overcomes a literally bone-breaking giant of a problem through cleverness, gutsy determination, and imagination. Like the "roll of dimes in the hospital" story, here again we see that Joe was ingenious at empowering his daughter with a sense of courage, competence, and industry.

While there, I chauffeured him around, helped him into the car, drove him to Mass in the morning.

Anyway, he was very appreciative of the way I handled everything. He said, "If you ever need anything or want anything, give me a call." So I called him and said, "I want to take my daughter over," and he said, "Bring her over." We went over. That's the kind of guy he was.

PAT: That was fun. I knew meeting him was a big event, and I had a good time. I don't remember getting dressed up, but it made me feel kind of special. (Of course, he was very friendly with the Kennedy family. When John was sworn in, he said all the prayers and everything.)

JOE: He was a special guy, and we got along with him very well. One of the special events in our life.

Encouragement of Schooling and Reading

PAT: I went to elementary school in the record book, but . . . .

JOE: She had tutors here at home for a long while, and she read a lot.

PAT: I went to kindergarten, and I went to the first grade. Then I would be out for a while, then I was back in for a while. I remember going to the seventh grade and on through high school.

JOE: Her mother made sure she got to school and was doing well. Even when the tutor was here, her mother made sure that everything was set, it was quiet, things were adequate.[11]

PAT: He did give me funny books, every one with the top missing. Hundreds of them, I mean, every kid in the neighborhood just said, "Wow," you know, but we shared. Hundreds of them.

JOE: The tops of the covers were missing because the tops had to be returned to the dealer for the distributors to get credit. So I brought the remaining stacks of comics home for the kids to read.

PAT: We "distributed" them through the neighborhood. Everybody had comic books.

Family Fun

PAT: Remember you were the coach of the team, and I was the scorekeeper? Billy, my brother, was the ball player. Basically, I was

11. Joe here acknowledges his wife's role in caring for and promoting Pat's intellectual-academic development.

a glorified secretary, but I thought I was the scorekeeper, and I'd sit there on the bench. He'd say "You paying attention? That was a K."[12]

JOE: Oh my. That was Little League. Your first team was sponsored by . . .?

PAT: Harvard Cleaners. He was the coach and I was the scorekeeper.

JOE: I also remember teaching you how to pitch a baseball.

PAT: You tried.

JOE: I tried.

PAT: He was a Little League coach, and then a manager, and then, a League President, and then the Commissioner that oversaw the leagues. He is still involved.[13]

JOE: Right now the only time I'm involved is when tournament time comes. In every tournament game, there has to be a tournament director because there's no protest. If there's a rule, and you can't answer it, you call the district director, and if you can't get the district director, you call directly to Williamsport, Pennsylvania, but that game has to be settled, that day, that time. You have to make a decision, and that's why I get involved at tournament time.

PAT: I remember another crazy story. When did you go to Maine? What summer was that? The summer that you worked up in Maine, off and on.

JOE: Oh, I don't know. You were young.

PAT: I remember I was young; Billy and I were about 3 and 5 and Ginger was a baby. I thought it was great when you came back. He walked in with this brown box, and everybody was happy to see him because he had been out of town for awhile, and he took out a white rabbit and a black rabbit.

JOE: Yeah, yeah, yeah. The menagerie.

PAT: We were all excited. We each had a rabbit, running around in this apartment, okay? This was great. Then he went back out to

12. K denotes a strikeout. As scorekeeper, Pat was using a notation system to maintain a precise play-by-play record of a baseball game. The complicated system of abbreviations would have been, for Pat as a child, a significant intellectual task.

13. Joe used baseball as a forum for parental generativity, and it subsequently evolved into a forum for societal generativity. He encouraged Pat's physical-athletic development at a time when many men would not have done that for their daughters. He also took time to be a coach to other children. His parental generativity subsequently was followed by clear societal generativity as he also took responsibility for the well-being of coaches and other adults.

the car again, and walked in again, and you had a coop with a half a dozen chickens!

I thought my mother was just about ready for a straightjacket (laughter). (Actually, to this day, I don't know if my mother got a phone call and knew, or if she was absolutely shocked.) Well, at this point Billy and I started feeling bad for my father, but we knew we couldn't defend him on this one. As if that wasn't bad enough, he went back out to the car again, and he came in with turtles! All for us kids, because he had been away. God, it was just wonderful!

JOE: I think the chickens were ducks. They were supposed to be ducks but they looked like chickens, and they sounded like chicks. I said, "They don't go quack, quack, quack."

PAT: You kept saying, "I wonder if they can swim?"

JOE: I put the ducks in the tub that time, and I'm saying, "They said they were ducks; they said they were ducks." So I turned the water on to see if they were going to swim. I remember that. They didn't want to swim.

PAT: We had ducks in this kitchen, we had rabbits, we had turtles. All these were in the house as pets. Of course, my brother and I thought this was heaven, right? Like dying and going to heaven. "Call the rabbit, where's the rabbit?" "Isn't he cute now," and "Their mess is so small."

JOE: Then we had to get those special pellets to feed the rabbits.

PAT: That's right, that's right. The rabbits wouldn't eat carrots, and the ducks wouldn't swim. I remember that was comical. But they grew up. Ate carrots and swam.

JOE: The ducks ended up as six very beautiful white ducks. We brought them up to the summer house in New Hampshire.

PAT: They went swimming on the lake. Oh, my mother loved it. And my grandfather, his father, built a hutch in the yard for the rabbits. Oh, it was a riot. Everybody in the neighborhood came to visit them.

Grandfather's Ongoing Involvement

PAT: You and Granddad forced me to learn how to play the saxophone one year.

JOE: Oh yeah, yeah (laughter).

PAT: My grandfather was in the firemen's band and he played the saxophone. So they decided, Pat can play this!

JOE: You spent time with your grandfather, too.

PAT: I remember around age 5, he was building the summer house in New Hampshire. I remember us all being up there while they were digging a well, and I can remember sifting dirt and finding coins. He also taught me how to fish. My grandfather is quieter, more into himself than my dad. He's always happy to see you, but he's better if you're involved in an activity. As long as there was an activity, it made up for conversation almost, instead of just having to talk one on one. He couldn't just sit at the table and talk to you for long periods.

I can remember being real young and when my grandmother would go in town shopping, he and I making up a batch of stout beer, and doing it quick before she got home and putting it downstairs and then acting like something was absolutely wrong with her when she wanted to know what the smell was in the house: "I don't smell anything. Do you?" It was fun type stuff, and meanwhile we know there was beer brewing or cooking downstairs. He was very good to me. I would go up and visit them every night or just about. He would treat you like an adult. When you walked in, the first thing he would do would be offer you a cold drink. Then, "You want something to eat?" or "Have a piece of cake?" He didn't ignore you because you were a child.

Helping Father's Political Campaign

PAT: How about the nomination papers between the mattress and the box springs?

JOE: Between the mattress and springs? What was that?

PAT: When you were getting nomination papers signed, to run for office?

JOE: Oh, yeah.

PAT: You said there was no sense in telling Mom, because you might not get enough signatures anyway? (laughter).

JOE: So I hid them (laughs).

PAT: I remember the day you decided that we were going to make signs, and I was going to help. So you had a piece of silkscreen made up with—what was it? "Vote right, vote for Bright" or something like that?

JOE: "Elect Bright."

PAT: Yeah. They were blue and white. We had clean newsprint paper, and we'd have to squeegee out these signs that were *huge*. I mean, to me they were huge, so I must have been little. Then you'd have to carry this wet, painted sign . . .

JOE: . . . and hang it up or lay it out to dry.

PAT: They were laid all over this house! That was a lot of fun. I thought, "This is great, this is terrific, Dad!"

JOE: Then I'd go out and hang them that night.

PAT: And we'd have campaign rallies. I remember the clambake in Uncle Josh's yard. That was fun. When you ran for public office. That was a lot of laughs.

JOE: We had some good moments.[14]

Joint Reflections on the Second Decade
Father Stayed Engaged

PAT: When I got older, Oh God, he still was great. He would tease, he was helpful. He was basically omnipresent. If we weren't in the house, and if my friends weren't in the house, and if we were outside someplace—he loved doing this to us—he would drive by in his car and act like he was just driving around. He'd drive by and do one of those wolf whistles, and I'd turn around, and he'd go, "Ah ha! Caught you all looking!" And he'd just keep going on. Actually, I usually guessed it was him whistling, but he'd always make it seem like I'd turn for anyone who would whistle (laughter). I don't know. He was really good. Most of the time, he wanted to help. He'd want to. He'd say, "Well, I'll volunteer to chauffeur you girls down there." He was pretty much omnipresent. Same as he is now.

JOE: I made a point to be a part of her life, all of their lives. They all knew that if they went out, I just might opt to show up at that affair, wherever it was, and I made it a point to be seen. Everywhere. Not that I wanted to know what they were doing—they understood that they were trusted all the time—but rather that I would be around and that I was available. Show up at a dance, just walk in, go to the

14. Joe's interest in serving the public through an elected office may have been an expression of his need to become societally generative. However, the interest brought out a direct act of parental generativity that promoted Pat's potential societal generativity. "Skills," Kotre (1984) elaborates, "are not transmitted in isolation. They bring in their wake symbol systems offering initiates something more than a sense of competence: a map of existence, a view of a place to settle on that map" (p. 22). When Joe demonstrated for his daughter how to run for political office, he was passing on a skill. As Pat's comments near the end of her interview will suggest, however, he was also passing on a belief in the generative ethic of care.

men's room and walk out, but they knew I was there. Most of the time they'd come running up to me, or Pat might announce, "There's my father!" But, every kid is different. Every one that we have is different in their activities, their behavior, all the way up the line. All of them are unique.

PAT: I remember you bought that motorcycle, motorbike. Remember the motorbike?

JOE: Oh, boy, here we go again.

PAT: I didn't have a driver's license, and I couldn't ride a bicycle, so I tried this. That didn't work out. That didn't work out at all.

JOE: You had an accident when it was four hours old.

PAT: Yeah. (I think we all had an accident the first day; Billy, me, everyone.) Drove it into a wall.

JOE: Kabang!

PAT: Yeah, I was going real fast!

PAT: I remember when I was in high school, he would always get involved in helping on school projects, like prom time, anything like that. He would show me how you go about running an ad page to generate money and how you go out and solicit donations from various businessmen. That was real good.

JOE: That's right.

PAT: He also lined me up with summer jobs with the park department, so I worked in a park environment with younger children.[15]

JOE: I introduced you to Tony C., remember?

PAT: Tony Conigliaro, my first heartthrob, that's right. I think I was about thirteen then. That's when he made it in the big leagues, the Red Sox. He was a real home-run hitter. He was also much older, of course, so all I could do was drool over the pictures.[16]

JOE: Then he got beaned—the end of his career. But we had had him in Little League when he was a boy, so I knew him. When he

15. Joe had found satisfaction in his summer camp work with younger children when he himself was a boy. Here we see that he encouraged Pat to replicate his experience by lining her up for a summer park job working with younger children.

16. Tony Conigliaro (1945–1990) was a local boy who achieved his dream of playing for the Boston Red Sox. He was a star homerun hitter and outfielder until he was beaned in 1967. The tragic blow to his head, which caused severe injuries, finished him for the season. While he made comeback attempts, his subsequent blurry vision eventually ended his baseball career. Red Sox fans also knew that his misfortunes continued: heart attack and subsequent nursing care, and finally kidney failure, which ended his life at age 45.

made it with the Red Sox, I introduced Pat to him. She liked the Red Sox, so we got season tickets and we'd go to the games.

PAT: Mmm. Still do.

JOE: She still loves baseball. All the kids still like to watch baseball. My father also loves the Red Sox.[17]

To me *major* league ball is one of the most boring sports in the world. Just sit there. . . . I enjoyed what I was doing with the Little League, coaching and organizing, but given all the professional sports, I'd prefer hockey, football, or even soccer. My father loves to sit down and watch baseball, so I'll sit there and watch it with him. He'll start talking about players and I'll say, "Who?" (Laughs.)

But Pat loves baseball! Maybe, in some ways, she's probably got a little bit of my father. You know, once she sets her mind to doing something, she does it. He does pretty much the same. And she's very independent. Self-supporting, in many ways like my father. She works hard for what she's getting. But, of course, she is basically *unique*.

Ensuring Appropriate High School Experience

JOE: I remember a mistake that I made. I put her in the public high school. I took her out before the end of one marking period and put her right back in the parochial school system. See, when she graduated from Holy Innocents at the eighth grade, we had the option of going to the public high school or staying at Holy Innocents for the ninth grade and high school. I figured it would be good for her to go to the public school, but that lasted less than one marking period.

She was happy; it was a new experience. But, at that time, the public school was starting to get the wise guys. You know, don't turn in your homework, don't do this, don't do that, and she started to get influenced by that. I was sitting there, doing my own homework, and I asked her about hers. She said, "Dad, nobody turns in homework." And I said, "Is that so?" So I went up, and I saw her teacher and I said, "What's the story?" "Well," he said, "I don't make them, I just give them D's." I said, "What do you mean, 'Don't make them?' Do you know that my daughter has her homework done every day?" "She

17. As the *Boston Globe* columnist, Mike Barnicle, once observed, "Baseball isn't a life-and-death matter, but the Red Sox are" (Angell, 1972, p. viii). Baseball during the years that Pat and the other children in this study were growing up is captured in Roger Angell's (1972) classic, *The Summer Game*.

doesn't turn it in." I said, "Why?" He said, "Don't ask me why." I said, "Look, you're the teacher. You're supposed to know what's going on. Don't give me any bull." So he said, "That's the games they play," and I said, "Well, you're not going to play them with this girl." It is still going on today in the school system. You got clowns in there that don't want to teach.

I went down to the monsignor and said, "Monsignor, do you have an opening here?" And he said, "It just so happens, I have one opening," and I said, "Fine, it's full." He said, "Why?" And I told him the story. He said, "Glad to have her." Like that.[18]

PAT: I wasn't accustomed to being in any school, let alone changing to the public school, and so I wasn't used to structure. If you're not used to raising your hand and getting a permit to leave, and things like that, then why would you? At the parochial school, they were very, very flexible. They knew that I was there for all the right reasons and, so, no problem. It worked out; everything was great.

JOE: We made sure she was in a good school and made sure she passed. But I wasn't really that much involved with her courses.

PAT: He didn't really get involved in my school work until high school geometry (laughter). Then he called in the troops. Frank Haney had to come over, everyone had to help. We were going to learn, we were going to *learn* geometry. We got it.

Family Recreation

PAT: But, aside from geometry, most of my homework was done by the time I got home, and there were other things going on. Evenings and weekends were for swimming and stuff like that.

JOE: I would say we spent all weekend together. Whenever I was around, we spent time together: taking her to the ball fields, taking her everywhere. Mostly because she felt as though she fit in, you know, she wanted me there. But we were always together, I guess. All the kids. We all spent time together.

PAT: Yeah. For weekends, my grandparents had a summer place in New Hampshire, so we'd go up there. We'd do our trips to the zoo,

18. Religious institutions can provide important support for parents. They also have the potential to legitimize, promote, and support a better balance between men's work and family activities (cf. Ammerman, 1990; Browning & Browning, 1991; Slade, 1984; Thomas & Cornwall, 1991).

and our trips to the amusement park, and cookouts, and ball games, and swimming. Usually active every weekend: swimming, baseball, volleyball, horseshoes, or whatever.

Parental Discipline

JOE: My wife and I always worked together. She has been great.

PAT: My parents made it very clear, without saying it, that each other came first, and the rest of us as a group came second. That was clear. There was no doubt in any of our minds. There was no way you could run to one to get a different vote on it; if you say—"I want to go to the movies Friday night with my friends, go to Boston, we're going to take the T," and then my mother would say, "Absolutely not, that's out of the question, you're not going to be riding around in the train in Boston at night, you're too young. Come back with a better game plan than that." There was no going to my father to get an outruling, you just didn't bother. Things didn't shift that way. Similarly, I couldn't go to her and say, "He just doesn't understand." Because she'd just say to me, "You just don't make things clear then." I mean, there was none of this play Mom against Dad or Dad against Mom. It just didn't work. My mother is very laid back, but she's very supportive to Joe. Their relationship has always been pretty good. And it was always pretty clear that they were pretty important to one another. There was no game-playing with Joe and Connie.[19]

Daughter's Drive for Independence

JOE: Pat didn't try much of that kind of game playing, either, but she was a gutsy type of person. She was a pretty girl and everything but, with that little handicap, some people would probably have shied away from being popular, being active, going to graduation-type parties, going to a prom. Not her; it didn't bother her. I think it took a gutsy type of kid to behave that way. Especially when you start mixing with other girls and boys your age and they don't have anything wrong with them. She got along very well with people at school. Teachers. Students. I'd say she was very well liked. She had some sort of special strength.

19. Clearly, Joe and his wife, Connie, had a strong parenting alliance that enabled them to work together and mutually support each other in childrearing.

After her leg brace came off, Pat often did risky and adventurous things. I felt she should be more conservative. She wanted to be independent and she was headstrong about it. We had our arguments—each of us would take a strong stand.[20]

PAT: The thing is, once I was out of the braces, and able to get about, I wasn't going to go back. Never! You just can't. I was pretty independent even as a little kid; when they put me in braces and crutches, and I was able to get out of the wheel chair and grab onto a sense of independence. But without the braces, I just *FLEW* with it. I was not going to regress ever again. I just couldn't. I couldn't be in that dependent role.

Later, at one point, I just decided that I was going to pay my own dentist bill. My father said, "Why?" I said, "Because I want to." (Laughter) He wasn't delighted about that, and I probably only made twenty or thirty dollars a week, but I would give my mother five dollars a week to put toward the dentist bill. And on payday I'd bring him home all this candy, because he's a candyholic. The rest of it I would use for my lunch money and things like that.[21]

He also wasn't delighted when I had told him that I was going to apply for a job at Woolworth's. He said, "You can't get a job at Woolworth's, you're not sixteen, they won't hire you." But I knew that you can apply for a working permit, and get your working papers at fifteen and nine months, as long as you agree to not work after a certain hour at night in the city of Boston. So I—independently— went over and signed up for them. I came home and said, "I got a job at the five-and-dime store!"[22]

20. Pat's hard-won ability to stand on her own physically apparently also promoted her ability to take what her father calls a "strong stand" in arguments. During most of her school years Pat had to wear a laced leather brace, but she was able to discard it in high school. Even though that leg was still slimmer and more delicate than the other, it did not hamper her activities. In high school she was involved in cheerleading, hobby clubs, yearbook, and artistic activities. She also dated regularly and got along well with peers and teachers.

21. Pat's seemingly irrational insistence on paying her own dentist bill may have reflected her desire to symbolically pay back or express her appreciation to her parents for the very large hospital bills they had incurred from her various leg operations.

22. Educational and occupational mobility require a level of psychosocial development that enables a person to function autonomously, but extensive research indicates that adolescent girls often have difficulty with autonomy (Lasser & Snarey, 1989). Thus it is noteworthy that achievement of autonomy is a common theme in Pat's story, as seen in her insistence here and elsewhere upon employment and financial independence.

JOE: She showed me.

PAT: "They can't hire you! You're a minor!" And I said, "I got my working papers in Boston!" (laughs). So how do you deal with a daughter like that, right? He wasn't too thrilled about that.

JOE: She was in high school, and she didn't need to be indoors, waiting on cranky people. She needed to be out in the fresh air; she needed a balance. Why was I working, anyway? You know, I wanted her to be out in the fresh air, and do things with people, like in the parks, and recreation. It was healthy. Plus, I could keep an eye on her now and then.

PAT: Yeah, yeah, that pretty much followed.

Choosing a Nursing Career

JOE: I also had a hard time with her yearning to be a nurse. I resisted her doing so from the beginning—didn't want her on her feet so much doing disgusting tasks, like bedpans.

PAT: You made yourself real clear (laughs).

No, he didn't want me to become a nurse. No, no no no. I think he thought in terms of school teacher, you know, nice little secretary. Traditional female roles, you know. Airline stewardess was a little leftist for him, you know. The other girls could do that. Too much time on your feet. What do you want to be serving somebody drinks for, anyway? You know, nice traditional girlsy-type jobs.

When I decided to go into nursing—Oh, that was a riot; that was horrendous, horrendous. Oh, God, oh, what a year that was. I came into the house and said that I was going into nursing school. Oh, he had a fit. He had a fit. You see, this wasn't what he had planned for me. I was going to have a *good* job, I was going to be a school teacher; I was going to have the summers off, the weekends off, school vacations.

He said, "No daughter of mine is going to be an ass-wiper, bla, bla, bla." Well, I was horrified! I think it was the first time I ever even heard him use the word (laughs). Well, I just dug my heels in and said, "I'm sorry, I'm going to be a nurse." I said something to the effect that he wasn't even going to get involved in it. I had gone over and been evaluated by the New England Rehabilitation Foundation, and they were willing to consider assisting me in some fashion. But I didn't really have any answer, it was like limbo, my senior year. That summer was horrible. Everybody was up at the cottage having a great time swimming. I was working for the parks department and, at night and on weekends, I was working at a shop. It was crazy: stashing all my cash, and I didn't even know if I was going to be accepted into a school or what.

I can remember being here all alone. I got the mail: the New England University had accepted me. Then the phone call came in: The New England Rehabilitation Foundation was going to pick up the full tab for my entire education. I was here all alone and I just leaned against that wall [points to the wall] and slid down to the floor, because I was losing it. Here I was, saving all this money, not spending a cent—I mean, I was packing it because I was saying, "Well, geez, if anyone does take me into the program, I'll have to pay for this." Everybody's swimming up north, and I can remember calling my mother and telling her over the phone.

Then, my father lightened up for some reason about me becoming a nurse. During my freshman year, he drove me to school every day. *Every* day. Nursing wasn't in his bag of tricks for Pat, but he was going to help me do it.[23]

He was still always there. When I'd do hospital internships, he always got involved. He would show up at the dorm that I lived in near the hospital. Although it was an all-girls dorm and there were house mothers there, sure enough, every so often, I'd hear, "Shower inspector here! Shower inspector here!" It'd be my father walking down the hall. Just to let the girls know there was a man on the floor, and they knew him. They'd come out and say, "Hi, Mr. Bright, how are you?" "Just stopped by to say hello." Oh, he was a riot.[24]

College Graduation

PAT: He was very proud of me when I graduated from college. He was emotional that day. I know I felt real good about it, that he was that proud. He's not a person that's huggy, lovey, kissy. You sort of

23. Joe's parental generativity is shown by his support of his daughter's "dream" of adult life, even though that was not his dream (Levinson, 1978).

24. Part of Joe's watchfulness appears to be a carryover from when Pat was a little girl with a physical problem who was often hospitalized. Pat, however, appears to have had more than enough ego strength not to be overly bothered by what some college students would experience as intrusiveness. Joe's use of humor, of course, also helped to make him appreciated by Pat's friends.

have to tell by his eyes, or his face, how he feels about something. I think it was emotional for him. New England University, every year, has their graduation on Father's Day. So that heightens it a bit. And it's sort of fair. Because all of those fathers footing the tab for all those years. It's kind of a nice gift. So, that probably added to the emotion. Plus, at that time he was working for the *New England Tribune.* So he had all of his friends who were on the news staff show up with their cameras. It was as if it was the only graduation in the world, I tell you. It was a riot. Of course, everyone in my class and the Dean and everybody said, "This is incredible, Pat. You have the entire staff here from the *New England Tribune!"*[25]

JOE: That was a great day. But she didn't stop there.

PAT: After I got out of school, I decided that maybe I wanted to do a little bit more, so I had looked into schools of anesthesia, but there was a two-year wait, and then I thought about going over to Morgan—in a Nursing Home Administration Program, to get that certificate. But I was kind of saying, "Well, you know, it's a lot of money." My grandfather said, "Go," and he wrote me out a check for the tuition. Can you believe that? He was great.

Father-Daughter Similarities

PAT: I think we are similar in a lot of ways. Sometimes I wish I could be a little bit more like my mother, a little more of a blend of both parents. But I think I'm more like my dad.

I get involved in projects. A lot of nonpaying projects, "for the honor and glory," so to speak. I had watched him do that, growing up, "for the betterment of mankind," as he'd say. I feel like I'm like my dad, because he was my teacher. He was there.[26]

25. Joe was a high school-educated salesman for one newspaper during his first decade of childrearing and a minor supervisor for another newspaper during his second decade of childrearing. In both cases he was able to mobilize the resources of his place of employment on his children's behalf. Years later, at midlife, he went to college part time and earned a two-year college associate degree; he then became an assistant manager for a public enterprise that has provided him with greater opportunities for societal generativity.

26. Joe has successfully served several community organizations in a variety of roles (board member, committee member, chairperson, commissioner, president), all of which testify to his societal generativity. The association between Joe's parental and societal generativity is also seen in his daughter's adult behavior. Pat emulates her father's service-oriented and societally generative lifestyle.

Every once in a while, I get an inkling towards politics, and then I say "No, don't do that." I don't know if I back off because he wasn't successful at it, that he didn't win the final election, or if I back off because I just know that politics today is crazy. It's not just a community, a person trying to do for the better of the community. But that nudge, that interest, is similar to my father's. I've always been active in politics. I love it. I could thrive on it; if there could be more hours in the day, I'd be at a campaign headquarters. I'd be spouting the issues, defending the candidate that I felt confident in. Manning the phones. Oh sure. I know, I love it.

Current Reflections

The Father's Perspective

Oh, looking back, I guess what I wanted most for her, physically, was to have a good leg (laughs). Otherwise, to be what she is today—happy doing her thing. My main goal for her was for her to be *happy*, to do her own thing.

I think she did well, this far. She saw something that she wanted to do, and she's doing it. She has her own head screwed on right. She's a self-made, motivated person.[27]

I wouldn't have chosen that she become a nurse. But there's nothing wrong with it. If that's what they want, go to it.

I encouraged her to be the registrar of the board of nursing. "Keep your finger in with all the medical changes and everything," which she has. She writes the books now. People have the exams and so forth, while she just looks them over and approves them. I probably encouraged her to take this job because it would be easier for her, physically. Lifting people up on a bed, rolling over, it's tough. She's only, what? A hundred pounds?

She's a politician. I influenced her there. I was involved in politics myself, and she saw that. Actually she's a better politician than me, I would say. She learned very well.

Once she sets her mind on something, a goal or an objective, she goes after it. I'd say that I've done that many times myself. That was probably one of the traits that she picked up from me. You know, save for tomorrow, maybe, more than, say, the other children but, as I said

27. Joe also described his own father as a "self-made" person.

before, every one of them is different. And I would say that Pat plans probably more for the future, probably appreciates the things she has. She enjoys the good life, too, you know.

I place a lot of value on happiness. I tried to see that my children were happy. If they're happy, that's the important thing. You can't buy happiness; you have to make it, despite the inevitable ups and downs. Like I tried to tell them, you never win. You may think you win, but it is never over.

I still would say that it is important to always be available. I'm available, for whatever they want. Whether it be support or money or whatever. Even now, even though they don't need anything like financial support anymore, I am here and Connie's here, and we just try to make a family that they can rely on when they want and need it. Their mother feels the same way. Make them understand that family's very important, try to stick together.[28]

Basically, I try to be a good pal to them, you know. At a certain age you become more of a friend than a father. I think they look at you, and it's not a child to a father, but, sort of like a pal or a buddy. "Would you like to go to a game? You want to go down and do this? You want to get pizza?" You know, those type of things.

The Daughter's Perspective

How would my father describe me now? I don't think he's got any complaints. I think that he likes the job that I have today: I'm a state official, I'm second in command for nursing for the entire state of Maine. I serve on national committees, I'm flitting around the country, and I think that he thinks that's impressive. But I don't know why I was picked to serve at the national level. I'm not the smartest nurse in the country; I'm not the youngest; I'm not the oldest. I'm not the most articulate; I don't know why. But I was picked, and for whatever reason, I guess that's a reason to be proud.[29]

28. Joe's marital satisfaction was also, no doubt, increased by his and Connie's ability to function as a cohesive parenting team in their efforts to build a stable, reliable home for their children.

29. Pat's original interest in nursing and medical administration may be an example of mature altruism: it both replicates her positive experiences and compensates for her own suffering when she was in the hospital. Her father, for instance, described the nurses and doctors as "great" but the hospital director and administrators as "bastards." Pat herself became generative in a profession in which she experienced the effects of nongenerative administrators and caring nurses.

Why have I been so successful? I hear people say, "The right place at the right time." Actually, I've always kind of negotiated with myself; I don't kid myself into trying to think I'm anything special or the most deserving of this or entitled to that. I applied like everyone else, just throw my credentials out and answer the questions, and then I just take it each day at a time. I negotiated with myself before I went to nursing school. I said, I'll try one semester, and if I look like a fool at that university, I'll go to the airline (laughs). I negotiated with myself before I took my current position. I'll try one meeting at the national level, and if I clearly don't understand what these people are talking about, I'll resign, for personal reasons (laughs). I mean, I try to absorb as much as I can, and that's it. Sometimes I don't even know how I hold onto my job. If I truly sat down and thought about what I'm responsible for and what I do, I'd probably say, "You're crazy to do this." But you just don't, you take one day—you just do it. You go in the next day, and try to treat everybody alike; I try to give everybody a fair shake, no matter who they are. It seems to work out.

I think my father became more involved than many of my friends' fathers because he liked us. Actually, I don't really know what other fathers do; I watched what I was supposed to see, or what they didn't care that you saw, for other people growing up. But, I really think that he liked us, and, in all honesty, I think that he was having as good a time if not a better time than all of us, growing up. He was the first one dressed, and "We're going to be late, we're going to get on the road, there's going to be traffic . . . ." He was like the White Rabbit. Even today, a Saturday of activity and fun with Joe is still total exhaustion. First you got to play racquetball, then jump in the jacuzzi, you know, then we get in eighteen holes of golf. Then, if it's still warm out, you know, "Play a little tennis? How about croquet?" And you're like, "Uncle!" And he's saying, "What's the matter?" (laughs). So, I think he had a great time.

I think he's remained much the same. He's a rather strong figure. Most people, when they meet him, they know they've met someone. If they have any time to talk to him, he leaves an impression. When we weren't little kids anymore, he realized that we were young adults with our own ability to make a decision. I think that was probably the biggest adjustment for him. Where he wasn't making the plans and doing the sliding and the maneuvering and the steering of us. We entered or stepped into a level where we were making decisions on our own. Sometimes they probably weren't the best.

I don't think he expected me to become a nuclear physicist, God help the world! My father influenced me in the way I always saw him following through on everything. He never let anything burn away on the back burner. He never left anything incomplete. He's got basic home-made philosophies, like: "So what if you lose? Just go out there and play, who cares?" It was basically, as long as you do the best job you can, that's it. But make sure to finish it. So I guess that's what I've always done. I don't get involved in anything that I'm not going to finish. Or if I do volunteer for something or I get stuck with something that I know I'm not going to finish, I let people know right up front. I'll be able to do this amount of what you've asked, but at this point, somebody else can take over. It seems like it works. I don't end up getting frustrated, and nobody's disappointed.

It is important for a father to just be himself, to be authentic. He shouldn't try to act like "Daddy," or another role. He shouldn't try to tame it down or spruce it up because the child's there. Just be you throughout your life. Some of the friends that I've had were shocked when they found out what their father was really like, once they became an adult. I had no hidden surprises at the end. Joe was consistent. They found out that their father gambled or that he drank, and that their mother didn't say anything, but she cried at night when they were in bed, or that he beat her, or you know, he was just a different beast than the person they knew. I guess the most important thing I can see for a father is—I mean, unless there's something psychiatrically wrong with you—just be yourself. I think that's the most important thing because then all the rest of it is easy.

The Daughter Looks Ahead a Generation

I am *not* childless by choice. I'm determined to . . . . They don't know why, but it's certainly not by choice. I mean, I've even drunk Chinese syrups, stood on my head after intercourse, the whole nine yards. We never didn't try; we've never stopped trying. I haven't attempted in vitro fertilization, but I am exploring adoption.[30]

30. Pat's biological and parental generativity are out of synchronization. What is the implication of such a situation? "When movement along the generative tracks in a life becomes unsynchronized," according to Kotre (1984), "the stage is set for critical change" (p. 12). In Pat's case, her experience of biological generativity lagging behind her readiness for parental generativity affirms the reasonableness of her desire to change her family situation by becoming an adoptive parent.

We're flexible. It doesn't even have to be an infant. I mean, an infant is nice—it's like starting a garden from scratch, but, you know, I'm not adverse to buying the tomato plants already started. An infant would be great, but I would only draw the line at a child that was troubled enough that you had to cage them at night or that might try to burn the house down. But short of that, you know, "Send them all up!"

As a parent, I would only hope that I'd have my father's patience. I mean, he and my mother both have incredible patience. Just incredible. I could watch him with the younger kids because, while there is only a year and a half between me and Billy, there was 14 years between me and Kathy, even more between me and Carl. I could see that he *likes* kids, he was good with them.

I can remember when Carl, who's the youngest of us five kids, was a baby. The every-morning ritual was that he'd bring the baby in the bed with him and for half an hour just talk to that baby. I remember Carl was just 14 days old, and he was mimicking him in bed. It was a riot. He was repeating back what he was saying.[31]

And now I've been able to see him with his grandchildren. He loves kids, and kids love him. He's not intrusive, he's a pal, he's a real pal. He has common sense, the home-made theories as I call them. And he truly enjoys kids. So, in my having kids, I could only see it as even better because I'd also get to experience that pleasure that he has had.[32]

I would do some things differently—I would not allow my daughter to go to nursing school! I know that admonition didn't work with me, but I'd win. After years under his tutelage, I'd win. I'd handle it from a different approach.

But, I'd do most things the same as him. Well, a blend between him and my mother. I mean, you heard him say he didn't get involved in the school books. He didn't feel comfortable with the school sub-

31. Unlike the wives of some childrearing fathers, Connie did not work outside of the home during the years she and Joe were bringing up their five children. Nevertheless, Joe was still highly involved in all of his children's lives.

32. Pat's current development toward societal generativity without having experienced biological or parental generativity suggests that childrearing may not be absolutely essential for the attainment of genuine societal generativity. But her longing to get on with the business of parenting, and her previously mentioned specific interest in becoming an adoptive parent, are also expressions of her own sense of what she needs to sustain her adult development and to satisfy her need to maintain the life of the generations.

jects: geography, history. It wasn't active enough. (If you wanted to play horseshoes or volleyball, terrific.) So Mom did the book side of things if it was necessary. Only if it was necessary. Most of the time we were set up at the table, and we did our homework on our own. She'd proofread everything and help us out with stuff like that, but it wasn't like she sat here for 2 hours every night, reviewing lessons with us.[33]

He was always available. He's my conscience, even to this day. We'll talk back and forth, you know, from my office to his. When something comes up, he'll bang it off me. Which is kind of nice, that he's interested in my opinion, and vice-versa. I'd call him and say, "I'm not getting anywhere with the (so-and-so office)." And he'll say, "Try this and try that. And then, do this, and then, if they don't respond, then give them a little jab and do this." "All right, I'll try that." "Get back to me now! Give me a call."

I always liked being around him. I always enjoyed talking about him. I mean, always.

Concluding Query

Joe and Pat's story anticipates the primary topic of the next chapter—children's educational and occupational success by early adulthood. Conversely, the following chapter will bring some clarity to the following questions. In general, is it reasonable to speculate that Joe's childrearing participation actually contributed to the way his daughter later turned out? How might Joe's parental generativity have contributed to Pat's educational mobility? How might his childrearing participation have contributed to her success at work? Which specific types of Joe's childrearing activities probably contributed the most to Pat's success?

33. Even though Pat is not a parent yet, her thoughts here reveal her ideas about parental generativity. She, like most children, aspires to both model and rework the parenting she received. Pat's primary emphasis, however, is on modeling. She will probably do "most things the same as" her father, and so we may expect that she will raise her children to be just as determined as she was and find herself, like her dad, also unable to change their minds.

6

Early Adulthood Consequences of Men's Parental Generativity for Their Children

with Anthony Maier

The quality of a young adult's life may be linked, for better or worse, with the quality of the fathering he or she received as a child. What, empirically, does paternal childrearing predict about the ways the children subsequently succeed as adults? One of the most interesting questions from a child development perspective is how fathers' childrearing might advance their children's educational and occupational success. Here we report on the specific ways in which fathers' positive childrearing predicts their children's adulthood attainments.

What We Know from Prior Research

No published empirical longitudinal studies have documented how different types of fathers' parental generativity can predict, decades later, their children's educational and occupational success in adulthood. Nevertheless, prior studies of the significance for children and adolescents of varying levels of paternal childrearing participation have included consequences that have been linked to later social mobility. The following review will focus on these related dimensions (for example, intellectual competence, social-emotional maturity and self-esteem, sex-role flexibility, and motivation). The review branches out into studies of children 10 years old or younger (*excluding* infants) and studies of adolescents. Differences in results for daughters and sons are noted within each section. Wider-ranging reviews and edited volumes are available elsewhere (Belsky, 1991; Biller & Solomon, 1986; Cath, Gurwitz, & Gunsberg, 1989; Clarke-Stewart, 1980, 1988; Huston-Stein & Higgins-Trenk, 1978; Lamb & Oppenheim,

1989; Lamb, Pleck, & Levine, 1985; Lamb, Pleck, Charnov, & Levine, 1987; Parke, 1981; Parke, et al., 1989; Radin, 1981b, 1986; Ricks, 1985).

Childhood

The empirical research linking the behavior of childrearing fathers during their children's first decade of life with their children's subsequent capacities has produced three outcomes that are especially relevant to the present investigation: increased intellectual competence, increased social-emotional maturity, and greater sex role flexibility (Lamb & Oppenheim, 1989; Parke, 1981; Russell & Radin, 1983).

Intellectual Competence

Studies of parenting in relation to children's academic skills, IQ, and general cognitive development are especially useful for our purposes because intellectual competence is important for later social mobility through its effects on school performance. Several studies indicate, for instance, that parents' active involvement in their children's school work and academic skill development contributes to their children's level of elementary school success (for reviews, see Hoover-Dempsey, Bassler & Brissie, 1987; Irvine, 1990; Seginer, 1983). The research on parents' contribution to their children's intellectual-academic competence is still difficult to interpret, however, because of a shortage of longitudinal studies.

Whether fathers' and mothers' effects on their children's intellectual competence differ according to the gender of their children has been an active topic of research. A pioneer study by Bing (1963) reported the unexpected finding that the amount of time fathers spent reading was a strong predictor of their daughters' high verbal ability, suggesting that daughters may also model themselves after the opposite-sexed parent. This finding was noteworthy because the association did not hold true for fathers and sons, and the mothers' reading time did not predict either their daughters' or sons' verbal ability. Other retrospective studies have suggested that fathers' early participation in their children's lives predicts both their sons' and daughters' subsequent mathematical ability. Fathers' absence or limited presence during their sons' and daughters' childhood, for instance, is reported to predict that their children will subsequently score lower (relative to their peers) on math aptitude tests and other measures of quantitative ability (Landy, Rosenberg, Sutton-Smith, 1969; Biller, 1971, 1974; Radin, 1981b).

In another early correlational study of fathers' childrearing practices and the intellectual functioning of their 4-year-old sons, Radin (1972) found that the boys' IQ was positively associated with their fathers' nurturance and negatively associated with their fathers' restrictiveness. To gauge how fathers' involvement affected the IQ as well as the locus-of-control scores of 3- to 6-year-old boys and girls, Radin (1981a) observed and administered questionnaires to the children's fathers and mothers. The study assessed the degree of father participation by five indices: (a) physical care, (b) socialization, (c) decision-making, (d) availability, and (e) statements of father's involvement. All indices were combined to create a total childcare involvement index. The results showed that fathers' total involvement in childrearing was strongly associated with both boys' and girls' internal locus of control. Reported statements of fathers' high involvement were significantly correlated with girls' verbal intelligence, and fathers' responsibility for decision-making was significantly correlated with boys' verbal intelligence.

Using the longitudinal Berkeley Guidance Study data, Honzik (1967) extended this line of research by demonstrating that expressions of affection and the existence of a "close bond" between fathers and sons during early childhood were positively related to sons' IQ during later childhood, and that the less intense quality of genuine "friendliness" between fathers and daughters during early childhood was also positively related to daughters' IQ during later childhood. In retrospective studies, likewise, college women who scored better on tasks requiring analytic thought claimed that their fathers were challenging but not smothering or overly controlling during childhood (Heilbrun, Harrell, & Gillard, 1967).

Children's cognitive development and problem-solving behavior have also been shown to be positively associated with fathers' childrearing involvement and parenting characteristics (Easterbrooks & Goldberg, 1984). For boys, cognitive development generally correlates positively with fathers' nurturant behavior and negatively with fathers' restrictive control. For girls, however, the consequences of fathers' nurturant behavior are less clear. In particular, fathers' strong socio-emotional nurturance during their daughters' childhood years does not promote their daughters' cognitive development. This may be the case, in part, simply because paternal smothering harms daughters. Additionally, Baumrind (1978, 1980) has theorized that rough-and-tumble, "challenging" paternal behavior may promote the development of social independence in girls and make them less passively accepting of their environment. Similarly, as an extensive review of prior studies concluded, "it appears that paternal strictness in the context of warmth and moderate distance between fathers and daughters, as well as autonomy from fathers, are related to daughters' intellectual functioning, but even this evidence is tenuous" (Radin & Russell, 1983, p. 196). Fathers' direct influence on their daughters' social functioning and competence may therefore have an indirect effect upon their intellectual competence. Perhaps promoting social independence also facilitates intellectual independence.

Finally, the relationship between fathers' and their children's cognitive ability is illustrated by research on cognitive-moral development. This is especially relevant to Erikson's model of psychosocial development, which postulates a sequence of moral virtues arising in the course of the life cycle. A basic research approach within the psychology of moral development has been to evaluate parents' level of moral reasoning as a predictor of their children's level of moral development (for review, see Silberman, 1989). The results of this line of research are complex and have sometimes appeared inconclusive, because the impact of parents' moral reasoning upon their children's cognitive-moral development probably varies with the parent's gender and the children's age. Kohlberg (1963), for instance, originally theorized that mothers and fathers would have a "differential impact . . . upon their children's morality" (p. 310), and he observed that "the actual variations in the father's role which are important for morality seem to be variations in his affection" (p. 309). Empirically, in fact, Speicher-Dubin's (1982) landmark study demonstrated that the fathers' above-average standing in moral development, emotional warmth, and nurturance did not predict their children's subsequent moral maturity during late childhood or early adolescence, but the same paternal characteristics did significantly predict their older adolescent and young adult children's moral maturity. The contribution of fathers' maturity and nurturance to their offspring's maturity became measurably evident only when their children were older.

Social-Emotional Competence

Retrospective studies have shown that variations in fathers' participation in childcare are associated with children's social-emotional adjustment (for reviews, see Lamb, 1981; Maccoby & Martin, 1983). Santrock (1970) conducted a noteworthy retrospective study of 10-year-old boys. He examined the possible influence of losing one's father at various ages (0–2 years, versus 3–5 years, versus 6–9 years) on Eriksonian stage development. Santrock found that 10-year-old boys who experienced the onset of father-absence at ages 0–2 years showed significantly less trust (stage 1) than boys who had experienced the loss as 3- to 5-year-olds, significantly more shame (stage 2) than father-absent 6- to 9-year-olds, significantly more guilt (stage 3) than father-absent 6- to 9-year-olds, and significantly less industry and more inferiority (stage 4) than father-absent 3- to 5-year-olds. Santrock concluded that these findings provide "support for Erikson's contention that the development of basic trust in the child's early years serves as a foundation on which ensuing stages must build" (1970, p. 274). Among studies that have addressed father-daughter relations, for instance, Hoffman's (1975; 1970, 1981) research has shown that daughters' altruism (as indicated by the children's reputational ratings by their school peers) was predicted by their fathers' communication of altruistic values and by the fathers' use of victim-centered discipline (that is, directing the child's attention to the other person's plight). In contrast, other cross-sectional studies have suggested that fathers can have a deleterious influence on their daughters' social-emotional development by being overly involved with their daughters in ways that excessively protect them from experiences of failure, provide excessive direction, and generally inhibit their autonomy (for review, see Lamb, Owen, & Chase-Lansdale, 1979).

The findings from a longitudinal study begun by Sears and his colleagues are especially relevant to questions about fathers' influence on their children's social-emotional development. Sears, Maccoby, and Levin (1957) initiated in 1951 their study of the possible effects of childrearing on 5-year-old kindergarten children. They assessed the parenting of 379 children by interviewing each child's mother concerning her and her husband's parenting characteristics, and rating each parent on 150 childrearing practices. Among their cross-sectional findings, they noted the importance of fathers' disciplinary role and warmth for their children's sex-role identity development and the importance of mothers' interpersonal affective warmth for their children's social behavior maturity. Overall, maternal warmth was reported as having the most impact on their 5-year-old children. Seven years later, Sears (1970) assessed the children's early adolescent outcomes ($N = 160$). The results regarding the children's social-emotional development indicated that both maternal and paternal warmth were predictive of boys' and girls' higher self-concepts or self-esteem at age 12. Eleven years after this, Edwards (1973) assessed the children's early adulthood outcomes ($N = 64$). The results of this follow-up showed a trend for a mode of interpersonal interaction characterized by cooperation and that the resolution of social conflicts through personal sacrifice at age 23 was more common among men when their parents' childrearing practices had showed a minimum of sex-role differentiation at age 5, but among women when they had had a warm bond with their fathers at age 5.

A more recent follow-up of the Sears subjects, conducted 26 years after the original study, adds greater clarity to the contribution of fathers to their children's social-emotional development. Koestner, Franz, and Weinberger (1990) reported on the adult outcomes of 75 subjects who had been assessed at age 31 for empathy—"the tendency to experience feelings of sympathy and compassion for others" (p. 709). Using multiple regression analysis with stepwise entry, the researchers examined the children's adulthood empathy scores in relation to 11 dimensions of the parenting the mothers had reported for the children at age 5. They found that the dimension of parental involvement that accounted for the greatest percentage of the unique variance in these scores was *paternal* childrearing involvement. A higher paternal involvement rating simply indicated that the father stayed with the child when the mother was out, and that he did more to take care of the child on these occasions. "This single dimension," the authors emphasize, "accounted for a greater percentage of the unique variance in empathic concern scores (13%) than the three strongest maternal predictors combined" (p. 713). No significant interaction effects linked paternal childcare to the child's gender. In sum, both sons and daughters who experienced more paternal involvement as children were, as adults, more likely to report high levels of empathic concern for others. These findings are consistent with those noted above regarding fathering and cognitive-moral development.

The most recent follow-up study of the original Sears' children was conducted when they were 41 years old—36 years after the original interviews. This study by Franz, McClelland, and Weinberger (1991) of 89 of the 379 original children evaluated the childhood precursors of their midlife attainment of good social relationships. To define what constitutes such relations, the authors turned to Erikson's sixth stage of psychosocial development—intimacy, which they then operationalized in terms of conventional information obtainable from questionnaires (for example, having a long happy marriage, having children, engaging in recreational activities with nonfamily members) (see Vaillant, 1977). To assess the convergent validity of this social accomplishment index, they also rated subjects on generativity and work accomplishment ($N = 42$). Generativity ratings were based on the subjects' written statements of their hopes and dreams for the future; work accomplishment ratings were based on a number of characteristics such as work satisfaction, active leisure time pursuits, occupational status, and, for women, childcare as well as paid work. The results indicated that fathers' and mothers' parenting characteristics, especially *paternal warmth* assessed when the child was age 5, contributed significantly to the child's intimacy consolidation or conventional social accomplishments at age 36, regardless of the child's gender. Midlife intimacy was also found to be significantly correlated with midlife generativity, work accomplishment, and other psychological outcomes. The report, however, did not address the ability of parenting assessed at age 5 also to predict directly these other midlife outcomes. In addition, the ways in which Erikson's psychosocial stages were operationalized limit the study: the definition of social accomplishment confounded intimacy with biological and parental generativity, and the definition of work accomplishment confounded parental and societal generativity. Nevertheless, from a nontheoretical perspective, the report provides general support for the idea that fathers' contributions to their children's life outcomes are significant.

Sex Role Flexibility

Traditional fathers tend to promote their daughters' conformity to traditional sex roles, but highly involved childrearing fathers may have the opposite influence. Children's flexibility with regard to sex role attitudes and behavior, that is, is predicted by fathers' participation in childcare; this is highly relevant because this may be one of the linkages through which fathers also influence their children's career choices (Biller, 1981).

Sagi (1982) contrasted traditional with nontraditional families in Israel and found that, "involved fathers do not eliminate the feminine tendencies of their daughters, but add to the sex role orientation a masculine perspective as well . . . The less stereotypic models at home enabled [both sons and daughters] to perceive their fathers as maintaining dominance while being capable of reflecting love and warmth at the same time" (pp. 222–223). Ross (1982), for his part, has maintained that "it is closeness with the father and trust in him which ideally allow a boy [between 5 and 10 years] to temper the aggressivity of both his curiosity and his assertiveness" and internalize an image of fathering that is caring and competent (p. 250). Baruch and Barnett (1981) have found that greater father participation in childrearing was associated with less typecast views of sex roles in daughters. In Barnett and Baruch's later study (1988), father involvement predicted greater flexibility in sex role behavior among fourth-grade (but not kindergarten) children of employed mothers. As Lamb and Oppenheim (1989) conclude, "because the parents assume less sex-stereotyped roles, it is not surprising that their children have less sex-stereotyped attitudes themselves about male and female roles" (p. 21). What is surprising in the prior research findings is the relative neglect of the probable association between sex role flexibility and parents' support of their daughters' and sons' physical-athletic development. Biller and Meredith (1974) are a striking exception. They suggest that "fathers have a unique and powerful role to play" in promoting their children's physical fitness and athletic abilities and that, in particular, fathers who encourage their "daughters to engage in athletics" help to alleviate sex bias (pp. 182, 194). Evidence in support of this idea also comes from a study by MacDonald and Parke (1984), which indicated that daughters who are exposed to higher levels of paternal physical play tend to be more popular and assertive with their peers.

Perhaps the most notable longitudinal study relevant to the area of fathers' influence on their children's sex-role development is an 11-year follow-up study of sex-role flexibility by Williams, Radin, and Allegro (1992; Radin, 1991). They retested the children in Radin's (1981a) original study of young two-parent Michigan families. The fathers in the top third of childrearing participation were, by a narrow margin, the primary caregivers in their families: they assumed, on average, 57% of the childcare; the mothers were clearly the primary caregivers in the families whose fathers ranked in the lower third of childrearing and assumed, on average, 22% of the childcare. The parents were tested on three occasions. At Time 1, 59 parents of 3- to 5-year-old children were interviewed (Radin, 1981a, 1982). At Time 2, 47 parents were reinterviewed; their children were then 7 to 9 years old (Radin & Goldsmith, 1985). At Time 3, 32 parents and their children (now aged 14 to 16 years) were both reinterviewed (Williams, Radin & Allegro, 1992). The findings most relevant to the present study were that higher levels of fathers' childrearing participation when their children were 3 to 5 years old predicted that those children as adolescents would hold less traditional views of their future employment patterns (for example, greater approval of dual-earner couples). Higher levels of fathers' childrearing participation when their children were 7 to 9 years old predicted that those children as adolescents would hold less traditional views of their future childcare plans (for example, greater approval of nontraditional childrearing patterns, including shared childcare plans). These findings, according to Williams, Radin, and Allegro (1992), suggest that long-term change in gender-stereotyped roles is possible because an apparent preference for nontraditional patterns of parental generativity is being passed on from one generation to the next.

Adolescence

In their second decade of life, both daughters and sons separate from their parents and face the difficulties of forming intimate bonds with peers, adopting more adult social roles, and establishing their own identity. Several studies, however, offer tentative evidence that fathers can continue to function as important role models for their children during the adolescent years (Brooks-Gunn & Furstenberg, 1989). The general argument has been made that parents who have been authoritative and have provided positive models of adaptation to larger social demands will have relatively more influence over their adolescent children, compared to parents who have been authoritarian or permissive (Baumrind, 1980). The following studies address the significance of fathers for their adolescent daughters' and sons' intellectual-academic competence, social-emotional development, and work-role success.

Intellectual-Academic Achievement

Fathers' and mothers' own levels of education and their simple recognition of their children's achievements (complimenting, expressing pleasure, praising) have been shown to predict their children's realistic educational expectations, ideal educational aspirations, and actual school grades. All three outcomes were included, for instance, in Smith's (1989) elegantly succinct sociological study of 185 sixth-, eighth-, and tenth-grade students and their parents. Using multiple regression analysis, Smith found that a total of 27% of the variance in the students' educational expectations was accounted for by the students' personal characteristics, their fathers' level of education (zero-order $r = .40$), fathers' recognition of their children's achievement ($r = .24$), and mothers' education ($r = .32$). Similarly, Smith was able to explain 18% of the variance in students' educational aspirations and 17% of the variance in students' school grades; in both cases the fathers' recognition of achievement ($r = .22$; $r = .25$) and the mothers' level of education ($r = .27$; $r = .23$) made significant contributions to the explained variance beyond that contributed by a student's gender and year in school. Overall, mothers' level of education and fathers' recognition of their children's achievement made a significant contribution to the explained variance for all three student outcomes, while fathers' level of education made a significant contribution to the explained variance in one of the outcomes, and mothers' recognition of achievement did not make a significant contribution to the prediction of any outcome. In contrast, however, the role of fathers' level of education was more robust in a five-year longitudinal study of middle-class girls whose career aspirations were assessed during late childhood (Ehrhardt, Ince, & Meyer-Bahlburg, 1981) and again during middle adolescence (Sandberg, Ehrhardt, Mellins, Ince, & Meyer-Bahlburg, 1987). Among the almost two-dozen predictor variables under consideration, fathers' education was the only variable that significantly and positively predicted whether a girl aspired to enter a higher status male-dominated career at her childhood assessment and again at her adolescent assessment.

Cross-sectional and short-term studies have also indicated that parents' childrearing behavior remains important during the adolescent years. In general, parents who treat their adolescent children warmly, democratically, and firmly tend to promote their children's academic success (Baumrind, 1973; Dornbusch, Ritter, Leiderman, Roberts, & Fraleigh, 1987; Lozoff, 1974; Steinberg, Elmen, & Mounts, 1989). Parents' general involvement with their children's homework, at least during early adolescence, continues to benefit their children's academic performance (Leone & Richards, 1989). Fathers' strong involvement, in particular, also continues to predict that their adolescent sons and daughters will score significantly better, compared with those of boys and girls whose fathers are not highly involved, on math aptitude and general academic achievement tests. For instance, Goldstein's (1982) study of adolescents aged 12 to 17 documented that fathers (more than mothers) promote their sons and daughters' mathematical abilities, and that this pattern is maintained even after controlling for educational, occupational, and family structure differences.

The configuration for daughters, however, has some additional complex features compared to the picture for sons (Bieri, 1960). For instance, Lozoff (1974) retrospectively studied the impact of fathers on three groups of intellectually able college women. The first group consisted of female students who were achieving academically and were effective interpersonally. They tended to recall their fathers as energetic and ambitious men whose fathering style was active and encouraging. These daughters, however, frequently disagreed with their fathers. Students in the second group were achieving intellectually but were less competent interpersonally. These women tended to recall their fathers as aloof, self-disciplined, and often demanding. Finally, students in the third group were not achieving academically but were described by their peers and professors as interpersonally competent, well-organized, and reliable. These women tended to recall traditional fathers who adhered to rigid sex-role definitions and who did not reinforce their daughters' academic achievement.

Social-Emotional Development

A developmental task of adolescent boys is to achieve a significant degree of psychosocial independence from their fathers and indeed fathers seem to play a decreased, although still positive, role in their adolescent sons' social-emotional development. One example of how a positive model offered by fathers may influence their early adolescent boys is given by Feldman and Wentzel (1990) in a study that focused on the association between parent-son relationships and their children's friendships with peers. They observed that both fathers and mothers appeared to promote their sons' positive regard among their peers through child-centered practices (defined as acts which place a high premium on promoting the child's personal interests, happiness, and psychosocial development). Only fathers' child-centeredness, however, also predicted their sons' self-restraint (defined as impulse control and prosocial behavior). In addition, use of harsh discipline by fathers, but not mothers, predicted that their sons would be disliked by their peers.

Bronfenbrenner (1961) studied the contribution of parental behavior to adolescents' responsibility and leadership among 400 tenth-grade students. His findings showed that the types of parenting that promote these indicators of social-emotional maturity among sons are different from the parenting that promotes the same behavior among daughters. He concluded, "The major obstacle to the development of responsibility and leadership in boys stems from inadequate levels of parental support and authority." In contrast, "for girls, the principal danger lies in the possibility of over socialization through an overdose of parental affection and control" (p. 268). Most relevant for the present study, Bronfenbrenner concluded that "fathers show greater individual differences in parental behavior than do mothers and thus account for more of the variations in the behavior of their children" (p. 268).

Several other theorists have noted that fathers have a unique role in their adolescent daughters' social-emotional development (Chodorow, 1978, 1981; Deutsch, 1944; Johnson, 1975). Deutsch (1944) was one of the first to clarify that the typical nature of the mother-daughter relationship creates the basis for the girl's psychological shift toward her father. The girl's experience of self, and self in relation to her mother, prompts her to perceive her father as a symbol of freedom from dependence and merger with her mother. Her differentiation from her mother is promoted by identifying with her father, in particular with his power. Johnson (1975) also saw the father as promoting independence from the mother while reinforcing sex-differentiated behaviors. Chodorow (1981) further argued that a father's low positive emotional involvement in his daughter's life may predispose her to have difficulty with autonomy.

Lasser (1986; Lasser & Snarey, 1989), in a qualitative study of older adolescent girls, provides some support for these conclusions. Comparing girls at three different levels of ego or psychosocial maturity, she reports that the most mature girls had fathers who remained consistently involved in their lives from childhood through adolescence. These girls often participated in dyadic athletic activities with their fathers and were able to disagree with them openly. At the middle or conformist levels of social-emotional maturity, adolescent girls reported having fathers who were critical, gave inconsistent messages, and undermined their self-confidence. Finally, adolescent girls at lower stages of psychosocial maturity reported having cool and remote fathers.

The above findings can be interpreted as providing evidence that the contribution of fathers to their daughters' adolescent social-emotional development is significant. In particular, they clarify the father's important role in promoting his daughter's ability to gain a margin of separation from her mother without undue threats to her identity.

Work Role Success

Cross-sectional and retrospective evidence indicate that fathers' involvement with their adolescent children is positively associated with their work success and occupational competency as young adults. One of the few longitudinal studies, devised by Bell (1969), recorded the degree to which fathers, other adults, and siblings served as role models for boys when they were freshmen in high school and again when they had been out of high school for 7 years. At the latter time, he also measured six aspects of their vocational adjustments and behaviors. Of all the occupational role models that subjects reported at the first period, only fathers' role-modeling was associated with their sons' vocational behaviors a decade later. The most positive role models were more likely to have sons who attained their occupational goals and showed clear job satisfaction. Interestingly, fathers had ceased to be the most important role models for these subjects during early adulthood. They were replaced by teachers, employers, other adults, and peers.

Heath's (1976, 1978, Heath & Heath, 1991) longitudinal study of

Haverford College men also included a retrospective look at the fathers of those students who had succeeded vocationally. Heath found that Haverford men who had succeeded in their work during early adulthood or who were the most mentally healthy were also significantly more likely than the other men in the study to remember their fathers as available, accessible, and affectionate. These fathers helped the boys with their homework and encouraged their physical-athletic growth (1991, pp. 286–290). It is notable that the effective fathers of Heath's subjects, in our terminology, exercised all three types of parental generativity and, thereby, cared for and promoted all three domains of their sons' development—social-emotional, intellectual-academic, and physical-athletic. However, when the Haverford men's memories of their fathering were reexamined in relation to their later work success at midlife, their fathers' contribution to their vocational accomplishment was no longer statistically significant.

Tessman (1982) further clarifies the fathers' impact on their daughters' orientation to work. She points particularly to the father's ability to respond to the daughter's "endeavor excitement," which promotes her development toward autonomy. "More salient than a distant pride in her achievement is his willingness to involve himself in the process. . . . Women who emphasize their father's contribution to their enthusiasm in work usually stress . . . his treatment of her as an interesting person in her own right . . . his trust in her developing autonomous capacities during joint endeavors; his own capacity for excitement or enthusiasm about discovery in work or play" (p. 227). Tessman insightfully points out that daughters seek out and respond to two kinds of appreciation from their fathers, one related to their sexual identity, the other to the growth of their own mastery of the world around them.

Tessman's (1989) empirical research among young adults aimed at determining how their fathers' participation in their adolescent development was transformed into energy for work during adulthood. Her subjects (high-achieving women students from the Massachusetts Institute of Technology) typically described their fathers as "encouraging or stimulating her curiosity, exploration, or independent judgment; as involving her in joint endeavors with him; as showing trust in her growing capacities; and, finally, as enjoying a playful attitude or being playful with the daughter" (p. 204). These women, as adults, were highly productive at work and, in Eriksonian terminology, were clearly societally generative. Similar findings have been reported for female managers (Hennig & Jardim, 1977) and other groups of unusually competent women (for review, see Barnett & Baruch, 1978).

Douglas Heath's study of Haverford men also provides important data on the possible influence of fathers on women's work success because he and Harriet Heath expanded the longitudinal study to include the men's wives (Heath & Heath, 1991). When these women entered the study at midlife, they were asked to recall the parenting they had received. The Haverford subjects' wives who succeeded in their work, in contrast to those who were less successful, showed many "more enduring 'effects' of their fathers" than of their mothers (p. 287). These vocationally successful women recalled that, when they were children, their fathers "firmly . . . held them to high expectations, actively spurred their academic achievement, and stringently disciplined them for failing" (p. 298). Likewise, fathers who urged their daughters to participate in athletics appear to have contributed more to their daughters' subsequent adult success. These same women recalled fathers who "valued their daughters' intellectual development, actively participated in educating them, and opened up the outside world to them" (p. 287). Finally, the fathers provided important work-related advice: "They talked to their daughters about how to get a job, prepare for an interview, dress appropriately, get along with men and their bosses, deal with male ways of being critical and supportive, read the financial pages, ask for a raise, invest their money for income and capital gain, make alliances, and anticipate . . . changing office politics" (p. 288). The report does not make clear if the recalled fathering was different during the childhood and adolescent decades but, in our Eriksonian terminology, it is clear that these fathers provided all three types of parental generativity—support of intellectual-academic, social-emotional, and physical-athletic development. Interestingly, there is no clear indication of warm, tender father-daughter relationships among the high-achieving women.

In summary, the preceding studies differ in fundamental ways but they generally agree that fathers who are available provide important experiences and models for children that can help them gain greater competence and maturity. In terms of the present longitudinal investigation, it is perhaps most important to note that prior studies provide tentative evidence that the responsive participation of fathers in their children's lives, both when they are young and when they are adolescents, has a significant impact on those children's later lives and will be evident years later during their children's early adulthood years. Here we intend to explore longitudinally how fathers may contribute to their daughters' and sons' educational and occupational success.

Research Questions

Prior research, primarily cross-sectional, suggests that fathers may influence their children's adulthood outcomes. The following two questions, which provide a foundation for the portion of the study reported in this chapter, use the most realistic criteria available to assess the study fathers' possible contributions to their children's adulthood outcomes. They address the relationship between what the fathers did during childrearing and how their children did as adults. **Question 1: Does fathers' parental generativity predict daughters' educational and occupational success?**

Several recurrent themes in the literature tentatively suggest that daughters whose fathers were more involved in general, and specifically more involved in forms of childrearing that challenged the girls through less traditionally feminine activities, will achieve more mobility than will daughters of less participatory or more traditional fathers. **Question 2: Does fathers' parental generativity predict sons' educational and occupational success?**

Again, on the basis of several recurrent themes in the above literature review, it is reasonable to theorize that sons whose fathers were more involved in general, and specifically more involved in childrearing patterns that challenged them through less stereotypically masculine activities, will achieve a higher level of upward mobility than will sons of less participatory or more traditional fathers.

The general expectation regarding children is that the gains children acquire from involved fathers in their first two decades of life will remain with them and be evident as direct and indirect adulthood outcomes. In particular, men's parental generativity will contribute to the children's upward educational and occupational mobility by early adulthood.

How the Study Was Conducted
Subjects

When the relation of the men's generativity to their children's achievement was considered, the sample was restricted to fathers with an adult daughter or son (aged 25 or older) whose early adulthood educational or occupational outcomes were known. Among the 240 child-rearing fathers in this study, educational outcomes were available for 206 of the men's first-born children (an equal number of daughters and sons). The children's adult occupational outcomes were available for 176 of the men's first-born children, including 82 daughters and 94 sons. At the time of their adulthood assessment, the daughters ranged in age from 25 to 37, with a mean age of 29; the sons ranged in age from 25 to 38, with a mean age of 29.

Because the adult outcomes were known for far fewer later-born children, this study confined itself to these first-born children. When the backgrounds of the fathers of the adult children in the study were compared with the backgrounds of those of the excluded children, there were no significant differences.

Rating Scales

The fathers' adult children were rated on their educational and occupational mobility outcomes, which served as measures of early adulthood success or achievement (Commons, Armon, Richards, & Schrader, 1989). Control variables included both general and decade-specific family background characteristics. The three types of paternal generativity in each decade functioned as predictor variables, allowing us to evaluate their ability to account for variance in the men's adult children's mobility outcomes while controlling for differences in family background. All ratings were made by judges who were blind to other aspects of the fathers' lives and also to the ratings made by other judges. The interrater reliability reported for each variable, unless indicated otherwise, is the correlation coefficient based on a comparison of the ratings assigned by the original rater with the ratings assigned by a second rater to the same randomly selected subgroup of cases.

Children's Adulthood Outcome Variables

The daughters' and sons' mobility attainments were assessed as follows.
Adult child's educational mobility. Each father's oldest adult child was rated on his or her level of education, on the educational subscale from the Hollingshead's Index of Social Status (1959, 1975). The

original scale was reversed so that it ranged from 1 (low) to 7 (high). The interrater reliability coefficient for the educational ratings was estimated to be .96. The degree of educational mobility for each child was estimated by subtracting the average of the father's and mother's Hollingshead educational rating (described below) from the child's own adult rating, and then adding 7 to the difference to create a scale ranging from 1 (extreme downward educational mobility) to 7 (perfect stability) to 13 (high upward educational mobility). To ensure a minimal number of years for educational mobility to occur, adult children were at least 25 years of age at the time of the assessment.

Adult child's occupational mobility. Each father's oldest adult child was rated on his or her level of occupation, as situated on the occupational subscale from the Hollingshead Index of Social Status (1959; Haug, 1972). The scale, as used, ranged from 1 (low) to 7 (high). The interrater reliability was estimated to be .94 for occupational ratings. The degree of occupational mobility was estimated by the same procedure outlined above for calculating educational mobility. The resulting scale ranged from 1 (extreme downward occupational mobility) to 7 (perfect stability) to 13 (high upward occupational mobility). Although the subjects were all 25 years of age or older at the time of the assessment, it is important to note that occupational mobility typically continues well after the mid-twenties. Therefore, the assessment of the adult children's occupational mobility should be understood as a preliminary estimate.

Family's General Background

The analysis controlled for the general background of the families, including the fathers' and their wives' levels of education and occupation and the fathers' marital affinity.

Father's occupational and educational levels. The fathers were rated on their occupation and level of education, using the same scales from Hollingshead's Index of Social Status (1959, 1975). The scales ranged from 1 (low) to 7 (high). Interrater reliability was estimated to be .92 for occupation and .98 for education.

Wife's occupational and educational levels. The Glueck subjects' wives were rated on their occupation and level of education, using the same scales. Wives' premarital occupations were used for women who never worked outside of the home after marriage. Interrater reliability was estimated to be .75 for occupation and .75 for education.

Father's marital affinity. The father's marital affinity or commitment was assessed through his self-reports on the possibility of divorce. On the basis of interviews that took place during his first two decades of childrearing, each father was rated as to whether divorce had been: (1) seriously considered, (2) casually considered, or (3) never considered. The rating was based on combined assessments because sufficient information was not uniformly available for each separate assessment. Interrater agreement was .75, using Cohen's kappa which corrects for chance agreement.

Family's Specific Background

The analyses also controlled for the wives' employment, the children's ages, and the number of children in each family at each longitudinal assessment.

Wife's employment outside of the home. Each wife was rated at each longitudinal assessment as follows: (0) wife not employed outside of the home, (1) wife employed part-time outside of the home, and (2) wife employed full-time outside of the home (see also Chapter 4).

Child's age. Because the time when the men began their families varied, the ages of their children were not the same when the men were assessed for their participation in childrearing during the first decade and during the second decade of their child's life. The age of the child at each longitudinal assessment was thus included as a control variable.

Number of children. The men's parental generativity with the first child and the impact of their childrearing might have changed according to the total number of children for whom they were eventually responsible. Thus the number of each father's children was also monitored at each longitudinal assessment to control for this variation statistically.

Father's Parental Generativity Variables

The analysis used the three different types of parental generativity (social-emotional, intellectual-academic, and physical-athletic), each rated during the 2 decades of childhood and adolescence, to assess the ability of varieties of fathers' childrearing participation to predict the early adulthood life outcomes of their sons and daughters. (See also Chapter 2.)

What We Found:
Consequences of Fathers' Childrearing
for Their Children

The children were, on average, upwardly mobile more than one educational level above that of their parents (daughters, M gain = 1.2; sons, M gain = 1.4). This often meant that a father and mother who had finished the tenth grade had a child who was a high school graduate and may have attended a year of college or obtained an associate degree. Forty-seven percent of the first-born children attended college for at least one year, 23% of the children earned a four-year college degree (B.A., B.S.), approximately 10% obtained additional professional training, and 5% went on to earn an advanced graduate degree (M.A., M.S., M.Ed., M.Div.).

In terms of occupations, the children were also, on average, upwardly mobile by approximately one occupational level above that of their parents (daughters, M gain = 1.1; sons, M gain = 0.8). This frequently meant that a child whose father and mother held semiskilled or skilled blue-collar jobs became a technician, an owner of a small business, or a semiprofessional. During early adulthood, 15% of the first-born children entered the major professions (for example, accountant, architect, counselor, educator, lawyer, clergy), 21% became semiprofessionals (dental hygienist, court reporter, mortician, business manager), 36% became technicians or owners of small businesses, 19% entered the skilled trades, and 9% were semiskilled or unskilled workers.

Did the fathers' participation in childrearing make a measurable contribution to their children's early adulthood educational and occupational outcomes? The results of a series of regression analyses of the adult children's mobility are reported below. General control variables included the prior educational achievements of the fathers and their wives and the father's marital affinity. Decade-specific control variables included the wife's work outside of the home, the child's age, and the total number of children in the family. The analyses are presented separately for educational and occupational mobility.

Predicting Educational Mobility

The following analyses consider the contribution of fathers' generativity to explaining differences in their daughters' and sons' early adulthood educational mobility, after we controlled for the contribution of background characteristics.

Daughters' Educational Mobility

The regression analysis relevant to daughters' educational mobility is summarized in Table 6.1. The total model, with all control variables entered into the equation before the childrearing participation variables, accounts for 54% of the variance in educational mobility [$R = .737$, $F (15, 87) = 6.91$, $p < .001$].

The contribution of the daughters' general family background to their educational mobility is both quite substantial, explaining 33% of the variance, and significant ($R = .577$, $F = 16.52$, $p < .001$). Secondary analysis of the block of family background variables, using a stepwise entry procedure, showed that the major portion of this explained variance (26% out of 33%) could be attributed to the fathers' own level of education ($R = .509$, $F = 35.44$, $p < .001$).

The block of family context variables during the childhood decade does not make a significant contribution to the explained variance, but the individual contribution of wife's employment outside the home is significant and negative. Secondary analysis indicated, however, that a mother's employment outside of the home did *not* make a significant contribution to a daughter's educational mobility when it was entered into the equation alone. Rather, there was a weak interaction in which maternal employment outside of the home made a small negative contribution (3%) upon the daughter's educational mobility only when the daughter was in late childhood, and there were a number of other younger children in the family (R^2 change = .026, F change = 3.96, $p < .05$).

Fathers' generativity during their children's first decade contributes an additional 7% to the explained variance in their daughters' educational mobility after controlling for the contribution of background variables (F change = 3.80, $p < .05$). Secondary analysis, using stepwise entry for the block of three types of parental generativity, indicated that the strongest contributor was the fathers' high level of care for physical-athletic development (R^2 change = .03; F change = 4.22, $p < .05$), followed by their relatively low level of care for childhood social-emotional development (R^2 change = .02; F change = 3.95, $p < .05$). The positive contribution of the fathers' support of intellectual-academic development did not remain statistically significant after

Table 6.1 Predicting daughters' educational mobility: regression analysis

Independent variables, listed in order of entry[a]	Beta[b]	R	Cumulative variance explained[c]	New variance explained[d]	F change
Block 1. Family's general background:					
Father's education	-.452***				
Father's marital affinity	.183*				
Wife's education	-.248**	.577	.33	.33	16.52***
Block 2. Family context, childhood decade:					
Number of children	-.109				
Wife's outside employment	-.172*				
Child's age	.173	.610	.37	.04	1.96
Block 3. Father's childrearing, childhood decade:					
Physical development support	.151[e]				
Social development support	-.184*				
Intellectual development support	.145	.663	.44	.07	3.80*

	b		c	d	
Block 4. Family context, adolescent decade:					
Child's age	-.054				
Wife's outside employment	-.057				
Number of children	-.104	.671	.45	.01	.53
Block 5. Father's childrearing, adolescent decade:					
Intellectual development support	.076				
Physical development support	.310***				
Social development support	.191*	.737	.54	.09	5.90***

a. Hierarchical regression model; blocks are entered in historical order, while individual variables within each block are entered in order of decreasing tolerance.

b. Final standardized regression coefficient and significance level of t for each variable.

c. R^2 statistic.

d. R^2 change statistic.

e. Approached significance ($.05 < p < .10$) under forced entry of the block as a whole, *and* attained significance ($p \leq .05$) under stepwise entry of the individual variables within the block.

*$p \leq .05$, **$p \leq .01$, ***$p \leq .001$; $N = 103$.

controlling for the contributions of the other childrearing variables. The overall contribution of fathers' childrearing was positive, but it is important to note that the specific contribution of fathers' care for their daughters' childhood social-emotional development was negative (final beta = $-.184$, $t = -2.21$, $p = .029$; beta on entry = $-.166$, $t = -1.98$, $p = .049$).

The block of family context variables during adolescence does not make a significant additional contribution to the explained variance.

After controlling for all prior (blocks 1, 2, 3) or concurrent (block 4) family variables, the fathers' adolescent-decade childrearing participation still explains an additional 9% of the variance in the daughters' educational mobility, and the contribution is consistently positive (F change = 5.90, $p < .001$). Secondary analysis, using stepwise entry with three types of paternal generativity, confirmed that the two significant and positive forms of childrearing were high levels of care for adolescent physical-athletic development (R^2 change = .06; F change = 10.20, $p < .01$) and adolescent social-emotional development (R^2 change = .03; F change = 4.96, $p < .05$).

In sum, a total of 16% of the variance in daughters' educational mobility is contributed by the fathers' childrearing participation after the imposition of all concurrent or historical control variables. Fathers who gave their daughters more support for physical-athletic development during *both* the childhood and adolescent decades and who provided social-emotional support at relatively lower levels during childhood but at high levels during adolescence, made a major positive contribution to their daughters' subsequent upward educational mobility. If the variance explained by the fathers' own level of education is added to this finding, the fathers' characteristics together contribute 42% to the predicted variance in their daughters' educational mobility.

Sons' Educational Mobility

The analysis of sons' early adulthood attainment of educational mobility is summarized in Table 6.2. With all control and predictor variables entered into the equation, the total model accounts for 40% of the variance in the sons' educational mobility [$R = .631$, F (15, 87) = 3.83, $p < .001$].

The sons' general family background explains 25% of the variance in their educational mobility ($R = .498$, $F = 10.88$, $p < .001$). Secondary analysis using stepwise entry indicated that the major portion of this explained variance (22% out of the 25%) could be attributed to the fathers' level of education ($R = .471$, $F = 28.79$, $p < .001$).

The childhood block of family context variables does not make a significant contribution to the explained variance.

After controlling for all prior or concurrent family variables, the fathers' childhood-decade childrearing participation still accounts for 7% of the variance in the sons' educational mobility (F change = 3.02, $p < .05$). The contribution of childrearing support of intellectual-academic development is significant. Secondary analysis, using stepwise entry for the block of three childrearing variables, confirmed that it was one of the major contributors to sons' educational mobility (R^2 change = .03, F change = 3.96, $p < .05$). Additionally, fathers' support of social-emotional development entered the equation (R^2 change = .03, F change = 4.32, $p < .05$).

During the adolescent decade, the block of family context variables does not make a significant additional contribution to the explained variance.

After controlling for both historically prior and concurrent family background characteristics, the fathers' support of adolescent intellectual-academic development is the only statistically significant form of childrearing during the second decade to predict their sons' educational mobility. The overall block of childrearing variables during adolescence did not achieve statistical significance. An auxiliary analysis, using stepwise entry, confirmed that the individual contribution of fathers' care for intellectual-academic development was statistically significant, explaining 4% of the variance in educational mobility (R^2 change = .04, F change = 5.86, $p < .05$).

In sum, fathers' childrearing contributes a total of 11% to the explained variance in their sons' educational mobility. Fathers who provided high levels of intellectual-academic support during both childhood and adolescence, as well as high levels of social-emotional support during childhood, had sons who achieved greater educational mobility. If the variance explained by the fathers' own level of education is added to this finding, the fathers' characteristics together contribute 33% to the predicted variance in their sons' educational mobility.

Table 6.2 Predicting sons' educational mobility: regression analysis

Independent variables, listed in order of entry[a]	Beta[b]	R	Cumulative variance explained[c]	New variance explained[d]	F change
Block 1. Family's general background:					
Father's education	-.439***				
Father's marital affinity	.038				
Wife's education	-.163	.498	.25	.25	10.88***
Block 2. Family context, childhood decade:					
Wife's outside employment	.108				
Number of children	-.018				
Child's age	.104	.522	.27	.02	1.09
Block 3. Father's childrearing, childhood decade:					
Intellectual development support	.183*				
Social development support	.173[e]				
Physical development support	.076	.581	.34	.07	3.02*

Block 4. Family context, adolescent decade:					
Child's age	.101				
Wife's outside employment	.141				
Number of children	-.085	.600	.36	.02	1.10
Block 5. Father's childrearing, adolescent decade:					
Intellectual development support	.204*				
Social development support	.040				
Physical development support	-.038	.631	.40	.04	1.77

a. Hierarchical regression model; blocks are entered in historical order, while individual variables within each block are entered in order of decreasing tolerance.

b. Final standardized regression coefficient and significance level of t for each variable.

c. R^2 statistic.

d. R^2 change statistic.

e. Approached significance (.05 < p < .10) under forced entry of the block as a whole, *and* attained significance ($p \leq .05$) under stepwise entry of the individual variables within the block.

*$p \leq .05$, **$p \leq .01$, ***$p \leq .001$; $N = 103$.

Predicting Occupational Mobility

The following analyses consider the contribution of fathers to their daughters' and sons' early adulthood occupational mobility outcomes, after controlling for background variables.

Daughters' Occupational Mobility

The regression analysis of daughters' occupational mobility is summarized in Table 6.3. The total model, with all control variables entered in the equation before the childrearing participation variables, accounts for 61% of the variance in occupational mobility [$R = .781$, $F (15, 66) = 6.87$, $p < .001$].

The daughters' general family background is important. The father's occupational level, his marital affinity, and the mother's occupational level together explain 37% of the variance in the daughter's occupational mobility and the contribution is significant ($R = .611$, $F = 15.56$, $p < .001$). Secondary analysis of the block of family background variables, using a stepwise entry procedure, indicated that the major portion of this explained variance (19% out of 37%) could be attributed to the fathers' occupational level ($R = .437$, $F = 18.92$, $p < .001$).

Family characteristics during the daughter's childhood decade contribute an additional 10% to the explained variance (F change = 4.26, $p < .01$). Secondary analysis indicated that the major portion (8% out of 10%) was due to a negative association between mobility and the number of siblings in the family (F change = 11.41, $p < .001$).

Fathers' parental generativity during the first decade, after the imposition of control variables, makes a marginally significant positive contribution to the explained variance in their daughters' occupational mobility (F change = 2.54, $.05 < p < .10$). Secondary analysis, using a stepwise entry for the childrearing variables, showed that the trend primarily reflected the marginally significant contribution of fathers' care of their daughters' childhood physical-athletic development to their daughters' occupational mobility (R^2 change = .03; F change = 3.93, $.05 < p < .10$).

The adolescent block of family context variables does not make a significant additional contribution to the explained variance.

The contribution of fathers' adolescent-decade childrearing to their daughters' occupational mobility is consistently positive and explains

Table 6.3 Predicting daughters' occupational mobility: regression analysis

Independent variables, listed in order of entry[a]	Beta[b]	R	Cumulative variance explained[c]	New variance explained[d]	F change
Block 1. Family's general background:					
Father's occupation	-.402***				
Father's marital affinity	.204*				
Wife's occupation	-.424***	.611	.37	.37	15.56***
Block 2. Family context, childhood decade:					
Wife's outside employment	-.138				
Child's age	.250*				
Number of children	-.347**	.682	.47	.10	4.26**
Block 3. Father's childrearing, childhood decade:					
Physical development support	.165				
Social development support	-.144				
Intellectual development support	.116	.718	.52	.05	2.54
Block 4. Family context, adolescent decade:					
Child's age	-.051				
Wife's outside employment	-.080				
Number of children	.087	.725	.53	.01	.45
Block 5. Father's childrearing, adolescent decade:					
Intellectual development support	.036				
Social development support	.235*				
Physical development support	.298**	.781	.61	.08	4.71**

a. Hierarchical regression model; blocks are entered in historical order, while individual variables within each block are entered in order of decreasing tolerance.

b. Final standardized regression coefficient and significance level of t for each variable.

c. R^2 statistic.   d. R^2 change statistic. $*p \leq .05$, $**p \leq .01$, $***p \leq .001$; $N = 82$.

an additional 8% of the variance in mobility, even after controlling for all background variables and for childrearing participation during the childhood decade (F change = 4.71, $p < .01$). Secondary analysis, using stepwise entry with the three types of parental generativity, confirmed that the significant contribution was due to two types of childrearing participation: support for physical-athletic development (R^2 change = .05, F change = 7.95, $p < .01$) and social-emotional development (R^2 change = .04; F change = 5.80, $p < .05$).

In sum, the contribution of fathers' childrearing is not measurably significant during the childhood decade but is significant during the adolescent decade, explaining 8% of the variance. Fathers' strong support for their daughters' physical-athletic and social-emotional development contributed more to their subsequent occupational mobility. If the variance explained by the fathers' occupational level is added to this finding, the fathers' occupational and childrearing characteristics together contribute 27% to the predicted variance in their daughters' occupational mobility.

Sons' Occupational Mobility

The results of the regression analysis pertinent to the sons' occupational mobility are shown in Table 6.4. After all control and predictor variables were entered into the equation, the total model accounts for 37% of the variance in sons' adulthood occupational mobility [R = .606, F (15,78) = 3.02, $p < .001$].

One quarter of the variance in the sons' occupational mobility is explained by their family's general background (R = .500, F = 10.01, $p < .001$). Secondary analysis of the block of family background variables, using a stepwise entry procedure, revealed that the major portion of this explained variance (19% out of the 25%) could be attributed to the mothers' occupations (R = .430, F = 20.92, $p < .001$).

The childhood block of concurrent family context variables does not make a significant additional contribution to the explained variance.

After controlling for all prior or concurrent background variables, fathers' parental generativity during their sons' childhood accounts for an additional 6% of the variance in occupational mobility (F change = 2.68, $p < .05$). Support of physical-athletic development was the primary contributing variable, as stepwise entry also confirmed (R^2 = .04, F change = 5.23, $p < .05$).

Table 6.4 Predicting sons' occupational mobility: regression analysis

Independent variables, listed in order of entry[a]	Beta[b]	R	Cumulative variance explained[c]	New variance explained[d]	F change
Block 1. Family's general background:					
Father's occupation	-.268**				
Father's marital affinity	.021				
Wife's occupation	-.354***	.500	.25	.25	10.01***
Block 2. Family context, childhood decade:					
Wife's outside employment	.002				
Number of children	.052				
Child's age	.067	.509	.26	.01	.36
Block 3. Father's childrearing, childhood decade:					
Intellectual development support	.158				
Social development support	.026				
Physical development support	.191*	.569	.32	.06	2.68*
Block 4. Family context, adolescent decade:					
Child's age	.026				
Wife's outside employment	.170				
Number of children	-165	.596	.36	.04	1.34
Block 5. Father's childrearing, adolescent decade:					
Social development support	-.024				
Intellectual development support	.113				
Physical development support	.006	.606	.37	.01	.45

a. Hierarchical regression model; blocks are entered in historical order, while individual variables within each block are entered in order of decreasing tolerance.

b. Final standardized regression coefficient and significance level of t for each variable.

c. R^2 statistic. d. R^2 change statistic. *$p \leq .05$, **$p \leq .01$, ***$p \leq .001$; $N = 94$.

During the adolescent decade, the block of family context variables does not make a significant contribution to the explained variance.

After controlling for all prior or concurrent background variables, including childrearing participation during the childhood decade, the fathers' adolescent-decade childrearing participation does not make a significant additional contribution to the explained variance.

In sum, fathers' care for and promotion of their sons' development during boyhood explain 6% of the variance in their sons' occupational mobility. In contrast with the results for the sons' educational mobility, only boyhood participation accounts for variance in the sons' occupational mobility. If the variance explained by the fathers' occupations is added to this finding, the fathers' occupational and childrearing characteristics together contribute 20% to the predicted variance in their sons' occupational mobility.

For all of the above hierarchical regression analyses, it is theoretically possible that an enhancing effect could be at work in which the strength of one type of participation may be increased when other forms of participation or background characteristics are present. Except for gender, however, no tested interactions were statistically significant.

Discussion of the Findings

The contribution of fathers' parental generativity to their children's educational and occupational outcomes was assessed after statistically controlling both for parents' occupational and educational levels and for the enduring characteristics of the fathers. Consistent with prior research, the fathers' and mothers' levels of education negatively predicted their daughters' and sons' educational mobility. Similarly, the parents' occupations negatively predicted their daughters' and sons' occupational mobility (Featherman, 1980; Jencks et al., 1972). These negative associations may seem counterintuitive because parents' educational and occupational *status* is positively correlated with their children's *status* in our society, reflecting the fact that children's status is partially inherited from their parents. In contrast, however, parents' *status* and their children's *mobility* are negatively correlated in our society because mobility is based on the *difference* between the parents' status and their children's adulthood status. Parents' and children's status levels are positively correlated, that is, because the higher a child started out in life the more likely he or she was to end up at a higher social class, but parents' status and their children's mobility are negatively correlated because the lower a child started out in life the more likely he or she was to be more upwardly mobile.

The findings, more originally, also show that fathers' parental generativity contributes significantly to their children's educational and occupational mobility success. Paternal childcare variables, that is, have significant coefficients, and make a significant contribution to the explained variance. This remains true even after pre-existing characteristics of both parents and of the family, any of which could be expected to shape daughters' or sons' upbringing and achievements in many unmeasured ways, are entered in the equation.

Daughters' Mobility

During the childhood decade, the fathers' childcare made a significant contribution to their daughters' later educational but not occupational mobility. First, daughters' educational mobility was negatively predicted by one fathering style: high levels of social-emotional support. While the association was significant, a majority of the daughters (55%) still advanced one or two educational levels regardless of variations in their fathers' social-emotional support. Second, when fathers' support of childhood physical-athletic development as a positive predictor of their daughters' educational mobility was reconsidered using stepwise entry, its contribution to the explained variance also attained significance ($p < .05$). During the adolescent decade, two fathering styles also made significant positive contributions to both the educational and occupational dimensions of their daughters' social mobility. First was support of their physical-athletic development. Although a traditional father may enjoy a vigorous catch with his son, these nontraditional fathers also enjoyed pitching a baseball or engaging in other athletic activities with their daughters. Second was fathers' care for their social-emotional development. During adolescence, that is, the upwardly mobile adolescent daughter was also relatively close to her father.

The previously weak negative contribution of social-emotional support during childhood and the continuous positive emphasis upon promoting physical-athletic capacities during both decades, however, suggests that the nature of this relationship is as affirming of the daughter's ability to function autonomously and competitively as it is nurturant. Most athletic activities are by definition competitive, and Monsaas and Engelhard (1990) have shown that the competitiveness of high-achieving men and women is significantly predicted by the degree to which their parents modeled, reinforced, and valued competitiveness. Insofar as this type of paternal support given to daughters predicts their higher achievements, it suggests that the fathers contributed to their ability to compete with men beyond the family sphere.

These findings are generally consistent with prior studies. Crouter and Crowley's (1990) study of young adolescents suggests that these styles of support may be effective, in part, because girls with greater one-to-one involvement with their fathers simply felt closer to them. In contrast, they found that boys' feelings of closeness with their fathers were not linked to levels of duo involvement. Heath and Heath (1991) report that fathers who urged daughters to participate in athletics contributed more to their daughters' subsequent adult success, but that social-emotional tenderness was not typical of the fathering characteristics recalled by the successful daughters in their study. In contrast to our findings, however, the Heaths report that the father-daughter identification was still highly conflicted for vocationally successful daughters. It is possible that this contrast reflects a cohort effect. The daughters in our sample, born between 1946 and 1964, were members of the baby boom generation that experienced the women's liberation movement, but the women in the Heaths' sample, born during the 1930s or early 1940s, were members of the silent generation that provided little support and harsher penalties for violations of traditional gender roles.

Sons' Mobility

Sons' social mobility was predicted by fathering styles during the childhood decade that were different from those that predicted daughters' mobility. Sons' educational mobility was significantly forecasted by their fathers' care for their childhood intellectual-academic development and social-emotional development. Their occupational mobility was predicted by their fathers' care for their physical-athletic development. Thus, all three types of fathers' participation during the childhood decade made a significant contribution to some form of their sons' social mobility. Boys, that is, appear to benefit from all types of positive interaction with their fathers, and boys who received all three forms of paternal nurturance thus had an advantage over boys whose fathers provided only traditional forms of childrearing participation. Whereas traditional fathers may be nurturant with their little girls and supportive of their little boys' athletic development, the most effective fathers broadly cared for their boys' development across all domains of development—academic, physical, and social.

During adolescence, in contrast, it was only the care for intellectual-academic development that predicted the sons' mobility. Boys' adulthood mobility thus benefits from intellectual-academic support received from their fathers during both childhood and adolescence. Fathers' fostering of their sons' social-emotional and physical-athletic development during adolescence did not make a significant contribution to their educational or occupational mobility. It is important to clarify that support of adolescent physical-athletic development was the least frequent type of childrearing for all adolescents; this does not mean, however, that fathers provided significantly less support to their sons than to their daughters (see Chapter 1). Rather, support for social and physical development during adolescence simply did not make a measurably significant contribution to their sons' mobility outcomes, while the same types of care did make a significant contribution to their daughters' mobility. The dynamics underlying this and other gender differences will now be considered.

Gender Differences in Consequences

Fathers in this study displayed a lack of gender bias in the level of care they provided; it was the same for daughters as for sons for any of the three types of paternal generativity across two decades (see Chapter 1). Yet the various types and separate decades of paternal childrearing participation had a different impact for each gender. Three of the four significant childrearing predictors of boys' mobility were from the childhood decade, but four of the six significant childrearing predictors of girls' mobility were from the adolescent decade. The types of childrearing that were significant predictors of mobility during both decades also differed for sons and daughters.

Eriksonian Patterns

Our findings fit well with Eriksonian theory, which clarifies why daughters and sons appear to need different types of paternal support during different decades.

During childhood, both sons and daughters need their fathers' support to negotiate the first four of Erikson's psychosocial tasks. But the types of fathering that promote sons' and daughters' development are not always identical. For sons, the early portion of the childhood decade requires them to separate from the mother and identify with the father, the same-sex parent, as part of the boy's gender identity development. Fathers' warm, close, guiding support encourages their sons' acceptance of them as their primary models. Fathers' broad support of their sons' physical-athletic, intellectual, and social-emotional development promotes this transition and the continuation of their boys' sense of basic trust and autonomy (Erikson's stages 1 and 2); it also fosters the successful achievement of a basic sense of initiative (stage 3, paralleling Freud's Oedipal years). The later childhood years also encompass the mentorship period when boys, striving to achieve a sense of industry (stage 4), again turn to their fathers for guidance and training (Ross, 1982).

In contrast, the daughters' primary identification remains with their mother during childhood. Fathers' friendly but not extremely warm or tender childrearing support does not draw them away from this primary identification, while their rigorous physical-athletic interaction also helps them to avoid an extremely traditional sex-role identification. Fathers who provide secure excitement during infancy and optimal freedom during toddlerhood contribute to their daughters' achievement of favorable ratios of trust over mistrust and autonomy over doubt. During early childhood, fathers are also an important resource for daughters' achievement of a favorable ratio of initiative over guilt. There is evidence, for instance, that girls aged 3 to 5 whose fathers engage in considerable physical play (wrestling with the child, swinging the child in the air, and so on) are more assertive in their peer interactions, as well as more popular with their peers and teachers (MacDonald & Parke, 1984).

During adolescence, sons and daughters alike are striving to establish their independence and distinctive identities. The type of fathering that will help their adolescents fulfill these tasks, however, differs for sons and daughters. The sons' psychosocial task includes achieving a significant degree of separation from their fathers. Their fathers' encouragement from the sidelines, for instance, would support their ability to achieve such a significant degree of separation from them while also providing them with a firm bridge back to the family. No wonder that fathering during adolescence has a weaker impact on their sons—that is, sons are preoccupied with achieving a degree of physical and emotional differentiation from their fathers during their adolescent years. It is likely, that is, that adolescent sons themselves contribute to the weakened impact of their fathers' involvement. One of the processes by which this may be accomplished is suggested by Erikson's observation that adolescents sometimes "artificially appoint perfectly well-meaning people," such as their fathers, "to play the role of adversaries" (1950, p. 261).

For adolescent daughters, it is fathers' active, energetic involvement on life's playing fields that can promote their ability to achieve a significant degree of separation from their mothers and establish a bridge to the outside world. It is in adolescence that paternal childrearing participation can function as a possibly crucial conduit or bridge from the mother to the larger society, allowing the young women to successfully negotiate the establishment of an autonomous identity and providing opportunities for them to have constructive, assertive interactions with males. In this study, the findings indicate that fathers' support of physical-athletic and social-emotional development during adolescence was significant only for girls. It seems that fathers who continuously engage their daughters in positive interaction without smothering them support their adolescent girls' successful identity achievement. This interpretation recalls early research (Hetherington, 1972) that showed that the negative effects of father's absence on daughters did not become markedly evident until girls reached adolescence.

Nontraditional Continuities

Fathers' support of physical-athletic development during both childhood and adolescence was only significant for girls. Fathers' support of intellectual-academic development during both childhood and adolescence was only significant for boys. While previous research has shown that a traditional father promotes his daughter's expressive behavior and his son's instrumental behavior (Lamb, 1981), the present findings suggest that the types of childrearing support from which the daughters and sons benefit most are nontraditional: physical-athletic for girls, and intellectual-academic for boys. Counterbalancing traditional sex-role patterns of socialization also clarifies why continuity in the types of childrearing that were significant predictors of mobility during both decades also differed for sons and daughters.

These findings are generally consistent with the research reviewed in this chapter. Prior studies suggested that fathers who are involved with their children in less traditional ways promote their children's success: fathers who exhibited less sex-role stereotyped behavior with their daughters promoted their daughters' development of a more balanced (less stereotypically feminine) sex-role orientation, and fathers who supported their sons' intellectual competence contributed to their sons' academic performance. The findings are also congruent with Radin's (1981b) more comprehensive earlier review of the literature, in which she concluded "that paternal warmth is seldom negatively associated with cognitive functioning in boys whereas there are indications that too much warmth may be detrimental to the development of intellective capacity in young girls" (p. 400). Radin offers a thoughtful summary of diverse interpretations of the general trend that young daughters benefit from friendliness but not from very close social-emotional relationships with their fathers during childhood. One possibility is that this type of balance reinforces the importance of girls forming their primary or original identification with the same-sex parent during their early years. It is also possible that fathers' excessively nurturant behavior during the childhood years may hinder girls' educational achievement because it draws them into more traditionally feminine roles. More positively, fathers who allow their daughters more distance and autonomy may give them the intellectual freedom necessary to develop analytic thinking.

The contrasting nontraditional patterns in the present study may also function to help the boys and girls become well-rounded and highly adaptive adults. The fathers who filled in the gap left by common social practices (for example, more community and school programs for boys that emphasized physical-athletic skills) may have provided something needed by all children for optimal educational and occupational success and generational succession. This interpretation is consistent with the previously reviewed longitudinal study of

Haverford College men (Heath, 1976, 1978) and their wives (Heath & Heath, 1991) who, despite their economically advantaged position, also grew up in communities with noninclusive sex-role expectations for children and parents. It is notable that the fathers of vocationally successful Haverford men, like the Boston fathers of upwardly mobile sons, cared for and promoted all three types of their sons' development—physical-athletic, social-emotional, and intellectual-academic. The Haverford subjects' wives who succeeded in their work, like our Bostonian fathers' daughters who evidenced upward occupational mobility, showed "more enduring 'effects' of their fathers" (p. 287) when these had actively fostered their development and promoted their entrance into the outside world. Despite the clear social class differences between the Heaths' Haverford sample of upper-middle- and upper-class men and the Gluecks' Boston sample of working-class men, therefore, the fathering that the Heaths' occupationally successful husbands and wives recalled receiving was similar to the fathering of the Glueck men's upwardly mobile sons and daughters.

Maternal Differences

This investigation is unable to address adequately the role of mothers in their children's lives. However, two indices of the study fathers' relations with their wives add to our understanding of the difference that mothers make in the life outcomes of their daughters and sons.

Marital Affinity

The finding that fathers' marital affinity or commitment was a significant predictor of both educational and occupational mobility for daughters but of neither form of mobility for sons also confirms that the mother is important in different ways to daughters and sons. This finding suggests that daughters especially need their parents' relationship to be relatively stable or compatible.

This interpretation is generally consistent with previous research. Elder (1974) also reported in his study of children of the Depression that "girls appear most responsive to family relations" when "forming evaluations of parents" and that the father grew less attractive than the mother for "girls who reported a high level of family conflict," while "no meaningful variation was found among boys" (p. 100). In more contemporary cohorts, these general findings regarding the special importance of the parents' marital relationship for daughters are also consistent with some of the unexpected findings of prior research. Several studies report that father-son relations were related to the son's identity development, but father-daughter relations, mother-daughter relations, adolescent-sibling relations, and parents' marital relationship all contributed to the daughter's identity development (Grotevant & Cooper, 1986; Hauser, Jacobson, Noam, & Powers, 1983; Powers, Hauser, Schwartz, Noam, & Jacobson, 1983). In addition, several studies of adolescent and adult women have shown that academic or career success was associated with a significant father-daughter relationship that took place within the family context of a strong marital and parenting relationship (Hennig & Jardim, 1977; Honzik, 1967; Lasser & Snarey, 1989).

Building on this pattern, one may also speculate that men who are on good terms with their wives are likely to be on good terms with their daughters as well (Brody, Pillegrini, & Sigel, 1986), and that the daughters' positive outcomes may be credited in part to the family context that was made possible by the fathers' positive marital adjustment (Lamb & Oppenheim, 1989). Previous studies, in fact, have shown that father-child relations are more systematically associated with patterns of marital adjustment and satisfaction than are mother-child relations. The linkage between marriage and fathering actually looks more robust than the connection between marriage and mothering in a number of studies (Barber, 1987; Belsky, 1979b; Belsky, Gilstrap, & Rovine, 1984; Dickie, 1987; Goldberg & Easterbrooks, 1984). This may occur because a man's effectiveness as a husband and as the father of a daughter reflects his heightened ability to understand and relate to women. Alternatively, the explanation may be that fathers' roles are less scripted by society than wives' roles, and thus fathers are more able to adapt sensitively to the influence of their primary social support, the marital relationship (for review of interpretations, see Belsky, Youngblade, Rovine, & Volling, 1991).

Although fathers' marital affinity or commitment was not significantly associated with their sons' mobility, their parents' strong marriage is not irrelevant to the sons' other life outcomes. A retrospective study has clearly suggested, for instance, that men whose parents got along well were significantly less likely as new fathers to experience stress or decline in their marital relationships during their own transition to fatherhood (Belsky & Isabella, 1985).

Maternal Employment

Wife's employment outside of the home (only during the childhood years) made a significant, small (3%), *negative* contribution to daughters' (but not sons') educational mobility, but only if the daughter was in late childhood, and there were other younger children in the family. Why there would be a significant negative contribution under this one specific condition is open to speculation. Girls may especially need their mother's presence and attention during puberty and transition to adolescence, but this explanation does not take into account that girls without younger siblings did not experience the same negative impact on their later educational mobility. More likely, it is that older girls with younger siblings must assume additional maternal and housekeeping roles. This is especially plausible for the present sample since all of the daughters were first-born. Their added home responsibilities may have prompted them to take on traditional feminine roles prematurely. It is also possible that the burden of their housework made it difficult for them to excel in school in the same way that part-time work has been shown to usually negatively influence most aspects of school performance (March, 1991).

Consistent with the present findings, previous studies have usually shown that mothers' employment status as such does not have a negative impact on their children's development (Gottfried & Gottfried, 1988; Hock, 1980; Hoffman, 1984; Schubert, Bradley-Johnson, & Nuttal, 1980). Researchers on maternal employment have found inconsistent results when they studied its possible effects on children's subsequent achievements during adolescence and young adulthood (for review, see Lamb, 1982, pp. 59–60). Some broadly based studies agree with the present findings, and others disagree.

In a cross-sectional study, Kogos (1991) reported that mothers' work during the childhood decade negatively predicted daughters' (but not sons') early adulthood moral development. Crouter, MacDermid, McHale, and Perry-Jenkins come to a different conclusion in their cross-sectional study (1990). They reported that school-aged boys (but not girls) are sometimes negatively affected by mothers working outside of the home because the boys are less well monitored (less well supervised, less parental interest shown in the child, less communication with the child). Several studies do confirm that a mother's employment, resulting in a dual-earner family, initiates a shift of more responsibilities for both housework and personal care to the children (Douvan, 1963; Elder, 1974; Propper, 1972; Woods, 1972). Elder (1974) also notes that, among children of the Great Depression, family size (three or more children) was a major predictor of children's sex-typed work roles, with daughters being assigned domestic roles in larger families. In contrast to this study's findings, however, some of these prior studies also note a general or overall *positive* influence of these responsibilities upon children's development, but none of these studies considered the possible contribution of maternal employment to their first-born children's long-term outcomes as mediated by an interaction effect between gender and age.

Finally, beyond whether wives or mothers worked outside of the home, it is important to recall that the occupational level of the Glueck wives was a major contributor to the explained variance in daughters' occupational mobility, and it was the major contributor to the explained variance in sons' occupational mobility. The present longitudinal findings show that a small adverse effect of maternal employment upon children is indicated only for first-born daughters who are in late childhood and have younger siblings, but it is more than counterbalanced by the consistent and stronger positive contributions to children's mobility by increased levels of fathers' parental generativity.

Placing the Findings in Context

Leo Tolstoy, like Freud, suggested that "one can live magnificently in this world if one knows how to work and to love" (in Troyat, 1967, p. 158). We have used educational and occupational mobility as measures of successful early adulthood outcomes, and success as a student and employee certainly requires the ability to love (that is, to engage in team work, to be in relationship, connected, attached) and the ability to work (to engage in individual labor, to be independent, autonomous, exploratory) (Hazan & Shaver, 1990; MacKinnon, 1991). Thus it is reasonable to speculate that the findings reported in this chapter suggest that fathers contribute to their children's ability to work and to love. Nevertheless, it is also reasonable to speculate that the findings may assess most directly the work side of adult functioning. We must therefore exercise great caution in any attempt to generalize the findings to more narrowly defined adulthood social accomplishments, such as marital happiness.

It is also reasonable to speculate that the contribution of fathers' parental generativity to their children's educational and occupational mobility would be generally the same in more recent cohorts as it was in this sample because we took into consideration and statistically controlled for many characteristics of the children's family backgrounds. However, other historical factors not addressed by this study are, no doubt, also at work. Only a minority of the mothers in this study worked outside of the home, and when they did, nearly all of the children were still cared for by other family members and within the home. In fact, only 2% of the preschool children in the general population were cared for by a daycare facility when the study's children were growing up (Strauss & Howe, 1991, p. 305). Today, 24% of preschool children attend group care centers or nursery schools (institutional daycare) and another 36% are cared for in the homes of nonrelated caretakers (family daycare) (Bureau of the Census, July, 1990). Furthermore, the potential of children today for future educational and occupational mobility may be more limited. Fewer economic resources may be available to them because many more children are born outside of marriage and raised in single-parent households. In 1950, for instance, 4% of all births were to unmarried women. The figure rose to 11% in 1970, 18% in 1980, and 26% in 1988; today, that is, about one out of four children are born to unmarried mothers (Select Committee on Children, Youth, and Families, 1989; National Center for Health Statistics, 1990c). The number of children raised in economically marginal single-parent households looms even larger, of course, when one considers that "divorce and separation have historically created a dramatic situation in which women and children have lost economic security" (Couture, 1991, p. 41). At the same time, children's life chances today may have improved because of less peer competition within their smaller cohort. The birth rate peaked in the late 1950s at about 12 births per 100 women (aged 15 to 44), then sharply declined, and stood in 1990 at about 7 births per 100 women (National Center for Health Statistics, 1991a, 1991d). All of these factors suggest that generalizations must be quite tentative.

7

Peter and Peter Jr.: Remodeling Lives

This portrait of a father-son relationship is, in part, the story of
the son's upward move from a respectable working class family
to an upper middle class profession. This account also provides a
particularly vivid picture of the benefits and conflicted tradeoffs inherent in the relationships of many white-collar sons and blue-collar
fathers. It weaves uncommon and intricate patterns. Yet it also advances Erikson's simple but profound insight that "life cycles are
embedded in generational cycles" (1980, p. 213).

Sandy-haired Peter Sr. is a 59-year-old, well-paid skilled worker
who takes considerable pride in his work. Son of a trucking-company
foreman, Pete completed high school and then worked as a skilled
craftsman during his childrearing years. At the time of this interview,
his health was poor. He has been married for over 35 years, and he
and his wife, Martha, have raised three sons.

The first-born son, Peter Jr., is a 34-year-old man with an imposing
physique and a sensitive spirit. He graduated from college, completed
his master's degree, and now directs the guidance counseling program
and coaches at an urban high school. He is also currently developing
his abilities in the skilled trades. Pete Jr. has been married for less
than a year.

Peter Sr.'s private interview primarily took place over a cup of tea
at the kitchen table in the family's Boston homestead, where he
himself had grown up, and where he and Martha reared their children.
Pete Sr. and Pete Jr.'s joint conversation took place in the son's new
condominium, and much of Pete Jr.'s private interview was completed
during a stopover at an airport while he and his wife were traveling
on vacation.

Early Memories
The Father Looks Back a Generation

My father was a foreman for a big trucking company in this part of
Boston. They had . . . lots of drivers, mechanics. It was a big, enormous

company. My father was not just a simple foreman; he ran the schedule for the interstate and local trucking. It was a tough job in them days, more than it would be today.

Probably my earliest memory of him would be meal times in elementary school. We didn't see much of him because he worked all the time. But he worked local, so he was there for all the meals. People on the street used to say they knew what time it was when they'd see Thomas O'Brien, my father, walking by on his way to work every day. They could set their alarm clock when they'd see him walking by: "Quarter to six." He was home every day at 12:05. My mother and sisters had dinner waiting for him. He'd eat fast and by 12:30 be back down there. Then he'd come home about 5:30 to eat, be back down there by 7:00, and be back home around 9:00, 10:00 at night. I can remember him sitting at the table, drinking a little brandy or a little highball, smoking a cigar, and reading his paper. That was his day, five days a week, sometimes six days a week, and occasionally Sunday if a truck would break down or something.

I remember my father as a very stern, strict man. (He came from Ireland.) If your schoolwork was behind, he let you know, or if your report card wasn't right, or if you hooked school or something, and he got word of it, he'd let you know. He made sure we done our homework; he made sure we were in all right. If we were to be in at 7 o'clock, you were in at 7 o'clock, not 7:30. If you weren't, you wouldn't go out the next day; you'd be punished that way. You looked out the window at the kids playing football or baseball down the street, but you couldn't go out. Eventually, you smartened up, I guess.

He was 6'2", 6'3", and pretty stern, but my *mother* was the disciplinarian. He made the money, and my mother ran the house. That was about it. My father would come into the argument if he had to, but my mother handled all these. My father was stern, but he never took a bat at you or nothing. (My mother would, but he wouldn't.) He would just discuss it with you, stern look on his face, and if you did something you weren't supposed to do, he let you know in his voice. He'd just discuss it with you and give up and throw his hands up in the air.

Every time I got in trouble at school, I used to take my older brother, who looked a lot like my father (we all had premature gray anyhow). I got away with it for four or five years. Nobody found out until (laughs) probably '48 when I took him to the banquet. It was a father and son deal for the all-Boston football team and that's when the principal met him, you know (chuckles). The principal done a double take; he said, "Who's the guy I've been dealing with the last 4 years then?" I said, "Ah, that's my older brother. This is my father." It didn't bother my father; he got a chuckle out of it later on. The principal, at reunions in later years, often told that story![1]

Growing up, we didn't see a whole lot of my father, except on weekends. But he always had time to take us on picnics. Even though he worked all week, we never missed a Sunday without the beach or a picnic, or horseshoes, or something. He piled us all in a big '38 Buick Roadmaster (or whatever he happened to have; he always bought the big Buicks) and went out for the day: a picnic on the side of the road, farmland, up to Lexington, beaches, the Cape, and mostly we'd go to Revere Beach, Nahant. Later on, even when I started driving, we still went out with the family. He was a family man. He just lived for his family.

He liked keeping his property up. He had a lot of pride in his property. Always shedding the roof and shingling it, and having work done on the house. We never wanted for nothing. We were the only family on the street that was never on welfare. I'd go up to the welfare lines with all my gang, and we would wait up by the fire barn, and they would give you sneakers about eight sizes too big and pants that didn't fit you. I mean, those were welfare days, and we never seen welfare, we never hurt for food. We always used to give food out to the neighbors, like Mrs. Murphy across the street who had eight or ten kids and her husband died young, plus was an alcoholic anyhow. My father helped bring up most of that family. We kids could go to him for anything we wanted. He was always a great man for giving us a half-dollar, if we were looking for ice cream or something. When we got a little bigger, he would give each of us an allowance. "You always got to do your work."

In the winter, it was always a warm house. You could bring your gang in for cocoa, every day in the cold weather. They used to have an old custom of tea every day at three o'clock. We'd have the mailman in, the insurance man in, the ice man in; whoever was in the neighborhood would come in for tea. We'd have a couple of those Irish breads

1. This story is consistent with Pete Sr.'s longitudinal records in which his father is described as distant, yet firm and kindly in his supervisory style. His father also used physical punishment.

there and it was a ritual. People knew that they could hit O'Brien's house for tea any day of the week. There was always tea on, same as my house now.

I think my father set an example for the way I raised my kids. I was probably more of a disciplinarian than he was. Between me and my wife, who was also a disciplinarian (my wife more so than me), we tried to know where our guys were all the time. The boys had to be in by ten o'clock. If they weren't in at five past ten, I was out looking for them, and I didn't allow them to hang around on the corners. I mean, you get those guys on the street corner, they come from all over the town down there. You get a couple of trouble makers down there, and the next thing you know you got big trouble on your hands. If they wanted to hang on my doorway, hang in the yard, fine. But not the street corner.[2]

When I was a teenager, my father went to a lot of my games. I played a lot of football, baseball, in high school, and some tournaments around here. My father didn't really know what football and baseball were. My mother and father didn't understand football, but they'd be there anyway. Of course, compared to my father, I was more heavily involved with our kids in sports, which I'm a real firm believer in. I think that burning their energy up in sports, working out, helped them develop their own traits, plus the fact that we knew where they were at all times. They played hockey, football, baseball. I worked with Little League baseball for about ten years; I ran Senior Little League for a while. I had Pete Jr. playing for me, and Andy and Kevin. I was heavily involved with baseball in those days.[3]

2. On the basis of his personal observations of children in his urban neighborhood, Pete Sr. formulated a street-wise philosophy for parenting his son that has turned out to be consistent with research findings. Glueck and Glueck (1968), in their original study of delinquent versus nondelinquent boys, found that "almost all delinquents (95.2%) were in the habit of hanging around street corners compared with 58.4% of nondelinquents" (p. 35). Subsequent research has shown that "poor parental discipline and monitoring practices" during middle childhood are among the primary factors predisposing a child to engage in delinquent behavior in adolescence (Dishion, Patterson, Stoolmiller, & Skinner, 1991). Preliminary research findings also suggest that once a child has reached adolescence, "the positive impact of parent's [authoritative] behavioral control is stronger for boys than girls" (Steinberg, Elmen, & Mounts, 1989, p. 1430).

3. Baseball seems to have generally had a special role in the lives of many post–World War II fathers and their baby boom children, judging by the expansion of Little League Baseball: from 306 leagues (with 12,000 players) in 1950, to 5,542 leagues (with 550,000 players) in 1960, to 6,432 leagues (with 1.3 million players)

Especially with sports equipment, my father probably would describe me as a spendthrift. He was always a great guy for watching
the penny, "If you watch the pennies, the dollars will take care of
themselves." He probably wouldn't like the way I spend money
(chuckle), I suppose. When my boys were kids, they got the best.
When they wanted sports equipment, they got the best. They may not
have been the best players up there, although they all held their own,
but they had the best equipment. When I go to buy, I buy the best
the first time, and it usually pays off in the long run. They had the
best bikes, the best hockey equipment, the best baseball equipment
money could buy.[4]

Both my dad and I managed people quite a bit, at work, but he had
a much bigger crew than I got. I got 30 guys over there; I'm in charge
of heating, ventilation, air conditioning. Basically, I'm an electrician
and a supervisor in charge of 30 maintenance men, all tradesmen.[5]

I work for a large medical center; it's one of the largest buildings
in the New England area. Most of my men are the greatest guys in
the world. These guys can't do enough for you; ask them something
and it's done before you turn around. I brought a lot of them into the
job out of the kitchen help. I helped them get into maintenance,
encouraged them to go to school and helped them get reimbursed. A
couple of them are fine tradesmen now. Some of them are making
twice the money they made as kitchen help. One guy was a cook in
the kitchen. He was making decent money, but he came in our place
as a general mechanic, wound up painting. I got him into a trade
school. Then he ended up over in my department and now he's my

---

in 1970 (Weller, 1991). Little League Baseball has remained popular; today there
are 7,500 leagues (with 2.5 million players); the additional growth during the last
two decades, however, is accounted for by the addition of girls' softball teams,
which were first officially fielded in 1974 (Weller, 1991).

4. From the longitudinal records, it appears that Pete Sr. and his father,
Thomas, are actually similar in this regard. Both were generous with their money,
especially with their children, but both also were able to manage their money with
sufficient skill to build up a significant "nest egg." Earlier in this interview, in fact,
Pete Sr. had described his father as generous.

5. After completing high school, Pete worked as an appliance service man and
an electrician's helper. He then became a licensed electrician, which was his
major occupation throughout his first two decades of childrearing. At midlife,
however, he was promoted to supervising foreman, replicating his own father's
job title. Pete's own father supervised more men, as he states, but Pete supervises
more highly skilled tradesmen who perform more complex tasks than those performed by the men his father supervised.

lead mechanic. He went from $18,000 in the kitchen to between $45,000 and $50,000 now as a lead mechanic. He is a hard worker.[6]

My father liked traveling, but local; my wife and I do a lot of traveling, too, but we also go further afield. When the kids were small, we went to the West Coast by car a couple times. We went to Seattle, Washington, for the World's Fair; we went down to Texas; we went to Disneyland; up over the Rockies; to Boys' Town, Nebraska. We piled the kids in the car and headed across country, would be gone for three weeks. Even now, we're always like two years ahead on our trips. We're going to Florida in October, on a cruise in February, to England next September. These things are all in the works already. I read up, and I plan way ahead on these things, and I work hard. I make a lot of money. I work hard for my money, but I spent a lot on us, on traveling, and the house, and kids.

I am basically more easygoing than my father. I don't know that he'd call me easygoing, but I can roll with the punches. I don't let myself get upset. I go for a walk by myself. I'm not stern like he was. But I think if he took a look at my family—my three boys, my two granddaughters, and my two grandsons, he'd probably feel that something went right along the way. We've got a nice family. We never had any problems with any of our kids, other than normal growing-up problems, which everybody has. I think he'd probably be pleased with the way my life turned out.

I don't think I am like my father completely. I don't think I'm as dedicated as he was. I'd like to think I am, but I don't know if it's his constitution—I wish I had it. I set three alarms in the morning to get out of bed, and I hate to get up then, but he got up with no alarm. He was a workaholic. I guess I'm a workaholic, too, but I think he was more family dedicated, oriented. He lived for his family. I live for my family, but I live for myself, too. I like to travel. I like to do things. I like to play; I don't go play ball now, but I go to games. I do a lot of things that maybe somebody might say could be a little selfish or something. I take care of myself, which my father never did. He took care of my mother and the kids. He took heart medicine for years and kept himself in good shape, but he didn't really give a hell about

---

6. As Pete describes his men, he also provides a vivid portrait of one blue-collar context of generativity. He not only monitors his men's progress; he promotes their development. Pete has also demonstrated his societal generativity by coaching athletic teams and serving on workplace and community committees.

himself. . . . I'm a lot like him, but, like I say, I am not a carbon copy of him by any means.[7]

I think my son is more like my father than I am. Because he's on top of everything, too. He's more nervous than I am. I think my father would describe himself as a little nervous because he ran so many things. He had so much on his mind. My son likes to plan things. If he's going to put a nail in there, he's going to measure it three times—unbelievable to me. I'd have that thing up and down in two minutes, and he's still studying it. Yeah, I'd say he's more like my father, than I am, because of some of his habits. He plans things well ahead and he follows through.

The Father's Earliest Memories of His Son

My earliest memory of Pete is when he was *born!* I was 25 years old; we had been married 5 years, but my wife and I had had two miscarriages before he was born. Then, when Pete was born, it was like *heaven* opened up! Ah, feeding and diapering him, and giving him all the attention!

One of my best memories of him as an infant was going for walks out in the carriage. We used to put him in the carriage and go for a walk around the town almost every night of the week. I can still picture walking with him.[8]

After waiting five years, we sure were glad to see him. Yeah. Well, we had trouble getting over the miscarriage. You wonder, when you're young, why the hell it happens, you know . . . . You're twenty years old, twenty-one, twenty-two years old, looking forward to having the kid, and you don't know why you carried for three or four months and then a miscarriage. Nobody ever had any trouble with a miscarriage, not in our family, and it's just kind of hard to accept it.

7. Pete Sr.'s modest description of his parental generativity actually parallels Erikson's emphasis: adult maturity involves attaining a favorable ratio of generativity over stagnation, not a collapse of all ego-interests toward generativity. Mature generativity requires that the scales be tipped toward care for others, but it simultaneously requires a significant degree of care for one's self.

8. Erik and Joan Erikson (1981) observed that "when you see young fathers going around holding babies in a perfectly natural and lovely way you would be tempted to say how motherly they can be" (p. 269). This was probably true of some who saw Peter Sr. strolling by with his infant son. "But," the Eriksons also tell us, "we may just as well recognize it as a paternal expression of a generative drive" (p. 269).

So, we thought his arrival was wonderful! I think it kind of changed me. I think we changed our lifestyle a little then. (Martha and I were kind of young and carefree until we started having the kids.) I started looking forward to someday they're going to go to college, going to get married, and to helping them out.[9]

Oh, he was a good kid. He did exactly what he was told. Martha could put him in the doorway, and he'd be there two hours later. He never left. He just sat there. As a young boy, I guess Pete was easygoing, but he didn't ever back down to anybody. He never backed down to a soul. Around this town, if you aren't able to hold your own, you're in trouble anyhow. He was very active in sports; always playing ball out in the streets. When he wasn't playing regulation ball, he'd be playing halfball.[10]

He went to the Boys Club, swimming a lot, basketball in the Boys Club. He was an exceptional player, no matter what he did: Midget hockey, Little League baseball, Pop Warner football.[11]

You couldn't match the guy. He had an awful desire to win. He was a competitor at all risk. He tore his knee up one day blocking a guy at home plate, and he ended up in the operating room. He was only ten years old at the time that happened. He eventually had both of his knees operated on. He was a great competitor. That made me proud of him because I was a competitor myself when I played sports. I hated to lose. I think my biggest pride in him when he was growing up was the sports he was involved in and the fact that he was a fierce competitor. He could do anything: He could pitch. He could play short, catcher. No matter where you put him, he was at home. He was just an all-around ball player. I have to say to this day, he could have been a professional ball player if he had wanted it.

He got a lot of awards, small trophies and stuff, for being an All-Star. He always got picked for the All-Star teams, and I can remember a lot of banquets we went to. Every time he got an award, he'd be ten feet tall, at least, because not every kid in this part of town got the

9. From Pete Jr.'s birth, Pete had aspirations that his son would achieve more academically than he himself had.

10. Halfball is a local variant of baseball. The father and son will explain it during their joint conversation.

11. Pop Warner Football is a youth league named after Glenn "Pop" Warner (1871–1954), a creative Hall-of-Fame coach who, having no children of his own, took a fatherly interest in all of his players (Warner, 1934). Children enter the league as Mighty Mites when they are seven to nine years old.

awards. He was very well liked, too. He was well liked by the coach. He was well liked by people who'd choose him because he's an outstanding player in different things. I think maybe we probably came to expect it of him. I was proud but not surprised. I knew.

The Son's Earliest Memories of His Father

I remember my father remodeling my bedroom on the third floor. When I was at a very young age, I remember him coming in and doing the walls over: removing the old mop boards at the base of the walls, redoing the walls with paneling, drop ceilings, and so forth. I remember, as I was watching him do it, he was banging away with a hammer and then he dropped the hammer down inside the wall. I remember he started to curse (smiling broadly). Nothing out of the ordinary; he was always doing something around the house with a hammer. I don't know why that stands out.[12]

I remember being proud of him because anything that had to be fixed, he could fix it. If something went wrong, something broke, "Don't worry, Dad's coming home, he'll take care of it." Sure enough, he'd know what was wrong and he'd fix it. The average person can't do that. He could. Whatever had to be taken care of, he was always there to take care of it. (Hell, he's still like that today.) I was proud as a peacock that he was my dad.

When I was growing up, he was a real friendly, active type of father. He always loved sports, loved me getting involved in them. He loved adventure, things that kids like too, things I liked. I'd say if there was anything you had to fault him on, you'd probably say he wasn't an early riser. He doesn't like to get up real early; I don't either. So once in a while he'd sleep a little late, and we'd be late for things.[13]

He has always had a big heart; he's a real kind guy. There's not many people who don't like him. Friends everywhere. People always have a good word to say about him, very few if anybody would say he's an S.O.B.

---

12. "First" memories and perhaps other early memories "are more than representations of the past. Very often they are metaphors for narrators' unconscious intuitions about major life motifs and about the present conditions of their lives" (Kotre, 1984, p. 143). As it will gradually become apparent, this is certainly true of the relation between Peter Jr.'s first memory and current struggles.

13. When he was late, Pete Jr. was severely reprimanded by the nuns at school.

I always remember that he wasn't one to just go out and work and let the wife take care of the kids, no. He wanted to be around us. He enjoyed his kids. He liked coming home and seeing us, talking to us, finding out what was happening with us. He'd sit down and build the model plane with you. He usually had as much fun at it as I did! So it wasn't like he was always sacrificing; it was a labor of love.

He was always the one that I could get things out of or get to and talk to and get him to give me whatever I needed. He is a softy like that; he's got a big heart.

Joint Reflections on the First Decade
Extended Family

PETE SENIOR: Well, Pete joined a big Irish family when he was born. The whole family was close; we all took care of each other.[14]

PETE JUNIOR: I remember going as a young kid with my father, over to my grandfather's house and having tea. Every night they'd sit down and they'd have tea and toast, and all my aunts would come down, my father, and my uncles. Whoever was around could do it, would go over there at ten o'clock. You never knew who was going to be there. A couple of the grandchildren, and then there would be a crowd of people having tea, every night, you know? It was a time to kibitz, talk, and catch up on what happened during the day and what's going on. It was a real social event. It was great. I miss that.

PETE SENIOR: When I was a boy, my father sometimes used to take us all down to Isaly's for ice cream. So, when we got big, he took our children, his grandkids. He was the family patriarch: he used to take 13, 15, then 18 grandchildren for Sunday morning ice cream, bought them all a cone. He handled them all by himself. How the hell he crossed the streets and stuff I'll never know.

PETE JUNIOR: I remember my grandfather pretty well; I was under his influence a lot. Every Sunday, he used to take us for ice cream after church; all the grandchildren would meet. I was four or five the first time I went. We'd meet Sundays right out front of my house. All of his sons and daughters lived in the same block. Definitely

14. Ethnicity plays a central role in the keen sense of intergenerational continuity between Thomas, Peter Sr., and Peter Jr. The grandfather, an Irish immigrant, retained a connection with Ireland and passed it on to Peter Sr., who visited Ireland with his son, and to Peter Jr., who also traveled there as an adult.

an extended family. He'd walk us right down the street to Isaly's, eventually twenty of us, for heaven's sakes, and buy us all ice creams. We did it every Sunday. It was great—I got to be with all my cousins and my grandfather. He was as proud as a peacock showing off all his grandchildren. I mean, it was unbelievable. I remember that vividly.

He was a very gentle man, very caring, and a smart man. He always took care of the family, finances, working, and stuff. I remember looking up to him. You always knew everything was going to be okay because Granddad was around. My grandfather just had this calming influence over everybody.

I see a lot of my granddad in my dad. He looks a lot like him. Like my granddad, my dad is a really hard worker. My granddad had a lot of skills, and people who knew him always tell me that he ran a quality operation, that he really knew what he was doing. My dad is a skilled craftsman and does quality work; he really knows what he is doing. Lots of other similarities: the same mannerisms, the way he handled the grandchildren, being a hard worker and good provider, taking care of the family.[15]

PETE SENIOR: My father, he's been gone 25 years. They just don't make 'em like him no more.

PETE JUNIOR: He died five days after my ninth birthday, but I remember it like it was yesterday. I was there the day he died. He died right out in the street. I was in the back yard building a model that I'd just gotten for my birthday. I was building a model plane, and I heard the ambulance. I went running out in the street and they were carting him out. He was dead then.

PETE SENIOR: When he died, about a hundred truck drivers walked behind the hearse (the custom in the old days) from St. Margaret's church to the square near our house. He was right well liked. We waked him at home, and about three or four in the morning, knocks on the door were road drivers coming in from New York, New Jersey, to the wake to see him. He was that well liked.

PETE JUNIOR: I remember they waked him in the house. (Talk about Old Irish.) They don't do that any more. (We didn't wake my

15. The three-generation parallels are obvious but powerful: Peter Sr. admires and values the parental and societal generativity of his own father, Thomas, whom he tends to see in heroic terms. Pete Jr. admires and values the work of his father and grandfather, both of whom provided Pete Jr. with models of exemplary adulthood.

grandmother.) We waked him in the house. Geez, my aunts, my uncles, they were heartbroken when he died. I just remember them. When you wake someone in the house, it's a 24-hour wake. It was long. Some are out in the living room, crying. One house, you know? So we'd be sitting in the back of the house where the kitchen and dining room were, having tea or eating, trying to get through the night, and the front was where the wake was, and my uncles were all up there. Very emotional time. I remember it like it was yesterday.[16]

Childcare Activities

PETE JUNIOR: When I was a boy, my mother worked part time, nights, so he'd come home from working all day, and she'd go out to work nights. He'd be home with us, taking care of the family—doing house stuff and playing with us.

PETE SENIOR: She worked from six to ten at night and I was working days. So I'd be at home and have the kids. When they were young, we used to play soldiers and stuff like that. The boys were always playing soldiers. (You know, I made them lead soldiers, and then when they got older they learned to pour the lead molds and make more little soldiers.) Other nights I would be with the kids at the park, or at the playground, or in the yard. I made sure they were in the house on time, and in bed on time.

PETE JUNIOR: We played a lot of games at the kitchen table.

PETE SENIOR: Different board games, Monopoly and all that stuff, when they were old enough. We also had trains set up around the house. I think that I was probably a little closer to them then but, of course, one of us was always there. Martha was always a good mother; she played a lot of house games with the boys during the day.

PETE JUNIOR: Her job really made it financially possible for us to travel every year, unlike most of the people in the neighborhood.

Family Trips

PETE SENIOR: We did a lot of traveling across country. We went to Florida two or three times. I think '55 was the first year we went

16. I have observed that when men talk seriously about childrearing, they tend to include as many stories of deaths as they do of births. Perhaps, as Kotre (1984) has remarked, this "should come as no surprise, for the turnover of generations is accomplished by death as well as by birth" (p. 112).

down there, when Pete was a baby. We put the crib in the back seat and took him along with us.

PETE JUNIOR: I remember as a young kid sitting in the back seat of the car all the time and driving through endless fields of corn in Nebraska, and all throughout the whole country. I remember reading books and talking, and talking sports, and maybe having an argument here or there.[17]

PETE SENIOR: Right. When we traveled cross country, we had some arguments. But we also became close . . . A lot of trips stand out in my mind. We went to the Grand Canyon; saw the Rocky Mountains. We went to Disneyland. We went to the Seattle World's Fair. Pete went to Ireland a couple of times with me when he was small, and he's been to Ireland on his own since then.

PETE JUNIOR: Those trips were tremendous.

PETE SENIOR: We had a lot of fun. I think we all enjoyed them. The kids got used to traveling. They saw things that a lot of the other kids in this part of town will never see, never see them even today.

PETE JUNIOR: I remember all that when I was a kid. We went around the country two or three times, I'd say. I remember coming back all the time and going to grammar school and talking about what you did for the summer. "I went to Ireland!" I always had the best stories to talk about, traveling and all. The kids used to look at me, and I felt very fortunate that I was able to travel.

PETE SENIOR: Driving is a great way to see the country: California, Washington, New Mexico, Florida. You learn things; like he said. We saw the corn fields in Nebraska and Iowa! Who would intentionally go to see corn fields? You had to see them nevertheless, they were part of the country. The Rocky Mountains were gorgeous. The Grand Canyon; we went down there and watched the sunset and then we woke up early and went to the canyon wall to watch the sunrise. We stayed at a nice motel near the edge. Texas, we went through Texas. The arch of St. Louis. Seattle and the World's Fair. We just like traveling.

PETE JUNIOR: I remember one time when we went down to North

17. Like sports, travel can be an activity which allows parents to be involved in every aspect of their child's development. Being together in close quarters for extended periods of time provides opportunities for talking and listening, for perfecting methods of conflict resolution, and for sharing experiences which will form unusually vivid memories that have the power to intensify existing bonds.

Carolina. Remember we went down to Sliding Rock, down there in a place called, I think, it's Transylvania? Is that right?

PETE SENIOR: Yep, that's it. Sliding Rock. We stopped down there. Stripped the bottoms off our bathing suits sliding down it! (laughter).

PETE JUNIOR: Sure, we had great times down there. I remember us going down the rock, and the next thing I know, we're all running around with our fannies showing through big holes in our bathing suits (laughter).

PETE SENIOR: Yep. Two or three rides down there, and your bathing suit was no good anyhow. We would slide down there, and like he said, we had a lot of fun.

PETE JUNIOR: Right, right. It was a great experience. It was a lot of fun. I miss those days. I looked forward to the summer every year. We always went someplace nice.

PETE SENIOR: We were very close, literally, living in a hotel room. It's close quarters and (chuckles) so you learn to get along. All of us, Martha and myself included, also saw things we probably never hoped to see. I still love to travel. I travel every year if I can.

PETE JUNIOR: I do too. Every year.

Baseball Encouragement

PETE SENIOR: I was still playing ball when Pete was a little kid. We played semi-pro softball; I was a catcher. His mother used to bring him over to see me play ball. Then, when he got a little older, I was *his* catcher.

PETE JUNIOR: I have a lot of memories of my father when I was practicing for Little League.

PETE SENIOR: I was catcher all the time . . .

PETE JUNIOR: . . . and I used to pitch. He used to come out, after working all day, to catch me for an hour or two. Then, I expected it.

I think about it today: after he worked all day, to come out and catch me for an hour or two. I can remember going out there for hours and pitching to him. It's amazing how he did it; I mean, I know I'm tired when I finish working a full day.

PETE SENIOR: I enjoyed catching for him.

PETE JUNIOR: He was always encouraging me. He tried to instill a lot of confidence in me. I had confidence, but I didn't have as much as you'd like to see a young athlete have in order to try to excel as much as he can. Confidence is a big thing in athletics, a main thing, especially at a young age. I was always unsure as a young kid, and he was always trying to boost my confidence. He never criticized me. Some times, he'd tell me how to do things a little better, and I always listened. I remember that vividly: playing baseball, and he'd be out there catching; playing football, and he'd be out there throwing the ball around. Sports; that was a big connection; sports and traveling.

School Problems

PETE JUNIOR: I didn't like grammar school. I just hated school. The school was run by nuns, by the way. I was sort of a lazy kid in grammar school. I wanted to go out and play ball. I wasn't very enthusiastic about school, mainly because of the nuns. The nuns were very detrimental to me. I was often late for school, so they humiliated me. I still remember many experiences when they humiliated me. They would stand me in front of people and destroy me psychologically and talk about keeping me back.

I told my parents that I did not want to go any more. "I want to quit. I hate this world." They didn't know what was going on, so they went to the nuns to get help. When the nuns found out that I had complained to my parents, I got humiliated again. It was really bizarre. They should have talked to me about my feelings, but they just humiliated me. I *hated* grammar school. I couldn't stand it. Remember how I used to try and stay home all the time?

PETE SENIOR: Pretending to be sick?

PETE JUNIOR: Yeah. Sick, or I didn't feel good, or whatever. Once in a while I used to sneak down to the cellar, remember, Dad?

PETE SENIOR: (chuckles) You see, he went to St. Margaret's. The nuns were tough. They were tough teachers. Their reputation was tough. Plus, they were Catholic nuns and you were a Catholic kid from a Catholic family. You had no choice anyhow. A few of the nuns would whack you around with a ruler or a stick or anything else.

PETE JUNIOR: My parents were pretty upset. My mother was more angry and mad. My father was never really that angry, but he was upset. He tried to talk to me about it, tried to rationalize things with me. My mother was the emotional one. He understood why I hated it. He explained that it was something I had to do. I had to go and couldn't get out of it. I didn't like it. He used to sit down and talk to me and tell me it was something you got to do, you know, got to make it through school, make good grades, and whatever. That was that.

I also remember that whenever I'd come home from school with a 100%, or a sticker, or stars on my work, he'd say, "Oh, that's great!" Pat me on the back, give me strokes. He'd verbally do that for me.

PETE SENIOR: I also remember the day I took you out of school and we took off to go get a Christmas tree (both laugh). First, we went to the pancake house, up on Route One. It cost me about ten dollars for breakfast. We drove all the way up to New Hampshire, to maybe three different tree farms. They were either closed or they didn't have anything worth buying. The pick was gone. It was way up in the boonies too. Then on the way back, we went into a skid. I can still remember the driveway coming down from a lady's house. I went right up, skidded right up some lady's driveway. We almost got in an accident (joint laughter). We came all the way back and stopped at the Valley Diner and had dinner. We *still* didn't have a tree. We ended up in the neighborhood market buying a tree for thirty bucks or something (all laugh). Which we should have done in the first place. The day cost me about a hundred dollar bill. I don't think I ever told my wife!

PETE JUNIOR: (Turns to father.) Occasionally, not often, but once in a while, you used to take me with you to work, too. Remember?

PETE SENIOR: Yeah. You would go on service calls with me.

PETE JUNIOR: "Out sick for the day." We had some good times when he got me out of school and took me with him. We'd go out and pick up his parts in the morning and go on the call. I'd hand him tools and help him. I liked that much better than I liked going to school. I really enjoyed just seeing what he was doing, being with him. I didn't like the idea of sitting in a classroom, listening to these nuns. I'd rather be with him.[18]

Joint Reflections on the Second Decade

PETE SENIOR: Things did get better eventually.

PETE JUNIOR: They had a few good teachers. My seventh grade

18. Perhaps because of his own school experiences, Pete seemed to understand that Pete Jr. needed to get away from school occasionally. The hooky episodes may have also functioned, however, to give Pete Jr. a double message. His father told him, verbally, to go to college and not be a worker like him, but, nonverbally, he may have communicated that he would be proud if Pete Jr. became a skilled

teacher was a regular guy. He was a good influence. He came out and played ball with us. He was my first male teacher, and I could identify with him. Anyway, he was a person you could really talk to.

Then, my eighth grade teacher was exceptional. She was fantastic. A good person. She built your ego up—positive, positive, positive, all the time—she encouraged me to go to Catholic Latin High School, which is a very good college prep school. She told my parents that I could do it if I wanted to. I was smart, I had the ability, but I was just a little bit lazy. She encouraged me to see that I had the ability. So I had a choice in the eighth grade, and I decided that I really wanted to go to CL.

Family Financial Responsibilities

PETE JUNIOR: I think my being a teenager affected my father's work life. The financial burden was there. He had my tuition. I was at an expensive high school. Then there was college tuition coming up, he had car payments, trying to fix the house up (back then, we gutted the house out on the second floor). So he felt the financial burden. My mother also worked full time, days, when I was older, to increase the family income.[19]

PETE SENIOR: Yeah, later on she went to working full days when the kids were in high school.

PETE JUNIOR: My parents had a few arguments over me and all of us. There was a conflict between trying to make the financial commitments (like tuition payments) and wanting to remodel the house. My mother wanted the house done, but he didn't want to get a big contractor and have to pay big money. He wanted to just do it himself. So it never got done; it *still* isn't finished.

PETE SENIOR: Yeah, the first floor is gutted right now.[20]

---

blue-collar worker like him. While this is pure speculation, it is consistent with the tensions that Pete Jr. later experienced.

19. Pete's wife, Martha, worked part time during Pete Jr.'s childhood and full time during his adolescence. Her job as a clerk carried important bookkeeping responsibilities. This gave Pete Sr. the chance to have sole responsibility for the children at night and to instill in them an appreciation for sex-role flexibility.

20. As interviewers have noted, it seems to be part of his father's charm that at literally every interview time during Pete O'Brien's participation in the study as an adult, the interviewer assigned to visit him observed that some portion of his home was in the process of being remodeled. He apparently began by remodeling the floor of their original apartment during the years before he and his wife had a successful pregnancy and, subsequently, "doing the house" has literally spanned decades.

Father-Son Sports Participation

PETE JUNIOR: During the early teen years, when I was playing in the street, he would come out and play halfball with us. We'd go right around the side of the house and play, right?

PETE SENIOR: Oh, we'd play for hours. Halfball is a unique game around here. You cut a pimple ball in half and you scale it, and you hit it with a broomstick.

PETE JUNIOR: A pimple ball is a little rubber white ball with these little pimples on it.

PETE SENIOR: Yeah. You cut it in half with a razor blade to make it nice and neat and you try to hit it with a broomstick. You play it off a wall. The Halfball Tournament made national TV for a while, "The World Series in Halfball." In a tournament they had on TV, he hit a single or a double, and a home run.

PETE JUNIOR: Halfball was invented here. They still play it today.

PETE SENIOR: Still a great game. Not only that, it gives a kid great coordination for hitting a baseball. If you can hit a halfball, you can hit a baseball.

PETE JUNIOR: He also coached baseball—Senior Little League during my early teenage years. I played all through Little League, and then I went on to Senior Little League. He coached a team, and naturally I played for him. We won the District Championship a couple of times. He was always helping other kids and coaching them and trying to teach other kids, always good like that. Then he would take me and the other kids out afterwards. "Let's go for an ice cream" or something.

PETE SENIOR: Yeah. When our team got something, I'd take his whole team down and buy them pizza and a Coke on a Saturday noon, or something like that.[21]

Philosophy of Raising Teenagers

PETE SENIOR: Also, I don't know what the worst years are in terms of bringing kids up (they talk about the terrible twos), but my

21. In this discussion of Pete's parental and societal generativity, there is perhaps a parallel between his Saturday trips with a group of his players for pizza and his own father's Sunday trips with a group of his children and later grandchildren for ice cream. These outings served to communicate to the children that they and their efforts were valued.

whole theory in life is you got to control them in the early teenage years—13, 14, 15. If you didn't control them then, you've lost them. I've seen this happen around my neighborhood. I've seen teenagers who are in jail today because their mother and father never knew where the hell they were. These are the rebellion years; they're the years they tell you they might want to take you on or they might feel you're an old-timer or you're being old-fashioned, or something. They're the years they're going to get involved with bad gangs. They're going to get involved in trouble. Some of my friends' kids, today, are still in jail doing time, serious time, and yet when they were that age they were running around ten, eleven o'clock at night. They were out in the streets drinking beer and everything else, and my kids weren't. I made damn sure they weren't. I'm not saying they didn't sneak a beer once in a while.

PETE JUNIOR: (Laughs.) I'll never forget the first time he found me drinking. Boy, he scared the hell out of me. He threatened to put the strap to me for a bit, and then walked me around the house and around the street. I think I thought he was going to kill me. I was about 13 or 14; you grow up quick around here. I never will forget that. I've never seen him that mad, ever before and never again since. Whew! I didn't drink for a long time after that, even though my friends were still doing it all the time.

I never really got into much trouble, but, I think my mischief created the fear that I might get into a little more trouble than I had bargained for. In this neighborhood, a lot of kids crossed the line from mischief to crime. One of my best boyhood friends ended up in jail for years; a lot of my old friends got into major trouble. I changed friends at about age 13 . . . My new friends, they were all athletes too, we still got into fights and mischief, but we never took it a step further. But a lot of my old friends did. They started doing crime, and some of them ended up in jail. I didn't take that path because I could see what was coming. Depending on your perspective, I wasn't stupid or crazy enough or I didn't have enough guts to do it. Plus, I really didn't want to hurt my father and mother. I just didn't have it in me to hurt my family.

College Prep School

PETE SENIOR: He went to Catholic Latin High School, which was roughly ten miles away from us. He traveled by train every day;

it was an hour to and an hour back. That school was also very tough; they were tough on marks and loaded them with homework. (He didn't like homework, of course.) And he also always had practice: football practice, or hockey practice, or baseball practice; the nights he didn't have practice, he had a game. During baseball and football season, he left at six in the morning and he didn't get home until seven at night. So we didn't see as much of him.

PETE JUNIOR: He told me I could go to any high school I wanted to go to. He would pay. He also helped to finance my college education, and he would have helped more if I wanted him to. I grew up with him telling me that I would never do the kind of work that he is doing. Sometimes I regret it because there are things that I don't know how to do. But he pushed education. He didn't want me to be a worker, with his hands, like he had to do. He saw education as the gateway to success and really encouraged me to be educated, to meet college people, to go to college.

PETE SENIOR: I encouraged him, but I wasn't really that involved in the homework side of things. Yet, he knew how we felt about education. We sent them all to private high schools. From day one we planned for them all to go to Catholic prep schools.

PETE JUNIOR: When I went to high school, I became more aware of people from different economic backgrounds because—well, I went to elementary school here. This is basically a working class community; my Dad is a *skilled* craftsman. But my high school was basically an academic school, and there were kids from other neighborhoods. Most people in this town are civil servants: firemen, policemen. I went to Catholic Latin High School, which is a college prep school. Kids were from all over the city, and I got to see kids from all the suburbs, exclusive areas, and so forth. I went over to their houses and saw how they lived, and that was the first time I got a feel for the class structure.

I am a very proud person. Most people from this part of town are proud. At times I was bitter, at times I was jealous, at times I was happy for them. But I was always proud. You know, act tough, be tough; growing up around here is not easy on the streets, even though it was also a lot of fun. Anyway, people from the suburbs also respected me because I was from this part of town. People from here are supposed to be tough, so that was basically my façade, how I dealt with my negative feelings about them. I wished I had what they did, but, when I was 14 or 15, I didn't admit it at all.

Father-Son Sports' Memories:
Hockey, Baseball, Football

PETE JUNIOR: My neighborhood hockey team played for the National Hockey Championship out in Minnesota, at about that time. He and my mother flew out to watch me.

PETE SENIOR: Oh, that was really something. He was about 15 or 16. The kids won the Midget Title unexpectedly. (We had all the different divisions in amateur hockey: Mites, Bantam, Midget. The Midgets are the older kids.) We played Crestwood Vale up there for the New England Midget Championship. We were expected to lose, naturally. The Crestwood Vale's team even had all the buses ready to go from that night's game out for the National Championship playoffs. It was like a nine or ten o'clock game at night at Crestwood Vale, and they had the buses outside, marked "Minnesota-bound," figuring they were going to take the Crestwood Vale team out there. Well, they did their best to beat us. They had us down to three men in the last two minutes: my Peter and the defense men, Patrick O'Neill's and Jim Martin's kids (all three of them had played hockey together as they grew up). Crestwood Vale had five on three the last two minutes. Even then, you know, they still couldn't beat us. We beat them.

We almost had to fight our way out of there. It was an angry mob up there—an all-Crestwood crowd. Thank God the cops were there.

PETE JUNIOR: The entire team consisted of 15 guys from one square mile from this part of town. We played for the New England Championship; we were never expected to win but we won it. We won it, 2 to 1; it was a great game. Then the whole town raised all kinds of money to fly the entire team out to play the National Championship. My parents flew out.

PETE SENIOR: Yeah. We took Andy and Pete, and went out there. The kids played some tough games out there. Pete was a hell of a hockey player. He was tough as nails, and big and strong. We didn't win the Championship, but we came in second or third.

PETE JUNIOR: It was a great experience to play for the Championship. We went 2 and 2 up there. That is a great memory. This part of Boston is a great hockey town; it was a real close-knit community and they really stood behind us. We had a great time out there.

PETE SENIOR: We had a bunch of guys for chaperons: Father Kelly was the spiritual leader. We had a hell of a weekend out there:

we took them sight-seeing, and they played a lot of hockey on the weekend, and stayed at a nice motel. We had three or four rental station wagons, and chauffeured them around. It was a really good weekend.

PETE JUNIOR: We still practiced baseball together, too. He still caught for me.

PETE SENIOR: Until he got too fast for me! Later he got too fast for me and then I couldn't catch no more. I tried to bounce them off my knees. I used to try to catch them all even . . .

PETE JUNIOR: . . . even on the sidewalk . . .

PETE SENIOR: I caught all my life, too. But he could play any position. He could play any place you put him. But, all my life, catching was my favorite position and I used to try to catch him. Then, like I say, as he got older he got a little too fast for me. I'd be kind of ducking them. It was time to quit then (chuckles).

PETE JUNIOR: During later adolescence, as I played a lot more ball, he came to more sporting events to watch me. From age 15 on he was more of a spectator at my games. He made time to go see me play sports. It was important to me, it was important to him. He'd always go to my baseball games, football games in high school and college, and hockey games in high school. Then I played semi-pro hockey for a while; he always made time to go to as many as he could. It was great; he was always involved. Like I'd say, "Dad, I need a ride to Melrose to go to a game tonight at eight, can you do it?" "Ah, yeah, I'll do it." So six guys would go in the car, you know, and he'd watch the hockey game on a July night in the summertime, you know?[22]

PETE SENIOR: Many nights I dragged my wife down to a game. Even if we would rather be home watching TV or down in the yard working, we got our fannies down there for the game. We were down there watching those games. We always enjoyed watching Pete and our other children play, but who the hell wants to go to watch hockey when it's two o'clock in the morning? Sometimes you had to when they played at two o'clock in the morning. You drive them there,

22. Even when Pete Jr. was separating from his family during adolescence, his father was able to use sports to stay connected with him. Being in the stands and seeing Pete Jr.'s experiences on the field as they happened must have functioned to help keep the communication lines open. Frequently, what being a good father comes down to in various situations is maintaining good father-child communication, a principle that is also stressed in the more father-helpful "how to" books on parenting (Biller & Meredith, 1974; Levant & Kelly, 1989; Lickona, 1983).

watch them, and bring them back. It was just a part of our life together.[23]

PETE JUNIOR: He and my mother also used to come and visit me when I was playing college football. That was a big social event—coming for a weekend football game, usually. They usually came once during the spring, too.

I remember one time that he, my uncle, one of my little brothers, and one of my uncle's sons came out to Notre Dame. They watched the game, and then we all went out on the town to eat. We had a real nice time, just spending time together and joking around. (We're a family of pranksters; we're always joking around.) Just being together—nothing special, but it really made me feel happy. It made me feel wanted and cared for, you know. It was important for me to have my father come to see me play, to be around him. He was proud of me, and it made me proud to have him there. (Especially if I had a good game.) I played well for him; naturally, I played with a little more emotion, hit a little harder, if I knew my father was watching.[24]

PETE SENIOR: Yeah, we used to go and watch him play college football. Freeze our fannies off, sitting there, watching the game. We took them out to dinner at a barbecue mansion, stuff like that. My wife went out once or twice, most of the time the trip was too much, because of little Kevin, you know, lugging him with us. So, I went out and watched him play a few games. Probably we made three trips in a season, from September to June. Then he'd come home, you know.

Academic Ambivalence and Success

PETE JUNIOR: My first year at college got my credits doing very little; I managed to get anywhere from a D– in Theology to an A in Classic Sociological Theory. I did next to nothing in most courses. I wanted to transfer back here. I wasn't studying; I was playing football and partying and chasing girls—everything but what I should have been doing. He didn't want me to come home. It was important for

23. Pete Sr. often refers to his wife in his conversation, and his longitudinal records confirm that his marital affinity or commitment has been continuous throughout their marriage, despite having their share of disagreements.

24. By playing college football, Pete Jr. was doing what his father had passed up.

him for me to graduate from Notre Dame. I started valuing it later on, but I didn't at the time.

I had a lot of doubts when I was going through college: was it really for me, was I smart enough to do it? Finally, I went to a lot of encounter group sessions that helped me to get my head in shape. I decided I wanted to prove to myself that I could do it. So I went every day, I didn't miss a class. I worked hard. I never applied myself prior to that. I took a lot of tough courses and I passed them.[25]

I really put my nose to the grindstone, I was elected to a national honors society. I graduated. My father was so proud of me the day I graduated from college, he was as proud as he could be. Geez, he was proud of me.[26]

PETE SENIOR: Once he got his priorities straight, he seemed to do well in school . . . We all went out for the graduation and spent the week out there.

PETE JUNIOR: When doing my master's degree, I had more confidence in my potential but I still had to prove something to myself.[27]

Current Reflections

The Father's Perspective

I think we wanted our son to have success in life. My wife and me were hell-bent on college education for all of them. (My wife felt that

25. Pete Jr.'s college transcript bears out his testimony. During his freshman and sophomore years he received an A in two courses in his major, but otherwise he received straight D grades. During his junior year, however, he received an A in 24 of his 36 course credit hours (most of which were in upper-level philosophy, sociology, or political science courses), although Ds still accounted for his other grades (most of which were outside his major). Of course, despite his dramatic turnaround, his grades were still completely polarized: he received either an A or a D in every single course (while never failing a single course). During his senior year, however, Pete was less ambivalent and his grades were less polarized. At the end of his last year he was elected to a prestigious honors society.

26. For Peter Sr., as for many other fathers, parental generativity was more central than career success or creativity in his midlife expression of generativity. As Erikson and his colleagues remind us (1986), economic or social conditions often make it "difficult or even impossible for many [parents] to pursue their own educational and professional goals while raising families" (p. 82). Thus it is understandable that they will "reconcile facets of their own generativity by taking overwhelming pride in their children's academic . . . and professional accomplishments" (p. 82).

27. His graduate school records shows that he was an outstanding student who graduated with a 3.7 grade point average.

way from the day we got married.) The two of us never went to college.
I had a chance to go on a football scholarship down in Georgia, but
I never took them up on it. At least we were going to help our boys
go if they wanted to have a good education.[28]

And we wanted to see them happily married and growing up in a
family, and a little bit of financial success, if it's possible. They all
seem to be doing well so far. Pete's doing well, and so are his two
brothers. We just made sure they went to good schools. We made
sure they did their homework. We went to the PTA meetings, and all
that stuff with them. But, when they got older, I didn't sit down at
night at the table with them. I wouldn't know half the homework
anyhow, to be truthful with you (chuckles). I would have liked to sit
down and say, "Are you getting the most out of this?" or "What are
you getting out of this?" I don't think I've ever done that. I put their
report cards out, I looked at their papers occasionally, but Martha did
most of that kind of work.

I took Pete with me on jobs and stuff a few times. He showed some
talent but not a lot of interest at that time. My wife used to get mad
that I didn't take the kids on jobs with me, but I wouldn't take them
away from sports in order to take them with me. The kids would rather
be out playing hockey or hardball or doing something on the street.
They never showed an interest to learn a trade until more recently.

Even now, Pete went to school last year to study carpentry. He
worked this summer with a contractor in his time off from school
teaching, worked damn near all summer with this guy in a whole new

28. As Pete Sr. notes, his and his wife's educational histories are relevant here.
Martha attended the same high school as her husband through the 11th grade,
when she apparently dropped out of school. She later returned and completed her
GED high school diploma. Pete Sr. also had his school difficulties. During junior
high school he had been tracked into the noncollege course sequence (although
his IQ was far above average). When asked at age 25 about his frustrations or
dissatisfactions, he still recalled his regret that his junior-high principal had not
allowed him to enter the college preparatory course. This barrier was apparently
not insurmountable, however, in that he gained admission to the University of
Georgia on an athletic scholarship. At age 25 Pete Sr. said that he was still
interested in going to college and "getting a degree in electrical engineering" but
that he "felt" that his "family could not send him." During that same interview,
he also noted that his father was "strong for education and would be willing to
give me the money to go to college today if I wanted to." He was never clear why
he "never took them up" on his apparent opportunity to attend college, but the
implication was that he was giving priority to staying with his family, to marrying
his high school sweetheart, and to starting his own family.

field until he went on his honeymoon. I consider myself a carpenter, too, I guess, but he went to school over at McCutchan to learn the trade. He took two or three courses over there, and now he's putting it to use; so he's got another field going, which will give him summer employment, and maybe some day even start his own contracting business.

Pete is working with carpentry now, and he's going to be working downstairs; we tore the whole four rooms out. But, I had a serious heart attack and pneumonia and stuff, and right now I ain't able to work. I'm dying to get working again, but I've got to pace myself a lot different now. I never finished this house in all the years I've been here. I get started, and then I rip out something else, and I put something in and change it around, and I'm like that anyhow, but I enjoy that work a lot.

Well, I don't know why Pete has been so successful. I would like to think that maybe I set an example—I'm a hard worker. I worked hard all my life. I worked something like my father. Whenever I'm not working at work, I'm working at home. He's helped me remodel from the days when he was four years old. I tore this house apart. I built a homemade slide in there for him. He was like four, five years old. I'd be tearing down plaster walls. He'd be in there with me. He didn't do that much that young, but he'd be there with me, and he could swing a hammer when he was a little kid same as I could. Pete enjoys, even now, this job we're tackling. We were always doing something, you know.

I think the most important thing for a father to do is to maintain the father position and still be close to them, but eliminating this buddy-buddy, which I've seen a lot in my town. I try to impress on them, "I'm still your father, I ain't your buddy." If I can be your father and friend, I'm your father and friend, but I ain't your buddy. You're still their father, you still must earn their respect. I like to think that over the years that I've earned their respect and friendship.

I'm well pleased with him! He's done real well. There aren't too many from our town who are living where he is living or doing what he is doing. He helps others, he is the guidance director at Core City High School.[29] He knows how to handle money a lot better than I do.

29. Pete Jr., his father, and his grandfather, Thomas, represent three generations of men who helped other people: Thomas helped his neighbors in his Irish community, especially during the Depression; Pete Sr. helped his "neighbors" in

I won't say he's thrifty, but he knows how to handle his money well; he lives within his means. He's got a lovely wife, Molly, who is also a local girl; a pretty girl, a real nice woman.

I believed that each of my three sons needed or deserved guidance, and direction, and someone they could relate to. I wanted that for my family. I was brought up with my father knowing where we were, and we knew where they were in turn. So I just made sure I was around when my kids needed me; if they didn't need me, I was around *anyhow*.

When my son becomes a father, I hope he'll be the same way. I'd like him to know where his kids are at all times. I hope he takes time out to smell the roses along the way with his kids. You can't just let the kids grow up without you because one day they're going to wonder, "Who are you?" You got to be on top of their situation, you got to be with them, you got to grow up with them, you got to always spend time with them. You won't come this way a second time . . .

I have no regrets in my life. I wouldn't change my life one minute. If I lived all over again, I don't know what I would do different. We were close to them; I like to think we're still close.

The Son's Perspective

My father always encouraged me to be the best I could be. He always told me to never quit anything I have started. "No one's better than you," that type of thing. My mother always encouraged me as well, in the same ways. They worked together. Beyond that, I am also pretty competitive. I have that competitive spirit; I hate to lose anything. So I have had the encouragement and I have a drive, in that sense, to be successful.

I think just the respect I have had for him, for being the type of person that he is, made me always want to do as well. I guess the values and virtues he had and the way he conducted himself was an example for me. I don't want to let him down.

I think my father was able to stay with me through my ups and downs and rough passages. As I went through the different phases of development, he adjusted with me. Like I mentioned, I remember the

---

the kitchen at his place of employment to get ahead; and Pete Jr. helps working-class high school youth become upwardly mobile. Curiously, Pete Jr. also became the good guidance counselor that his father regretted not having had in school (see prior note).

first time I came home with booze on my breath: It shook him up a little bit, but it also opened his eyes a little bit. He stayed in touch with what I was up to.

My dad was a realist, too. He didn't believe me when I didn't think I could do it. I could never pull any wool over my dad's eyes. He knew what was happening, he knew the score, and he was always encouraging me.

I think he wanted me to be the most I could be, to get the most out of myself. I think he saw himself with a lot of potential, but hadn't taken advantage of it. He taught me to take advantage of a lot of things that he could have. He could have been pretty well off today if he had done things a little bit more aggressively or did things that he put off because of things I already explained to you. I think he wanted me to take my abilities and my whatever and apply myself, which I never did in school. He just wanted me to be successful and to get what I wanted. Education was seen as the key to both personal fulfillment and economic gain.

I am like him; very much so. Like, my father always takes on other people's problems; he has a big heart. He tries to be the person who deals with problems in a level-headed way. He doesn't lose his cool, he stays rational about himself. Also, he is always ready to take on a new challenge. He was a good athlete. A hard worker. Not many people dislike him. I feel like I am similar to him in all those ways. Maybe I take on too much of a burden. (I worry about everyone's problems, I worry about everything too much.) Maybe there are a couple of people I have alienated over the years (laughter), but I am fortunate to have some pretty good friends. I'd like to think I am somewhat the same way as him.

I just wish I had more knowledge of tools, and the trades, like he does. I am trying to get like that. I should have done it when I was younger, but I was too busy playing ball to learn that. He would want me to work with him but he wouldn't want me to work with him, if you know what I mean. He would never make me work with him. He knew I'd rather be with my friends, he knew I'd rather be out playing baseball, hockey, football, or something, and so he did it himself. He sacrificed for me that way. As I look back, I wish I had been told to do it or made to do it.

I would say, when I was captain of the high school football team, he was especially proud of that. He was proud when we played in the state championship—we lost, but he was proud; he was proud when we played in the national championship in hockey; in baseball, the All-Star team; any accomplishment. He has taken pride in anything I've ever done: I got a college degree, regardless of what I did, I never flunked out of school; I got the master's; I became Director of Guidance at the high school; I am also a high-school coach. He's proud of any accomplishments that I've made. It makes him proud to know that his kid has succeeded.

Some of my friends tease me; they call me a "lifer." They assume that I'll be a guidance counselor forever. I don't really know if that is true. If I could afford to do it forever, I probably would. I love working with the kids. I think if I had a better guidance counselor, you know, I would have done better earlier. I have seen that talking with a guidance counselor can really help a person; I have seen it influence kids, motivate kids, give them relief by providing an opportunity to get things off their chest. They know they can come in and talk, come in and cry, come in and laugh. But the salaries in education are abhorrent. The salaries are disgusting.

My father always pushed me towards education because he wanted me to go to college and get the white collar job and not kill myself. But I wish today I had worked with the tools and knew a little more than I know. He worked on his hands and knees—fixing dishwashers and disposals and washing machines and all kinds of other appliances—and he didn't want me doing that. I used to see him bending over there and trying to fix this and fix that. My dad is a jack of all trades. Well, I am trying to develop that.[30]

The Son Looks Ahead a Generation

I just got married and so I have been giving some thought to becoming a father. I'll work to meet the challenge. There's a lot of things that

30. Peter Jr. was originally attracted to counseling working-class high school students because, in helping those who were in a position in which he once was, he was able to maintain a significant degree of continuity with his past. Although he receives many benefits from this altruistic orientation to his work, it seems especially unfortunate that his job pays so poorly, at least compared to the income of blue-collar aristocrats like his father. Peter's choice of a second line of work (a blue-collar trade) is also one that will function to ward off a divided ego by providing a reasonable degree of continuity between who he was as a boy and who he is as an adult (Sennett & Cobb, 1972).

are going on now that were different when I was a kid. I think, no matter what, you're going to have a new role, fatherhood. You have a son that's yours and you'd have to deal with him, but you still have your own father and he'll always be my father. In some basic sense, I don't think our relationship will change. It'd be just another thing to deal with: my father will be his grandfather; my kid will be his grandson.[31]

I hope I can be as good a father as he's been. I hope my children get to know and enjoy him and my mother for a long time. There are probably a thousand things I'll do the same. I hope I can take as many trips and take my kids places and buy them things and show them the love and affection and the care that he's given me—support and encouragement. As a kid you take it but you don't appreciate it till later on, until after you're older.

Of course, I might not send my kids to a Catholic grammar school (laughs). I'll also value open communication more than my father did, communication of feelings. I will hug my kid. I will always hug him. I think I will go out of my way to do things like that. I will value that type of communion. That openness. That is something that I am going to try my best to do.

Feelings are very important because, if you have an understanding of your son's feelings, you are going to begin to understand him as a person. People actually strive to communicate their feelings all the time; it is a need; it is an imperative.

You know, he's never told me he loves me; I've never told him I love him. I never go around hugging my father or tell him I love him; we haven't done that in years. That's just not the way he is. That's just something we don't do, but it's there; the feelings are just pouring out. It's shown in other ways. It's funny, I don't know if it is the Irish-Catholic background, or the working-class background, or what. I don't know what the hell it is, but that's the way it is. Something I plan on doing is outwardly showing my affection to my kids, hugging and kissing, and telling them that I love each one. We don't do that.

Right now, of course, my biggest concern is my father's health. I

31. Pete Jr. leaves little doubt about his preference regarding his first-born child's gender. Equally notable, however, he himself has no doubt that he wants to be a childrearing father, just the way his father was with him. He does speak of some reworking, however, as he wants his relationship with his "son" to be more affectionate, less stereotypically masculine.

want him here forever. I don't ever want him to leave (misty-eyed). In the hospital recently, when I thought he was dying, I told him that I loved him. Just squeezed his hand. He smiled, nodded. He had tubes in his nose and down his throat, pacemaker in his chest, breathing apparatus, the whole intensive-care works. But he accepted it. It's so important to be able to do that. It's something that's always hurt me. But I know it's there in other ways. It's there, no question about it. My father is a hard-working, sensitive, loving-in-his-own-way person.

There is another important thing for a father to do: to make sure you finish what you started on the house (laughter). That's also why I took the builder's courses and am getting the builder's license. Because I want to finish the house. Other reasons why I did it—self-fulfillment, I always wanted to learn how to do those things. But also, deep down inside, I knew I was going to carry the ball and provide some of the labor and skills to see that the house was eventually finished.[32]

I've already started and it will get done. I have the skill to do it now. I don't need my father to do it for me or tell me how to do it. I can do it myself.[33]

Concluding Query

The story of Pete Sr. and Pete Jr. also forecasts the themes of the next chapter—biological generativity and infertility. In this light, several questions are raised. Would Pete Sr. have been as highly and carefully involved in parental generativity if generativity chill had not been part of his previous experience? Did Pete Sr.'s biological generativity make

32. Pete Jr. has come full circle in his interview. He began by sharing an early memory of his father remodeling the house and now he closes with his own remodeling dream. Maintaining the "nest," owned by his father and originally purchased and maintained by his immigrant grandfather, may be a symbol for Pete Jr. of the legacy that he has received and of his commitment to carry on their work. By picking up and "carrying the ball," he is also modeling himself after them and figuratively paying back his father and grandfather for the sacrifices they made to provide for the ongoing life of the generations. As he and his new wife look forward to starting their own family, Pete Jr. is also preparing to pass on the legacy through his own parental generativity.

33. Here Peter Jr. states clearly that he is now an adult. He is now ready to stand as the generative link between his ancestors and descendants. He is now ready to take responsibility for his family's ongoing history, symbolized by the house itself.

a unique contribution to his midlife achievement of societal generativity? Is it reasonable to speculate that his early adulthood style of coping with the threat of infertility, which included devoting parent-like attention to his house, also forecast his midlife societal generativity?

8

Early Adulthood Barriers
to Biological and Societal Generativity

with Linda Son

Early adulthood is the time when most men experience the first type of generativity—becoming birth fathers. Many more couples, however, are delaying their entry into parenthood until well after the peak years of their fertility, and consequently many among them experience difficulty achieving their first live birth (Mosher & Pratt, 1990). What is the impact of involuntary childlessness on aspiring young fathers' subsequent generativity? The experience of marital infertility is an obvious major threat to biological, and thus parental, generativity, but it may also make an important contribution to a man's becoming societally generative at midlife. In this chapter we will describe the different coping styles of the husbands who experienced involuntary childlessness and thus were not able to make the transition to fatherhood in the way they had expected. We will then evaluate how various ways of coping with infertility may have contributed to men's subsequent success in achieving societal generativity.

What We Know from Prior Research

Primary infertility refers to the inability to become a birth parent; secondary infertility refers to the inability to have a second or additional child. The American Fertility Society (1988) estimates that the national primary-infertility rate is approximately 15% among couples of childbearing age; similar figures (14%, 16%) have been reported by the National Center for Health Statistics (1982, 1987). Yet although infertility is experienced by about one out of every six couples, psychological studies of its consequences have been rare. The following review of prior research focuses on studies that have considered the psychological experiences of men. Previous research on the psychological experiences of infertile women in particular and the medical dimensions of infertility in general has been reviewed elsewhere (Feuer, 1983; MacNab, 1985; Matthews & Matthews, 1986; Mazor & Simons, 1984; Menning, 1977; Noyes & Chapnick, 1964; Simons, 1982; Stangel, 1979; Wright, Allard, Lecours, & Sabourin, 1989).

Coping with Generativity Chill

The concept of generativity chill (introduced in Chapter 1) refers to a type of ego anxiety arising from the moments when an adult faces the possibility of losing the child he or she has helped to create, whether the threat comes in the form of a fertility problem preventing the birth of the child who has already been psychologically conceived, or strikes in the form of a near-death accident to the living being that one has biologically conceived. The psychosocial study of infertility is, therefore, a specific case in the study of biological generativity chill.

Biological infertility is a basic threat to men's sense of contributing to the life of the generations. It is capable of engendering intense anxiety, as suggested by their psychological reactions to thwarted procreation. Mahlstedt (1985) found that the psychological impact of infertility begins as soon as a man recognizes that conception has not occurred as soon as expected. A group of 30 infertile men studied by McNab (1985) initially experienced a sense of shock, disbelief, and helplessness, a feeling that their ability to control their lives and choose their destiny had been suddenly denied (see Kraft et al., 1980). Several authors have described the substantial sense of loss that is experienced in infertility (of status or prestige, self-confidence, hope of fulfilling an important goal) as a key factor in the depression felt by many men and women (Berger, 1980; Mahlstedt, 1985; Mazor, 1979, 1980). Feuer (1983), who studied the experiences of 93 infertile men, found that each man could identify some aspect of his life that was negatively affected by infertility, and that virtually all experienced depression. The level of psychosocial stress associated with infertility may still be higher among women than men, according to a review of prior publications (Wright, Lecours & Sabourin, 1989). But the reviewers also note that studies that "included . . . social desirability scales invariably found that men scored high, suggesting that men tend to downplay the psychosocial impact of infertility" (pp. 132, 137). This psychological reaction to downplay the stress also tends to foster emotional withdrawal which, Osherson (1986) notes, ironically becomes an "obstacle to learning more about the male experience of infertility" (p. 97).

Some men also associate infertility with their masculinity or male sex-role adequacy (Humphrey, 1977; Mahlstedt, 1985). Several studies report that most men viewed their infertility as severely threatening to their masculine self-image and to their body image, apparently regardless of whether it was the husband or wife who was infertile (Kraft, et al., 1980; Mazor, 1979; Platt, 1973). Mazor and Simons (1984) also concluded that poor body image and low self-esteem, in turn, foster a general sense of unproductiveness in other areas of life. In general, MacNab (1985) found that infertility represents the most significant lapse in mastery since youth.

An aspiring father's infertility is also nested within a broader family network. Depending on who is "at fault," a husband may feel guilty for depriving his wife of a child or feel resentful of his wife for depriving him of a child (Mazor & Simons, 1984). Mahlstedt (1985) suggests that "being infertile, living on such an emotional roller coaster, upsetting their spouses, disrupting so many aspects of their own lives, and disappointing their families" can prompt feelings of guilt (p. 341). Parents and grandparents may add to a man's sense of disappointment if questions about fertility are insensitively asked, if the problem is considered a taboo discussion topic, or if pressure is exerted to provide grandchildren or great-grandchildren.

Long-Term Impact

Consequences of infertility can go beyond feelings of having disappointed the prior generation. DeAngelis (1990) has noted that men "can experience their loss as a break in the continuity of the life cycle" (p. 25) that cuts them off from making any contribution to the continuity of the generations. This observation is consistent with Erikson's (1950, 1969a) suggestion that the achievement of generativity becomes more difficult, although not impossible, without the experience of parenting children. However, longitudinal research reports have not considered whether the way men cope with the threat of infertility to biological generativity predicts the subsequent attainment of societal generativity.

In summary, cross-sectional research has documented the psychosocial stress resulting from infertility, but little is known about variations in coping strategies, especially among men. No published research has longitudinally documented the phases of coping, variations in coping strategies used during each phase, and their long-term significance for a person's subsequent psychosocial adult development. Yet it is possible to learn much from infertility. As Parke and Beitel (1988) have suggested, "an examination of how the transition to parenthood is modified or exaggerated by unusual events," including how fathers manage stressful, unexpected misfortunes such as reproductive difficulties, can provide "new insights into the nature of . . . paternal roles" (p. 221).

Research Questions

Our investigation is a part of the larger consideration of how unexpected difficulties in the transition to parenthood can shed light on the normal, expected paternal life cycle. We limit ourselves to the two questions that follow. Together with speculative predictions based on prior research, they provide a foundation for this portion of the larger study.

Question 1: How do men cope when infertility threatens their biological generativity?

It is expected that the ways men initially find to cope with the threat of infertility and their long-term approach to resolving their need to become parentally generative will be interrelated. Initial coping strategies may foreshadow parenting resolutions because both decisions reflect, in part, the men's orientation to generativity.

Question 2: Do different strategies of coping with infertility affect the subsequent realization of societal generativity at midlife?

Coping patterns may, in effect, mediate the impact of biological infertility upon societal generativity. How men cope with their infertility and desire for a parenting role may ultimately determine the significance of infertility for predicting men's psychosocial development. On the basis of Erikson's theoretical work, we hypothesize that the sociological experience of fathering rather than the biological fact of fatherhood, provides many of the prerequisites for midlife societal generativity.

In sum, this study uses longitudinal data to question the short-term and long-term implications of biosocial infertility on psychosocial generativity. Parenting is hypothesized to function as a contributing precursor or critical foundation, although not sufficient condition, for the subsequent achievement of societal generativity.

How the Study Was Conducted
Subjects

The sample requirements for this portion of the study are different from those reported in previous chapters. Parental generativity ratings were not required for all subjects and, in fact, many men who experienced infertility would not have had complete childrearing ratings because they started their families after the first adulthood longitudinal interview or because they remained childless. The files for 343 of the men were sufficiently complete to evaluate reliably whether they had experienced infertility in their first marriage; the total included the core 240 fathers and 103 of the previously excluded subjects.

Of these 343 subjects, the subgroup of men who experienced infertility in their first marriage represent the core sample for this chapter. Those who did not experience infertility, but for whom childrearing ratings are available, will serve as a comparison group. The actual sample sizes will be reported as part of the results section.

Rating Scales

All subjects were first rated for biological generativity or fertility. The fathers who experienced infertility in their first marriage were also rated on their medical backgrounds, social backgrounds, their infertility coping strategies and parenting outcomes, as well as on societal generativity. All ratings were made by judges who were blind to other aspects of the fathers' lives including the ratings made by other judges. The interrater reliability coefficient reported for each fertility-related variable was based on 20 randomly selected cases that were rerated by a second rater. Disagreements between raters were resolved by consensus, after a subject's blinded file was reexamined.

Biological Generativity

Biological generativity was measured by the simple existence of a live child whom a subject biologically fathered and helped give the initial care necessary to ensure its biological survival. From the detailed long-term information on each man in the study, it was possible to assess a man's biological generativity with unusually high reliability.

A couple was considered to have primary infertility if they had no children and had been either unable to achieve a pregnancy after trying for at least 18 months, or the mother was unable to carry to term. This definition is slightly more conservative, but probably also more reliable, than that of the conventional medical definition of an infertile couple as one that has not achieved a successful pregnancy after having had 12 months or more of unprotected intercourse (see Menning, 1977; Potter & Parker, 1964; Taymor, 1969). A positive rating indicates that the files contain a self-report of difficulty or inability to achieve a successful pregnancy, or the presence of clear medical evidence of a fertility problem, or both a self-report and independent medical evidence. Self-reports and discussions of infertility by the Glueck subjects were usually given in response to questions regarding their children or plans for children, their wives, or their personal medical histories. Otherwise, the men were not systematically questioned about their fertility.

All 343 cases were examined by two independent judges. Their ratings were compared, and, for those cases in which there was disagreement (approximately 6%), the files were restudied, and a final rating was made by consensus. For the minority of Glueck subjects who were rated as infertile, 51% of the judgments were based solely on self-reports, 11% were based solely on their medical records, and 38% were based on both a self-report and medical records. Thus a clear self-report of a fertility problem was present in 89% of the cases, and independent medical evidence was present in 49% of the cases. Cases of secondary infertility were not included in this study.

Medical Condition and Context

Those cases rated as infertile were also rated on the medical context of their experience. These ratings were based on a subject's combined adulthood interviews and medical files.

Medical diagnosis. A judgment, based on the available self-report and medical evidence, was made on whether the medical problem resided in: (1) the wife, (2) the husband, or (3) both the husband and wife. The third category also included those for whom the couple's physi-

cian had been unable to identify a specific medical problem. Exact interrater agreement was 80%; interrater agreement was estimated to be .66, using Cohen's kappa which corrects for chance agreement.
Medical prognosis. A judgment was made on the degree to which the original medical diagnosis provided a sense of hope, and classified as follows: (1) no realistic possibility for an eventual conception and successful birth, (2) uncertain or unclear medical hope of an eventual successful pregnancy, or (3) a good possibility of an eventual conception and successful birth. Comparing the level of agreement between the two raters, there was 70% exact agreement and 90% agreement within one adjoining ordinal level. Interrater agreement was estimated to be .61 using Cohen's kappa.
Years without children. Each subject was rated on the number of years he devoted to trying to have children, that is, the number of years before an eventual birth, adoption, or a decision to stop trying and live childfree. The interrater reliability was estimated to be .81. For contingency table analysis, the following three categories were used: (1) 4 years or less; (2) 5–8 years, and (3) 9 years or more. These intervals were chosen after examination of the continuous data indicated that there were natural breaks in the distribution between the fourth and fifth year and between the eighth and ninth year, and that a fairly equal number of subjects fell into the three resulting categories.

Social Context

To control for social class as a background variable, the following two indices were used.
Childhood social class. This rating is an index of the Glueck subjects' parents' social class: (1) lower class, (2) working class, (3) lower middle class, (4) middle class, and (5) upper class. (Levels 3 to 5 were combined into one middle-class category for purposes of contingency table analysis.) The rating uses Hollingshead's Index of Social Status (1959, 1975; Haug, 1972; Hollingshead & Redlich, 1958; Landecker, 1960). The occupational and educational categories used to assign membership in a particular class are understood as "signs" reflecting differential social values, attitudes, and behavior patterns associated with each class. The index also takes into consideration marital status and gender in order to yield a social class position for a family unit.

It is essentially an average of a subject's father's and mother's social position as recorded in interviews held with the parents when the subjects were 14 years of age. The interrater reliability coefficient was .71.

Adult social class. This rating uses the same Hollingshead 5-point ordinal scale as above. The index is based on a combination of the previously reported occupational and educational achievement levels as indicated in the subjects' interview at age 47. Interrater reliability was .93.

Infertility Coping Strategies

Clinical observations and the unblinded examination of the files of infertile Glueck subjects not included in this study (because their interviews at age 47 were incomplete), led us to conclude that men who experience generativity chill in the form of infertility typically go through at least two primary phases in their coping behavior, following their initial shock and denial. First, men choose or unconsciously adopt some form of substitute activity to help them cope with the inevitable waiting that occurs after the problem is discovered. As Erikson (1980b) has also noted, when young adults are not parenting, they "must sublimate some of their procreativity" (p. 216). Second, they eventually choose a parenting solution and often speak of it as the way they resolved their problem. The men in this study were rated on both phases in order to assess the various social strategies used to cope with the problem of infertility. The ratings were based on their interviews at age 25 and age 31.

Initial parenting substitutes. The men were rated for their *primary* or dominant style of using substitutes after the discovery of a fertility problem and before a final resolution, such as a birth or adoption. The following substitution styles were identified: (a) substituted self by treating himself as the only child (for example, preoccupation with personal body building, health foods, macho behavior); (b) substituted a nonhuman object, treating it as his pride and joy or referring to it as his "baby" (for example, parent-like devotion to house, pet, garden, or car); (c) substituted a child or other appropriate person by becoming involved in vicarious childrearing activities with the children of others (for example, leading a youth group, teaching Sunday school, becoming the equivalent of a Big Brother to a neighborhood boy).

There was 80% exact agreement between the two raters. Interrater agreement was .69 using Cohen's kappa.

Biological generativity resolution. The men were also rated on the resolution of their desire to become parents. This variable included the following categories: (a) childless (the couple failed to conceive and chose to live without children); (b) birth parent (the couple decided to wait for an eventual birth, rather than choosing adoption, and did eventually achieve a successful birth); (c) adoptive parent (the couple brought a child into their family by adoption). Exact agreement between the raters was 95%; recording error correction raised interrater agreement to 100%.

Psychosocial Development

Two stages from Erikson's model of the life cycle were used to assess each subject's psychosocial development during both boyhood and adulthood.

Boyhood Eriksonian industry. To control first for variations in psychosocial development prior to the experience of infertility, the subjects' boyhood rating on industry, Stage 4 in Erikson's developmental model, was used. For purposes of contingency table analysis, the 9-point scale was collapsed into three equal categories: (1) industry low, (2) industry moderate, and (3) industry high. (For a more detailed description of this variable, see Chapter 2.)

Societal generativity at midlife. Each man was assessed for the achievement of societal generativity based on his age 47 interview. The rating included the following categories: (1) generativity failed or clearly absent, (2) generativity unclear or weak, and (3) generativity clearly achieved. Childrearing activities were excluded from consideration. In essence, the criterion that differentiated the generative men was their assumption of responsibility for other adults beyond the sphere of the nuclear family (see Chapter 1).

Parental generativity during adulthood. Post-hoc analyses will also use the ratings of three different types of parental generativity (support of social-emotional development, support of intellectual-academic development, and support of physical-athletic development) during the two decades of childhood and adolescence to assess the contribution of infertility to predicting the involvement of late-birth or adopting fathers in childrearing participation. (These ratings were fully described in Chapter 2.)

Statistical Procedures

The statistical analyses reported in this chapter primarily rely upon contingency table analysis because of the nominal (that is, named or classified into categories) nature of the biological generativity resolution outcomes; chi-square or Yates corrected chi-square was used as a test of statistical significance and Cramer's *V* or phi was used as a measure of strength of association. As a practical rule, it is usually recommended that all expected cell counts equal or exceed 5. Most, but not all, of the cross-tabulations reported in this study satisfy this criterion. Thus, it is important to note that Cochran (1952), Camilli and Hopkins (1978), and others have demonstrated that contingency tables give accurate probability statements, even when the expected frequencies in a minority of the cells are as low as 1 or 2. All of the analyses presented more than satisfy this criterion.

A proportional-reduction-in-error (PRE) measure, based on lambda, is also presented to summarize each series of analyses (see Goodman & Kruskal, 1954, 1972; Reynolds, 1977). The PRE is a method of assessing the cumulative contribution that a series of independent variables makes beyond chance to improving the prediction of a dependent variable.

What We Found:
The Relationship Between Infertility
and Generativity

Biological Infertility

Of the 343 men, 15.5% (*n* = 53) experienced infertility in their first marriage. The rate of infertility was lower among the childrearing fathers (9%; 22 of the 240 men experienced reproductive difficulties before becoming fathers) and higher among the men excluded from the study (30%; 31 of the 103 men) because the experience of infertility delayed or prevented their childrearing involvement.

Medical and Social Background

The origin of each couple's fertility problem was derived from the men's self-report interviews and their personal medical records. Only 21.5% of the 53 husbands in the sample were identified as having a fertility problem (due, for example, to subnormal spermatogenesis, injuries, congenital anomalies). In contrast, 51.5% of the 53 men had wives with a fertility problem (such as malfunctioning ovaries or fallopian tubes, miscarriages). Finally, in 29% of the cases, both the husband and wife most likely had a medical problem. National statistics on which partner in a couple is infertile are inadequate, but it is often estimated that in 30–40% of the cases it is the husband's problem, in 30–40% of the cases it is the wife's problem, and in 20–30% of the cases it is a joint problem (see Dublin & Amelar, 1972; Roland, 1968; Taymor, 1978). If this is correct, the number of infertile husbands may be underrepresented in the sample. Alternatively, some husbands may have found it difficult to identify themselves as the sole source of the problem, or the male medical establishment, especially during the 1950s, might have been more inclined to identify the wife as the source of a couple's infertility.

Of the 53 men who experienced infertility, 85% married during their twenties (*M* age = 26), as did 89% of the fertile men (*M* age = 24). Approximately 66% of the infertile men began trying to start a family during their first 2 years of marriage, and all had begun trying by their fifth year of marriage. Men who experienced infertility but eventually became birth fathers ranged in age from 23 to 32 at the time of their child's birth (*M* age = 28), while men who did not experience infertility ranged in age from 17 to 36 at the time of their first child's birth (*M* age = 25). Among the involuntarily childless couples, the number of years spent trying to have a child—before an eventual birth, adoption, or decision to live childfree—varied greatly. The findings indicate that 34% of the couples devoted 4 years or fewer to the problem, 42% spent 5–8 years, and 24% spent 9–12 years. Almost half (49%) of the couples were given medical hope that conception and a successful pregnancy would eventually be achieved, 21% were given virtually no hope of an eventual successful pregnancy, and 30% experienced an uncertain hope because their medical condition or diagnosis was unclear.

Parenting Substitutes

A minority of six men (11%) primarily substituted themselves as an initial means of coping with their marital infertility and their need to be parents. A majority of the men (*n* = 31; 58%) primarily substituted a nonhuman object that was treated as if it were their baby, and about one quarter of the men ($n = 12$; 23%) primarily substituted parenting-like activities with the children of others. A rating was not possible for four of the men (8%) because their early interview files were incomplete. No significant relation was found between the type of parenting substitute chosen and any of the three medical background variables or the three social background variables.

Predicting Biological Generativity Resolutions

In 24 cases (45%), couples decided to continue trying rather than adopt and finally did achieve a successful pregnancy. This figure was followed by 16 cases (30%) in which the eventual decision was to remain childless rather than to adopt a child. Finally, a quarter of the men ($n = 13$; 25%) chose adoption. Almost half of the men in the infertile sample ($n = 26$; 49%) eventually became birth fathers. This included 24 (60%) of the 40 men who did not adopt and only 2 (15%) of the 13 men who did adopt (this latter figure contradicts the notion that adoption is often followed by a pregnancy).

Table 8.1 summarizes the relation of the three types of parenting resolutions with the background variables and prior substitution-coping strategies. The relation between who (husband or wife) was infertile and biological generativity outcomes is weak and nonsignificant. Secondary analyses did indicate that the association of an individual (husband or wife) or joint (husband and wife) infertility problem, cross-tabulated with a childless or adoption outcome, approached significance, χ^2 (1, $n = 29$) = 3.48, $.05 < p < .10$. The trend indicated that couples with a joint medical problem were more likely to choose to remain childless rather than adopt, and couples in which only one spouse had a medical problem were more likely to become adoptive parents.

Table 8.1 also shows that the relation between having been given medical hope of eventually having a child and the type of parenting outcome chosen is strong ($V = .52$) and highly significant ($p < .0001$). As shown in the second cross-tabulation in Table 8.1, childlessness rather than adoption was chosen by the majority ($n = 7$; 64%) of the 11 men who were given no medical hope of eventually having a child. Adoption was chosen by half (50%) of the 16 men who were given uncertain medical hope that their wives could have a successful preg-

Table 8.1 Predicting fathers' biological generativity resolutions: cross-tabulations

Prior independent variables	Biological generativity			n	df	χ^2	V
	Childless	Birth father	Adoptive father				
Medical background							
Who was infertile				53	4	8.97	.29
Wife	7	14	6				
Husband	3	2	6				
Both	6	8	1				
Hope of conception				53	4	28.84***	.52***
None or low	7	1	3				
Unclear, uncertain	6	2	8				
Good or high	3	21	2				
Years trying				53	4	14.83**	.37**
4 or fewer	4	9	5				
5 to 8	3	14	5				
9 or more	9	1	3				

Psychosocial background							
Childhood social class				44	2	3.83	.30
Lower	8	17	10				
Working	5	3	1				
Boyhood Eriksonian development				52	4	2.65	.16
Industry low	2	2	1				
Industry moderate	11	14	7				
Industry high	2	8	5				
Adulthood social class				53	4	5.16	.22
Lower	5	2	2				
Working	9	13	7				
Middle	2	9	4				
Coping strategies							
Parenting substitutes				49	4	14.23**	.38**
Self	1	5	0				
Object	12	15	4				
Child	2	3	7				

Note: $^*p \le .05$, $^{**}p \le .01$, $^{***}p \le .001$.

nancy, and almost all (*n* = 21; 81%) of the 26 men who were given good or clear medical hope resolved to wait for an eventual birth.

Table 8.1 next shows a moderately strong (*V* = .37) and significant relation (*p* < .01) between the number of years spent trying to have a child and the type of parenting resolution reached. Of those who spent more than 8 years trying to conceive, only 7.6% eventually became fathers through birth and 23% through adoption. In contrast, 78% of those men who spent 4 or fewer years trying to have a child and 86% of those who spent 5–8 years trying became birth or adoptive parents. Examination of the continuous scale, for instance, indicated that there were two to six births per year for each additional year of trying up to 8 years, but there was only one birth among the men who persevered more than 8 years. In sum, couples that spent more than 8 years trying to have a child were significantly more likely to end up childless.

The association is weak and nonsignificant between type of parenting resolutions and all social background variables.

Finally, Table 8.1 shows a moderately strong (*V* = .38) and significant (*p* < .01) association between the type of initial parenting substitute used and the type of biological generativity resolution reached. None of those men who initially used self-centered substitutes ever adopted, and only 13% of those men who initially substituted a nonhuman object became adoptive fathers. In striking contrast, 58% of men who substituted parent-like activities with the children of others eventually adopted.

The ability to predict correctly an individual's parenting outcome from these findings can be summarized by using a PRE procedure. The PRE was .41 for the association between medical hope as the independent variable and parental resolution as the dependent variable. Knowledge of the number of years spent trying to have a child improved the PRE value to .48. Finally, adding parenting substitutes improved the total predictive value to 65% in the correct prediction of biological generativity resolutions.

Predicting Societal Generativity Outcomes

A total of 52% of the men who experienced infertility subsequently achieved some degree of societal generativity by midlife. The precursors of societal generativity will now be examined, together with their relationships with biological and parental generativity. Table 8.2 summarizes the findings, showing that the achievement of societal generativity is not significantly associated with any of the medical background variables, with boyhood social class, or with boyhood psychosocial industry. (Note, however, that boyhood industry was significantly correlated with adulthood societal generativity among the men in the larger fertile sample, $r = .16$, $p < .005$.)

Other than the medical and boyhood variables, all three of the remaining variables shown in Table 8.2 are significantly associated with the achievement of societal generativity at midlife.

First, a significant ($p < .005$) and moderately strong association ($V = .38$) is found between adult social class and psychosocial development. No one in the lower class achieved clear societal generativity, only 26% in the working class, but 67% in the middle class clearly reached this stage. It must be remembered, however, that all of the subjects began life in the lower or working class, so their adulthood middle-class rating was an achieved status. It was previously demonstrated in Chapter 2 that personal psychosocial development is highly correlated with social mobility, even when social class of origin is controlled for. It is primarily social mobility, rather than social class, that underlies the present association.

Second, the type of parenting substitute chosen is significantly associated with societal generativity (see bottom section of Table 8.2). None of the men who used self-centered substitutes achieved clear societal generativity by midlife, and only one of these men evidenced any societal generativity. In contrast, 28% of those who substituted an object and 75% of those who substituted a child were clearly generative at midlife ($p < .005$).

Third and finally, biological generativity resolutions and subsequent societal generativity are moderately and significantly associated ($V = .34$, $p < .02$). Of those men who remained childless, 81% completely failed to show evidence of societal generativity. In comparison, 38% of those who waited until the birth of their first child and 23% of those who adopted completely failed to evidence societal generativity at midlife ($p < .005$). Stated in positive terms, a rating of "clear" generativity was attained most frequently by the adoptive fathers (53%), followed by the birth fathers (42%), and then the men who remained childless (6%). Similarly, using the more generous criterion of having attained some degree of generativity, generativity was again

Table 8.2 Predicting fathers' societal generativity outcomes: cross-tabulations

Prior independent variables	Societal generativity			n	df	χ^2	V
	Absent	Unclear	Clear				
Medical background							
Who was infertile				53	4	0.89	.09
Wife	13	4	10				
Husband	5	3	3				
Both	7	3	5				
Hope of conception				53	4	3.21	.17
None or low	6	2	3				
Unclear, uncertain	8	1	7				
Good or high	11	7	8				
Years trying				53	4	6.15	.24
4 or fewer	7	4	7				
5 to 8	8	5	9				
9 or more	10	1	2				

Psychosocial background

Childhood social class				44	2	2.05	.22
Lower	14	7	14				
Working	6	1	2				
Boyhood Eriksonian development				52	4	5.04	.22
Industry low	1	1	3				
Industry moderate	16	8	8				
Industry high	7	1	7				
Adulthood social class				53	4	15.56**	.38**
Lower	8	1	0				
Working	15	6	8				
Middle	2	3	10				

Parenting strategies

Parenting substitutes				49	4	14.42**	.38**
Self	5	1	0				
Object	18	5	8				
Child	1	2	9				
Biological generativity resolutions				53	4	12.08*	.34*
Childless	13	2	1				
Birth father	9	5	10				
Adoptive father	3	3	7				

Note: *$p \leq .05$, **$p \leq .01$, ***$p \leq .001$.

attained most frequently by the adoptive fathers (77%), followed by the birth fathers (63%), and then the men who remained childless (19%).

When a PRE procedure was used to summarize variation in societal generativity that can be explained by the variables significantly associated with societal generativity, it was found that the PRE was .29 for adulthood social class, with societal generativity as the dependent variable. The addition of the parenting substitutes further improved the PRE to .44, and the addition of biological generativity resolutions (parenting outcomes) further improved the cumulative predictive value to .52. Biological generativity alone, prior to controlling for social class and parenting substitutes, accounts for 18% of the variance in societal generativity.

Biological and Parental Generativity as Precursors of Societal Generativity

It is revealing at this point to compare the mean levels of societal generativity attainment among the three subgroups of the 53 men who experienced infertility (16 childless *vs.* 24 birth *vs.* 13 adoptive fathers) with the fathers in the childrearing sample who never experienced infertility ($n = 218$ of 240). The rate of societal generativity achievement was highest among the infertile adoptive fathers ($M = 2.31$), followed by the initially infertile birth fathers ($M = 2.04$) and the fertile birth fathers ($M = 1.54$); the lowest mean level was shown by the infertile subjects who remained childless ($M = 1.25$). A series of t-tests (separate variance estimate) comparing the mean societal generativity scores of alternate pairs of subject subgroups further justifies the idea that biological generativity achievement is a precursor of societal generativity achievement. The mean level of societal generativity achieved by the infertile men who remained childless was significantly lower than that among the birth fathers who never experienced infertility ($t = 1.90$, $df = 19.10$, $p < .05$). The mean level of societal generativity also was significantly lower for the birth fathers who never experienced infertility compared with the infertile men who eventually became birth fathers ($t = 2.60$, $df = 26.70$, $p < .01$) and compared with the adoptive fathers ($t = 3.16$, $df = 13.17$, $p < .01$). The difference between the mean levels of societal generativity among the infertile men who became birth fathers versus those among adoptive fathers, however, was not significant ($t = 0.88$, $df = 26.07$, $p = $ N.S.).

Sample restrictions make it difficult to test directly the possible contribution of infertility to predicting subsequent parental or societal generativity. It was possible to determine fathers' longitudinal child-rearing ratings for only 22 of the 53 infertile men. Simply comparing the mean ratings on the six varieties of childrearing participation for these 22 men who experienced infertility with the fathers who did not experience infertility showed that only one of the six comparisons indicated that the means were significantly different. The mean level of care provided for their adolescent children's intellectual-academic development was significantly higher among fathers who had experienced infertility than among fathers who had not experienced infertility ($t = 1.78$, $df = 22.75$, $p < .05$). Fathers who had experienced infertility, however, also had somewhat higher mean levels of paternal care on all six varieties of childrearing participation. The statistical probability of this consistent pattern occurring by chance is .05 (sign test). Furthermore, the total quantity of all types of *parental generativity* combined was significantly higher among fathers who had experienced infertility ($M = 11.9$, $n = 22$) compared with those who had no such experience ($M = 8.9$, $n = 218$) ($t = 1.77$, $df = 23.30$, $p < .05$). This relationship may have contributed to the equally interesting finding that the mean level of subsequent *societal generativity* was significantly higher among these same 22 fathers who had experienced infertility ($M = 2.27$, $n = 22$) compared with those who had no such experience ($M = 1.54$, $n = 218$) ($t = 3.75$, $df = 24.32$, $p < .001$).

Discussion of the Findings

Infertility was experienced by about one out of six men in the larger sample during their first marriage. The analyses identify several factors that shed light on the ways in which married men cope with the problem of infertility as a threat to biological generativity and the significance of infertility for predicting the subsequent achievement of societal generativity.

Coping with Generativity Chill

The presence or absence of medical hope, as one would expect, is an important factor in how men cope with biological infertility. In this sample, the men who were given medical hope of having a child in the future were more likely to wait for the birth of their child than they were to consider adoption or living childfree. The men with more severe medical problems and little or no medical hope of having a child in the future were more likely to remain childless. They were not likely to turn to adoption. The rate of adoption was highest among those whose medical condition was unclear and whose hope wavered; those who did receive clear medical hope may have felt less need to take additional action beyond medical treatment to resolve their infertility. MacNab's (1985) study of involuntarily childless men also reports that a definite positive medical diagnosis seems to provide a couple with a sense of "resolution" to their infertility and promote their ability to get on with other areas of their lives. Similarly, those with the clear negative diagnosis, because of the lack of hope, may have come to feel more decisive about reapplying their energies to other areas of their lives. In contrast, the experience of generativity chill in a situation of fundamental uncertainty appears to leave a husband and wife with some degree of personal control or responsibility and motivates them to consider adoption.

In terms of medical hope, it is also noteworthy that almost half of the infertile couples in the sample eventually achieved a successful pregnancy, a figure which is only slightly lower than the current rate. Only 15% of the adoptive fathers subsequently became birth fathers, however. This rate may seem low in view of the common myth that a pregnancy usually follows an adoption, but comparable low post-adoption conception rates (usually ranging from 10% to 20%) have been consistently reported in previous empirical studies (for reviews, see Aaronson & Glienke, 1963; E. J. Lamb & Leurgans, 1979; Mac-Nab, 1985; Mai, 1973; Mazor, 1984; Noyes & Chapnick, 1964; Simons, 1982).

Another interesting finding is that the number of years spent trying to have a child is associated with the parenting outcome. Few couples achieved a pregnancy after trying for 8 years or more. This is generally consistent with the increase in reproductive difficulties as a couple becomes older (only 2% of married couples are infertile among wives aged 15 to 19, while 27% are infertile at age 40; National Center for Health Statistics, 1987). Adoption, however, was also least likely for those couples who spent more than 8 years trying to have a child. Although men who did not adopt may simply have had a greater investment in wanting only their biological children, another possible explanation for this difference in adoption rates may be the consequence of aging while waiting more years to begin a family. One man, for instance, reported at age 30 that he and his wife were still trying to have children because a recent stillbirth, although painful, had made him believe that it was "not hopeless." But after several additional years had passed without a successful birth, he reported not only that he and his wife had stopped trying but also had decided that they were "too old now" to start a family—the socially appropriate time had passed.

Those who try longer are not only older when they finally consider adoption, but also tend to be exhausted by the stress of constant anxiety over their thwarted generativity (see Wicks, 1977). For instance, when the interviewers described the subjects' feelings during the years prior to achieving some resolution, the most common term used was *anxious*—anxious to have children, anxious over their childless marriage, and anxious over the outcome of their medical treatment. Such anxiety, over an extended period of years, obviously drains the couple's energy. Furthermore, many of the men tended to feel "off time," that is, they were behind where they should be in the socially defined life cycle. At the same time, some of those who failed to achieve a pregnancy or to adopt for many years also appeared to want to "catch up" by skipping the phase of parenthood (LaRossa, 1983; Neugarten, 1969, 1979).

Predicting Societal Generativity Outcomes

The initial parenting substitute proved to be a very good predictor of the men's subsequent parenting resolution and societal generativity attainment. Men who used self-centered substitutes were most likely to remain childless and to fail to achieve societal generativity in later life. Men who used object substitutes were less likely to remain childless and somewhat more likely to evidence some degree of societal generativity at midlife. Men who used parent-like substitute activities with the children of others were the least likely to remain childless, the most likely to adopt a child, and the most likely to evidence clear societal generativity at midlife. In fact, half of the men who initially substituted parent-like activities with the children of others eventually adopted in early adulthood; three-quarters achieved clear societal generativity at midlife; and nine out of ten showed some degree of societal generativity at midlife. One husband, for instance, became involved in extracurricular childrearing activities during the course of his medical treatment. When he "realized [that] no children were possible" he and his wife immediately adopted. Two decades later he was judged by blind raters to have a very stable family, and clearly to enjoy his marriage.

Furthermore, and of greater theoretical importance, the findings lend support to the Eriksonian idea that the experience of parenting serves as a foundation for the subsequent achievement of societal generativity at midlife. Infertile men who became fathers, either by adoption or birth, were more likely to be generative in middle adulthood than were childless men. Moreover, this subsequent societal generativity is not associated solely with biological fatherhood. Overall, the rate of societal generativity was the highest among the infertile adoptive fathers, followed by the thought-to-be infertile birth fathers, the fertile men in the overall sample, and lowest among the infertile men who remained childless. This suggests that the experience of generativity chill combined with the eventual experience of parenting may especially promote societal generativity. Furthermore, the three groups of men who eventually became fathers (with no problem, or by a happy resolution of the difficulties of procreation, or by adoption) were all significantly higher in societal generativity at midlife than were the men who remained childless. This suggests that the experiences of parental generativity do provide a partial foundation for subsequent societal generativity.

A competing interpretation of the relation between parenting and societal generativity, however, must be acknowledged. A man's initial coping strategy of becoming a parental figure to another child, that is, may be interpreted as an early sign of, or predisposition toward, societal generativity at midlife. From this perspective, one could argue that the predisposition toward societal generativity predicts the subsequent achievement of parenthood rather than that the parenting experience predicts the subsequent achievement of societal generativity beyond the family sphere. There is some evidence, for instance, that the adoptive process selects psychologically more mature and socially resourceful parents compared to typical birth parents (Levy-Shiff, Goldshmidt & Har-Even, 1991). The adoptive process, however, was not very selective during the time these men were becoming adoptive fathers because there was an excess of available infants. One must also note that the prior achievement of Erikson's fourth stage of development (industry), a more probable indicator of those who will develop societal generativity (Vaillant & Vaillant, 1981), was not a strong predictor of societal generativity in this sample. Additionally, one could also deny that the experience of working with the children of others as an initial parenting substitute was caused by a predisposition toward societal generativity but rather, that it engendered a disposition toward subsequent societal generativity. Furthermore, Erikson himself has always taken the position that all stages are present in some form or degree at all times of life, although their ascendancy to prominence follows a predetermined sequence across the life span. In sum, the detection of early signs of later societal generativity is theoretically complicated and empirically ambiguous.

Perhaps the most reasonable conclusion is that both parenting substitutes and parenting resolutions are markers of biological and parental generativity, and thus both make some contribution to predicting the achievement of societal generativity beyond the family sphere. On the one hand, a disposition toward societal generativity in early adulthood may be reflected in and reinforced by the parenting substitute chosen, particularly if it is parenting of others' children, and in the subsequent parenting outcome, especially the choice of adoption. Men who initially substituted parenting activities with the children of others and men who became adoptive fathers did in fact have the highest rate of societal generativity at midlife. Consistent with the definition of societal generativity, both stratagems involved going beyond the sphere of one's own family. On the other hand, the experience of parenting one's own children still makes an additional independent contribution to the subsequent midlife achievement of societal generativity. Men who became fathers—both those who initially experienced infertility and those in the larger fertile sample who experienced no delay in achieving parenthood—were significantly more likely to be generative at midlife than were those who remained childless. In sum, parenting one's children appears to provide a partial foundation for subsequently guiding other adults.

Finally, the exploratory analyses of our small subsample (the 22 men who had experienced infertility and whose subsequent childrearing ratings were available) suggest that the generativity chill apparently intensifies subsequent parental generativity and perhaps thereby also contributes to the later attainment of societal generativity. The psychological dynamics by which the specific experience of infertility may promote societal generativity are further suggested by MacNab's (1985) discussion of the "paradoxical" impact of infertility on men's adult development. "Men dealing with infertility concerns consider and reconsider the decisions of the generative stage of life. They have the unwelcome opportunity to know in great detail about their motivations for parenthood. More than their contemporaries who have children without difficulty, they must decide repeatedly that they want fatherhood. The many medical procedures, disappointments, and uncertainties of the process provide ample time to reflect on their willingness, readiness, and fitness for having children" (p. 158).

As the "movement into the generative period of life is slowed down or stopped," men must become more reflective about the meaning of biological, parental, and even societal generativity. MacNab also suggests that infertility's contribution to generativity may foreshadow the last stage in Erikson's model, integrity versus despair. "Men struggling with infertility have had a taste of the eighth stage of Erikson's developmental schema. They have a clearer picture than many of their contemporaries of the limits of the flesh and of the will. Erikson's description of the task of this stage [involves] the maintenance of ego integrity in the face of despair . . . Infertility teaches similar lessons about accepting this life as the one and only life cycle that one will live" (p. 159). MacNab suggests that infertility may paradoxically help men to affirm the integrity of their lives within a broader social context despite the obvious injustice experienced in their particular life. As Osherson (1986) also observes, "reproductive difficulties can help . . . us to understand that pain and vulnerability are a part of life" (p. 112).

To follow up the possible impact of reproductive difficulties upon men's generativity, infertility will be incorporated into a more inclusive index of threats to biological generativity in Chapter 10. Infertility, as such, will be counted as one among many possible general threats to a child's biological existence: this will allow us to assess the significance of generativity chill for parental generativity among all the fathers in the sample.

Placing the Findings in Context

The rate of infertility among the men in the Glueck sample is virtually identical to most estimates of the current national primary-infertility rate of 15% among all couples of childbearing age (Menning, 1980; American Fertility Society, 1988). This figure has remained fairly constant across historical and social contexts. A population study back in 1855 found the same statistic (cited in Shep & Ridley, 1965), and more recent surveys have not found significant social class differences in the rate of involuntary childlessness (Whelpton, Campbell, & Patterson, 1966). Currently, nevertheless, the actual number of couples who have, or will confront, reproductive difficulties has increased, because the large baby boom cohort has entered its childbearing years and because of delayed marriage and childbearing. The age of first marriage, for instance, was 23 years for the study fathers; it is 26 years for grooms in the general population currently (National Center for Health Statistics, 1990a, 1990d, 1991c).

Differences between the "silent generation" fathers and today's "baby boom" parents underscore that men's response to infertility cannot be separated from its historical circumstances. In the 1950s, in contrast to today, (1) fewer physicians specialized in infertility treatment (Aral & Cates, 1983); (2) fewer medical procedures and options were available (cf. Djerassi, 1990; Elmer-Dewitt, 1991; Medical Research International, 1990); and (3) the psychosocial supports available today did not exist (Glazer, 1990; Mazor & Simons, 1984; Menning, 1975, 1979; Porter & Christopher, 1984; Snarey, 1988). Conversely, infants were far more readily available for adoption during the subjects' childrearing years than they are to infertile couples now (Kirk, 1985; Martin, 1980; Paul, 1991). This change is primarily caused by the legalization of abortion and the lessening of the social stigma attached to unmarried mothers who are raising their children. For instance, out of every 100 unmarried pregnant women in the United States today, 64 will choose abortions, 35 will decide to give birth and keep the child, and only 1 will decide to give birth and place the child for adoption (Waldrop, 1989).

9

Jerry and Maria: Ties That Bind

This father-daughter story underscores, in part, the relevance of generativity chill for parental generativity. In part it is also a window on the interaction of social class and gender; above all it points to the importance of each husband and wife's parenting alliance in understanding fathers' contributions to their daughters' lives.

The father, Jerry, is a slightly edgy but playful and friendly man. His father, Steve, was a metal (copper) worker with a grade-school education, while Jerry attended but did not graduate from high school and then became a metal (steel) salesman for the same company all of his life. He started out as a laborer in the warehouse but became a salesman before the end of his first childrearing decade, a position he continued in throughout his later childrearing and midlife years. Jerry has been married for over 40 years. He and his wife, Gina, have two children.

His daughter Maria, in her mid-thirties, has abundant dark brown hair and attractive brown eyes. Her ready sense of humor and a little observable anxiety seem compatible with her father's personality. She attended but did not graduate from college and then became a semiprofessional health worker. Maria has been married for over ten years, and has two children.

All of the episodes in their story were shared in the comfort of Jerry and Gina's immaculately clean and elegantly decorated living room and dining room. Gina, while always very respectful and nearly always silent, was nevertheless present throughout the entire individual and joint interviews on the two occasions when they were held.

Early Memories
The Father Looks Back a Generation

My father, when he was about 13 or 14, went into what you call boiler making. He learned how to make boilers and fire extinguishers. He was a coppersmith, more or less.

I remember that he worked very hard and that he was a good man. He got up early in the morning and he came home late at night. He was a very, very good man, a happy-go-lucky guy. He had a very good sense of humor: always joking, always very, very happy and very light. Some men are heavy—demanding and very outspoken in the house. Well, he wasn't that type. Everything he did was on the light side. You knew when he was serious and you knew when he wasn't, but he didn't have to yell about it. He didn't say much but, when he said something, you knew when he meant business. He just spoke and that was it. You minded him. There were never any spankings as such because he wasn't the type to do that.[1]

He was good to the family. He was a good breadwinner. Them days it was tough anyway. Things were very, very bad. But he always gave the family a place to live and food and clothes. He did really everything more or less for everybody. The main things, essential things of life, and that was it.

He took the children to Revere Beach by public transportation. (In them days, Revere Beach was a place like Coney Island.) On Sundays once in a while we went over there. I was included in that, of course, but he never took one individual child and did something. There really wasn't too much he could do. I think my parents were very involved with us, as much as they could be. I mean, they couldn't go run to the schools like we could; they had five of us. But they were always there for us in every way. In those days, things weren't like it is today you know. We lived in a cold water flat, and there wasn't too much to do; there was nothing in the home to really do other than eat and sleep. We did nothing like families do today. They couldn't drive us to the beach, they couldn't take us up to New Hampshire or Maine, because we had no car. We had nothing. All he could do for us was give us a nice home and be a good parent. He was like any other father. I don't remember anything outstanding.[2]

We went to school and, in between, we helped as much as we could. Like, I shined shoes. Well, in all of the school years, I always

1. Jerry's boyhood records confirm that his father provided firm but kindly discipline and did not use much physical punishment. His mother's disciplinary and punishment styles were also the same as his father's, suggesting that they were able to work together as parents with at least some degree of harmony.

2. Jerry's longitudinal interviews confirm that his parents did not work together to do things as a family. In part, therefore, the Gluecks did *not* rate his boyhood home atmosphere as being cohesive or warm.

did something. I either shined shoes or I sold papers or I worked in the produce market. I did one of the three things all the time. I also did my homework. (But I didn't really have any chores at home.)[3]

I got to play basketball and football; that was park league. In those days they had park leagues, clubs. We had the Easthouse Club, which is a Boys Club which I belonged to. We played basketball there. I started at the clubs when I was about seven, and I stayed in the club all my young life.[4]

After we were married I got involved in the Boys Club; I gave a few nights a week. We had these little clubs and, after we were married, I helped out some. For these little kids have to come up, and you try to help them, the same as they helped us, you know. I did that for five or six, seven years. Then, once we had children, our lives were changed. Changed to a point where you're tied down more. In fact, though, I'm still an alumnus of the club today.[5]

But, getting back to when I was a teenager, my father wasn't that involved with me, individually. I hate to say this to make him sound ... He just was a general type guy. I mean, he never was an individualist. Never was. Not with the family. But we were happy. I think we were happier then than many kids are today, to say the least.[6]

I would say the way I raised my family was very similar to my parents. Gina knew my folks when she was young too, so we more or less followed their footsteps in being good parents. I think my father would say that I grew up to be what he wanted—a decent person. See, in those days, all they really were sticking for was somebody decent, somebody that didn't do anything wrong (in society, I'm talking about) and worked hard and took care of your kids and your wife and whatever. This is the way they were taught to bring up their

3. Jerry's longitudinal boyhood records also indicate that his attainment of Eriksonian industry was better than average, placing him in the top quartile of boyhood competence. His boyhood overall social-emotional health was rated as average.

4. Approximately 7 of every 10 fathers in this study, as youths, had made use of a local Boys Club or other supervised recreational facilities.

5. In response to the generativity chill of infertility, one of Jerry's coping strategies was to engage in parent-like activities with the children of others. The sense of continuity is also notable—Jerry became altruistically involved with the children who were now members of the same Boys Club to which he himself had belonged as a boy.

6. Jerry's longitudinal interviews also indicate that his relationship with his father during boyhood was apparently average.

children, and this is the way we try to bring our children up. I think I am like my father in a lot of ways. I think I'm similar to him in taking care of the household and the children and the wife.

He was a good man. We had a comfortable relationship.

The Father's Earliest Memories of His Daughter

I didn't sleep the night Maria was born. I remember that. I also remember taking her home from the hospital. We'd just had this house one year, and I took her in every room. I said to Maria: "This is your house. Welcome home." Then her belly button bled, and I gave her to her mother (laughter).

It took 8 years for Maria to come along; I was 30 years old.[7]

We had been checked and re-checked by doctors. Physically we were all right. There was nothing wrong with us. Either one of us was capable of having children. We both were healthy.[8]

According to the doctors we went to see, it was all just a natural thing that has to happen. It was just a question of the right thing happening at the right time. They claim sometimes with two people working, and the hustle and bustle of the making a living, you don't have the time to relax as much, you know. That was their theory.[9]

Maria was a normal child. She had her good days, her bad days. She was a good child. I mean, in the beginning everybody has their problems. They cry. You can't sleep. But I'm talking as they get older. They were just normal kids. She had her own little traits, but I just remember her as being a happy child.

Having a child made my wife and me even closer, in my opinion. We were very close before the children, too. We've always been close, but children, I think, do make you closer. With us, it did. Well, one

7. Jerry and Gina experienced recurring infertility. Their first child was born after 8 years of marriage, and they were rated as having devoted 5 to 8 years to trying to have children. Their second and last child was born after a wait of 4 additional years.

8. Jerry, therefore, would be rated as having been given high or clear medical hope that an eventual conception and successful pregnancy were possible.

9. The origins of Jerry and Gina's reproductive problems were unknown and, of course, could have been attributed to both or either. The suggestion that they just needed "to relax" could be interpreted as an example of physicians blaming the victim but, nevertheless, it also apparently functioned to leave Jerry and Gina with some sense of control over their reproductive outcome.

thing that I remember really well during the time we were waiting is that [my wife] wanted to adopt. She mentioned adopting children after about five or six years. Which I was against, at the time, because the doctor said we both were able to have children. If the doctor said we couldn't have children for some reason, then adoption would have been a different thing. But I didn't want to go through an adoption and then find ourselves doing two things at once, two babies at once. And it seemed to work out that way anyway; eventually we did have her.[10]

But, aside from our thinking on adoption, I would use the word "compatible" as best describing my wife and me. We both think about the same. We both enjoy the same things. She has the same sense of humor that I do. We have the same outlook in life. We have the same idea with the children. Everything was very similar. We laugh a lot, we joke a lot, even in the mornings when we separate. That's the way we live. And I mean it with all sincerity—just being with her, is enough.[11]

The Daughter's Earliest Memories of Her Father

As far as I can remember back, he was always there. When I was in kindergarten, I remember that he would always come to the plays and take time off from work to do that. When he came to see me at those elementary school plays, I knew he was sitting back saying, "That's my daughter up there," you know.

He was always nice. He would be the one that you would go to like if you wanted something. Just one little "Daddy" would do it. Not that he spoiled me. I mean, they always agreed, you know; I mean, if we asked for permission to do something, they would agree with each

10. Jerry's story illustrates the common pattern in which good medical hope of an eventual pregnancy predicts that a man will wait until he becomes a birth father, but his story is an exception to the common pattern in which the use of vicarious childrearing as an initial substitute predicts that a man will choose to become an adoptive parent. His reason for not adopting also illustrates the common myth that a pregnancy usually follows an adoption. This myth persists despite the low postadoption conception rates consistently reported in several studies (see Chapter 8).

11. Jerry's previous adulthood longitudinal interviews also confirm that his marital affinity was strong. The strength of his commitment was such that he had never considered divorce.

other. Basically, they kind of respected us, and we respected them. But he always wanted everyone to be happy.[12]

Joint Reflections on the First Decade

MARIA: Memories from the first ten years? (pause). UH! His earliest memory is when he is wanting to throw me off the porch because I was colicky. I don't remember that, though. Well, I don't remember the first three years (laughter). Do you remember?

JERRY: Those were the good years then! (joint laughter).[13]

Father-Daughter Companionship

MARIA: You'd take me to the store with you, all the time, when I was younger. I always wanted to go with him. Whenever he was going out, I always wanted to go.

JERRY: I took her, all the time. You can imagine what she was like in the store. She ran around like a cuckoo and I used to go chase her.

MARIA: Just about every Sunday he took us out for ice cream; that was something he did for the whole family.

JERRY: It became a tradition. Maria was about 6 or 7 when we started doing that and we did that for a long time. We used to take a ride on Sundays. It was a Friendly's Ice Cream, about thirty-five minutes away from here. We always went with the children, and on the way over we went by farms, and they saw the horses. (This was when they were young.) They remembered everything, and they enjoyed everything.

MARIA: It was always a fun day. We did that for a long time.

JERRY: We also took them to beaches up in Maine. (It wasn't just ice cream on Sunday.) We did a lot of other things.

MARIA: You also always came to see me in plays at school.

JERRY: Yeah. Every time she appeared on the stage for a little whatever, I took off from work and made sure I was there. I just told

12. Maria was 9 years old when her paternal grandfather, Steve, died, but her only memories of him are of him sitting quietly in a chair because he had been infirm for a number of years prior to his death. For a study of age as a modifier of grandfathers' interactions with their grandchildren, see Tinsley and Parke, 1988.

13. Steve, the paternal grandfather, had a playful sense of humor and, similarly, Jerry and his daughter Maria seem to have always been able to have fun together.

the boss, "I'm going to see my daughter on the stage, in school." I always left work to see her. I would take off from my work and be there in five or six minutes, stay there an hour, and then go back to work. It wasn't long distance. I always managed to get there.

Her first play was when she was in kindergarten. She did a little episode for our town, Arlington. She played a cheerleader; she had this little costume and she had the pom-poms. She was only in kindergarten but she did a cheer, shouting out the letters for our town: "Give me an 'A,' give me an 'R,' give me a 'L,' " and so forth. She did the whole thing.

I remember that made me very proud of her. We always said, "You did very nice; you did a good job," and the normal thing that you would tell a child if you really mean it. We meant it.

MARIA: Then there were my dance recitals . . .

JERRY: I always made sure I was there, but those were in the evening so I didn't have to take off. She took dancing lessons for a long time—from when she was about 4 to when she was about 10. I enjoyed going to all her dance recitals.

MARIA: He always came to father-daughter nights at Girl Scouts, too. I remember we danced at Girl Scout camp. I danced the Hokey-Poky with my dad! (much laughter). Whatever father-daughter things came up he would always take me.

JERRY: To be honest, the little things she was in, recitals and plays, all made me very proud of her. I know these things—singing, acting, and dancing—are common activities for children but that was something that I always wanted to see her do. When she was on stage, I always wanted to be there. Kids only come once, you know.[14]

Family Life

JERRY: We did a lot of picnics. We have a group that we went with (we still go with); four couples, and we make five, plus all the children. They're all related to me, either the men or the women. We've been going with these people for over 38 years, 40 years. Of course, all the kids are grown up now. We still all get together. The children don't, but we do.

14. Jerry's statement suggests that he took extra pride in Maria because of the couple's initial reproductive difficulties and delay in experiencing parenthood.

MARIA: They used to pick a place that had a swimming area and just spend the whole day having barbecues and swimming with all of my cousins. It was fun. We didn't see the cousins that much other than that. So, it was nice.

That brings to mind a humorous picture of him lurking around in the shadows, hiding in the shade. He can't go out in the sun, so he just has to hide under the trees, all day. He usually sat under the shade trees and did the cooking. He would never complain; he would let us swim and stay in as long as we wanted to, but you would never see him near the beach area. He can't even really walk in the sun because he would break out immediately. He just is not a summer man (laughs). But then again, he's not a winter guy either (joint laughter).

JERRY: I'd cook up a lot of things; then they would eat up a lot of things. We had some good times.

MARIA: He had a real good sense of humor all the time. I can remember that. He'd be out painting the house, and I'd be out riding my bike. We'd drive by a hundred times, "Hi, Dad." We'd tease him. He'd be like, "Well . . . I'm up here sweating and you're riding your bike. You having a good time?" We would always laugh. All my friends would always say, "Your father's so funny." "Your father's so nice." He could make us laugh. I don't know. He probably was dying for us to help him paint (laughter), but yet he felt, "I'll let them ride their bikes."

JERRY: Remember when I taught you how to ride a bike—the two-wheeler?

MARIA: Yeah, he helped me learn how to ride my bike, but all I remember is (laughter) falling . . .

JERRY: You kept falling, and I kept saying, "Get on the bike." You kept getting on, and you learned the same day.

She kept at it for quite a while before she got it, but she got it in *one* day. I don't know how she was, but I was pooped when I got home. But she got it. She rode home!

Joint Reflections on the Second Decade

JERRY: Gina, my wife, started working part-time when Maria was 7, 8, or 9 but she basically stayed home until the children were in their very early teens. When Maria was 16 and Tom was 12, my wife started working full time . . . But we still always had dinner together, and everything. I don't think the time we spent with Maria or Tom was hurt by Gina's working.[15]

MARIA: When my mother started working, he worked nights for a couple of years. So, I actually would be with him *more*. He went out to work, and then came home, and he was Dad. He wouldn't bring work home with him. When I got home from school, he would be here. You know, and we would just kind of have fun.[16]

Daughter's Sense of Responsibility

MARIA: I did most of my own homework. The only thing I might have had trouble with would be math. He would help me with math. He was good with math. But other than that, I was really independent, I think.

JERRY: Very smart girl in school. I'm not saying exceptionally smart but very smart. She took care of herself very well. Never had any real problems. She did good work, in school and out.

I also remember when our kids were in the teenage group, some parents would say, "Get home at 10. If you're not home at 10 you're going to be scolded . . . and this and that." We never did that. We talked to them; we told them what we believed was right and wrong. We said what we really believed. We told them to take care of yourself. Call us if you're going to be late. This is the way we brought our children up and we never had any problems. Maybe we were exceptionally lucky. I don't know. But this is the way we were and this is the way it is.

MARIA: I don't remember giving them a bad time. I mean, they never gave me an hour I had to be in because I never abused it. I

15. Gina, who worked as a part-time sales clerk, was a high school graduate. Jerry did not complete high school, however, and Jerry's parents never went beyond the junior high.

16. Survey research also has documented that fathers' participation in childcare is higher when husbands and wives work different shifts (Presser, 1988, 1989). Parenting and shift work are probably mutually reciprocal. Economic need may push a husband and wife to become a two-earner couple, but both parenting motivations and economic needs may prompt them to choose the pattern of a "two-shift" two-earner couple, because working different shifts allows a father to become more involved with his children and protects their second income from the added expense of an outside childcare provider.

never came in extra late where they had to say, "Be in at this time." So if I was going to be late, I'd call and just say, "I'm going to be a little late."

JERRY: Does it sound like she rehearsed this?

GINA: Terribly! (laughter). But that is the way it was.

JERRY: She never got in trouble as far as drugs or school. We were very proud of that, and I'm still proud of that, of both children. Very proud of them.

MARIA: Yeah. There was respect, you know. I never gave them reason to worry about me. Of course, all parents probably sit on the couch and worry, but I never gave them a real reason. From my teen years I mainly remember the little achievements that make parents happy, or make you feel proud. Like the day I got my driver's license. Like getting my first job.

Learning How To Drive

JERRY: Well, do you want to jump to driving cars? Just like with the bike, she had to learn it in a hurry (stifled laugh).

MARIA: Oh . . . I wasn't really in a hurry. Two weekends in a parking lot? (laughter). He used to bring me to a parking lot that was probably, well, it wasn't a huge parking lot.

JERRY: It was pretty big.

MARIA: Not that big! Not like a mall parking lot!

GINA: Not as big maybe as she thought she needed.

MARIA: Yeah (much laughter). We used to drive around the lot's two lamp posts a couple of times—up and down, up and down. Then he'd say, "I'll drive home now." Then next Sunday we'd do the same thing . . . and *he'd* drive home. So finally the third Sunday I said, "That's it. I'm driving home (laughter). I can't stand it any more" (much laughter).

JERRY: She drove home; that ended it.

MARIA: Just driving around the parking lot doesn't help you learn how to drive. I mean . . . once you learn where the brake and the gas is, that's it (laughter). You might as well get on the road and go. Right? (more laughter).

JERRY: I was teaching her how to park in between the lines, how to back up, and how to make a U-turn. That's why you were in a parking lot. But when you got through, you said to me, "That's enough.

I'm driving home." I said, "Well, if you have to drive home, drive home." When she did drive home, it was the first time she'd ever driven on the street with me, see? I thought we needed a couple more Sundays (laughter), but she fooled me. I tell you the truth. She drove home, and I said to her she didn't need any more lessons. That was it. She drove ever since.

MARIA: He taught Ma how to drive, too.

GINA: Yes.

MARIA: He taught everybody how to drive. (Turns to her father again.) You missed your calling. You should have opened a driving school (laughter).

JERRY: That's right. I taught my sister. I taught my brother. I taught just about everybody.

MARIA: Now Ma and I drive better than him (hilarious joint laughter).

JERRY: Star pupils always think they're better than the teacher (laughter). I'll tell you the truth. They're both good drivers, excellent drivers. I have to admit that (pause).

MARIA: You taught well.

He always let me use his car to go out.

JERRY: Right, I was very generous with my car to everybody. Then, years later, she told me about her "accidents" (laughter).

MARIA: It was just bumpers and little dingy accidents; no real need to tell you at the time (laughter). They weren't big accidents. It was like, backing up and "Oops, I backed up a little too hard."

JERRY: You did tell me about the time you thought you killed someone. That was a good story.

MARIA: I was working in a local bakery. He came in one day to pick up some rolls or whatever.

JERRY: She waited on me.

MARIA: I think it was like two weeks previously that I had used his car to go up to my girl friend's house. I made a U-turn on a main street and as I was making the U-turn—I had my pink slip at the time too. I didn't even have a license. As I was making the U-turn, there was a car parked. There was someone sitting in this car behind the driver's seat. I hit it—just made a little dent. It wasn't a bad hit but, obviously if you're sitting there, you get out of your car and yell or say, "What did you do?" Well, this person never moved. So I just backed up to where I was. I stayed there waiting for the person to get out. I thought, "Oh my God! He never moved. I must have killed him. He must have had a heart attack in the car" (joint laughter).

JERRY: She was just sixteen.

MARIA: I just sat there, and I didn't know what to do. I even got out and looked at my car. Nothing happened to my car. I looked over there, and there was a tiny dent in the door. Not bad but, if someone had hit me, I would have gotten out . . . Whoever it was just sat there. It was dark, and I couldn't see him or her very well, so I gave him five minutes. Then I said, "I'm getting the heck out of here" (laughter). I made that Uee and took off. Then later on, I started thinking, "Gees . . . I drove away with the lights on . . . and they could have written my driver's license plate number down and make up a big story." So I just mulled it over. A couple of weeks later it seemed like the perfect time: he came to buy dinner rolls (laughter). I was wrapping up his dessert or whatever, and I said, "Daddy! Two weeks ago, I think I killed somebody." He said, "WHAT?" (uproarious laughter).

I told him the story, and his first question was, "WITH MY CAR?" (more hilarious laughter).

JERRY: Then I said, "After two weeks, honey, they would have had you by this time. If they haven't called you yet, don't worry about it."

MARIA: I said, "Really?"

JERRY: She was crying . . . but, obviously, she hadn't hurt anybody. If anyone was really sitting in there, they were sleeping, or preoccupied, or just didn't want to get out in the dark.

MARIA: Yeah, that was such a relief.

Daughter's First Job

JERRY: She started to work at 14.

MARIA: I got working papers at 14 or something—as soon as I could. My mother always said, "Don't work, you're going to work for the rest of your life." But I always wanted to, so I did.[17]

17. How soon Maria could work was defined primarily by the Fair Labor Standards Act which was enacted in 1938 (Silver, 1991). It and state laws help to protect children from prematurely entering the labor force. At the time of this study, Maria and other Massachusetts residents aged 14 or 15 were required to obtain a special work permit, which only allowed employment within many protective restrictions. Children aged 16 to 18 years were also covered by special protection, including a prohibition from working in hazardous occupations. Maria's father was also protected by this enactment; he left high school at age 17 to help his financially strained family, but he might have continued in school longer

JERRY: She was a good teenager. She worked hard; she worked in a bakery and did a lot of odd jobs. She saved her money on her own; she paid for college. She tried to help herself. She did a good job. She really did.

MARIA: I saved all my money. I used to take vacations with my friends. I had money in the bank. I just wanted to have my own money. I just never liked asking for money. Oh, they would offer to give me money. If I was going out, my father was the first one with his hand in his pocket. "Here, take money." "Well, I have money, Dad." "No, you have to have extra. Take extra." So it wasn't because they didn't give it to me. It was just that I never wanted to take their money, or ask. I wanted to make my own money. I think that was just the only reason. I guess that I was real independent.

Father-Daughter Sports Events

JERRY: We went to a lot of football games. I took you to the football game on Thanksgiving Day. We'd be out in the freezing ice watching football. We used to freeze our buns off. It was so cold. Throughout high school that was a highlight. Every year we'd sit together, and every year we'd get sick together.

MARIA: We always seemed to catch it together. There we were sitting around the holiday table, snorting and barking together (laughter).

JERRY: She's got a lot of genes that I have.

MARIA: He also took me to wrestling. Well, he *made* me go to wrestling. (Breaks into laughter and claps hands.)

JERRY: Did you ever see a light go on when someone lies? (laughter). Her face should be lit up.

MARIA: No, no, no. He took us to all the sports events: Red Sox games, Celtics games. Then he thought he'd introduce WRESTLING.

JERRY: I am a sports fan so I took her along. I thought she loved wrestling. She sounded like she was having a ball. But do you know what she told me afterwards? She said, "I really went for the food."

MARIA: I love sports. But wrestling? It was all right. It was OK.

---

if his first job at the warehouse had been classified as a hazardous occupation. Maria's grandparents were not protected by these policies and entered the work force without going beyond grammar school. Social policies, obviously, have the power to change people's life courses.

(Turns to father.) But mainly I used to go along to give you company, Dad (pause), and to have pizza and popcorn and Coke (laughter).

JERRY: I found that out years later! (laughter).

Family Vacations

MARIA: He and Mom also took us on a lot of vacations—to Florida, to Hawaii on their 25th anniversary.

JERRY: To Hawaii!

MARIA: How old was I? Seventeen? They took me and my brother to Hawaii with them. Still to this day I don't know why they did that, but they did (laughter).[18]

JERRY: We did that because we wanted to share it. That's why. (Gina nods in agreement.)

MARIA: So they took us and we stayed at a real nice hotel. They took us everywhere sightseeing. We went one day to this Pearl Harbor tour that the Navy puts on.

JERRY: The *Arizona*.

MARIA: We got on the boat, and there were three Navy men on the boat. My father was speaking to one of the Navy guys, joking around with him, and later the same Navy guy started speaking with me, which my father didn't know. So we got off the boat and he goes, "What a nice guy he was." I said, "Yeah, Dad. He asked me out for tomorrow night. There's a group playing." He goes, "No, no. I didn't like him that much" (laughter). He goes, "You can't trust those Navy guys. I was a Navy guy. Forget it" (more laughter).

Funny how his opinion changed (laughter). Anyway, I had told him that I wouldn't go out with him.

JERRY: See? She believed me. Right?

MARIA: No. No. No. I just wouldn't go out with somebody, one night, in a strange place (pause).

Dating

MARIA: Then I started dating Mark. Mark had a convertible that used to leak a little bit and, of course, we'd come home from dates and it might be 11, and we'd sit in the car for like half an hour . . .

18. Taking their children with them on their "second honeymoon" indicates how important the children were in their lives.

45 minutes, and Dad would come home. Sometimes we wouldn't even see him pull up. He'd come to the car (giggles).

JERRY: They were parked out here. I drove right by them and right into the driveway!

MARIA: We were deep in conversation. We didn't notice (laughter).

JERRY: . . . right, right . . . (more laughter).

MARIA: . . . and then all of a sudden we heard a knock on the window! He knocked on the window and asked, "What are you sitting in the car for? It's cold out."

JERRY: No. What it was . . . She's making it sound worse than what it is. It was in mid-winter . . . and it had to be five below zero that night.

MARIA: We were warm (laughter).

JERRY: They had to be making their own heat (laughter). That convertible he had, believe me, wasn't warm at all. So I thought, "Why don't you go upstairs? Instead of freezing in the car?"

MARIA: You thought? You forgot to think back when you were that age!

JERRY: That's right. That's the reason she said . . .

MARIA: "No, we're fine Dad. I'll be up in a little while" (laughter).

JERRY: Oh, the windows were all frosted and steamy; I had to scrape to get . . . (much laughter).

MARIA: Get out of here.

JERRY: That's the reason why I knocked on the window. That was the only time I ever did that, but it was so cold—I was worried about them.

MARIA: I don't think you were worried that we were cold though. More that we were too warm? (much laughter).

JERRY: Yeah. [Father is apparently slightly embarrassed.][19]

Rejection of Mother's Request

GINA: Should we tell about how I asked for room and board? Oh yeah, go ahead.[20]

---

19. A brief paragraph has been deleted at this point.
20. It was not long after Jerry's embarrassment that Gina gave Maria permission to tell an equally embarrassing story about her. In this way, she affirmed her daughter's honesty while also providing evidence that Jerry had also been an unusually wise parent at times. The role Jerry played in this incident also provided

MARIA: All right, you asked for it (laughing). I guess I was probably sixteen or so, and my mother came up with the idea that I should start paying room and board. Out of the clear blue, she said, "Now that you're working and you're making money, I think we're going to ask for room and board." I just turned around and said, "ROOM AND BOARD?" (laughter). "For WHAT? WHY should I?" (laughter). "I don't understand. You had me. I'm your child. Now you want me to pay to live here" (more laughter). I just couldn't understand.

JERRY: That's the truth.

MARIA: It never clicked. I said, "I'm just not paying." I said, "I'm not paying to live here." Well, I just couldn't understand the motive.

JERRY: I come home from work . . .

MARIA: He came home, and I thought I better tell him about this idea (more laughter). I said, "You can't believe what Ma asked me. She wants money for room and board." I just couldn't believe it. He didn't know anything about it either. So that was good because he said, "Gina?" "What, honey?" "You think you want to start room and board?" I just told him, too. "There's no way," I said, "I just don't believe in that."

JERRY: She said to me, "I'm your daughter, did you know that?"

MARIA: "I'm your daughter. You had me. I live here." I said, "I don't think I overeat! I don't have to pay room and board. I save my own money. That's it."

Later, after that night, we discussed it together, and I told them how I felt and everything. Then Ma finally said, "You know, the reason I asked you was because I was going to save that money for you." She wasn't going to take it and spend it like some parents might do. She was going to take it and put it in a bank.

JERRY: That's what she always does.

MARIA: Her intention was to save the money for me. She didn't tell me that at the time. But I was saving money on my own. I always saved money. And my father, of course, just agreed. "Why should she?" (laughs). I thought that was good, but at the time I saved my own money.

JERRY: To be honest with you, we thought we were better off doing it for her. As it was, she did a good job. She really did a good job. She

---

him with an opportunity to rework the financial demands his own mother had placed on him during his adolescence.

was able to pay for college. When she got married she had money in the bank.

Support for College Attendance

MARIA: I went to Tufts University for two years. I was on such a crazy schedule at the time. You know, up at 6:00. He used to drive me to the bus. That was another highlight. Remember, Dad?

JERRY: Oh, how could I forget.

MARIA: I used to have to be at the bus stop by 7:00 or 7:30 and at the time he had to leave for work about the same time. Maybe 15 minutes earlier than that. So every morning I'd get up half awake, and I would just sit down to have my toast and juice, and he'd be, "I'm leaving. I'm leaving. I'm going to go in the car and you're not going to be ready in 5 minutes. I'm leaving. I'm leaving." I'd say, "Can I bite my toast? Can I have . . . OK. Leave. Go ahead and leave. I'll walk to the bus." "No. I'm telling you I'm going to leave." He would never leave but he would just keep telling me he was going to leave. Sometimes we would fight all the way to the bus stop (laughter). He'd drop me off. "Have a good day" (laughter). "OK." That would go on every morning that I was five minutes late.

JERRY: She was sitting there eating toast, like she had all day. "Move! It's time to go to work." I would never leave her. I'd never leave her mother either. I drive her to the bus now, every morning.

MARIA: When he says, "Gina, you ready? We're going to miss the bus." She just says, "There'll be another one." Right?

GINA: He's a wonderful man.[21]

MARIA: So during my college years I was busy. I left like at 7:00 in the morning and then used to go to work right from school. So I wasn't around home much. In and out.

I entered college majoring in speech and hearing therapy. I got a full scholarship to go. Half financial and half because of my grades. My second year of college I changed majors, mostly because of financial problems. The university dropped the scholarship and made it a loan. So I ended up having to take a loan out. It was a five-year

---

21. It is interesting to note that here and throughout the interview Jerry's wife never allows herself to side with her daughter against her husband. Even to this day she apparently maintains a clear parenting alliance (see Cohen & Weissman, 1984).

program, and I just couldn't see going that much into debt. So I switched over and went my second year in the Dental Program.

JERRY: Well, I was pleased with her really going to school and working for it. She was very, very good at it. I was proud of her doing what she did. She did what she wanted to do. She made up her mind she wanted to do work in a dentist's office, be a dental assistant, and she went to school for what she wanted. I never pressured her on doing anything else. The only thing I remember, maybe I gave her a couple of suggestions when she was getting into college about learning typing and learning secretarial work, which is a normal thing that a girl tries to strive for other than a career person. But other than that, no, she did what she wanted to do. We were proud of what she did. Everything she did, she did her way, but she did it well. She still works in dentistry. She's still independent.

MARIA: Also, although Mark didn't know it at the time, I thought we were probably going to get married. So, I didn't want to carry a big four-year loan into a marriage. We also wanted to have fun (laughs). Everyone—including my mother—kept telling me, and I tell everyone now, too: "Enjoy yourself now." Once you have kids, you can't do this, and you can't do that. So we took trips every year, and we had a really good time.[22]

Joint Vacations

JERRY: Before Maria and Mark had children, we traveled a lot together. We vacationed together. Once we took a car trip to Florida together.

MARIA: We had a good time. It was just the four of us, and my father had a big car, and we drove his car, and it was just fun. We got lost, and we just laughed. We just had lots of laughs. And, of course, once we got to Florida, my father was in the shade and we were in the sun! But it was fun. Luckily all of us were very compatible. My husband enjoys their company, and we had a good time.

22. Maria's upward mobility was above average. Nevertheless, her greater potential mobility was cut short by her decision not to complete a four-year college degree. Her family's traditional working class expectations (for example, family suggestions to take secretarial courses in high school and to marry at a fairly young age) hint at how socially defined sex roles can lower a person's life chances, even under otherwise unusually supportive conditions (compare Gronseth, 1978).

JERRY: We also took a trip to Puerto Rico together. We had a really good time. Lots of funny moments. It was like going with friends.

Current Reflections

The Father's Perspective

I enjoyed family life. That's what I wanted, and that's what I got, and that's what I enjoyed. That motivated me to work harder. Well, I always worked in one thing, which was iron and steel. I have sold steel for many years, but before those days I started out working in the warehouse, unloading and loading—getting stock ready to go out, getting materials into the warehouse, identifying materials and tagging them. I started there right after leaving high school, around 17. Well, I only worked there a little over a year and I was drafted.[23]

After the service, I came back to the same company. In those days warehouse work was actual real labor work. But I stayed, and one thing led to another over the years, and I became a foreman. Then, when I was around 32 years old, I got to a point where I wanted to go into sales. And that was my asking to go into it. I did take a deduction in pay at the time because I was making more money, but that wasn't the idea. The idea was that in the future there would be much more money for my family.[24]

The other reasons were that I liked selling, and I knew the product. Being a good salesperson is knowing the product, and I knew the materials in and out. I knew steel right from when I was a little kid, meaning 17, and I learned the materials and the grades and the specs and what have you. I am self-taught. I didn't go to any schools to learn how to sell, or how to identify materials, or whatever. I went through the book, I brought home all the literature I could find in the early years, and I studied and memorized the weights and specs on any kinds of material at all.[25]

23. He was in the Navy for three years during World War II and served part of his tour of duty overseas.

24. This occurred at a time that Levinson (1978) calls the "age-thirty transition," when men often either switch from an unsatisfying career while it is still possible to do so or intensify their commitment to their current career.

25. Jerry showed a significant degree of upward occupational mobility in his own life. His own father, a coppersmith, was a skilled worker with less than a seventh-grade education. Jerry started out as a laborer in the warehouse, after

I also developed my own contacts with different companies. They have certain ways of doing things and I have certain ways of doing things; we share each other's ideas and we might get a new idea. There's a lot of new materials that came out in the past 35 years that do different jobs, and by us learning the materials (what it could do, and what it can't do) we might get a new approach on things. In other words, there's the fabrication field, there's the construction field, there's forgers. There's so many things that people do with materials and by you knowing what the certain materials can do, and by learning all of this, you can help anybody that called you and said "I'm doing this, I'm doing that. What do you think the best material that I can use for that job?" The minute that I know what they're making or what they want to do with it, then I can tell them what material to use. The field that I am in, which I have stayed in all my life, is enjoyable to me even until today.[26]

Supporting the family is also a big part of being a good father with me. Because that's what my own father did, that's what I try to do. On one level, I really wanted both of my children to have a better life than my life, as far as wealth went. And I wanted her to have a good schooling. I never had college because we couldn't afford it. We didn't push them, but we were always real close and whatever she did, I'd tell her that we were proud of her. When she graduated, whatever it was, we were always there. She knew that we would be there because when she was little we were there. But everybody looks to help their children strive for much better.

On another level, when she was a kid, I just wanted my children to grow up as well as I did under my father and mother. In other words, I just wanted Maria to be a good person, to do her best, and to be happy.[27]

---

quitting school in the 11th grade to help the family. He later became a foreman in the warehouse, and eventually a steel salesman for the same company. He continued to work as a salesman throughout his later childrearing and midlife years. Yet all of his life, like his own father, he worked with metals.

26. Jerry has shown clear societal generativity at the workplace. By contributing to the useful life of the next generation of products, he took a conventional job and made it a creative calling. Jerry has also served as a town meeting member for his local community.

27. The intergenerational parallels are notable. The first aim he mentions is that he wanted Maria to be "a good person." The way he handled several dilemmas (setting curfews; paying board) also demonstrated his desire to impart to his

Well, she has succeeded on all levels: she is a good person; she respects other people; she is a nice person herself. She also did a good job in school, she's doing a good job as a homemaker, and she's good at her work in dentistry. I feel very strongly that she is doing a wonderful job; she really does an all-around great job. Finally, I think she's happy. The main thing that I remember about her wedding is that she was probably one of the happiest brides I ever saw. Really, seriously. I never saw anybody beaming the way she was beaming. She was extra happy, you know. She enjoyed every minute of it. We were pleased with the way it turned out. I am certainly pleased with the way she has turned out.

I think she's raising her children similar to the way she was raised. They're helped when they have to be helped. She teaches them right from wrong and, believe me, I mean that sincerely, she does a good job. I'm proud of what she's doing. In fact, she'll tell you . . . How many times have I told her I was proud of her? As a mother and as a homemaker. She did a wonderful job.

Oh, and I'm prouder than hell of her two children (laughter). I love those kids. I love my grandchildren the way I loved my children, only it's a different type of a love because we don't have to listen to them cry. It's a cliché, but it's true. We love them. They only live down the street, incidentally, and we see them every day, but we still live a different life. They live their life. We live ours. But I love them just as much as I love my children. Maybe I love them more than I did mine in a sense. What I'm saying is, you don't have that close relationship with them all the time so you try to give them a little extra love because you don't see them eight hours a day or whatever. They're both beauties, believe me.[28]

---

daughter a sense of decency. At the same time, he recalled that his own father's primary aim for his children was for each to grow up to be "a decent person." His second aim was for his children to do their best, and he previously commented that his own father had done the best he could, and we know that Jerry also tried to do his best. Finally, he sought his children's "happiness," and he previously described how his own father had contributed to his own boyhood happiness.

28. Jerry has transformed his childrearing generativity into a type of grand-generativity as he relishes his role as a grandfather. His affirmation of his daughter's own parental generativity is particularly important in this regard. "In the context of the generational cycle," as Erikson and his colleagues (1986) have suggested, "it is incumbent upon" elders to "to enhance feelings of generativity" in members of the younger generation (p. 74).

Now that she is an adult and a parent I would say that we get along as friends more than father and daughter. We really do. We don't act, you know, like some, you know, everything is done in formal ways. We don't do that. I enjoy her friendship and we really have a good time.[29]

If her success has anything to do with her parents, and I hope it did, maybe she saw us doing the best we could, and she probably was striving to do the best she could. I'll be honest with you. Everything I did was just trying to be a good father really. I don't know what I've achieved, but I do know that I tried to do the best I could. Yet, I don't remember doing anything really outstanding: I went into the service. I lived and came home. Got married and the family grew. That's all. [Gina enters the conversation.]

GINA: I want to say (turning to husband) you gave lots of love, and that was the most important thing of all.

JERRY: Yeah, but we both did, honey.

GINA: I think that's still special. I mean, lots of times fathers don't play that role. You were able to show your warmth and affection.

JERRY: But this is only normal for us.

GINA: That's true. [Gina and Jerry turn back to the interviewer.]

JERRY: The reason I say it was normal is because I was brought up in a home like that. Like I said before, we didn't have much when I was growing up, other than clothes and food and love. Expensive things we never had. But the love and the warmth that we received we also tried to give to our children.[30]

In turn, I can say that all I wanted for Maria was a good life and a happy life. I wanted her to be happy. That's the way I felt, and I feel

29. All of the fathers and children that appear in the self-portraits noted that their relationship became more collegial after the son or daughter became an adult. As Rubin (1982) has stated in a discussion of fathers and sons, for their "relationship to get better—or for it to remain good—it must change. A central challenge for both . . . is to transform a childhood relationship marked by the father's authority and the [child's] dependence to an adult relationship between two autonomous people" (p. 28).

30. Jerry apparently had no difficulty expressing his affection with hugs and kisses in his family of procreation. However, the longitudinal records of his family of origin indicate that his boyhood home was not rated as congenial or warm, especially in the sense that his parents seldom did things as a family. Jerry explained that his parents lacked the economic means to do much; nevertheless, he also clearly reworked and rectified this dimension of his family life when he became a parent.

very strongly she achieved it all. I'm very proud of her, just the way she is.

The Daughter's Perspective

I am independent and driven. I'm not one to sit down and do nothing. I don't think it was one thing that my father did that made me this way, or to turn out one way or another. He was more involved with us than a lot of fathers, but I think he just saw that as one part of us being a close family. He never did anything, you know, to stand up on a podium for. My friends would always say, "Your father's so funny. Your father's so nice." But basically he was just always there.[31]

I can see myself similar to my dad in a lot of ways! I think our personalities are a lot alike: the sense of humor and the nervousness. He tends not to find things in the house where it's in front of him, and I can be the same way; my mother can find anything. You know, personality wise, we are a lot alike.[32]

Like any parent, I think he always wanted the best for me. I don't think he ever actually said what he wanted for me. He just wanted me to do what I would be happy doing. That's more important. Just to be happy. He never forced anything on me, but I always had a goal in mind on my own. I suppose if I didn't have goals in mind, maybe he would have been giving me his opinion, but I always knew what I wanted to do. I think he just wanted me to do well in what I chose to do. And probably, of course, marry a nice, rich man (laughs).

I guess it's important for a father to just make sure his daughter knows that he is always there and is always willing to help. Just like my husband is with my daughter. He's just always there. He doesn't spoil her, but he does things that are important to her. And, all the time, hoping that she will go in the right direction as she gets older. And, all the time, hoping that she doesn't grow too far apart as she gets older.

31. Children of highly involved childrearing fathers typically are aware that their fathers were more involved than many other parents, but they always saw this as a reflection of their father's preferences and enjoyment. Their fathers, that is, did not make them feel burdened by the "sacrifices" they had made on their behalf. Rather, their fathers communicated that they generally preferred to be with them.
32. Jerry also attributed a sense of humor to his own father.

The Daughter Looks Ahead a Generation

Being a parent myself, now, it's nice. Of course, I usually feel *tired* (laughter), tired and mentally exhausted. It's harder than I thought it would be. Everything is real hunky-dory when it's just the two of you. When you add a child . . . then things become stressful at times. It adds happiness, too, but it also adds stress.

Now we have two children. Having two is more than twice as hard as having one. It's difficult. I guess I want to be like the perfect mother—I'm a perfectionist, I think. That's the problem with me. I want to have my house just so. The laundry has to be done. I want supper on the table at a certain time. Everyone has to be happy. It's like "Leave It To Beaver," you know? (Laughter.) So, that's why it's hard.

I think the way my father raised me has influenced the way I am raising my children. I basically do what he did. Like I said, you have to watch your kids. Each child is different. If your child is going along fine that way, then fine. You just follow it. I guess everything is just real home-oriented. Everyone eats together at night, and it's like a scheduled thing. I'm an organized person, and our family life is organized. You eat dinner at a certain time, and you go to bed at a certain time, and everyone just has their routine that they follow. That's the way I was raised. That's the way I like it for my children. I mean you just want the family to be happy.[33]

My father was not real rigid with restrictions or anything like that. Probably because I never took advantage. I guess you can start out that way. I can see myself starting out that way with my kids. Not giving them like, "Be in at 8 or else you're going to be grounded." I guess I'll start out the same way as my parents did, but it depends on your child. If your child takes advantage of it then you can't continue on that path. You have to change.

I think probably the only thing I do differently from my parents is that I try to put up with more from my children. In today's times, I think it is important to talk more, to reason more, to be patient and give them choices. Years ago, if you were in a store and a child wants

33. Maria follows her parents' childrearing practices, including her father's stress on happiness. Jerry also said that his parenting was modeled after that of his own father. When discussing being a good breadwinner, for instance, he said "That's what my own father did. That's what I try to do."

something, you just said "No. You're not having that. That's it. That's the final word." But now, parents need to do more reasoning. "Why don't we get ready to leave and go to the other store to buy our bread. Then we can get a cupcake there." Or, "If you want to do that, then you can't do this." I do a lot of that. You give them a choice and expect them to live with the consequences. Like, "You can have this toy or that toy, but not both. Which one do you want? You choose." I kind of make a couple of choices for them, and they decide which one they want. They think they are making a choice and, on some level, they are. Of course, sometimes it feels like I'll do anything just to keep them from screaming in a store (laughter).[34]

When I'm a grandmother I don't think I want to see my grandchildren every day (laughing). Right now I say that because I can see myself wanting a break from kids. But I think basically it's brought me and my father even closer and we can laugh at a lot of stuff that the kids do. He'd say, "You used to do that."

Now that I am a parent, I know what the heck they went through. Why they used to yell at us. Yeah, I can understand all that stuff now; sometimes I used to think when I was younger, "Oh, they're so mean." Now my son's saying that to me. So I can understand. Before I had a baby all I used to think about was a "baby," a little baby to hold and push in the mall. I didn't think about the baby growing up with walking and talking and answering me back. I didn't think about all this other stuff.

It's all cuddly and sweet. No one tells you you're not going to sleep for like three years, and they're going to answer you back. They're going to hate you at eight years old. I don't think you understand it until you're a parent. I have a friend that's single and as much as she'll come over and say, "Oh, how do you do it? You must be so tired. I have to go home and take a nap after I leave your house," I don't think she can really understand until she is in that circumstance, so it is hard.

I hope that my kids can just go to school and be successful at

34. Maria's discussion of childrearing practices reveals her special sensitivity to children's development and to the necessity of adjusting one's childrearing practices to accommodate individual differences and changing needs during the course of each child's development. Her practice of handling potential conflicts by offering choices, for example, is similar to the advice offered by moral educator Thomas Lickona in *Raising Good Children* (1983).

something. It doesn't have to be college and a degree. It can be becoming a plumber. Something to do that they *like*. I don't think I would ever tell them what to do, but they have to decide for themselves.

Concluding Query

Jerry's story provides many clues regarding the boyhood precursors and current adulthood promoters of unusually high levels of parental generativity. What are the connections between men's boyhood histories of fathering received and adulthood histories of fathering given? For instance, was Jerry patterning his own fathering after the model of his father? Or was his style of being "always there" a way of counterbalancing his own boyhood experience of a father who was always at work? What are the connections between men's ongoing family contexts and the fathering they provide? For instance, how did Jerry's wife contribute to the quantity and quality of fathering he gave to Maria?

10

Boyhood and Current Predictors of Fathers' Parental Generativity

with Carol Snarey

The genesis of good fathering represents one of the most intriguing puzzles in contemporary family studies. Why do fathers father the way they do? Why do some fathers spend more or better time with their children than do other fathers? This chapter unites both adult development and child development perspectives by treating fathers' parental generativity as the outcome variable and their boyhood and current family circumstances as possible predictors of variations in their parental generativity.

What We Know from Prior Research

Until the past decade, as Belsky (1991) wryly observes, "most investigators viewed parents as young children do, that is, as individuals without life histories that precede the role of parent and [without] identities that exist independent of it" (p. 123). The few studies that have attempted to understand the origins of variations in fathering, however, focus on two broad categories of factors thought to predict strong paternal generativity. In the first category the men's early experiences, typically in their family of origin, were believed to influence them to function in particular ways as fathers themselves. In the second category the contemporary circumstances in the men's current families of procreation were thought to dispose them to select particular levels or categories of participation in childrearing. The review below examines research on the prior and concurrent background characteristics of fathers that may lead to their higher levels of participation in childrearing. More comprehensive or differently focused reviews are available elsewhere (Booth, 1991; Berman &

Pedersen, 1987; Lamb, 1986; Lamb & Easterbrooks, 1981; Lamb, Pleck, Charnov, & Levine, 1987; Norton & Glick, 1986; Pleck, 1985; Radin, 1988; Russell, 1986).

Early Precursors

Two primary hypotheses are offered in the literature to explain the influence of early or boyhood experiences on men's subsequent level of investment in parental generativity (Barnett & Baruch, 1987; Radin, 1981a, 1981b; Sagi, 1982). First is the modeling hypothesis, which claims that fathers who are accessible, nurturant, and authoritative will serve as the most influential models for their sons. These sons, by a process of identifying with or modeling themselves after their fathers, will duplicate the fathering they received during their own childhood. Second, a reworking hypothesis has been proposed. It claims that sons of comparatively distant, nonnurturant, and powerless fathers will attempt to redress the fathering they received by giving their children the personal involvement that they themselves never received. These sons, by a process of compensating for or defending against their own fathers' shortcomings, will rework, improve upon, and rectify the fathering they received during their own childhood. The empirical evidence for these hypotheses is inconsistent.

Research on Modeling

Several studies report that men who experienced high levels of involvement from their fathers in their own childhood family of origin are significantly more likely to become highly involved with their own children (Cowan & Cowan, 1987; Kagan, 1958; Manion, 1977; Mussen, 1969; Mussen & Distler, 1959, 1960; Reuter & Biller, 1973; Sagi, 1982). Biller and Solomon (1986) reviewed several studies which indicate that fathers' nurturant behavior (affectionate, encouraging, attentive behavior toward his child) serves as a model for their sons; they are significantly more likely to identify with the male parenting role (to assume the role of the father doll in a doll-play activity and to score high on measures of masculinity). Manion (1977) further reported that a father's degree of participation was found to be positively associated with how much his own father had been involved in childrearing, thus suggesting the modeling thesis's relevance to boys own later behavior as fathers. The link between boyhood and adulthood was more directly addressed by Block's (1971) analysis of the Berkeley Longitudinal Study data. In brief, Block reported that boys who became the most well adjusted men were significantly more likely to have had strong, accomplished fathers who had shared with their wives the responsibility for childrearing.

Contrary to general public assumptions, however, less evidence supports a negative modeling hypothesis—that harsh, or uncaring fathering is usually replicated by a man in his own parenting. Studies that have used comparison groups, in contrast to weakly designed empirical studies or case studies of clinical populations, show that the great majority of men with childhood experiences of a severe or inadequate parent do *not* go on to replicate this pattern in their own childrearing behavior (Finkelhor, Gelles, Hotaling, & Strauss, 1983; Straus & Gelles, 1986; Straus, Gelles, & Steinmetz, 1980). Elder's classic longitudinal study of a Depression cohort (1974; Elder, Lilker, & Cross, 1984) also supports the idea that negative paternal models are *not* necessarily emulated. He showed, for example, that sons who grew up during the Depression did not repeat their own father's problem behaviors (for example, temper outbursts) in their own subsequent fathering.

Research on Reworking

Conversely, a considerable body of evidence supports the reworking hypothesis. Various studies report that men who experienced little paternal involvement during their childhood are more likely to compensate by becoming highly involved with their own children (De-Frain, 1979; Eiduson & Alexander, 1978; Baruch & Barnett, 1986; Biller, 1971; Hetherington & Frankie, 1967; Russell, 1982a, 1982b, 1985; for review, see Radin, 1988). The idea that negative role models may be counterbalanced or improved upon is supported by Baruch and Barnett's (1986) study of 160 middle-class families with kindergarten or fourth-grade children. They found that men who were dissatisfied with the quality of fathering they had received spent more time with their children. The process of reworking or counterbalancing for a negative role model was especially true of fathers in families with nonemployed wives, where the men did not necessarily have to become more involved.

Some cross-sectional and brief follow-up studies may even be interpreted as providing support for both hypotheses. For instance, in a study of families in which the father was the primary caregiver, Radin (1981a, 1982) originally found little relation between paternal involvement and fathers' recalled assessments of their own fathers. The study concluded, "The notion that the fathers of childrearing men would be unloving, unavailable, and powerless was unsupported" (1982, p. 197). However, a four-year followup assessment of these men indicated that the fathers who persisted as the primary caregivers, especially when they were rearing sons, also had reported at the prior assessment that their own fathers had not been nurturant (Radin & Goldsmith, 1985).

Modeling versus Reworking

It is quite difficult to resolve the apparently conflicting findings of the various studies. From a methodological perspective, one might be tempted to conclude that the majority of the studies are uninterpretable because they have relied heavily upon fathers' retrospective accounts of the fathering they received, and their recall could be quite distorted. Nevertheless, if one takes the findings seriously and examines the data closely, continuities within the inconsistencies can be seen. Sagi (1982) was one of the first to suggest that the modeling and reworking hypotheses "are not mutually exclusive" since "either process is possible depending on the circumstances" (p. 214). An unusually clear summary of this perspective has been offered by Belsky (1984): "Fathers who are warm, nurturant, and involved probably rear sons who identify with and model them, whereas noninvolved fathers, who in all likelihood generate a weak identification and a low probability of being modeled, perhaps stimulate a compensatory process that later prompts sons to parent in a manner expressly opposite that of their own fathers" (p. 86). Pruett (1989) also came to a similar conclusion, based on his small but pioneering longitudinal study of 17 fathers who were highly involved in childrearing: "Pleasant memories of being fathered, or conversely, lingering dissatisfaction with the relationship may impel a man either to repeat or to remake his past. A vital sense of fatherliness seems to have strong roots in either one's own father's caring or perceived emotional distance" (p. 402).

In sum, a reasonable interpretation of prior research is that the most consistent early antecedent of parental generativity is the fathering that the men received in their family of origin, and that this fathering motivation may be cited positively (as a model) or negatively (as something to be counterbalanced). This perspective was actually anticipated by Erikson himself who, as Roazen (1976) clarifies, described "the dependence of ego development on social models" and who also "described how the individual can transform his previous experiences by a process of organic growth" (Roazen, 1976, pp. 47, 55; see Erikson, 1950, 1968). However, given the primary basis of this interpretation—adults retrospectively reconstructing the parenting they received—it is not possible to assess clearly the degree to which fathers actually replicate or counterbalance the fathering that they themselves received. The present study is, therefore, of special interest because it will provide a four-decade longitudinal perspective on the question.

Current Circumstances as Predictors

The second broad category of factors embraces the current circumstances of the father and his family. The review will primarily examine those studies that address characteristics related to those variables included in this study: fathers' employment and socioeconomic status, wives' employment, fathers' marital affinity, and the number, age, and sex of the children.

Fathers' Employment

One of the earliest studies of the influence of socioeconomic status upon men's family roles was conducted by Komarovsky (1940), to gauge the negative effects of father's unemployment during the Depression on the father's status in the eyes of his children. Komarovsky concluded that the wife's attitude was a crucial mediating variable in the association between a father's economic status and family status. Elder (1974) also suggested that a father's loss of socioeconomic status decreased the quality of his relationship with his children, and his influence over them, relative to his wife's. More recent correlational studies confirm that a lower level of constructive fathering is predicted by financial strain and corresponding psychological depression (Conger, et al., 1990; Elder & Caspi, 1988; McLoyd, 1989, 1990;

Simons, Whitbeck, Conger, & Melby 1990). Flanagan's (1990b) study of the impact of the early 1980s recession upon parents and their adolescent children also documented how loss of work strained parent-child relations because fathers were less patient, less nurturant, and more irritable. Parent-child relations were further strained, Flanagan's data suggest, because sons and daughters had to restrict their achievement aspirations if financial resources to attend college were diminished when fathers were permanently laid-off, or when temporarily laid-off fathers did not feel free to encourage their children to attend college.

Other studies also show that a father's inability to meet the family's socioeconomic needs is a primary reason for wives' employment (Russell, 1982b, 1982c), although these patterns are not always strong enough to be replicated in socioeconomically homogeneous samples (Grossman, Pollack & Golding, 1988). Of course, even among working class wives, the motivation to seek paid work cannot be reduced to only financial need. Ferree's (1980) research has indicated that social and psychological needs also contribute to the preference most working-class women express for paid employment over housework.

For a comparison with families in the United States, studies of Australian and Israeli families are especially worthy of note. Russell's (1982b, 1982c) Australian study reports that mother's employment and economic potential were major contributors to a couple's decision to share childcare; in socioeconomically diverse families where the father was highly involved in childrearing, women had higher levels of education, higher status occupations, and, of course, higher incomes. Radin and Sagi's (1982) comparison of Israeli and American families also showed interesting association between childrearing participation and socioeconomic status. Fathers' socioeconomic status was negatively and significantly correlated with their participation in their daughters' childcare (Israel only) or their sons' childcare (United States only). It is unclear why there would be differences for daughters and sons between Israel and the United States, but Radin and Sagi note that the samples were self-selected and may be unrepresentative. Regarding the general negative association between paternal childcare and socioeconomic status, however, the authors note the two primary competing interpretations. Either fathers decide to "reduce their investment in their careers so they can spend more time" with their children, or "more fathers with a lower social status" decide "to become involved in childcare" (p. 132). (For a broader historical and cross-cultural review of the socioeconomic transformation of parenting, see LeVine and White, 1987.)

Mothers' Employment

Regardless of the socioeconomic and other motivations underlying maternal employment, numerous cross-sectional studies report that men are, in fact, more involved in childcare (but not necessarily in housework) when their wives are employed outside of the home (Barnett & Baruch, 1987; Baruch & Barnett, 1986; Bloom-Feshbach, 1979; Gottfried & Gottfried, 1988; Pleck, 1985; Russell, 1982b, 1982c; Zaslow, Pedersen, Suwalsky, Rabinovich & Cain, 1986). For instance, Crouter, Perry-Jenkins, Huston, and McHale's study of fathers with very young children (1987) reported that the men provided more solo childcare when their wives worked outside of the home, apparently because the demands of these "time-poor" dual-earner households necessitated the men's participation in childrearing. There are, of course, some anomalies in the literature. For instance, in Radin's (1981a, 1982; Radin & Goldsmith, 1985) study of intact upper middle-class families, economic considerations were seen as a minor factor in a father's decision to adopt a role-sharing parenting style. This sample was economically advantaged—all were in the "top classes" of Hollingshead's Index of Social Status, so only two of the wives said they "needed" to work for economic reasons. Radin (1981a) found, however, that women whose fathers had not been highly available (but were warmly experienced when they were present) reported that their husbands were active in childrearing. This was interpreted as reflecting the woman's desire to "create a less frustrating experience for her children" (1981a, p. 508). Radin (1981a, 1982) also reported that when a husband's mother and wife's mother had both been employed outside of the home, the husband was again more likely to be a childrearing father. Both of these patterns suggest that women's employment may condition men's parental generativity.

Additional studies of more representative samples directly addressed the possible moderating effect of wives' employment upon their husbands' parental generativity (Barnett & Baruch, 1987; Pleck, 1985). A study by Simons, Whitbeck, Conger, and Melby (1990) shows that fathers were more likely to engage in constructive parenting when they and their wives believed that paternal generativity would make an important difference in the way their children develop and mature (Pedersen et al., 1987). Barnett and Baruch (1987) also report that in dual-earner families fathers' involvement was predicted by wives' work-related characteristics and wives' attitudes, rather than by fathers' recalled socialization, or the number and age of children. When a wife's attitude was liberal, for instance, her husband was more involved in parenting. When her attitude was traditional, her husband did less (Feldman, Nash, & Aschenbrenner, 1983). National surveys also have confirmed that many wives do not desire or encourage their husbands to become more involved in childrearing (see Lamb, Pleck, Charnov, & Levine, 1987; Pleck, 1983). Barnett and Baruch (1987) further report that in single-earner families where the influence of maternal employment was absent, fathers' recollections of the quality of fathering they themselves received as boys was the most consistent predictor of their childrearing participation. Pleck (1985) similarly found that wife's employment had a moderating effect. In dual-earner families, wife's employment had an impact upon their husbands' level of involvement with their children, but when mothers were not employed, fathers' preferences had more impact on their childrearing. To summarize, in families in which the mother was employed, (1) the number of hours she worked and (2) her attitude toward the male role were the strongest predictors of fathers' participation in family work. In single-earner families, in contrast, the major determinant of father's high participation in family life was the father's perception of the quality of the fathering he had received as a child.

Father's Marital Affinity

The impact of fathers' marital affinity or commitment upon their parental generativity has been addressed directly and indirectly in several studies that generally show that marital happiness is associated with men's involvement in childrearing. However, because this body of research is generally cross-sectional in design (with marriages and parenting being assessed concurrently), it becomes equally plausible to interpret marital happiness as predicting husbands' childrearing, as to interpret father-child relations as predicting marital relations.

No doubt, reciprocal processes of influences exist, but the quality of the marital relationship is certainly one of the crucial positive factors influencing the way that fathers parent, because it functions as the primary social support system for parents (Belsky, 1984; compare Mitchell & Trickett, 1980; Powell, 1980). For instance, the esteem their wives held for their husbands predicted the praise the men gave to their preschool children (Sears, Maccoby, & Levin, 1957). Among fathers of older children and adolescents, high levels of marital discord predict the use of punishment rather than reasoning as a disciplinary style (Dielman, Barton, & Cattell, 1977; Kemper & Reichler, 1976; Johnson & Lobitz, 1974). These cross-sectional studies are generally consistent with three additional short-term *longitudinal* studies of first-time fathers, one conducted in Israel (Levy-Shiff & Israelashvili, 1988) and the other two in the United States (Belsky, Youngblade, Rovine, & Volling, 1991; Feldman, Nash, & Aschenbrenner, 1983). All three showed that marital affinity is a significant predictor of men's caregiving, playful behavior, and other aspects of fathering.

In sum, the pattern suggested by the above studies is that socioeconomic need is often a primary, but not sole, motivator of wives' employment. Wives' employment, in turn, decreases the family's financial strain and thereby may help to reduce the financially related psychological depression which generally hinders fathers from providing quality care. Furthermore, wives' employment also increases the need for fathers to contribute a greater share of their children's daily care. Fathers are especially likely to increase the quantity of their childcare when they are on good terms with their spouses and when their wives believe that fathers' parental generativity will benefit their children's development. Missing from this picture, however, are the characteristics of the children themselves.

Children's Characteristics

The children's demographic characteristics represent another set of predictors that has been considered in some research projects. The influence of the child's sex upon a father's childrearing involvement, for instance, has been investigated in several studies, but the results have been inconsistent: Some studies report that fathers prefer to interact with sons, but other studies report no significant paternal preference for sons or daughters. The age of the children involved in these investigations appears to explain some of the different findings. Fathers of infants often show more interest in sons than in daughters, while fathers of older children often show equal interest in sons and daughters (for review, see Chapter 2).

The number of children in a family and their ages also have been significant predictors of men's involvement in domestic labor, including childcare. Men with more children and younger children have been found to devote more time to housework and childcare (Barnett & Baruch, 1987, 1988; Coverman, 1985; Coverman & Sheley, 1986; Farkas, 1976), although this pattern has not been replicated in some studies (Russell, 1982b; Vanek, 1974). A problem with interpreting the inconsistent association between the age of a father's children and the amount of childcare a father provides is that "children" are not always distinguished from "adolescents," and the definition of older or younger children is unclear. A fourth grader, for instance, might be assumed in one study to be a younger child (compared with adolescents) but in another study assumed to be an older child (compared with preschoolers). Studies also have not clearly addressed the impact of the number of children in the family on the amount of childrearing support a father provides to each individual child.

In summary, several sets of factors have been hypothesized to explain the father's childcare behavior and involvement. Among them are included: (1) his early relationship with his own father and family of origin, (2) his socioeconomic background and status, (3) his wife's concurrent preferences and employment status, and (4) the sex, ages, and number of his children. Longitudinal data are needed to test these views, but most of the pioneering studies to date have had to rely on cross-sectional or correlational designs.

Research Questions

The inquiry in this chapter is organized around two research questions. The proposed answers are based on the observation of several suggestive themes in the literature.

Question 1: Does the fathering that men received during their own boyhood years predict their subsequent parental generativity as adults?

To the extent that boyhood histories of fathering received and adulthood histories of fathering given are related, it is possible that fathers will tend to imitate their own fathers' positive qualities (modeling theory) or to redress their own fathers' parenting deficits (compensation theory). Following Sagi (1982) and others (Belsky, 1984, Pruett, 1989), it is reasonable to hypothesize that the processes are not mutually exclusive. It is expected, that is, that highly involved fathers will seek to replicate what was positive in the fathering they themselves received and also to make up for what was distant or negative in it. In terms of the total quantity of all types of parental generativity, it is expected that fathers with unusually positive or negative experiences of being fathered will be more highly involved in rearing their own children, while fathers whose backgrounds were less remarkable will be less motivated to overcome the norms and constraints of our society that discourage paternal involvement with children.

Question 2: Among the concurrent variables, would the characteristics of the fathers themselves, or of their children, or of their wives be the best predictors of the fathers' parental generativity?

The coinciding characteristics of all persons involved will have significance for fathers because fathering is nested in a complex pattern of family relationships. Nevertheless, it is theorized that a wife's involvement in work outside of the home will be the primary concurrent predictor because, as prior cross-sectional research suggests, a wife's absence from the home is an unusually urgent incentive for increased paternal involvement.

How the Study Was Conducted

Subjects

The sample size was reduced from 240 to 231 subjects because complete background information on their families of origin was unavailable for 9 of the fathers. Aside from this missing information, however, no significant differences were noted between the included and excluded subjects.

Rating Scales

The outcome variables for this chapter are the six varieties of child-rearing participation and the fathers' total quantity of all types of parental generativity. The analysis involved 23 different predictor variables. These included the following 15 variables from the men's boyhood years: five indices of their boyhood personal or family characteristics, five boyhood assessments of their fathers' background or childrearing characteristics, and five boyhood assessments of their mothers' background or childrearing characteristics. The analysis also included eight concurrent predictor variables based on the simultaneous characteristics of the men's children, their wives, and themselves. All ratings were made by judges who were blind to other aspects of the fathers' lives, including the ratings made by other judges. The interrater reliability reported for each variable, unless indicated otherwise, is the correlation coefficient based on a comparison of the ratings assigned by the original rater with the ratings assigned by a second rater to the same randomly selected subgroup of cases.

Father's Parental Generativity Outcome Variables

The outcomes being predicted included the three types of parental generativity during two childrearing decades (care for childhood social-emotional, intellectual-academic, and physical-athletic development, and care for adolescent social-emotional, intellectual-academic, and physical-athletic development), as well as the global or total quantity of all forms of parental generativity during both decades. (To review detailed descriptions of the childrearing variables, see Chapter 2.)

Father's Boyhood Personal and Home Characteristics

Five characteristics of the men's boyhood personal and general backgrounds were included as predictors of adulthood parental generativity.

Father's IQ. Each of the Glueck subjects was given the Wechsler-Bellevue Intelligence Test when he entered the study (Glueck & Glueck, 1950).

Father's boyhood social-emotional health. This item rates each father during his boyhood in terms of his emotional character: (1) boy has problems that are significant (tics, phobias, bedwetting beyond age 8, dissocial); (2) average (problems known but not significant); and (3) boy is quite healthy (good natured, no known problems). The rating was based on the fathers' original boyhood case records. Multiple raters were used; all interrater reliability coefficients were equal to or greater than .70 (Vaillant, 1974, Vaillant & Milofsky, 1980).

Father's boyhood physical health. This item also has three levels: (1) severe or prolonged health problem (illness, disability, handicapping deformity); (2) minor illnesses (childhood diseases not marked); and (3) consistent good health (maximum of two minor childhood illnesses reported). The rating was based on the fathers' original boyhood case records. Multiple blinded raters were used; all interrater reliability coefficients were equal to or greater than .70 (Vaillant, 1974, Vaillant & Milofsky, 1980).

Father's boyhood Eriksonian industry. Each man was assessed for the boyhood achievement of industry (Stage 4), using a 9-point boyhood index (see Chapter 2).

Father's boyhood home atmosphere. This item rates each father's home in terms of cohesiveness and stability, on three levels: (1) noncongenial, noncohesive atmosphere (parents do not do things as a family, unintegrated family life, many moves); (2) apparently average home (does not stand out as good or bad); and (3) cohesive, warm atmosphere (parents work together to do things as a family, sharing atmosphere, maternal and paternal presence, stable home with few moves). The rating was based on the fathers' original boyhood case records. Multiple blinded raters were used; all interrater reliability coefficients were equal to or greater than .70 (Vaillant, 1974, Vaillant & Milofsky, 1980).

Father's Own Parents' Characteristics

Five characteristics of the Glueck subjects' own fathers and mothers, assessed during the Glueck subjects' boyhood years, are included as predictors of the men's subsequent adulthood parental generativity.

Relationship with his own father during boyhood. This item rates each boy's relationship with his father, as to whether it was warm and nurturant. The rating included three levels: (1) distant, nonnurturant, or unbalanced (paternal absence, overly punitive, expectations unrealistic or not what son wants for himself); (2) apparently average relationship; and (3) nurturing (warm, does things that promote the boy's autonomy or self-esteem, shows personal interest in the boy and discusses problems with him). The rating was based on the fathers' original boyhood case records. Multiple blinded raters were used; all interrater reliability coefficients were equal to or greater than .70 (Vaillant, 1974, Vaillant & Milofsky, 1980).

Relationship with his mother during boyhood. This variable, including the rating procedure and interrater reliability, is the same as the above parallel variable for the father.

Father's unsuitable supervisory style during boyhood. This is a dichotomous rating of a Glueck subject's own father's supervisory style, in which (0) firm but kindly is contrasted with (1) not firm or not fair. Fathers were rated as using an unsuitable supervisory style if their discipline was inconsistent, erratic, overstrict, or lax. The rating is based on a psychiatric interview with the boy, background interviews with the parents, and on social workers' observations of the family over an extended period of time. The interrater percent of agreement was between .91 and .94 (Delinquency Prediction Table, Glueck & Glueck, 1950; Craig & Glick, 1964; Vaillant & Milofsky, 1980).

Mother's unsuitable supervisory style during boyhood. This variable, including the rating procedure and interrater reliability, is the same as the above parallel variable for the father.

Physical punishment by father during boyhood. This is a dichotomous rating of the father's own father's disciplinary method, in which (0) father did not primarily make use of physical punishment or threats of physical punishment, contrasted with (1) father primarily used physical punishment or threat of physical punishment, which elicited fear in the boy. Physical punishment meant rough handling, strappings, and beatings, in contrast to reasoning, deprivation of privileges, or appeals to self-respect and ideals. The rating is based on a psychiatric interview with the boy at age 14 (+/– 2 years), background interviews with the parents, and on social workers' observations of the family over an extended period of time. The interrater percent of agreement was between .91 and .94 (Delinquency Prediction Table, Glueck & Glueck, 1950; cf. Craig & Glick, 1964; Vaillant & Milofsky, 1980).

Physical punishment by mother during boyhood. This variable, including the rating procedure and interrater reliability, is the same as the above parallel variable for the father.

Father's own father's educational level. The Glueck subjects' own fathers were rated on their level of education, based on the educational subscale from Hollingshead's Index of Social Status previously described (Chapter 6). Interrater reliability was estimated to be .92.

Father's mother's educational level. The Glueck subjects' own mothers' level of education were also rated according to the Hollingshead educational subscale. The interrater reliability was estimated to be .95.

Father's own father's occupational level. The Glueck subjects' own fathers were rated on their occupational level, based on the occupational subscale from Hollingshead's Index of Social Status (see Chapter 6). Interrater reliability was estimated to be .80.

Father's mother's occupational level. The Glueck subjects' mothers were also rated on their occupations according to the Hollingshead occupational subscale. Mothers' premarital occupations were used for those who never worked outside of the home after marriage. Interrater reliability was estimated to be .82.

Father's Concurrent Family Characteristics

Eight characteristics of the fathers' own families of procreation (four children's characteristics and four parental characteristics) were included as current predictors of the men's adulthood parental generativity.

Child's age. Because of variations in the time when the men began their families, the ages of their children varied when the men were assessed for their participation in childrearing during the first decade of their children's lives and during the second decade of their children's lives. The age of their children at each longitudinal assessment was thus included as a control variable.

Child's sex. The gender of the children was controlled for, when appropriate, using a constructed variable (coded 0 = female, 1 = male).

Number of children. A man's childrearing participation with his first child, and the significance of that childrearing, may be influenced by the total number of children for whom he is responsible. Thus the number of each father's children was also monitored at each longitudinal assessment to control for this variation.

Generativity chill. It is possible that generativity chill, defined as a threat to a man's biological generativity, would affect his commitment to parental generativity and societal generativity (see chapters 1 and 6). To explore the possible influence of generativity chill upon the fathers, each father was rated on whether he had experienced the threat of the loss of his first-born child during the first childrearing decade and during the second childrearing decade. The two ratings were based on the following ordinal categories: (1) his child had not experienced a major illness or a major injury, (2) his child had experienced a major but not clearly life-threatening illness or injury, or (3) his child had experienced a major and clearly life-threatening illness or other similar threat to existence. (First-decade threats to existence also included major fertility and prenatal problems, consistent with the findings previously reported in Chapter 6.) The interrater reliability was estimated to be .76 for the childhood decade and .71 for the adolescent decade.

Wife's work outside of the home. To evaluate the significance of her employment outside the home, each wife was rated at each longitudinal assessment as follows: (0) wife not employed outside of the home, (1) wife employed part time outside of the home, and (2) wife employed full time outside of the home. (For further details, see Chapter 2.)

Wife's education. The wives' levels of education were rated according to a subscale from Hollingshead's Index of Social Status (see Chapter 4); note that the wives' Hollingshead occupational status ratings were often made near the end of or shortly after the primary childrearing years and thus could not be used to predict fathers' childrearing.

Father's education. The fathers' levels of education were rated according to a subscale from Hollingshead's index (see Chapter 4); note that the fathers' occupational ratings were made near the end of or shortly after the primary childrearing years and thus could not be used to predict his childrearing.

Father's marital affinity. An index of the fathers' marital affinity or commitment was obtained through self-reports regarding thoughts of divorce at any time during his first two decades of childrearing. Each father was rated as to whether he had: (1) seriously considered divorce, (2) casually considered divorce, or (3) never considered divorce. (For further details see Chapter 6.)

What We Found: Precursors of Fathers' Childrearing

What accounts for variations in men's involvement in the rearing of their children? The correlations between the men's boyhood or current characteristics and their parental generativity outcomes will be examined first. To evaluate which predictor variables explain the greatest variance in the parental generativity outcomes, we will report a series of multiple regression analyses.

Correlations with Men's Parental Generativity

The correlations between the fathers' boyhood or concurrent background variables and the fathers' childrearing participation outcomes are summarized in Table 10.1. Among the 23 different boyhood and concurrent variables under consideration, a total of 15 (65%) are significantly associated with one or more of the parental generativity variables used to rate each father.

Only 1 (6.6%) of the 15 boyhood variables (IQ) is significantly correlated with the global summation of all types of childrearing participation. In contrast, 9 (60%) of the 15 boyhood variables are significantly correlated with one or more of the specific types of parental generativity. These include two (40%) of the five ratings of the father's boyhood personal characteristics, five (100%) of the five characteristics of the fathers' own fathers, and two (40%) of the five characteristics of the fathers' mothers.

In further contrast, five (63%) of the eight concurrent variables are significantly correlated with the global summation of all childrearing participation. Six concurrent variables (75%) are also significantly correlated with one or more of the fathers' subsequent types of parental generativity. In sum, the boyhood variables are more consistent predictors of specific types of parental generativity, while the concurrent variables predicted the global or total quantity of participation as well as specific types of parental generativity.

These correlation coefficients can be as confusing as they are helpful, because they do not take into consideration that boyhood variables occurred historically prior to the concurrent variables or that some variables may be partially redundant. They cannot tell us which variables account for the most variance from a longitudinal perspective. Regression analyses will be used to clarify the competing pictures of childrearing predictors.

Predicting Men's Parental Generativity

Seven multiple regression models were constructed to evaluate which predictor variables explain the most variance in the fathers' parental generativity outcomes. For each analysis, the variables were made available for entry into the equation in two hierarchical blocks. The first block included only the historically prior boyhood variables, and the second block included only concurrent variables. Within each block, stepwise entry was used. This procedure gives priority to historic characteristics over concurrent characteristics and only then gives priority within each set of characteristics to the stronger predictor variables.

The predictors of the total quantity of all varieties of childrearing participation were considered first. Then the predictors of each of the six specific varieties of childrearing participation were considered. As will be seen, the predictors of different varieties of childrearing participation sometimes contrast sharply with those associated with the total quantity of all childrearing activities.

Predicting Total Parental Generativity

The regression analyses reported in Table 10.2 show which boyhood and concurrent characteristics of the men and their families account for the most variance in the men's total quantity of parental generativity across their childrearing years. This analysis differs from all of the subsequent analyses in this chapter in that it addresses the global or overall parental generativity rather than variations in different types of parental generativity.

Six background characteristics account for over a quarter of the variance in total childrearing level [$R = .518$, $F (6, 224) = 13.68$, $p < .001$]. From the block of prior boyhood variables, the fathers' IQ is a significant positive predictor and the mothers' level of education is a significant negative predictor. Together those variables account for 5% of the variance. In addition, from the concurrent block of predictor variables, three positive predictors stand out: the father's marital affinity, the wife working outside of the home, and the wife's educational level together account for an additional 16% of the variance. Furthermore, the fathers' experience of a threat to their children's existence contributes an additional 6% to the explained variance in their total quantity of childrearing. The total model accounts for 27% of the variance in fathers' overall quantity of parental generativity.

Table 10.1 Predicting fathers' childrearing participation by boyhood and current characteristics: correlation coefficients

| | Fathers' childrearing support of: | | | | | | |
| | Childhood development | | | Adolescent development | | | |
Precursors	Social	Intellectual	Physical	Social	Intellectual	Physical	Global
	Father's Boyhood Family-of-Origin Characteristics						
Father's personal and home characteristics							
IQ	.130*	.203***	.075	-.030	.087	.019	.158**
Social-emotional health	-.132*	.062	.008	-.118*	.040	-.113	-.061
Physical health	-.038	-.064	.033	.008	-.050	-.005	-.038
Eriksonian industry	.098	.018	-.025	.098	.007	-.008	.052
Home atmosphere	.021	.033	.051	-.047	-.032	.068	.025
Father's own father's characteristics							
Father-boy relation	-.018	.015	.065	-.237***	-.087	.022	-.071
Provided unsuitable supervision	.036	.016	.141*	-.105	.017	.124*	.076
Used physical punishment	-.039	-.057	.079	-.058	.070	.152**	.053
His father's education	.161**	.029	-.102	.106	-.050	-.071	.009
His father's occupation	.034	.045	-.078	.178**	.114*	.011	.094

Father's own mother's characteristics

Mother-boy relation	.036	.059	.022	-.053	-.026	.002	.011
Provided unsuitable supervision	-.137*	-.090	.065	.002	.080	.116*	.020
Used physical punishment	.040	.015	.064	-.075	.002	-.014	.017
His mother's education	.020	.114*	-.132*	.011	-.147*	-.119*	-.099
His mother's occupation	-.007	-.003	-.011	-.011	.038	-.085	-.014

Father's Current Family-of-Procreation Characteristics[a]

Child's age[a]	.135*	.139*	.002	-.260***	-.124*	-.284***	.159[b]**
Child's sex (male)	.018	.054	-.029	.084	.062	.054	.073
Number of children	.025	.076	-.088	-.010	-.046	-.066	-.059
Generativity chill	.116	.087	.187**	.197**	.025	.254***	.262***
Wife's working	.060	.043	.136*	.099	.102	.248***	.187**
Wife's education	.057	.047	.052	.176**	.156**	.171**	.206***
Father's education	.054	.104	-.047	.085	.114*	.081	.081
Father's marital affinity	.305***	.060	.083	.340***	.114*	.096	.301***

a. The first three coefficients are based on the childhood decade ratings and the next three coefficients are based on the adolescent decade ratings when the ratings varied by childrearing decade.

b. Curvilinear (quadratic) correlation coefficient reported in this case; Pearson product-moment correlation coefficients are reported in all other cases.

*p ≤ .05, **p ≤ .01, ***p ≤ .001. N = 231.

Table 10.2 Predicting the total quantity of fathers' parental generativity: regression analysis

Independent variables, listed in order of entry[a]	Beta[b]	R	Cumulative variance explained[c]	New variance explained[d]	F change
	Fathers' Childrearing, Both Decades				
Block 1. Prior predictors					
Father's IQ	.166*	.166	.03	.03	6.55*
His mother's education	−.135*	.214	.05	.02	4.29*
Block 2. Concurrent predictors					
Father's marital affinity	.303***	.371	.14	.09	24.18***
Wife's employment outside home	.232***	.437	.19	.05	15.06***
Generativity chill (1st decade)	.247***	.500	.25	.06	17.77***
Wife's education	.133*	.518	.27	.02	5.32*

a. All 15 boyhood variables available for entry in first block and all 8 concurrent variables available for entry in second block; stepwise selection within each block, nonsignificant variables not listed.

b. Standardized regression coefficient, with significance level of t, for each variable upon entry.

c. R^2 statistic.

d. R^2 change statistic.

*$p \leq .05$, **$p \leq .01$, ***$p \leq .001$; $N = 231$.

Predicting Fathers' Care for Their Children's Social-Emotional Development

The results of the first two regression analyses in Table 10.3 show which boyhood and concurrent characteristics of the men and their families account for the greatest variance in the amount of care that fathers provide for their children's social-emotional development during the first and second decades of their children's lives.

Fathers' fostering of their children's social-emotional development during the first decade is predicted by two variables which explain a total of 13% of the variance [$R = .356$, $F (2, 228) = 16.51$, $p < .001$]. First, from the block of boyhood background variables, their own fathers' level of education enters the equation and explains 3% of the variance. Second, from the block of concurrent variables, the fathers' marital affinity accounts for an additional 10% of the variance.

Fathers' support of their adolescents' social-emotional development is predicted by six variables, which together account for 26% of the variance [$R = .508$, $F (6, 224) = 12.97$, $p < .001$]. In the first block, 12% of the variance is accounted for by three boyhood variables—the fathers' poor boyhood relationship with their own fathers, positive boyhood home atmosphere, and the men's fathers' occupational levels. In the second block, an additional 14% of the explained variance in fathers' support of social-emotional development is accounted for by three concurrent variables—having a high level of marital affinity, having a young teenage child, and having experienced generativity chill. In sum, fathers who became highly and positively involved in promoting their children's social-emotional development during adolescence tended to be men whose own fathers had been distant or nonnurturant, but whose own fathers had shown a significant degree of occupational achievement and who had otherwise provided them with a positive home atmosphere. These findings suggest that the men's own style of fathering was based on a mixture of modeling and of rectifying their own experience of being fathered. These men also tended to have a clear and positive marital commitment, to have a younger adolescent, and to have experienced generativity chill with their adolescent children.

Table 10.3 Predicting each variety of fathers' parental generativity: regression analysis

Independent variables, listed in order of entry[a]	Beta[b]	R	Cumulative variance explained[c]	New variance explained[d]	F change
Predicting Father's Support of Social-Emotional Development During Childhood					
Block 1. Prior predictors					
His father's education	.159*	.159	.03	.03	6.00*
Block 2. Concurrent predictors					
Father's marital affinity	.318***	.356	.13	.10	26.37***
Predicting Father's Support of Social-Emotional Development During Adolescence					
Block 1. Prior predictors					
His boyhood relations with his father	−.259***	.259	.07	.07	16.50***
His boyhood home atmosphere	.223**	.305	.09	.02	6.58*
His father's occupation	.171**	.348	.12	.03	7.17**
Block 2. Concurrent predictors					
Father's marital affinity	.287***	.446	.20	.08	22.13***
Adolescent's age	−.213***	.494	.24	.04	13.31***
Generativity chill	.118*	.508	.26	.02	4.09**
Predicting Father's Support of Intellectual-Academic Development During Childhood					
Block 1. Prior predictors					
Father's IQ	.183**	.183	.03	.03	8.01**
Block 2. Concurrent predictors					
Child's age	.171**	.251	.06	.03	7.11**

Predicting Father's Support of Intellectual-Academic Development During Adolescence

	b	R	R²	ΔR²	F
Block 1. Prior predictors					
Generativity chill	.225***	.225	.05	.05	12.31***
His mother's education	−.148*	.270	.07	.02	5.39*
His boyhood relations with his father	−.132*	.300	.09	.02	4.31*
Father's IQ	.133*	.328	.11	.02	4.41*
Block 2. Concurrent predictors					
Wife's education	.127*	.352	.12	.01	4.14*

Predicting Father's Support of Physical-Athletic Development During Childhood

	b	R	R²	ΔR²	F
Block 1. Prior predictors					
His father provided unsuitable supervision	.135*	.135	.02	.02	4.25*
Block 2. Concurrent predictors					
Generativity chill	.189**	.232	.05	.03	8.62**

Predicting Father's Support of Physical-Athletic Development During Adolescence

	b	R	R²	ΔR²	F
Block 1. Prior predictors					
His father used physical punishment	.148*	.148	.02	.02	5.13*
His boyhood social-emotional health	−.132*	.198	.04	.02	4.13*
Block 2. Concurrent predictors					
Adolescent's age	−.277***	.339	.11	.07	19.53***
Generativity chill	.217***	.402	.16	.05	12.52***
Wife's outside employment	.209***	.451	.20	.04	11.90***
Wife's education	.129*	.470	.22	.02	4.71*

a. All 15 boyhood variables available for entry in first block and all 8 concurrent variables available for entry in second block; stepwise selection within each block; nonsignificant variables not listed.

b. Standardized regression coefficient, with significance level of t, for each variable upon entry.

c. R^2 statistic.   d. R^2 change statistic.   *$p \leq .05$, **$p \leq .01$, ***$p \leq .001$; $N = 231$.

Predicting Fathers' Care for Their Children's Intellectual-Academic Development

The third and fourth regression analyses in Table 10.3 show which boyhood and concurrent characteristics account for the greatest variance in the fathers' support of their children's intellectual-academic development.

During the childhood decade, the amount of support for the children's intellectual-academic development is predicted by two variables which enter the equation. The fathers' boyhood IQ scores and their children's concurrent ages, together, explain 6% of the variance [$R = .251$, $F (2, 228) = 7.67$, $p < .001$].

During the adolescent decade, support for intellectual-academic development is predicted by five variables, which together account for 12% of the variance in this type of parental generativity [$R = .352$, $F (5, 225) = 6.36$, $p < .001$]. From the block of prior variables, four items account for 11% of the variance: a life threat to the child during the previous decade, the fathers' poor boyhood relations with their own fathers, the fathers' boyhood IQ, and the negative incentive of the fathers' mothers' level of education. One concurrent positive predictor—the wife's educational level—also enters the equation, bringing the total explained variance to 12%. It is noteworthy that the fathers' IQ was the only variable that predicted that fathers would promote their children's intellectual-academic development during both decades.

Predicting Fathers' Care for Their Children's Physical-Athletic Development

The fifth and sixth regression analyses in Table 10.3 show which variables account for the greatest variance in the amount of care fathers provide for their children's physical-athletic development.

Variation in the support of physical-athletic development during the childhood decade is explained by two variables [$R = .232$, $F (2, 228) = 6.51$, $p < .01$]. One boyhood variable enters the equation—unsuitable supervision by the subject's own father. One concurrent variable also enters the equation—generativity chill. Together, they explain 5% of the variance. It appears that the fathers attempt both to rectify their boyhood experience of their own fathers' use of erratic or extreme supervision and to adapt to the adulthood experience of having their biological generativity put in jeopardy by becoming highly and positively involved in their children's physical-biological development.

Support of their adolescent children's physical-athletic development is predicted by six variables which, together, account for 22% of the variance in fathers' childrearing [$R = .470$, $F (6, 224) = 10.55$, $p < .001$]. Two boyhood variables explain 4% of the variance—the fathers' poor boyhood social-emotional health and their own fathers' use of physical punishment. Four concurrent variables also explain an additional 18% of the variance—the age of the adolescent child, a life threat to the child's existence, the wife working outside of the home, and the wife's level of education. In sum, in this study men tended to become more highly and positively involved in promoting their adolescents' physical-athletic development when their adolescents were younger, when their own fathers had used physical punishment or fear to control them as boys, when they had experienced a threat to their biological generativity, and when their wives worked outside of the home and were better educated than most wives. The only variable to predict fathers' care for physical-athletic development during *both* the childhood and adolescent decades, however, is the father's experience of generativity chill.

Discussion of the Findings

Fathers' parental generativity is significantly predicted by a large number of background characteristics. The ability of these various boyhood and concurrent background variables to account for variations in the men's parental generativity was different for the total quantity of all childrearing activities versus specific types of childrearing. This underscores the importance of both boyhood longitudinal and concurrent adulthood perspectives on childrearing fathers.

Predicting the Total Quantity of Parental Generativity
Mothers and Wives

The characteristics of the women in the men's lives generally account for the largest amount of unique variance in the men's total quantity of overall parental generativity.

Education. Women's educational levels are important predictors of men's levels of childrearing participation. Fathers who are highly involved in childrearing are significantly more likely to have been raised by *mothers* who were *less* educated than most mothers. At the same time, highly involved childrearing fathers are more likely to be men whose *wives* were relatively *well* educated. It is interesting that the fathers' mothers' level of education was negatively associated with the men's parental generativity, while their wives' level of education was positively associated with it. (This pattern was also replicated with the specific types of childrearing. The repeated patterns apparently reflect multiple patterns of influence, which will be discussed later when discussing the prediction of specific types of childrearing.)

Marital affinity. Another important concurrent variable is marital affinity. High involvement in childrearing is closely related to strong marital affinity or commitment. The predictive importance of a father's marital affinity is consistent with reviews of previous research on marital contentment and related characteristics: they indicated that fathers who were supportive (emotionally and materially) of their wives tended to also care for and promote their children's development (Belsky, 1981, 1991; Cowan, 1988; Lamb, 1981). The working definition of marital affinity that is most similar to ours (infrequent consideration of divorce) is found in a study of 100 families by Belsky, Youngblade, Rovine, and Volling (1991). Each family was assessed at four points in time during their first child's first three years of life. These findings showed "that husbands whose love for their spouses declined over time and whose doubts about the durability and wisdom of their marriage . . . increased, behaved toward their young children in a more negative and intrusive manner than did other fathers." In contrast, husbands who showed no such declines "were disproportionately likely to express positive affect toward their young children and to interact with them in a sensitive, facilitating way" (p. 495). Furthermore, as in the present study, there were no significant gender differences; the pattern held true for both father-daughter and father-son relationships.

While parental generativity is similarly predicted by marital affinity among the study fathers, it is still likely that the fathers' marital affinity is, to some degree, a function of the fathers' parental generativity. Yet it is important to note that marital affinity is also the primary support system available to the fathers (that is, the marital relationship) and, as such, it would exert a direct influence upon fathers' parental generativity (Belsky, 1984; Power & Parke, 1984). Nevertheless, the reciprocal relationship of the two partners is the crucial factor: it is likely to be the reason that previous research has indicated that the quality of the marital relationship is one of the strongest and most consistently significant concurrent predictors of fathers' parental generativity.

Wife's Employment

A wife's employment outside the home is also a significant predictor of a father's childrearing participation. This finding recalls the general findings of prior research reviewed earlier in this chapter: (a) maternal employment increases the quantity of childcare that fathers provide; (b) fathers in dual-earner families are significantly more involved in the actual care of their children; and (c) wives' employment appears to moderate or condition the impact of childrearing precursors, including the impact of the fathering that the men recalled that they had received as boys. Still, the present longitudinal findings are different in that they indicate that wives' employment provides an immediate motivation for fathers to increase their childrearing participation, but that once this is set in motion, the fathers' boyhood backgrounds predict their preferred types or style of participation. "Compared to mothers," as Simons, Whitbeck, Conger, and Melby (1990) have noted, "fathers have a great deal of cultural license with regard to how they play the role of parent" (p. 387). Perhaps because of this significant social ambiguity concerning the details of fatherhood, the men's boyhood experiences of being fathered play an important role in predicting the types of parental generativity that will make up their parenting style.

Other Personal Factors

Apart from the effects of women in the men's lives, the characteristics of the fathers themselves and of their children also made a significant contribution to predicting their total quantity of overall childrearing activity.

IQ. Boyhood IQ scores were higher among fathers who later became highly involved in childrearing. The constancy of the link of fathers' boyhood IQ scores to their total quantity of all types of parental generativity (as well as their specific support of their children's intellectual-academic development) is, thus, one star in a constellation that includes three academic predictors—mother's education, wife's education, and father's IQ. Previous studies (Pleck, 1983) have suggested that more educated fathers are also more involved in childcare, but in the present analysis, which considered the father's IQ and the education of other family members, the positive association between fathers' education and childrearing did not remain strong enough to enter the equation. The three characteristics which did enter the equation suggest a tentative portrait of the underlying dynamics: men who are academically capable tend to value academic achievement for their children, and this is intensified when they compensate for their mothers' lack of education and appreciate their wives' educational achievement.

Generativity chill. The final significant predictor of overall childrearing is generativity chill. The total quantity of paternal generativity was intensified when a son or daughter had experienced a threat to his or her life during the childhood years. Generativity chill will be considered in more detail under specific types of childrearing.

Predicting Types of Parental Generativity

Predictors of variance in the specific types of fathers' childrearing participation are summarized below. They often contrast sharply with the predictors of overall or total quantity of parental generativity.

Fathers' Fathers

The greatest amount of unique variance in each of the different types of childrearing support is most generally accounted for by the characteristics of fathers' own fathers. These patterns suggest that fathers use childrearing to replicate the specific positive fathering they received *and* also to rework and rectify the specific unsatisfactory fathering they received.

Modeling. Ways of adopting and employing their own fathers' strengths are indirectly suggested by the following patterns:

   (a) Men who had relatively better educated fathers will themselves as fathers provide more childrearing support for their children's social-emotional development in childhood.

(b) Men who had relatively better employed fathers will provide more childrearing support for their children's social-emotional development in adolescence. The correlation may derive from the complexity of the better blue collar jobs, which has been shown to predict workers' psychosocial development and childrearing practices (Kohn, 1977, 1980; Snarey & Lydens, 1990).

(c) A cohesive boyhood home atmosphere in which the father and mother worked together predicts that the boy who grew up in it will provide more care for his own children's social-emotional development in adolescence. The experience of a boyhood family environment that promoted his own coping as a child is apparently passed on to his own children.

Reworking. Adapting by countering or reworking their own fathers' shortcomings is suggested by the following patterns:

(a) Having fathers who had been distant or nonnurturant predicts that men will provide high levels of care for their children's social-emotional and intellectual-academic development in adolescence. Men who had fathers who had provided average or above average nurturing relationships, in contrast, were almost equally likely to provide either low, moderate, or high levels of support for the same areas of adolescent development.

(b) Having fathers who had provided inconsistent or inadequate supervision predicts that men will provide high levels of care for their children's physical-athletic development in childhood.

(c) Having fathers who used or threatened to use physical punishment that instilled fear in them as boys predicts that men as fathers will provide high levels of care for their children's physical-athletic development in childhood.

Erikson had earlier suggested that *both* modeling and reworking processes direct the course of men's generativity (compare Browning, 1973; Wright, 1982). In his (1958) analysis of Martin Luther's life, *Young Man Luther*, Erikson elaborates a hypothesis of how the excessively harsh but attentive care provided by the boy's ambitious miner father, Hans Luder, subsequently contributed, primarily by a process of reworking, to Luther's theologically generative reinterpretation of his heavenly father as a God who was both genuinely just and unconditionally loving. Hans Luder's model of ambition, however, also likely contributed to Luther's determined rise to religious leadership. Similar processes are at work in Erikson's (1969b) mining of the father-son themes underlying middle-aged Gandhi's societal generativity. In *Gandhi's Truth* we learn how the Mahatma built upon the model of his "father's love" to construct a deeper understanding of the ethical principal of *ahimsa* (nonviolence, and respect for all forms of life), and also how Gandhi redeemed his father's "carnal weakness" through his own "superior character" and ethics (Erikson pp. 124, 127–128). A father's care for his child complexly influences the way his child subsequently extends care to others.

In addition to creatively modeling their own fathers' strengths and reworking their own fathers' limitations, the Glueck men also positively adapted to their own personal boyhood limitations. Specifically, fathers who had shown poor boyhood emotional health were more likely to care for and promote their adolescents' physical-athletic development. These findings indicate that boyhood problems do not necessarily prophesy adulthood difficulties. Elder, Liker, and Cross's longitudinal study (1984) similarly documented that children seldom replicate their fathers' negative disciplinary practices when they become parents themselves. As Elder and his colleagues note, "retrospective reports of uncertain quality claim that poorly treated children are at risk of becoming adults who relate to their own children as their parents did to them. But the evidence leaves much room for doubt" (p. 146). Previous studies conducted at high level of quality have documented the difficulty children experience in coping with inconsistent and arbitrary discipline (Rutter, 1980), but a review of previous longitudinal studies also found that the long-term effects of boyhood emotional problems upon subsequent adult adjustment are usually very slight (Kohlberg, Ricks, & Snarey, 1984). For instance, children who are referred to guidance clinics for emotional problems without concurrent cognitive and antisocial behavior problems are almost as likely to become well-adapted adults as is a random sample of the population. The Glueck men's parental outcomes, in sum, lead us to draw the same conclusion that George and Caroline Vaillant (1981) drew from their longitudinal study of Harvard men: "The things that go right in our lives do predict future successes and the events that go wrong in our lives do not forever damn us" (p. 1438).

Other Boyhood and Current Circumstances

Other than the direct contribution their fathers made to the men's subsequent choice of different types of parental generativity, several other boyhood and concurrent variables made a significant contribution to predicting their parental generativity.

Generativity chill. The near-loss of a child is a strikingly robust predictor. It forecasts all three different types of parental generativity. (The threat to a child's existence was also a positive predictor of men's total quantity of overall parental generativity.) There may be many reasons why brief or extended threats to generativity can have profound significance for fathers' childrearing participation. One of them, no doubt, is that the experience of generativity chill makes fathers realize how much is at stake. Whenever parental generativity is imperiled, for instance, other related psychosocial threats may not be far behind: a prior favorable ratio of intimacy over isolation (for example, marital happiness) may suffer, just as one's ability to become societally generative (for example, to mentor younger adults at work) may suffer. Most pointedly, however, the primary lesson taught by parental generativity chill may be simply that one should never take one's children for granted.

Age. The chronological age of the child is also a robust predictor of the pattern of a father's childrearing. Men are more involved in intellectual-academic childrearing activities with older rather than younger children (about ages 5 to 10) and more involved in social-emotional and physical-athletic childrearing activities with younger adolescents (about ages 11 to 15). This finding provides a sense of coherence to the variations in prior research previously reviewed. For the childhood decade, the findings may reflect the lack of confidence of some men to care for younger children, and for the adolescent decade the findings may reflect the need of older adolescents to separate from their parents. At any rate, the findings indicate that fathers are more involved in the middle years of childrearing (from about 5 to 15).

Marital commitment. Equally striking, marital commitment is the strongest concurrent predictor of the fathers' care for their offspring's social-emotional development during both the childhood decade and the adolescent decade. As previously noted, marital affinity is also one of the primary concurrent predictors of the men's total quantity of overall childrearing participation.

Gender. There were no significant sex differences. Gender did not predict variations in the fathers' total quantity or specific type of childrearing. In the present study, all children were their fathers' first-born, which may function to minimize possible gender differences. Yet, as noted previously, several prior studies have also reported no significant paternal partiality for sons or daughters after infancy.

Other variables. Other boyhood and concurrent characteristics that predict specific types of childrearing were previously noted as contributing to the prediction of the total quantity of all types of childrearing participation. The fathers' boyhood IQ predicts that they will provide more care for their offspring's intellectual-academic development during both the childhood and adolescent decades, just as it had previously predicted fathers' total level of childrearing participation. Their wives' educational level predicts the fathers' care for their children's intellectual-academic development and physical-athletic development in adolescence; their wives' employment outside of the home also predicts the amount of care fathers provide for their adolescents' physical-athletic development.

These patterns suggest that utilizing native abilities, correcting for boyhood deficits, and responding to concurrent characteristics all play a role in predisposing some fathers toward higher levels of childrearing participation. Equally noteworthy, the findings help to provide coherence to previous diverse studies that have focused specifically on only one of the predictors.

Continuity and Discontinuity

Factors that predict fathers' childrearing participation have been marked by both continuity and discontinuity, the combination of which may sometimes give the appearance of conflict. We will summarize the findings by considering three apparent polar tensions: total quantity versus specific types of childrearing participation, macroanalysis versus microanalysis, and constancy versus change.

When the patterns for the total quantity of childrearing participation are compared with those for specific types, some important differences are evident. On the level of the total quantity of all childrearing activities, fathers' participation was greater when (1) they had a higher IQ; (2) when they had experienced generativity chill; (3) when their mothers were more poorly educated; (4) when their wives were employed outside of the home and better educated than most wives; and (5) when the men themselves were relatively more committed to their marriages. In brief, four of the six significant precursors (66%) were related to the women in the fathers' lives. In contrast to the total, every specific type of parental generativity was predicted by some aspect of the fathering the men had received from their own fathers. In fact, all five of the variables describing the fathers' own fathers' characteristics (100%) predicted a specific type of parental generativity. Both total quantity and specific types of parental generativity, however, were related to their having experienced generativity chill. These patterns are consistent with an understanding that the dynamics of paternal generativity are quite complex and originate, at least in part, in two family systems—the men's family of origin and their family of procreation.

Our diverse findings are also consistent with the understanding that sociological and psychological levels of analyses are not incompatible (Belsky, 1981; Furstenberg, 1985; Minuchin, 1985; Moen, Kain, & Elder, 1983; Rossi, 1989). For instance, macro-level analyses of socio-economic pressures for fathers to be involved in childrearing in order to permit mothers to be involved in breadwinning are not incompatible with micro-level analyses of individual psychological motivations. Both psychological and sociological factors come into play in this study. Economic necessity and opportunity underlie three of the six predictors of higher levels of the *total quantity* of paternal childrearing. In contrast, more unique variance in the *specific types* of fathers' parental generativity is explained at the individual level primarily by the quality of the men's adaptation to their boyhood relationship with their own fathers.

It is also important to consider these findings within the debate over constancy versus change in life-span personality development (Brim & Kagan, 1980). The present longitudinal findings provide support for both modeling and compensation hypotheses and, in effect, illustrate both continuity and change from boyhood to adulthood. Because human development is characterized by both continuities and discontinuities, it seems less important to debate the relative balance of these patterns and more important to investigate the possible consistent processes that underlie and predict both change and stability in human development. Fathering is clearly an integral process within a complex multigenerational family system; psychological and sociological analyses of continuity and change are equally needed to understand childrearing fathers in particular and male generativity in general.

Placing the Findings in Context

Numerous historical circumstances qualify the findings on parental generativity among the Glueck subjects. Changing maternal employment, divorce, and infant mortality rates provide three examples: fewer than 2 out of 10 mothers with children younger than 10 years old were employed outside of the home among the 240 study families; 4 out of 10 mothers with children younger than six years old were breadwinners in two-earner families in 1970, and 6 out of 10 are breadwinners in two-earner families today (Select Committee on Children, Youth, and Families, 1989; Hayghe, 1986). This means, as Pleck (1987) has remarked, that the labor force participation of married women increased by 50% within the lifetime of their children, who are themselves parents during the 1990s. Very similar increases have characterized the number of marriages that now end in divorce (see Chapter 4), and thus the number of children affected by divorce has also increased. During each year in the early 1950s approximately 300,000 children were involved in divorces, but during each year during the late 1980s over 1,000,000 children were involved in divorces (National Center for Health Statistics, 1991b). Trends indicate that "59% of the baby boom's children will live with only one parent for at least a year before reaching the age of 18" (C. Russell, 1987). What is the likely impact of these changes upon childrearing fathers? Wives' employment makes it more urgent for fathers to become involved in childrearing, and divorce makes it more difficult for fathers to sustain their involvement in childrearing (Friedman, 1982). Children in single-parent homes are far more likely to live with their mothers than their fathers, and over half of these children visit their father less often than once a month (Russell, 1987; Parke, 1981, Ch. 6). Nevertheless, the number of children living with divorced fathers has grown from 177,000 in 1970 to 861,000 in 1988, a 386% increase (Select Committee on Children, Youth, and Families, 1989).

The concluding chapter briefly outlines the study's caveats. It then presents a lifespan overview of men's generativity that blends the singular father-child relationships revealed in the stories with the common father-child patterns revealed in the studies. This interweaving also clarifies what the research means for the experience of fatherhood today.

11

Advancing Generative Fathering: A Lifespan Review

Most men today want to be good fathers. Many also have come to see that fathering is potentially the most satisfying and probably the most demanding task that the life cycle has to offer them. They sense that the experiences of childrearing are about as enjoyable, and about as difficult, as life usually gets. More than a few contemporary fathers also have discovered that, rather than being a probable impediment to their personal careers, parental generativity is the royal road to their middle-adulthood developmental end-point—societal generativity or cultural fatherhood.

But there are difficulties—many of today's fathers, even the most highly motivated and clearest thinking, seem to feel unsure about whether to become fathers or how to be good fathers. Part of the problem is caused by stresses on their current nuclear families. Work responsibilities outside the home now usually fall on both spouses, as they try to provide for their family's economic as well as social-emotional needs; divorce affects many families; and so forth. These changing family patterns, even when they have some benefits, may make the attainment and maintenance of intimacy (Stage 6) more difficult, which, in turn, would hinder their ability to become parentally generative with their children during the next stage. Part of the problem also resides in their families of origin: because many of their own fathers (like many among the 240 fathers in this study) were not highly involved in rearing their children, many present-day fathers tend to fear that they must reinvent good fathering.

Why is it, however, that even men who, as sons, had fathers who were wisely and strongly involved in their lives, and who, as husbands, have made mature mutual commitments, are not spared the confusion about how to be good fathers? The problem, evidently, is made more complex by their cohort membership. Men who were reared by fathers of the 1950s, and came of age in the 1960s and 1970s, learned to focus on the differences and discontinuities between generations. Writing during the counterculture movement, Friedenberg (1969) observed that "young people today aren't rebelling against their parents: they're *abandoning* them" (p. 21). More recently, Strauss and Howe (1991) concluded that the baby boomers had waged a "consciousness revolution" against the prior generation, and their revolution "began within families, as a revolt against fathers" (p. 302). While none of these authors is suggesting that complex historical patterns can be reduced to one simple cause, there can be little doubt that campus protests during the 1960s were motivated in part by a rejection of the *in loco parentis* policies of overly parentalistic administrators. Today, buried remnants of distrust for the prior generation come up in the sons' own efforts to father the next generation.

Many of today's fathers also continue to believe that even the good fathers among the parental generation have nothing to teach the baby boomers about how to be good fathers because they are living in a different era. Of course, many historical factors do place limits on generalizing the childrearing practices of any cohort of fathers. The fathers of today's new fathers, like the fathers in this study, typically began their families during the 1950s. As documented in previous chapters, between the 1950s and the 1990s there have been striking *increases* in the number of children born outside of marriage, the average age at first marriage, the number of marriages ending in divorce, the participation of mothers in the labor force, and the participation of fathers in childcare. There also have been striking *decreases* in birth rates and infant mortality rates. Some of these changes are commonly judged as being for the better while others are condemned as being for the worse; nonetheless, all of these changes seem to make it easy to forget that yesterday's fathers and today's fathers are not different species. To some extent at least, the fundamental qualities of good fathering transcend generational differences.

The problem and its solution were well summarized by Bill Jr. as he thought about becoming a father himself:

> I was married for seven years before we had our first child, and that was a conscious decision. To be honest, I felt that I was too immature to have a child . . . My wife was into her late twenties and said, "I'd like to have a child before my thirties"; it got forced, in a sense, before I felt I was ready for it, because I was constantly questioning myself and saying, "Can I make a good father?" When I looked around at the models I saw around me, unfortunately, I felt that I was seeing more

negative models than positive models. And I was concerned, "Did I have the ability?" But I did have one very positive model, my own father. That's why [my children's] development is so important to me.

Bill Jr. has been able to successfully adopt his father's care for children's development as a model for his own fathering both because of and despite the fact that the most important historical variables have *not* changed. First, although the proportion of households accounted for by two-parent families had declined significantly (from 40% in 1970 to 26% in 1990; Bureau of the Census, Dec., 1990), the most common family arrangement for *children* today is *still* the two-parent family (60% of all children under age 18 live in this arrangement; Select Committee on Children, Youth, and Families, 1989). More important, as Bronstein (1988b) has observed, "the facts remain that men's jobs [still] generally can bring more income into the family, that the workplace is [still] less tolerant of men than of women taking time off from work for child care, and that society still does not sanction men's putting their family equal to or ahead of their career" (p. 5). The childrearing precursors, patterns, and consequences among today's fathers, therefore, will still reflect many of the same configurations that characterized the Glueck fathers. The story of Bill and Bill Jr., as well the stories of the other adaptive and path-breaking fathers featured in this book, demonstrate that some of the fathers of the 1950s passed on much to their sons and daughters. That is, these study fathers can serve as guides to many of today's fathers as they seek to be good fathers to the children of the 1990s.

The aim of this concluding chapter is to provide a practical chronological overview of a father's life course, from boyhood genesis to adulthood revelations, by weaving together the empirical study findings and case study findings, without being exhaustively or exhaustingly inclusive of all details. (For instance, references to prior research discussed in earlier chapters have not been repeated.) Before casting light on the art of being a good father today, however, it is necessary to summarize the study's caveats so that there is no doubt that we are engaged in a speculative process of interpretation.

The Research: Caveats and Qualifications

This study is based on a unique and rich data set. Without such a sample, it would generally be "impractical to study longitudinally" a model such as Erikson's because it covers such "broad periods of the life span" (Moss & Susman, 1980, p. 536). Yet, as with all studies, the data do not allow one to fully or directly apprehend reality.

First, as has been noted in every chapter, historical events place obvious limits on the confident generalization of the findings. It has been suggested, for instance, that because males born during the late 1920s suffered economic hardship throughout the years they lived with their family of origin, they experienced a significant weakening of affectional ties with their fathers and subsequently came to place high importance upon their family of procreation (Elder, 1974, 1979). One must always be cautious in generalizing the findings to historically different cohorts. Of course, there is always a positive side to specificity. Being part of the postwar baby boom, and growing up in the 1950s, 1960s, and 1970s, is consistent with the experience of many of today's fathers.

Second, the sample is not representative in terms of racial or socioeconomic backgrounds. There were no African Americans in the sample, and nearly all of the fathers were born into the urban working class. Although one fourth of them entered the middle class during early adulthood, this sort of mobility is not applicable to all groups. The achievement of educational mobility is an especially complex task for urban African Americans (Hogan, 1987; Irvine, 1990; Spencer & Markstrom-Adams, 1990). Therefore, one must be cautious in generalizing the findings to more diverse or differently advantaged populations. The working-class or "common-man" nature of the sample, however, is also a strength because these men represent one of the largest and most "typical" segments of the population. Furthermore, the previously noted parallels between the present findings and those reported in prior studies of socioeconomically advantaged cohorts of Haverford College men (Heath, 1991) and Harvard College men (Vaillant, 1977, 1978; Osherson, 1986), as well as of a disadvantaged Depression cohort born around 1920 (Elder, 1974), demonstrate that the study's findings have some relevance to different social classes. Although childrearing fathers have been occasionally dismissed as an exclusive phenomenon of the middle class, the existence of working-class childrearing fathers may help to confirm that, on some level, generative fathering transcends class boundaries.

Third, although the fathers' families of origin were otherwise ethnically and religiously diverse, a majority of the men also grew up in Catholic homes. Father-child church attendance was a common occurrence and, rated as providing social-emotional childrearing support, it was an important element of this type of parental generativity. Secondary analyses, however, showed that the father's religious affiliation did not make a statistically significant contribution to their own or their children's outcomes.

Fourth, the assessment of fathers' participation in childrearing did not include equivalent information on the mothers' childrearing activities. The data, therefore, do not permit an adequate assessment of the role that the men's wives played in the family system or on the fathers' and children's outcomes. Despite this significant limitation, however, variables that shed some light on the roles of wives and mothers were always included in the various segments of the study whenever it was possible to do so.

Fifth, it was only possible to study the men's first-born children. Some well-known studies, of course, suggest that first-born children are more likely to achieve upward mobility (Altus, 1965, 1966; McCall, 1984; Sutton-Smith & Rosenberg, 1970; Zajonc & Markus, 1975). This is a reason for caution, although most prior studies of fathers' participation in childrearing have been about first-borns (Berman & Pedersen, 1987; LaRossa & LaRossa, 1981; Pruett, 1989; Silverberg & Steinberg, 1990). However, some analyses of the literature on first-born children have shown that the impact of being first-born is not as substantial or enduring as has often been thought (Tierncy, 1983). To consider the relevance of being first-born to educational and occupational mobility in this sample, a preliminary test was undertaken: records of 25 randomly selected Glueck subjects who had been upwardly mobile, rising two or more classes, were compared with the records of 25 randomly selected Glueck subjects who were socially stable. First-born children were not significantly more likely than later-born children to be upwardly mobile in education or occupation. It is also worth noting that first-born subjects are increasingly representative of children today because, as family size continues to decrease, the percentage of children who are first-born will continue to increase. Today, "42% of births are first births. In the 1950s, just 25% of babies were first-borns" (C. Russell, 1987, p. 112).

Finally, although this study's longitudinal design permits a reasonable degree of causal inference because the historical sequence of the principal criteria or events for inferring cause is known, the results still do *not* establish causality. As with virtually all prior research in this field, for instance, children's genetically based dispositions, which may influence the way they are treated by their fathers, could not be separated from environmental influences on father's childrearing participation. McCall (1977a), who also believes that "the longitudinal method is the lifeblood of developmental" research (p. 341), has similarly concluded that "we must simply accept the fact" that, "from logical and practical standpoints," it is clear that "we will never unequivocally demonstrate" or literally "prove the sufficient or necessary causes for the naturalistic development of a host of major behaviors" (p. 336).

In sum, the original data source places restrictions on methodological rigor, and our interpretations, conclusions, and applications are, therefore, necessarily speculative. Given these caveats, we will now review the chronological life course of the study fathers, juxtaposing the quantitative data with vignettes from the self-portraits of Bill and Bill Jr. (Chap. 3), Joe and Patricia (Chap. 5), Peter and Peter Jr. (Chap. 7), and Jerry and Maria (Chap. 9), as well as the brief vignettes from the stories of Gordon and Gordon Jr., Maxwell and Cindy, and Harry and Bart given in Chapter 1. This interweaving will also provide opportunities to reflect on the possible practical implications for today's fathers.

The Boyhood Genesis of Fathering

Why do fathers father the way they do? What have we learned from the boyhood origins of these fathers' involvement in childrearing? What can fathers today learn from their own histories of being fathered?

Not only do fathers differ in the amount of time they spend in childcare, they also vary considerably in terms of their focus on renewing and developing their children's social, intellectual, or physical capacities during childhood or adolescence. Fathers' boyhood characteristics and histories explain the largest quantity of unique variance in the different types of paternal generativity. The discussion below, summarized in Table 11.1, provides an opportunity to reflect on the relevance of childrearing fathers' genesis in (a) their personal

Table 11.1   Overview of boyhood precursors of fathers' parental generativity

Boyhood precursors[a]	Types of parental generativity by decades[b]

Fathers as boys:

      high intelligence

      poor emotional health

Childhood social-emotional support

Fathers' fathers characteristics reworked:

Childhood intellectual-academic support

      poor father-son relationship

      poor supervision

Childhood physical-athletic support

      physical punishment

Fathers' fathers characteristics replicated:

Adolescent social-emotional support

      education

Adolescent intellectual-academic support

      occupation

      home atmosphere

Adolescent physical-athletic support

Fathers' mothers:

      little education

a. Unlisted precursor variables were not significant.

b. Some variables have been renamed so that all lines show positive relationships. Arrows represent direction of prediction, not necessarily causation, and are based on hierarchical regression analyses which controlled for background variables.

boyhood characteristics, (b) their fathers' characteristics, and (c) their mothers' characteristics.

Fathers' Personal Boyhood Characteristics
Intelligence

In the Glueck sample, fathers' boyhood IQ scores predict how strongly they will support their children's intellectual-academic development during both the childhood and adolescent decades and also predict the men's total level of overall parental generativity. The higher the father's IQ score, the more the father tends to promote his child's intellectual-academic development. For instance, Pete's boyhood IQ placed in the top 20% of the fathers, and, in turn, the extensive support he provided Pete Jr. also easily placed him in the top 20% of the fathers for promoting intellectual-academic development during the childhood and adolescent decades, and in his total level of overall childrearing activities. These patterns suggest that fathers' innate abilities are of some importance, in agreement with previous longitudinal studies (reviewed in Chapter 6), but these abilities are passed on through childrearing as well. Among the Glueck subjects, in sum, fathers who are "smarter" (at least in a limited psychometric or IQ sense) tend to be fathers who are highly involved in childrearing.

Emotional Health

In this sample, fathers whose boyhood emotional health was poorer than that of others are more likely to promote their children's physical-athletic development in adolescence. These findings show that boyhood problems are not predestined to become adulthood difficulties. Similarly, several prior studies (reviewed in Chapter 10) document that children do not generally or necessarily replicate negative childrearing practices modeled by their fathers when they become parents themselves. Fathers can also rework their personal boyhood limitations and thereby improve their related capacities. For instance, the boyhood social-emotional health of Joe was judged to be below average, but he was later rated as a well-adjusted adult who provided his children with above-average levels of care for their physical-athletic development.

The Fathers' Fathers

The characteristics of the fathers' own fathers made the largest contributions to the men's different types of childrearing activities. The patterns suggest that fathers use childrearing to replicate the specific positive fathering they received *and* to rework and rectify the specific unsatisfactory fathering they received. Of the six patterns discussed below, the first three suggest that contemporary fathers can rework or counterbalance their own fathers' shortcomings, and the last three patterns suggest that contemporary fathers can also model their own childrearing behavior after their own fathers' or boyhood family's strengths (Chapter 10).

Boyhood Father-Son Relationship

The findings suggest that fathers whose boyhood relationships with their own fathers were distant or nonnurturant are more likely as fathers themselves to provide their adolescent children with an above-average level of care for their social-emotional and intellectual-academic development. Compared with the fathers in the larger sample, for instance, the four case study fathers all provided above-average levels of care for either social-emotional or intellectual-academic development during their children's adolescent decade, and all also shared childhood stories in which they clearly acknowledged that their own fathers had been insufficiently present or inadequately attentive. Specifically, these childrearing fathers often described their own fathers as "hard-working" men (Maxwell) who left home "early in the morning and . . . came home late at night" (Jerry), "worked a lot" (Joe), and, because they "always worked so hard" (Gordon), were "pretty well tied up most of the time" (Bill), and their children "didn't see much" of them (Peter). Yet it is important that they all also noted with respect how their fathers had worked under different and difficult circumstances—very long hours for generally very low pay, at jobs which sometimes necessitated shift work, and at multiple jobs to assure their family's basic survival.

In this context, each father's early recollections of his own father contrasted with the way that his own daughter or son described him as being a father who was "omnipresent" (Patricia), a "companion" (Bill Jr.), "always there" (Maria), "always home" (Cindy), always "wanting to be around us" (Pete Jr.), and "always ready to have a good time with his kids" (Gordon Jr.). These fathers allowed themselves to be known and enjoyed by their children. Although the responsibility of breadwinning was not as difficult as it had been for their own fathers during the Great Depression, many still had to work two jobs at various times. Nevertheless, they still sought ways to be with their children every chance they could.

Poor Supervision

The findings suggest that fathers who received inconsistent or inadequate supervision from their own fathers were more likely to provide higher than average levels of care for their offspring's physical-athletic development in childhood. For example, Joe said that in boyhood he was an "athlete of the street" who was "out running around all the time" without any paternal supervision, but Joe in adulthood carefully monitored his daughter Pat's physical-athletic competence.

Physical Punishment

The findings suggest that fathers whose own fathers had used physical punishment or threats of physical punishment which they feared as teens were likely to rework or counterbalance their own experience (see Chapter 10 for review of related research). In particular, they were significantly more likely to provide above-average care for their children's physical-athletic development in adolescence. For instance, Bill Sr. told a story about his own father pulling him up the street by the ear because Bill was late coming home one evening. In contrast, Bill Jr. told a story about his father's patient and careful response to a more serious transgression (breaking into a boarded-up building to smoke cigarettes, narrowly escaping the police). Bill gave Bill Jr. social-emotional support, rather than emulate his own father's approach.

Own Father's Education

The findings suggest that fathers whose own fathers were somewhat better educated were more likely to promote their children's social-emotional development in childhood. Given that the average level of education among the fathers' own fathers was junior high school (and the most common endpoint was around seventh grade), this generally meant that fathers like Joe and Bill, whose own fathers had a partial high school education, were better able to provide social-emotional support to their children.

Own Father's Occupation

The findings suggest that fathers whose own fathers had better jobs were more likely to care for their children's social-emotional development in adolescence. Most of the study grandfathers were semi-skilled workers or machine operators; fathers like Pete and Joe, however, whose own fathers were skilled workers or blue-collar foremen, displayed greater ability to provide their children with social-emotional support during adolescence. The origins of this connection are unclear, but they probably reside in effects of the greater job complexity associated with being in more prestigious blue collar positions.

Home Atmosphere

The findings suggest that fathers whose own parents had worked together to provide their children with a cohesive and warm boyhood home are more likely to care for and support their own children's social-emotional development in adolescence. The experience of a boyhood family environment that promoted their coping skills as children is apparently passed on through their own subsequent parenting.

The Fathers' Mothers
Home Atmosphere

The atmosphere of the fathers' boyhood homes, discussed above, also depended upon the positive contribution of their mothers. Even though the emotional atmosphere of Joe's boyhood home was not rated as warm, for instance, Joe's recollection that his "mother was always there" softened his father's absence. Yet a genuinely cohesive home atmosphere requires the active cooperation of both parents to form an effective "parenting alliance." An effective alliance is an explicit effort at mutuality in childrearing decisions in order to not undermine each other as parents and to ensure that the quality of parenting is not dependent on the quality of the marital relationship. As Joe remarked, despite the fact that his marital enjoyment was at times uncertain, "My wife and I always worked together. She has been great." His daughter Pat then elaborated how her parents made it very clear that "there was no way you could run to one to get a different vote on it . . . I mean, there was none of this play Mom against Dad, or Dad against Mom. It just didn't work." By working together, Joe and his wife were able to give Pat and her siblings what Joe had missed as a boy. The menagerie story illustrates a warm home atmosphere, Joe's ability to know what his children would enjoy, and his wife's ability to go along and enjoy it with them. It contrasts with Joe's reminiscence of his own father; he enjoyed taking things apart and liked to make his son watch him do that, apparently unaware that Joe was thoroughly bored. Joe's wife also contrasts with his mother who was apparently unable to help Joe's father connect with his children in a warm and meaningful way.

Mother's Education

The findings show that fathers are significantly more likely to provide relatively high levels of care for their adolescent children's intellectual-academic development when their own mothers had relatively low levels of formal education. Their own mothers' lower levels of education also predicts that the men will have higher levels of overall childrearing activities. For example, Joe's mother quit school after the eighth grade, and Jerry's mother had an elementary school education, but both men were highly involved in childrearing. They easily ranked higher than three-quarters of the other men in the study in their total level of childrearing participation in general and in their support of intellectual-academic development during adolescence in particular. The importance of a mother's level of education will be reconsidered in a later discussion of the importance of wives' education.

Possible Underlying Dynamics

The characteristics of the fathers' parents predicted important aspects of how the Glueck subjects would father their own children. Clearly, fathering is a complex process that spans the three-generational family system. In particular, the intergenerational transmission of fathering from grandfather, to father, to son deserves further attention.

Modeling and Reworking

The intergenerational flow of successful fathering appears to follow two primary patterns: (a) modeling, in which a man replicates the strengths of the fathering he himself received, and (b) reworking, in which a man rectifies the limitations of the fathering he himself received. The four self-portraits provide numerous examples of both continuities and discontinuities between generations, many of which are likely indicators of modeling or reworking. Some of these possible generative parallels are summarized in Table 11.2.

When he was a boy, Bill Sr. found his own father, Thomas, to be a role model with whom he could identify. In general, his father believed that hard work was the basis for a successful life, a model that guided Bill Sr.'s own breadwinning behavior and which he passed on to his son. Similarly, his own father loved music, and Bill also provided his children with a musically rich family life. However, Bill Sr.'s own upbringing also provided him with opportunities to rework or improve upon his history. His own father used physical discipline, but Bill Sr. did not; although he punched a wall on occasion and he taught his son to fight back, he primarily focused on supporting Bill Jr.'s physical-athletic development. His own father was not able to become very involved in Bill's boyhood life or activities, but Bill actively encouraged his son to do his best, and spent a lot of time playing baseball and other sports with him. His father died when Bill was only fifteen—a most painful blow to an adolescent—but his wife, Betty, helped him to overcome this wound and remain able to support Bill Jr. in his adolescence. Bill Sr.'s patterns of replicating and reworking are also evident in the life of his son. Bill Jr., in most ways, has modeled his parenting on the fathering he received (no physical punishment; promoting a love of music; supporting his son's personal interests and activities; passing on a love of reading; spending time with his son playing baseball and other sports). Bill Jr., however, has reworked some aspects of the fathering he received so that his own childrearing style is also different. He is somewhat more attuned to his children's social-emotional lives, actively encouraging them to talk about their feelings; he is also more probing with regards to his

Table 11.2 Generative parallels: possible patterns of modeling and reworking

Father's own father (the grandfather)	Father himself (the Glueck subject)	Father's offspring (first-born son or daughter)
Richard, Bill Sr., and Bill Jr.		
Loved music, as had his own father; loved to dance	Loves music and tried to pass an appreciation on to his son; he and Betty also enjoy going dancing	Loves music; enjoys going dancing
—	Paper carrier as a boy; encouraged son to do the same	Paper carrier as a boy
Died when Bill was only 15 years old	Dropped out of high school when his father died; eventually passed GED	Dropped out of college; eventually finished B.S. degree
Could not spend much time with his son; average father-child relationship	Spent lots of time with his children; unusually warm father-child relationship	Spends lots of time with his own children
Was a hard worker; Bill admired him for this quality	Is a hard worker; also admires his own son's workplace initiative	Is an aggressive worker; also admires his father's workplace initiative
Had little time for play in general	Admires his son's ability to play and enjoy children	Admires his father's ability to play and enjoy children
Used physical discipline	Seldom used physical discipline; supported his son's physical development	Does not use physical discipline; supports children's physical development
Little time spent playing ball with son; not a sports fan	Spent every spare moment playing baseball with son; avid fan of Boston sports	Coaches his children's ball teams; avid fan of Boston sports
—	Avid reader, loves science fiction, taught his son to enjoy reading	Avid reader, loves science fiction, teaching his children to enjoy reading
—	Empathetic; mentored fatherless boys	Empathetic; reading tutor for nonadvantaged children

Father's own father (the grandfather)	Father himself (the Glueck subject)	Father's offspring (first-born son or daughter)
Richard, Bill Sr., and Bill Jr. (continued)		
—	Interested in science; loves the ocean, gave son his first snorkel mask	Interested in science; loves the ocean, continues to go diving
Patrick, Joseph, and Patricia		
Christmas most important family holiday; stayed home for the day	Christmas most important family holiday; earliest memory	Christmas most important family holiday; earliest memory
—	Boyhood athlete, played baseball	Girlhood physical disability, scorekeeper for baseball team
—	Teenage counselor for children at summer camp	Teenage counselor for children in city park program
—	Teenage after-school job at a local store	Teenage after-school job at a local store
Did not complete high school	Very active in high school activities such as sports, yearbook	Very active in high school activities such as cheerleading, yearbook
Not involved in childrearing; home 1 day every 2 weeks; but became an active grandfather	Consistently highly involved in rearing his children; enjoys children and is able to be patient with them	Wants children very much; accepting of children's behavior
Quiet, serious	Playful sense of humor	Playful sense of humor
Enjoys watching baseball, but never directly involved	Enjoys coaching baseball, does not like to just watch	As adult still enjoys baseball, has season tickets to games
—	Involved in politics and civic activities	Interested in becoming involved in politics
Independent, a gutsy fighter	Relationship-oriented, a politician	Independent but relational, a resourceful fighter

Table 11.2   (continued)

Father's own father (the grandfather)	Father himself (the Glueck subject)	Father's offspring (first-born son or daughter)
	Patrick, Joseph, and Patricia (continued)	
Highly motivated; described as a self-made, self-taught man	Highly motivated; described as successful, respected	Highly motivated; described as a self-made person
—	Discouraged Pat's interest in nursing	Pursued nursing despite discouragement, but would discourage her daughter from the field
	Thomas, Peter Sr., and Peter Jr.	
Purchased family house and cared for maintaining it	Concerned with maintaining and remodeling the family home	Concerned with maintaining and remodeling the family home; earliest memory
Traveled locally, was Irish immigrant	Travels widely; took his son to visit Ireland	Travels widely; visited Ireland on his own
Made use of physical punishment	Minimized use of physical punishment; stressed support of son's physical development	—
Did not play ball with his children; did not actually understand baseball or football	Played ball with his children; very knowledgeable about sports	Looks forward to playing ball with his children; very knowledgeable about sports
Distant; monitored his children but did not have time to enjoy parenting	Close to his sons; took great pleasure in parenting	Expects to be close to his children; looks forward to becoming a parent
Relished role of grandfather; took grandchildren for ice cream after church	Relished role of coach; took sons and his players for pizza after ball games	Enjoys coaching; also takes his players out for a treat

Father's own father (the grandfather)	Father himself (the Glueck subject)	Father's offspring (first-born son or daughter)
	Thomas, Peter Sr., and Peter Jr. (continued)	
Did not accompany son to sports banquets	Accompanied his son to sports banquets	Accompanies his players to sports banquets
Stern	A "softy" but finds it difficult to show emotions	Intense, but able to show his feelings
Altruistic; financially supported neighbors in need	Altruistic; "has a big heart"; volunteered time	Altruistic; volunteers time
Hard-driving; a planner	Competitive	Competitive; a planner
—	Regretted having had a poor guidance counselor in school	Became a good guidance counselor for students
	Steve, Jerry, and Maria	
Was a good breadwinner	Was a good breadwinner	Is a hard worker
Good sense of humor	Playful sense of humor	Playful sense of humor
Dropped out of elementary school to begin work	Dropped out of high school to help support his family	Dropped out of college to avoid bringing a debt into her marriage
Did not use physical discipline	Did not emphasize support of daughter's physical-athletic development, but did take her to sporting events	—
—	Did not use physical punishment; emphasized role of good communication	Emphasizes role of reasoning in disciplining her own children
Did not do many things together to build a cohesive family unit	Close family; did many things together as a family; enjoyed family life	Close family; does things together as a family; enjoys family life

Table 11.2   (continued)

Father's own father (the grandfather)	Father himself (the Glueck subject)	Father's offspring (first-born son or daughter)
	Steve, Jerry, and Maria (continued)	
Took his family to the beach every once in a while on Sundays	Took his family out every Sunday; always strove to be a good parent	Always striving to be a good parent
Wanted his son to grow up to be a decent person; remembered as con- tributing to his son's happiness	Wanted his daughter to grow up to be a good person who would be happy and enjoy her work	Wants her children to be happy adults who enjoy their work
Found it difficult to show affection	Openly expressed his affection by giving his children lots of hugs and kisses	Openly affectionate with both her par- ents and her chil- dren
Recalled as being a typ- ical father	Sees daughter as a unique, indepen- dent, individual	Described father as an ordinary man who was a special father

children's intellectual curiosities, using Socratic questioning to stimulate them to think for themselves. Bill Jr. also goes beyond both modeling and reworking to raise a more fundamental question, "Why do we have children?" He posits that, "if it's a conscious effort, we have children to further the interests of society and the world and our own personal interests as well . . . If my child develops, the child will be giving something back to me by giving me the satisfaction. Not the satisfaction in that they achieved this certain goal that I set for them, but rather the satisfaction that they became people of value." Here Bill Jr.'s answer to his own question intuitively links parental generativity, societal generativity, and an ethic of care.

It is not surprising that men's ability to be effective fathers is strengthened by memories of their own fathers' sustaining care. But it is not expected that men's capacity to be effective fathers may be strengthened as much by their own fathers' shortcomings. The childrearing fathers in this study did not dismiss or deny the difficulties of their boyhood experiences, but neither did they grant them the power to determine their lives. Rather they turned their fathers' weaknesses into their own strengths. A review of prior research on parents' characteristics linked to their childrearing behavior uncovered a similar pattern and drew an equally applicable conclusion: "Adults who acknowledge and seem to have worked through the difficulties of their childhood are apparently protected against inflicting them on their own children" (Belsky, 1991, p. 124). The judgments the fathers made of their own fathers when interviewed as adults were usually quite consistent with the facts as recorded in their boyhood interviews, perhaps surprisingly consistent given the distortion that is often attributed to recollections. The style in which they told their fathers' stories, however, had typically changed. By midlife, the men had placed their own fathers' shortcomings in context and thus were able to take extenuating circumstances into account. There was a sense in which they had forgiven and become reconciled with their fathers. As Gordon explained, his own father had worked during "tough days" and his breadwinning difficulties were not unique because, "right after the Depression, times were tough for everyone." In effect, the typical childrearing father now understood that his own father had usually done his best, and he certainly no longer believed that his own father should have been perfect. The fathers reworked the shortcomings in the fathering they received by becoming the kind of fathers to their children that they wished their own fathers had been, and by transforming their anger with their own fathers into a sense of sadness for and understanding of the conditions under which their own fathers had functioned. "Those who successfully reworked [their] heritage," as Kotre (1984) has observed, have "the satisfaction of knowing their children would not suffer precisely as they did. Progeny, in fact, [give] those standing between generations a way of mastering a painful past" (p. 168).

In sum, fathering received appears to provide a model of fathering to be given. Positive fathering received provides a direct picture or model to be passed on. Negative fathering received provides a negative picture that must first be reworked, as if reversing the negative of a photograph, but then is also able to provide a reworked, positive model of fathering to be passed on. It is also important to note, however, that these joint processes can never be completely successful. Good fathers, no matter how well they adapt, never become perfect fathers, and so they always provide their children with material to be reworked.

Grandfathers

In some cases, when the fathers' fathers became grandfathers, they recognized their earlier childrearing shortcomings and also began to rework their pasts. Perhaps prompted by their own current psychosocial task of achieving a sense of integrity, some saw that the second chance at a kind of "grand-generativity" offered by their grandchildren was also a second chance to get it right and make peace with their past (E. Erikson, J. Erikson, & H. Kivnick, 1986, p. 74). Russell's (1985) study of grandfathers, for instance, found they often "reported that they regretted not having been more involved with their own children, and that they enjoyed their grandchildren more than they had enjoyed their own." In fact, "many grandfathers appeared to view being involved with their grandchildren as a way of making up for opportunities that they felt they had lost with their own children" (p. 257). As Kotre (1984) also has observed, some grandfathers use this "second chance" to "make up for generative damage they [had] inflicted" (p. 169). Perhaps, in turn, some childrearing fathers further master their grief and experience further healing as they watch and vicariously enjoy their own fathers doing with their grandchildren what they themselves had missed years ago.

The self-portraits provide some evidence for the preceding interpretations. Recall the references to the paternal grandfather in the self-portraits provided by Pete Jr. and by Pat. Pete Jr. was 9 years old when his father's father died, but the grandfather had been vitally involved during his last years and he was vividly remembered by his grandson, particularly as he paraded down the street with Pete Jr. and a flock of other grandchildren to buy them all ice cream every Sunday. The grandfather may have spent more quality time with his grandchildren than he did with his children. In the story of Joe and Pat, however, we see a clearer picture of a man who was now, as a grandfather, taking hold of his second chance to be more supportive. During her childhood years, Pat's grandfather taught her how to fish, allowed her to join him in his clandestine but exciting attempt to make a batch of stout beer, encouraged her to visit him and her grandmother regularly, and, after "the menagerie" episode, built a hutch in the backyard for Pat's and her brother's rabbits. During her adolescent years he was mentioned less frequently, but when Pat was uncertain about how she could finance her desire to do advanced studies in nursing administration, "he wrote . . . out a check for the tuition." To this day, he still collects pictures of his son that occasionally appear in a local newspaper, continuing one of the apparently few activities that communicated his pride in Joe as a boy. The grandfather may have never achieved Joe's uncanny ability to understand children's interests and to take their perspective, but he still made a success of his "second chance" with his grandchildren, and this appears to have helped Joe renew his relationship with his own father. Not all grandfathers, however, are able to experience such a second chance. Maria's paternal grandfather was infirm for several years and died when Maria was still young, so she simply remembers him sitting quietly in a chair; Bill Jr. never met his paternal grandfather.

Becoming a Father in Early Adulthood

What have we learned from the ways the study fathers initially approached fatherhood, and from the ways they coped if they faced reproductive difficulties, that is relevant to fathers today? In Osherson's succinct wording, for instance, "what [does] not being able to have children tells us about all men"? (1986, p. 96).

Becoming a birth father, even without having reproductive difficulties to overcome, represents a significant psychosocial milestone for most men. When they recalled their earliest memory of their firstborn, for instance, the self-portrait fathers easily relived their initial experiences of intense joy and relief. Joe thought his newborn, Pat, "was great!" and went on to describe in rich detail her fingernails, chin, eyes, and hair. Peter Sr. exclaimed that Pete Jr.'s birth made him feel "like *heaven* [had] opened up!" Jerry told of bringing Maria home and, in his excitement, literally introducing her to "every room" in their house; he made it clear that this was her home. Gordon, recalling the day he became a father, exclaimed, "Oh, I felt great! Oh, God, yeah!" He also went on to describe his infant's physical appearance in detail. They, like most fathers, were fascinated, captivated, and engrossed by their infants. The immediacy of their feelings suggests that they had become bonded to their child even before it was born (Greenberg & Morris, 1974/1982; Biller, 1974).

The baby's birth also brings forth a number of initial stresses and strains (Grossman, 1988), although the self-portrait fathers seldom dwelled on them. In the recollections of Gordon Sr. (Chapter 1), however, memories of intense joy in becoming a father were balanced with memories of the initial barriers to fatherhood. The employment system did not permit him to leave work and join his wife and newborn son immediately; the medical system did not permit any fathers to be in the delivery room; and the gender role system poked fun at his lack of knowledge about what an infant should look like. New fathers today also need to be told about the everyday physical, psychological, and social strains of becoming a father and caring for an infant because forewarning renders these difficulties less stressful (Belsky, 1986; Grossman, 1988).

Fathers' bonding to their infants, their infants' becoming attached to them, and the initial stresses of fatherhood all prepare the way for eventual parental generativity. Unlike some men, however, the self-portrait fathers did not allow themselves to be left out of childcare during even the earliest months. Reflecting on his experience when Pete Jr. was born, for instance, Peter Sr. relived his pleasurable memories of "feeding and diapering him, and giving him all the attention!" Research by Pedersen and his colleagues (1987) suggest that fathers may even foster an unusually close relationship between themselves and their children through such early one-to-one interactions that occur without the mother.

A stress relating to biological fatherhood, one that was never forgotten by the fathers who experienced it, was the unexpected threat of possibly never having memories of feeding or diapering. The pain of infertility is fleshed out in Pete Sr.'s experience: "You wonder, when you're young, why the hell it happens, you know . . . You're twenty years old, twenty-one, twenty-two years old, looking forward to having the kid, and you don't know why the hell you carried for not longer than three or four months and then miscarriage. Nobody ever had any trouble with a miscarriage, not in our family, and it's just kind of hard to accept it." Approximately 15% of the men in the study (like 15% of couples of childbearing age in the general population today) experienced reproductive difficulties in their first marriage (Chapter 8). The longitudinal follow-up of the men clarified the significance of biological generativity difficulties for their later attainment of societal generativity.

Resolving Infertility

Among husbands and wives who experience the crisis of biological infertility, those who are given medical hope are more likely to wait for a successful pregnancy, and couples with little or no medical hope are more likely to remain childless. Of greater interest from an Eriksonian perspective, however, the rate of adoption was highest among those whose medical condition was unclear and whose hope was uncertain.

Few couples in this study realized a pregnancy after trying for 8 years or more. Adoption, however, was also least likely for couples that spent more than 8 years trying to have a child. It was unfortunately not possible in this study to control for their wives' desire to adopt but, generally, research suggests that wives tend to yield to their husbands' preferences for becoming adoptive parents (Gerson, 1985).

For men who experienced fertility difficulties and then became fathers, either by birth or adoption, the arrival of a baby released their pent-up feelings of nurturance. Pete Sr. recalled, "One of my best memories of [Pete Jr.] as an infant was going for walks out in the carriage . . . I can still picture walking with him."

These findings have implications for couples today. First, because infertility increases with age, the trend to delay beginning a family until after early adulthood means that more couples are going to confront reproductive difficulties. Second, the very low conception rate after years of trying suggests that, at some point, a couple that has encountered infertility must begin to consider adoption or they will risk ending up childless, perhaps unable to realize the potential to care for the next generation that Erikson sees as a distinguishing mark of midlife maturity. Joe's daughter, Pat, seemed to understand this intuitively as she and her husband considered adoption.

Forecasting Biological, Parental, and Societal Generativity

Men who experience reproductive difficulties typically select a substitute activity to help them cope with the unavoidable waiting. The type of substitute chosen, as summarized in Table 11.3, is a remarkable predictor of the men's later generativity outcomes.

Table 11.3   Overview of relations between biological infertility and societal generativity

Infertility	Societal generativity

Coping strategies

Self substitute

Object substitute

Child substitute

→Absent

→Unclear

Biological generativity

Childless

→Clear

Birth parent

Adoptive parent

Note: Lines show positive relationships. Arrows represent direction of prediction, not necessarily causation.

Biological and Parental Generativity

The findings show that men who primarily used self-centered substitutes are most likely to become birth fathers and least likely to become adoptive fathers. Men who primarily used object substitutes are more equally likely to become birth fathers, to remain childless, or to adopt. Men who primarily substituted parenting other children are the least likely to remain childless and also the most likely to become adoptive fathers. For example, Jerry became active in a parent-like way with a local boys club when his need to become a parent was temporarily frustrated. As he told us, he tried to help "these little kids . . . come up" but "once we had children, our lives were changed to a point where we were tied down more." Men like Jerry, in effect, often become the psychological fathers of other children until they can become actual parents, through birth or adoption.

When parental generativity ratings of men who experienced infertility but eventually became fathers and men who became biological fathers without difficulty were compared, the findings showed that fathers who experience infertility subsequently become more highly involved in all types of childrearing, and especially in support of intellectual-academic development during adolescence.

The above findings suggest that if a man is using vicarious childrearing activities to cope with an infertility problem, he might also consider that becoming an adoptive parent would be an appropriate resolution. (The same may be equally true of women. Pat, Joe's daughter, has shown considerable use of altruism—her community service activities and service-oriented occupation—and she is also considering adoption.) However, these findings should not be used to rule out anyone for adoptive parenthood since exceptions can be found to virtually all of the patterns.

Societal Generativity

Men who eventually became fathers (with no problem, or by waiting for an eventual birth, or by adoption) were more societally generative at midlife than the men who remained childless. In addition, adoptive and birth fathers who initially experienced infertility were more societally generative at midlife than were birth fathers who never experienced infertility. Pete Sr., for instance, was able to acknowledge his pain and later to modify his lifestyle to adjust to the needs of his infant and become a caring, active father. Subsequently he also became societally generative at work and in the community. As Pete Jr. remarked, "My father always takes on other people's problems; he has a big heart."

These findings support Erikson's idea that the experience of parenting serves as a foundation, although not as a sufficient condition, for the later attainment of societal generativity at midlife. In sum, coping with biological infertility in a generative style (sublimating through activities with the children of others), actually becoming biologically generative ("having" a child, either by birth or adoption), and becoming parentally generative ("rearing" a child, as indicated by childrearing participation) appear to contribute to the building of an adequate foundation upon which to develop societal generativity—caring for and promoting the development of other adults.

Fathers' Current Circumstances

What have we learned about the everyday or concurrent characteristics of the study fathers that promoted their increased participation in childrearing? How are these patterns relevant to fathers today?

Fathers' participation in childrearing is predicted by a variety of concurrent background characteristics, summarized in Table 11.4, and which underscore the complexity of the forces that motivate childrearing fathers. In contrast to the boyhood variables previously summarized, current variables are better able to account for the total

Table 11.4 Overview of concurrent adulthood predictors of fathers' parental generativity

| Concurrent predictors[a] | Fathers' varieties of childrearing participation[b] |

Fathers
marital affinity → Childhood social-emotional support
→ Childhood intellectual-academic support

Fathers' sons and daughters
age (older child or younger adolescent) → Childhood physical-athletic support
generativity chill[c] → Adolescent social-emotional support
→ Adolescent intellectual-academic support

Wives
education → Adolescent physical-athletic support
employment →

a. Unlisted predictor variables were not significant.

b. Lines show positive relationships. Arrows represent direction of prediction, not necessarily causation, and are based on hierarchical regression analyses which controlled for background variables.

c. Generativity chill during the childhood decade and generativity chill during the adolescent decade have been combined for this summary table.

quantity of men's childrearing than for variation in specific types of childrearing (see Chapter 10).

Fathers' Adult Characteristics
Marital Affinity

Fathers who are highly involved in childrearing are likely to have strong marital commitments. Marital affinity or commitment is the strongest concurrent predictor of fathers' care for their children's social-emotional development during both childhood and adolescence. Marital affinity also predicts the total quantity of all types of parental generativity. Pat described her father and mother's relationship in these words: "My parents made it very clear, without saying it, that each other came first and the rest of us as a group came second." Clear marital affinity does not necessarily mean that a father always enjoyed his marriage. Rather, it means that he remained thoroughly committed to his wife despite the inevitable ups and downs in any family. The assessment of marital affinity is also an indirect indicator of the quality of the principal support system available to the fathers, and, as such, it appears to exert a direct influence upon fathers' parental generativity. For instance, all four of the childrearing fathers in the self-portraits were rated high on marital commitment, and all four provided their children with high levels of support for social-emotional development during both the childhood and adolescent decades.

Both the statistical analyses and life stories suggest the special importance of the parents' marital relationship for daughters. This apparent intermingling of intimacy and autonomous identity achievement is consistent with Gilligan's (1982) interpretation of an Eriksonian anatomy of human development. She states that for women, in contrast to men, "intimacy goes along with identity, as the female comes to know herself as she is known, through her relationships with others" (p. 12; see Gilligan, Ward, & Taylor, 1988). Building on this pattern, one may also speculate that men who are on good terms with their wives are likely to be on good terms with their daughters.

Sons and Daughters

Child's Age

In this sample, the age of a child contributes to the prediction of the degree to which the father provides social-emotional, intellectual-academic, and physical-athletic childrearing support. Overall, fathers are more involved with their children in the middle years (ages 5 to 15). More specifically, men are more involved in intellectual-academic childrearing activities when their children are between 5 and 10 years old, in social-emotional and physical-athletic childrearing activities when their adolescents are 11 to 15. Possibly, some men lack confidence to care for very young children. Recall that after Jerry welcomed his daughter home by taking her into every room, he said, "Then her belly button bled and I gave her back to her mother." The adolescent pattern probably reflects the need of older adolescents to separate from their parents, as well as the older fathers' lower physical energy. The sons and daughters in the father-child self-portraits often held jobs during their adolescence as well. To pay his tuition to a parochial high school, Bill Jr. worked as a delivery boy at a jeweler's and ran a paper route—two jobs just like his father had at the time. His father commented, "I was working more then, too. I don't think we did get together too much during his late teen years." Maria reported, "I got working papers at 14 or something—as soon as I could. My mother always said, 'Don't work, you're going to work for the rest of your life.' But I always wanted to, so I did." Pat also got her working papers as soon as she could; she decided she was going to use the money she earned working at Woolworth's to pay her own dental bill and to help pay for her college tuition. These teenage jobs reduced the amount of time they were home and available to spend time with their parents.

While this pattern of part-time employment during high school suggests that the adolescent is able to identify with adult roles and responsibilities, it does *not* indicate that a job during high school is inevitably a constructive experience that all fathers should urge upon their children during their high school years. The self-portrait children with part-time jobs worked to achieve personal educational goals. In contrast, however, research has shown that working while in high school, during the school year, and for reasons other than to attain educational goals usually predicts poorer educational outcomes

(Marsh, 1991; Mortimer, Finch, Shanahan, & Ryu, 1992; Steinberg & Dornbusch, 1991).

Generativity Chill

Statistically, generativity chill predicts that fathers will provide high levels of physical-athletic support during both the childhood and the adolescent decades of childrearing, and also high levels of social-emotional and intellectual-academic support during their children's adolescent decade. In addition to predicting all three different types of parental generativity, it also predicts the fathers' total quantity of overall childrearing participation. The sudden awareness of death, it seems, prompts a renewed giving of life through parental generativity. At the minimum, it promotes some men's realization that parental generativity should not take a permanent back seat to anything.

Somewhat surprisingly, such threats to generativity also were evident in all of the father-child self-portraits: Bill recounted how when Bill Jr. was quite young he became so sick that they were afraid that they "might lose him." Before Pat was five years old, "she was hit with . . . pseudarthrosis," which entailed several subsequent operations. The birth of Peter's son occurred under the threat of another miscarriage, and in childhood Pete Jr. also experienced more than his share of athletic injuries and operations. Jerry faced the possibility of not having children because of infertility.

The Wives

Two characteristics of the fathers' wives are also related to the fathers' parental generativity.

Wife Working

The more wives are employed outside of the home, the more fathers will engage in overall childrearing in general and care for their adolescents' physical-athletic development in particular. The present longitudinal findings reveal that wives' employment provides an immediate motivation for fathers to increase their childrearing participation; once this is set in motion, it is the fathers' boyhood backgrounds that predict the style of their participation. This is so because fathers in our society still have more freedom than mothers in choosing the specific ways in which they will be involved with their children. These choices, we now know, are patterned in part as responses to their boyhood experiences of being fathered.

While some fathers of infants and younger children prefer that their wife remain home, surveys have also suggested that some fathers do not become equally involved in childcare because their wives do not really want their equal involvement. Thus it is also important to consider that the apparent influence of a wife's employment outside of the home upon her husband's childrearing participation may also reflect a couple's liberal or open attitude toward gender roles (for literature review see Chapter 10). Although Pete Sr. enjoyed feeding and diapering his new son, the other fathers retained more traditional habits. In general, however, it appears that the wives of childrearing fathers are sufficiently secure in their femininity not to be overly threatened by a husband's caregiving, just as their husbands are sufficiently secure in their masculinity not to be overly threatened by a wife's breadwinning. Their mutual willingness to share the primary caregiver role was a progressive exception to the conventional norms during their childrearing years. "Just a generation ago," Lamb (1982) reminds us, "the working mother (especially one with young children) was considered selfishly derelict in her maternal responsibilities, and her husband . . . was considered a shamefully inadequate provider and . . . a weak husband because he 'permitted' his wife to work" (p. 46). Nevertheless, the distinction between a mother with young children staying home and a mother with teenagers working outside of the home was observed by some families in this study, even during times of economic difficulty. When Peter's wife, Martha, worked from 6:00 to 10:00 P.M., Peter had sole responsibility for the children, and he enjoyed taking them to the park, playing games, and putting them to bed. Nevertheless, Martha did not begin "working full-time days" until Pete Jr. and his brothers were teenagers. Similarly, Jerry's wife, Gina, started working part time when Maria was about 8 years old, but did not work full time until Maria and her brother were in their early teens.

Wife's Education

Wives' educational level predicts the study fathers' care for their adolescent children's intellectual-academic and physical-athletic development. Wives' education also helps predict the fathers' total quantity of participation in all types of parental generativity. Wives of highly involved fathers have *more* years of education than wives of less highly involved fathers. The father-child stories also confirm that a wife's level of education may positively contribute to her husband's support of intellectual-academic development and, in turn, to her children's educational mobility. Bill acknowledged that it was his wife who first wanted to send their children to a private parochial elementary school. Peter Sr. also mentioned that his wife was "hell-bent on college education" for their children, as he says, "from the day we got married."

Conversely, the *less* educated a father's mother, the more highly he will be involved in childrearing. Both Joe and Jerry, for instance, were the sons of mothers with less formal education than most of the men in the study, and they were also the husbands of wives whose education was equal to or higher than that of most the other subjects' wives. Joe and Jerry, of course, were also well above average in their level of childrearing participation. This thought-provoking pattern characterized the specific types of childrearing in addition to the total level of parental generativity and suggests that the fathers compensate for their mothers' educational deficits by marrying women with more education and supporting their wives' educational ambitions for their children. Additionally, wives with higher levels of education are also more assured of obtaining an acceptable job outside of the home, which, in turn, would provide an additional impetus for fathers' childrearing involvement. The original analysis, however, did show that the contribution of the wife's education still remained significant after their employment was controlled for statistically.

In sum, the combined findings suggest that making use of natural abilities, correcting for boyhood deficits, and responding to concurrent characteristics all play a role in predisposing some fathers toward higher levels of participation in childrearing. Analyses of social trends, such as the economic pressures for fathers to support mothers' breadwinning involvement, do not contradict analyses of individual psychological motivations influencing men who wish to care for and promote the next generation. Today's childrearing fathers should not allow themselves to be robbed of the integrity of their choice to actively participate in childcare. The economic pressures are real, but not all paternal childrearing motivations can be reduced to them alone. Men's personal histories also count; their fathering behavior is predicted by their personal boyhood characteristics as well as the characteristics of their own fathers, mothers, wives, and children.

How Their Children Turned Out

What have we learned about how fathers effectively contribute to their children's realization of their educational and occupational potential? What might today's fathers learn from the study fathers about caring for and empowering their children?

Paternal Generativity Consequences

Fathers in this study displayed a lack of gender bias in the level of care that they provided daughters versus sons on all six varieties of childrearing participation. In contrast, however, gender made a remarkable difference in the apparent importance of different types and decades of fathers' childrearing participation for the mobility of their sons versus daughters (see Table 11.5). The significant childrearing predictors of boys' mobility were from the childhood decade, but the majority of significant childrearing predictors of girls' mobility were from the adolescent decade. Equally striking, daughters and sons appear to need different types of childrearing support from their fathers during the same decades of life. Fathers' support of physical-athletic and social-emotional development during adolescence was only significant for girls, while fathers' support of intellectual-academic development during both childhood and adolescence was only significant for boys (see Chapter 6).

Childrearing Contributions to Daughters

During the childhood decade, the study fathers contributed to their daughters' educational mobility by providing high levels of care for their physical-athletic development. For instance, Joe taught Pat how to pitch a ball, row a boat, and swim even though her medical condition, at various times, required corrective shoes, a cast, and leg braces (before she was able to step away from orthopedic supports during adolescence).

Daughters' educational mobility, however, is negatively predicted by one type of fathering during the childhood decade. Girls who

Table 11.5　Overview of consequences of fathers' parental generativity for their children

Fathers' childrearing	Child's outcomes

Childhood social-emotional support

Childhood intellectual-academic support

Childhood physical-athletic support

Adolescent social-emotional support

Adolescent intellectual-academic support

Adolescent physical-athletic support

Son's educational mobility

Son's occupational mobility

Daughter's educational mobility

Daughter's occupational mobility

Note: Solid lines show positive relationships and broken lines show negative relationships. Arrows represent direction of prediction, not necessarily causation, and are based on hierarchical regression analyses which controlled for background variables.

received high levels of support for social-emotional development from their fathers early on attained relatively lower levels of education in early adulthood than those who did not receive such support. One Eriksonian interpretation is that daughters' primary psychosocial identification should be with their mothers during childhood. Another hypothesis is that fathers who are rated high on social-emotional support during childhood may actually create an overly controlling, smothering, environment which does not promote their daughters' intellectual autonomy or psychosocial industry necessary for educational mobility. It is also at least theoretically conceivable that a father's high level of social-emotional childrearing support reflects an attempt to compensate for a wife's inadequate maternal skills—a lack which actually underlies the negative association. The present study, of course, cannot resolve such competing interpretations. Perhaps what is most important to note here is that the negative contribution to differences in daughters' mobility was not large; most of the daughters in this study were upwardly mobile regardless of differences in the level of childhood social-emotional support they received from their fathers.

During their daughters' adolescence, fathers' care for both physical-athletic and social-emotional development promoted girls' later educational and occupational mobility (see Table 11.5). Upwardly mobile girls have a generally high level of one-to-one involvement with their fathers during the adolescent decade. The strong emphasis upon promoting physical-athletic capacities during both decades suggests that the nature of the father-daughter friendship was more challenging, affirming the daughters' ability to function autonomously and vigorously. This physical rigor is evident in Pat's story. "Even today," she explains teasingly, "a Saturday of activity and fun with Joe is still total exhaustion. First you got to play racquetball, then jump in the jacuzzi, you know, then we get in eighteen holes of golf. Then, if it's still warm out, you know, play a little tennis." At various times during her adolescence, Pat also played baseball, volleyball, and horseshoes with her father. The link of fathers' physical-athletic support to daughters' high achievement suggests a contribution to their ability to compete with men beyond the family sphere. These fathers may also promote and legitimize a greater sense of assertiveness in transcending culturally determined gender roles. Girls raised by traditional fathers, in contrast, may remain at a competitive disadvantage with men.

From an Eriksonian perspective, girls do not separate from their mothers until early adolescence. At this time, fathers' social-emotional support can function as a "bridge" from the mother to the larger society, allowing daughters to successfully negotiate the transition to autonomy and providing opportunities for constructive interactions with males. Joe, for instance, passed on his ability to interact with businessmen in the community by showing Pat "how you run an ad page to generate money and how you go out and solicit donations from various businessmen."

In sum, study fathers promoted their daughters' developing autonomy by inviting them to participate in nontraditional areas of mastery with them, such as active athletic play. Mothers can also be athletic, of course, but when this care comes from the father it also promotes his adolescent daughter's ability to launch out of the mother-child orbit into the world outside the family. The changing roles of women in the world beyond the family, however, may modify these dynamics in the future.

Childrearing Contributions to Sons

Fathers can promote their sons' later educational or occupational mobility by providing in their childhood high levels of care for their social-emotional, physical-athletic, and intellectual-academic development. Several childrearing fathers, for instance, made the substantial commitment to coach one of their son's athletic teams at some point during the late childhood or very early teen years. Bill and Peter coached their sons' baseball teams, and Gordon Sr. coached his son's football team.

From an Eriksonian perspective, in the early years of the childhood decade boys need to separate from the mother and identify with the father, the same-sex parent, as part of the their gender identity development. Fathers' broad support of their sons' physical-athletic, intellectual, and social-emotional development promotes this transition, the maintenance of their boys' sense of basic trust (Stage 1), autonomy (Stage 2), and the successful achievement of a basic sense of initiative (Stage 3). The later childhood years also encompass the mentorship years when boys, striving to achieve a sense of industry (Stage 4), again turn to their fathers for guidance and training.

During their boys' adolescence, fathers significantly promoted their sons' later educational mobility by providing strong support for their intellectual-academic development (see Table 11.5). The self-portrait fathers, for instance, monitored their sons' academic progress in high school. As Pete Jr. explained, his father "saw education as the gateway to success and really encouraged me to be educated, to meet college people, to go to college."

The fathers' possible impact upon their sons' occupational mobility was not evident in this study. This may be because occupational mobility is less reliably assessed during early adulthood, especially among members of the baby boom cohort who have delayed commitments to careers. From an Eriksonian perspective, the adolescent boy now must also separate from his father. It thus follows that fathers apparently had a weaker impact on their adolescent sons, preoccupied as these were with achieving a degree of physical and emotional differentiation from their fathers. Pete Sr. tells us, "All of my life, catching was my favorite position." He caught for his son for years until Pete Jr.'s pitches "got too fast for me and then I couldn't catch no more." The pride in his son's ability may have been mingled with regret, yet apparent acceptance, that his own skills were diminishing. "I tried to bounce them off my knees . . . I'd be kind of ducking them. It was time to quit." Yet these sons' separations were still accomplished with sensitivity. There was a constant sense of engagement with the father, while each son was becoming his "own man." As the father-child stories also showed, effective childrearing fathers managed to maintain a genuine connection with their adolescents even during turbulent times. Bill Jr. remembers that he "was into rebellion" during the time of the Vietnam War. He let his hair grow long and his course grades drop; his "hippie style" provoked some arguments with his parents, particularly his mother. When he moved out of his parents' house into his own apartment with a girl friend, his father visited him. As Bill Jr. recalls, "As I was striving to be different, I still could have a conversation with him."

In summary, the present findings show that the types of childrearing support of greatest benefit are relatively nontraditional, especially in nonadvantaged families: physical-athletic for girls, and intellectual-academic for boys. But, obviously, these contrasting father-daughter and father-son patterns do *not* mean that fathers should not provide support in the traditional domains of fatherly concern. Rather, the contrasting nontraditional patterns in the present study suggest that fathers' support in these unconventional areas helps their sons and daughters, in part, because they are giving their children what they may not be getting elsewhere. Therefore, they function to help their sons and daughters become balanced adults.

Maternal Predictors

The roles that fathers play in their sons' and daughters' lives are part of the dynamic triad of father-child-mother. The relative balance between autonomy and attachment within this triadic system changes from childhood to adolescence to adulthood, with different patterns of change characterizing the development of daughters versus that of sons. To promote their daughters' and sons' autonomy and attachment, or identity and intimacy in Erikson's terms, fathers must concurrently recognize and affirm that their children are, on one level, always fully separate independent beings and, on another level, always bonded to them, and on still another level, always bonded to their mothers. Thus it is not surprising that maternal variables, including the fathers' marital relationship, also contribute to predicting children's outcomes.

Marital Affinity

Fathers' marital affinity or commitment is a significant predictor of both educational and occupational mobility for daughters, but not for sons. This observation points to gender differences in the role of the mother in her children's lives and suggests that daughters need their parents' relationship to be relatively stable or compatible. Such an interpretation is consistent with prior studies (for review, see Chapter 6), but it does not mean that the fathers' marital affinity is irrelevant to their sons' other life outcomes: some evidence indicates that the sons of parents who got along well are themselves, as new fathers, able to make a smoother transition to parenthood.

Wife's Employment

Maternal employment outside of the home (only during the childhood years) made a significant, small (3%), but negative contribution to daughters' (but not to sons') educational mobility under *one* condition—the daughter was in late childhood and had younger siblings in the family. It is likely that first-born daughters with younger brothers and sisters assume some maternal and housekeeping roles when their mothers become employed outside of the home. These home responsibilities may prompt them to commit themselves to traditional feminine roles prematurely, as well as make it difficult for them to excel in school. Previous studies have usually shown that mothers' employment status in itself does not make a negative contribution to their children's development (see Chapter 6). The negative adverse effect of working mothers reported here occurs only under one very specific condition; moreover, that negative contribution is more than counterbalanced by the consistently positive and stronger influence of paternal care that also results, in part, from the mother's working.

Beyond Social Mobility

Children's occupational and educational attainments are important because they reflect aspirations that most parents have for their children. What parents want *from* their children is culturally quite diverse, but what they want *for* their children is far less variable. As LeVine (1988) has clarified,

> What parents want for their children . . . can be conceptualized as universal: survival and health, the acquisition of economic capabilities, and the attainment of whatever other cultural values are locally prevalent. These goals form a rough hierarchical sequence in the course of development, since parents might reasonably want to be assured of infant survival before attending seriously to the child's capabilities for socioeconomic participation, and they might well give priority to the child's future economic security over the development of culturally defined virtues.   (p. 4)

The childrearing fathers in this study did in fact give considerable attention to helping their children secure the traits and skills necessary to adapt successfully to life in a class society. Their orientation, however, can be criticized from two perspectives—elitist and practical.

The elitist position essentially questions whether social mobility is an appropriate indicator of successful parental generativity. Certainly, to the degree that socioeconomic security is both abundant and inherited, people from more advantaged social classes can afford to ignore social mobility as a measure of children's life outcomes, while less advantaged parents cannot afford to be so indifferent. In fact, however, the childrearing fathers in this study gave considerable attention to other attainments as well. Beyond promoting mobility and socioeconomic independence, all of the men in the father-child life stories demonstrated that their childrearing aims included diverse cultural ideals and character virtues: personal and family happiness, intergenerational continuity, ethical sensitivity and compassion, community responsibility, religiosity, and a sense of humor.

From the practical position the criticism consists in questioning how significant is amount of variance a father's childrearing actually explains in his child's life outcomes. Here it must be acknowledged that the translation of statistical significance into psychological significance is relative and a matter of judgment. If a father could improve by approximately 10% the speed with which his child mows the lawn, he probably would conclude that it really doesn't matter; but if a father could improve by approximately 10% his child's level of educational or occupational mobility, he would be more likely to conclude that it really does matter (see the statistical procedures section in Chapter 4). Of course, in some cases, when some boyhood deficits fail to show up in negative adulthood behavior, one could also take courage from the fact that men's experiences of being fathered do not predestine how they turn out as fathers.

These findings for the childhood and adolescent decades and subsequent social mobility are consistent with the research of Youniss and Smollar (1985), to the effect that parents and their children are "in alliance together against society" (p. 78) while the children are in high school and college. The self-portraits, however, extend this pattern in a way that is also consistent with the claim of Frank, Avery, and Laman (1988) that "by the end of the third decade of life the children are more willing and able to rely on their own resources" (p. 736). The fathers and children who appear in the self-portraits all noted that the father-child relationship changed to some degree after the son or daughter became an adult. After the childrearing years, effective fathers generally develop a less directive and more collegial relationship with their adult sons and daughters (see Roberts & Zuengler, 1985).

Midlife Revelations from the Fathers

What have we learned about the importance of parental generativity for the study fathers' own maturity, and perhaps for today's fathers as well? Table 11.6 summarizes the findings relevant to this question in the areas of men's marital enjoyment, occupational mobility, and societal generativity (see Chapter 4).

Marital Success

The more fathers participate in childrearing during early adulthood, the more likely they are to be happily married at midlife. Fathers' care for their children's social-emotional development during childhood and adolescence, and their intellectual-academic development during adolescence forecasts fathers' later marital stability and happiness.

Table 11.6   Overview of consequences of fathers' parental generativity for fathers
themselves

Fathers' childrearing	Fathers' midlife outcomes

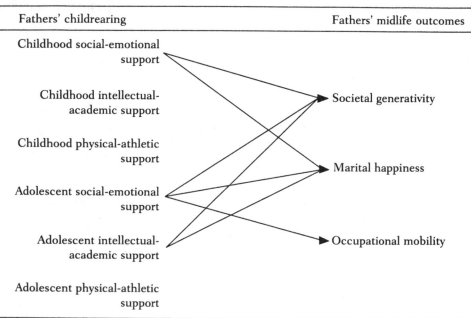

Note: Lines show positive relationships. Arrows represent direction of prediction, not necessarily
causation, and are based on hierarchical regression analyses which controlled for background
variables.

Together, these three varieties of childrearing account for almost a
fifth of the variance in the fathers' midlife marital outcome even after
taking into consideration or controlling for differences between the
fathers' backgrounds.

The social-emotional support provided by Jerry, for instance, was
higher than that provided by three out of every four fathers during
the childhood decade, and higher than nine out of every ten fathers
during the adolescent decade. The intellectual-academic support provided by Jerry was also higher than three out of every four fathers
during the adolescent decade. Jerry, in turn, was not only still married
at midlife (as were a little over 80% of the other fathers) but he also
was rated as clearly enjoying his marriage (as were almost 30% of the
other fathers). Jerry, himself, felt there was an association between
the two: "Having a child made my wife and me even closer, in my
opinion. We were very close before the children, too. We've always

been close, but children, I think, do make you closer. With us, it did."
They did have different perspectives on the urgency of starting their
family by adopting a baby, but he nevertheless was able to comment,
"I would use the word 'compatible' as best describing my wife and
me."

Occupational Success

Greater childrearing participation does *not* generally translate into
lower occupational mobility for fathers. In fact, contrary to the speculation that family participation will hinder men's careers, fathers
who cared for their children's intellectual development and their
adolescents' social development were more likely to advance in their
occupations. Otherwise, the findings regarding occupational mobility
are generally consistent with prior research in which the primary
predictors of a father's occupational mobility are his boyhood family
occupational levels, his boyhood IQ, and boyhood psychological competence.

It is difficult to know whether the economic cost of childrearing
participation for fathers in this sample of men who moved from the
lower and working class to the working and middle class would be
different from the economic cost to fathers who begin life in the
middle class or work as professionals. The opportunity cost to fathers
may vary with socioeconomic status. The men in the sample, for
instance, generally held jobs with regular hours (say 8:00 to 4:00),
while persons in the professions are seldom able to limit their work
to regular hours. Attending soccer practice with one's daughter in the
evening may have higher career costs for professionals. It is also
possible, however, that the greater time flexibility inherent in many
professional roles may permit father's participation at crucial times
without any significant career sacrifice. One of the conditions for
men to become and stay highly involved in childrearing is for their
work hours to be and continue to be flexible. Such time flexibility is
also one of the benefits experienced by some full-time professionals.
(See the Afterword for a brief review of father-supportive workplace
policies.)

Contrary to the stereotype of a rigid work-family tradeoff, a positive,
reciprocal interaction may exist between childrearing and breadwinning. Men who are better fathers to their children probably also learn

something from their families about how to be better mentors to their staffs or junior colleagues. Men who value democracy in workplace management probably also learn something about how to be more caring and inclusive in family decision making. Prior research on men who have performed well at work also suggests that they are men who have done well by their children (for review, see Chapter 4).

Erikson's (1950) original conception of adult development and generativity advanced Freud's thesis that the ability to work (breadwinning) and to love (childrearing) are integrally linked (compare discussion of agency and communion by Kotre, 1984). The dynamic processes through which childrearing may promote effective breadwinning are suggested by Philip Cowan's (1988) discussion of fathers' self-concept development among the men in his study of new fathers:

> Before they became fathers, the men did not appear to be conscious that home and work life often require different personal qualities. In their work lives, men tend to believe that they should be independent, aggressive, and self-focused; the men in our study who were not becoming parents tended to bring this persona home. By contrast, new fathers were usually painfully aware of the needs of others, experiencing a pull to be caring and empathic even when their own resources were depleted . . . They began, [for instance], to describe themselves as more aware of their personal relationships on the job, and [also] more able to use some of their managerial skills in the solution of family problems. (p. 24)

While it is reasonable to assume that childrearing will have a negative impact upon daily work life, it appears that childrearing actually makes a small but significant positive contribution to successful careers. The possibility that this significance may become larger with time, especially as fathers enter midlife career changes, was further suggested by the self-portrait fathers. Two of these four men evidenced new occupational mobility after midlife when their children were gone from home.

The further possibility that effective parenting and occupational success may interact in mutually supportive ways was illustrated even across generations in the story of Joe and Pat. Recall Pat's deeply moving story of how her father had given her a roll of dimes and taught his young daughter how to negotiate as a patient in the hospital:

> When he'd come to visit me at each hospitalization, he'd bring me a roll of dimes. He'd write his work telephone number on the roll of

dimes, and the home phone number, and I was all set. He'd say, "Anyone wants to do anything, and you don't want that going on [or] . . . you're not satisfied with their reason, just tell them, 'Time Out.' Tell them they need to get you a pay phone, you just need to talk to your father and discuss it, you're not satisfied with their explanation, and you'll be back." That was it. I was young, I was in a wheelchair, . . . but . . . I have my dimes, so Dad's right there, so I can handle this. It was great . . . When I did call, I just explained the situation, and we'd talk. He'd tell me how to handle it, and I'd go back and negotiate. He'd say, "I want you to call me back and tell me how it worked out."

Joe himself subsequently showed additional upward mobility after his childrearing years by completing an associate degree from a junior college and then assuming a new supervisory role which required keen negotiation skills. Pat, as a young adult administrator, was still able to turn to her paternal mentor for administrative advice. As she explained,

We'll talk back and forth, you know, from my office to his. When something comes up, he'll bang it off me. Which is kind of nice, that he's interested in my opinion, and vice-versa. If I call him and say, "I'm not getting anywhere with the so-and-so office." He'll say, try this and try that. And then, do this, and then, if they don't respond, give them a little jab and do this. "All right, I'll try that." "Get back to me now. Give me a call."

Joe also treated his adult daughter as a professional colleague and felt free to ask for her advice. Parenting and breadwinning were in harmony. It is also noteworthy that the two case study fathers who evidenced additional occupational mobility well after their children were launched from the nest, both moved into more societally generative occupations.

Societal Generativity

The most important finding of this study is that fathers who participate strongly in childrearing are also more likely to become societally generative at midlife. Fathers' care for their children's development explained about one-sixth of the variance in psychosocial generativity beyond the family sphere, even after controlling for background variables. This finding is consistent with Erikson's idea that the experience of parenting serves as a foundation for generativity at midlife, although it does not guarantee its attainment. Of course, it cannot be claimed that parental generativity literally causes societal generativity (see Chapter 4).

The self-portrait fathers exemplify this pattern. All gave significant attention to their children's social-emotional care during both child-rearing decades and showed some evidence of societal generativity at midlife. The stories of Bill Sr., Joe, Pete Sr., and Jerry are all, in fact, dramas about caring fathers who have promoted the life of the generations. Societal generativity was also evident in the lives of Gordon Sr., Maxwell, and Harry, whose stories were only briefly introduced. It seems that these men discovered for themselves what Erikson has called the Golden Rule of generative ethics: "Do to another what will advance the other's growth even as it advances your own" (1980a, p. 56). "The ethical rule of adulthood," that is, "is to do to others what will help them, even as it helps you, to grow" (1978, p. 11).

Conclusion

The story of childrearing fathers has been the story of men who did not expect their wives to do all the work of parenting. These men took responsibility for encouraging a child who was afraid of the dark and helping an adolescent who was afraid of a neighborhood bully; for reading books to a small son and discussing books with the teenage son; for showing a small daughter how to throw a ball and teaching the teenage daughter how to improve her throw so that she could make pitcher for her softball team (Chapter 2).

Generativity

The findings of this study are quite complex. Fathering, like most aspects of family functioning, is multiply determined and has multiple consequences. Yet the overall pattern is quite simple: children are psychologically highly significant to fathers and their psychosocial development, and, in turn, the impact of fathers' participation in childrearing is positive and significant for their sons and daughters, their families, and the larger society. Fathering is an integral process within a complex multigenerational family system, and both psychological and sociological levels of analysis are needed to account for the complexly intertwined personal and social facts of fathers' child-

rearing in particular and male generativity in general. Equally important, these findings offer much hope that men can rework their past
and provide better fathering than they themselves received. The findings also offer little sustenance for anxious predictions that the impact
of highly involved fathers would be negative.

Integrity

The strengths of generativity may be finally reintegrated into an even
more encompassing sense of integrity and wisdom. Beyond generativity, that is, Erikson relates human development during the senior
adult years to the attainment of a favorable balance of integrity over
despair (Stage 8). Erikson's stage of integrity involves "the acceptance
of one's one and only life cycle as something that had to be and that,
by necessity, permitted no substitutions" (1950, p. 268). In contrast,
"despair expresses that feeling that time is now short, too short to
attempt to start another life and to try out alternative roads to integrity" (1950, p. 269). Given the clear attainment of societal generativity
by many childrearing fathers, one would speculate that integrity will
also "ripen" in their lives.

The virtue or ego strength of integrity is a comprehensive sense of
wisdom, which Erikson describes as a "detached concern with life
itself, in the face of death itself" (Erikson, Erikson, & Kivnick, 1986,
p. 37). It seems fitting to close with the seasoned wisdom of two
study fathers for today's fathers. Their wisdom is inclusive of both
generativity and integrity. Bill Sr.'s advice is so explicitly generative
that it could have been written by Erikson himself:

> I believe a father should really show his love to his children a lot. To
> be around and loving, I think, would be the most important thing.
> Because I think it gives them a feeling of wanting to find it in themselves
> to pass it on to the next generation. You know, to emulate that with
> their own children, to be loving and thoughtful and raise them well, to
> be with them when they need it.

Pete Sr.'s advice further links the spirit of generativity to the later
adulthood goal of integrity:

> I believed that each of my three sons needed or deserved guidance,
> and direction, and someone they could relate to. I wanted that for my
> family. I was brought up with my father knowing where we were, and

we knew where they were in turn. So I just made sure I was around when my kids needed me; if they didn't need me, I was around *anyhow*.

When my son becomes a father, I hope he'll be the same way. I'd like him to know where his kids are at all times. I hope he takes time out to smell the roses along the way with his kids. You can't just let the kids grow up without you because one day they're going to wonder, "Who are you?" You got to be on top of their situation, you got to be with them, *you got to grow up with them,* you got to always spend time with them. You won't come this way a second time . . .

I have no regrets in my life. I wouldn't change my life one minute. If I lived all over again, I don't know what I would do different. We were close to them; I like to think we're still close.

Pete Sr., from his current vantage point of living with a life-threatening illness and recovering from a recent heart attack, is able to see the life cycle with simple clarity. Good fathering, it seems, really does matter. It matters over a long time, over a lifetime, and even over generations.

Afterword:
Parent-Supportive Workplace Policies

Father-child relationships, like mother-child relationships, have moral significance. By this I mean that fathers directly experience the moral claims of their children and are personally obligated to their children. Erikson's psychoethical model suggests to me that our society is now providing men with unprecedented opportunities for parental generativity. However, parents in our society frequently find that their primary obligations—breadwinning and childrearing—are in conflict. Fathers as well as mothers face numerous practical moral dilemmas because they cannot do all the things they ought to do. Conflicts in moral obligations are inevitable, of course, but they seem to be unnecessarily intensified for parents in our society at the present time.

Erikson's model further suggests that our society is now in the midst of a crisis of societal generativity. As Browning (1973) originally observed, "Modern man . . . cares so poorly for that which he creates" (p. 164). This study has demonstrated that men's parental generativity is linked to their own subsequent societal generativity, but, of course, parental generativity is also linked to some degree to the prior generations' successful societal generativity. In brief, today's fathers need the support of yesterday's fathers. But many social institutions today are headed by persons who were never significantly involved in childrearing. Quite simply, some (but certainly not all) administrators and policy makers are handicapped in their ability to be genuinely societally generative. Some supervisors seem to find it all too easy to ignore the suffering that their bottom-line policies often inflict on employees who are parents, and many of them literally do not realize that this suffering inevitably trickles down to employees' children.

To be sure, all social entities and public policies may function in ways that hinder parental generativity. Even institutions and policies that aim to promote men's ability to be good fathers may be administered by nongenerative adults whose decisions regularly inhibit good fathering. Consider the coach or administrator of a children's athletic league who makes decisions by the criteria of what is most likely to promote his or her own sense of importance and trouble-free existence, instead of considering what is most likely to promote children's self-esteem and sense of competence. Consider a government welfare policy that functions to pressure an unemployed father to "abandon" his family so that they will qualify for public assistance. Although public policy reform is greatly needed, however, many of the most common and serious problems derive from *workplace* policies that are insensitive to family life. The workplace is especially significant simply because the majority of fathers and mothers work outside of the home. Thus the principal nonhome setting in which most fathers and mothers live their lives is the workplace. New policies must be developed to make the workplace more favorable to a workforce that includes childrearing fathers and mothers (Scarr, Phillips, & McCartney, 1989; Stipek & McCrosky, 1989; for annotated bibliography see Hansen, 1991).

The first step toward workplace policies that promote parenting, paradoxically, is to affirm both women's and men's commitment to their work. Parenting involves, and women's and men's psychosocial health may require, both breadwinning and childrearing. "To assume that work is central in the life of a man while home is central in the life of a woman," as reviews of prior research conclude, "is contrary to the data" (Crosby, 1991, p. 122). The work lives of men and women must not be casually derogated as they occasionally are by otherwise sensitive and perceptive students of family life. It must also be understood that, to the degree that our society requires trade-offs between work and family life, the arrival of a child intensifies the cross-pressures in *both* men's and women's relationship to the workplace. New mothers typically experience additional pulls toward the workplace, for instance, because of their increased "need for additional income in order to support children, but they are pulled away from the work force by their primary responsibilities for child care" (Couture, 1991, p. 42). Typical new fathers also want to be home with their children, but they also know that now, more than ever, others depend upon them to be successful "hunter-gatherers." As all the case studies showed, each new father felt a new weight added to the importance of his success in providing for his family economically as well as psychosocially. Balancing these counterforces is not simple because one of the first obligations of any parent is to provide adequate food, clothing, shelter, and medical care and, in our society, competition for these resources is keen.

The next step is to change the actual environment of the workplace, not just our attitudes about what constitutes men's and women's work. As Okin (1989) has forcefully argued, "employers must . . . be required to make positive provision for the fact that most workers, for differing lengths of time in their working lives, are also parents" (p. 176). The primary need is for policies that function to increase the flexibility of all parents' jobs. If both husbands and wives are given more control over their work schedules and work environments, they will be able to create a better balance between work and family life. A number of policy options should be explored.

Infant-care leave (both paternity and maternity leave) is one of the policy options that has the potential to enhance fathers' and mothers' control over their work-family balance and promote the quality of their parent-child relations. A gender-inclusive parental leave policy provides the flexibility needed to allow fathers as well as mothers to form early, firm bonds with their newborn or newly adopted infants, and to allow infants to become equally bonded with both of their parents. Such gender-fair policies also implicitly promote the understanding that both fathers and mothers are their children's care givers from day one. Unfortunately, both unpaid short-term paternity leave and paid short-term maternity leave are options that are still only available to a minority of workers (Biller & Solomon, 1986; Curran, 1989; Hyde & Essex, 1991; Pleck, 1988, 1990; Schroeder, 1989; Zigler & Frank, 1988).

Alternative work schedules are even more essential. Fathers will be able to come up to the mothers' level of childrearing participation if *both* are able to make the necessary adjustments in their work schedules to allow some degree of shift work. Some of the policy options include: flex-time or flexible hours, flexible sick-leave options to care for a family member, job sharing, compressed work week, permanent part-time jobs with pro-rated benefits and without loss of advancement opportunities, and flex-place or home-based work (for reviews and evaluations, see Christensen, 1989; Deutschman, 1991; Parke, 1981; Pleck, 1986, 1990; Staines & Pleck, 1983; Schroeder, 1989).

Family support services should be added to the workplace to counterbalance workplace structures that make it difficult for men and women to bring their childrearing concerns, let alone their children, to the workplace. Generative policies and programs are needed to build an ethic of parental generativity into the structure of the workplace. Some of the policy options for improving the workplace include: new-father and new-mother classes; support groups for fathers and for mothers; affordable, quality on-site nurseries; paid leaves for family-related matters; on-site or near-site childcare centers; and daycare as a standard benefit (for a review of family-supportive policies and services, see Galinsky, Hughes, & David, 1990; Zedeck & Mosier, 1990; for an evaluation study, see McBride, 1990).

Looking into the future, there is reason for optimism. Many of today's parents learned to question conventional values before they came of age; they have the skills necessary to convince policymakers of the detrimental consequences of today's nongenerative policies. One could also hope that, as more childrearing fathers and mothers launch their children from the nest and begin to take on positions of broader social responsibility, they will draw on their generative values to promote positive institutional changes. This is happening very slowly, but it is happening. Such societally generative administrators are hastening the approval of enlightened workplace policies which acknowledge the priority of family life and promote the common good of children, parents, and society as a whole. Ethically, in terms of parental generativity, such policies recognize that *"parents,* rather than *mothers,"* are responsible for their children's care and development (Couture, 1991, p. 183). Ethically, in terms of societal generativity, such policies recognize that we are *all* parents of *all* children.

References

Index

References

Aaronson, H. C., & Glienke, C. F. (1963). A study of the incidence of pregnancy following adoption. *Fertility and Sterility, 14*, 547–553.

Altus, W. (1965). Birth order and academic primogeniture. *Journal of Personality and Social Psychology, 2*, 872–876.

—— (1966). Birth order and its sequelae. *Science, 151*, 44–49.

American Fertility Society (1988). *Infertility: An overview.* Birmingham: The American Fertility Society.

Ammerman, N. (March 1990). "Women, men, and families in changing congregations: A research agenda." Unpublished paper, Emory University, Atlanta, GA.

Angell, R. (1972). *The summer game.* New York: Penguin Books.

Anthony, E. J., & Benedek, T. (eds.) (1970). *Parenthood: Its psychology and psychopathology.* Boston: Little, Brown.

Aral, S., & Cates, W. (1983). The increasing concern with infertility: Why now? *Journal of the American Medical Association, 250*(17), 2327–2331.

Atchley, R. C. (1989). Demographic factors and adult psychological development. In K. W. Schaie & C. Schooler (eds.), *Social structure and aging: Psychological processes* (pp. 11–34). Hillsdale, NJ: Erlbaum.

Baier, A. C. (1987). The need for more than justice. *Canadian Journal of Philosophy, 13*, 41–56.

Bailyn, L. (1977). Involvement and accommodation in technical careers: An inquiry into the relations to work at mid-career. In J. Van Maanen (ed.), *Organizational careers: Some new perspectives* (pp. 109–132). London: Wiley.

—— (1978). Accommodation of work to family. In R. Rapoport, R. N. Rapoport, & J. M. Bumstead (eds.), *Working couples* (pp. 159–174). New York: Harper & Row.

Baker, B. O., Hardyck, C. D., & Petrinovich, L. F. (1966). Weak measurement vs. strong statistics: An empirical critique of S. S. Stevens' proscriptions on statistics. *Educational and Psychological Measurement, 26*, 291–309.

Barber, B. J. (1987). Marital quality, parental behaviors, and adolescent self-esteem. *Family Perspective, 21*, 244–268.

Barnett, R., & Baruch, G. (1978). *The competent woman: Perspectives on development*. New York: Irvington.

————— (1987). Determinants of fathers' participation in family work. *Journal of Marriage and the Family, 49,* 29–40.

————— (1988). Correlates of fathers' participation in family work. In P. Bronstein & C. P. Cowan (eds.), *Fatherhood today: Men's changing role in the family* (pp. 66–78). New York: Wiley.

Barringer, F. (1991, November 3). A drop in births is reported, and the recession is blamed. *New York Times,* pp. 1, 18.

Baruch, G., & Barnett, R. (1981). Fathers' participation in the care of their preschool children. *Sex Roles, 7*(10), 1043–1055.

————— (1986). Fathers' participation in family work and children's sex-role attitudes. *Child Development, 57,* 1210–1223.

Baumrind, D. (1973). The development of instrumental competence through socialization. In A. Pick (ed.), *Minnesota symposium on child psychology* (Vol. 7, pp. 3–46). Minneapolis: University of Minnesota Press.

————— (1978). Reciprocal rights and responsibilities in parent-child relations. *Journal of Social Issues, 34,* 179–189.

————— (1980). New directions in socialization research. *American Psychologist, 35,* 639–652.

Bell, A. (1969). Role modeling of fathers in adolescence and young adulthood. *Journal of Counseling Psychology, 16,* 30–35.

Belsky, J. (1979a). Mother-father-infant interaction: A naturalistic observational study. *Developmental Psychology, 15,* 601–607.

————— (1979b). The interrelation of parental and spousal behavior during infancy in traditional nuclear families: An exploratory analysis. *Journal of Marriage and the Family, 41,* 62–68.

————— (1981). Early human experience: A family perspective. *Developmental Psychology, 17*(1), 3–23.

————— (1984). The determinants of parenting: A process model. *Child Development, 55,* 83–96.

————— (1986). Transition to parenthood. *Medical Aspects of Human Sexuality, 20*(9), 56–59.

————— (1991). Parental and nonparental child care and children's socioemotional development: A decade in review. In A. Booth (ed.), *Contemporary families: Looking forward, looking back* (pp. 122–140). Minneapolis: National Council on Family Relations.

Belsky, J., Gilstrap, B., & Rovine, M. (1984). The Pennsylvania infant and family development project: Stability and change in mother-infant and father-infant interaction in a family setting at one, three, and nine months. *Child Development, 55,* 692–705.

Belsky, J., & Isabella, R. (1985). Marital and parent-child relationships in family of origin and marital change following the birth of a baby: A retrospective analysis. *Child Development, 56,* 342–349.

Belsky, J., & Pensky, E. (1988). Marital change across the transition to parenthood. *Marriage and Family Review, 12,* 133–156.

Belsky, J., & Rovine, M. (1990). Patterns of marital change across the transition to parenthood: Pregnancy to three years postpartum. *Journal of Marriage and the Family, 52,* 5–19.

Belsky, J., Youngblade, L., Rovine, M., & Volling, B. (1991). Patterns of marital change and parent-child interaction. *Journal of Marriage and the Family, 53,* 487–498.

Berger, D. M. (1980). Couples' reaction to male infertility and donor insemination. *American Journal of Psychiatry, 137,* 1047–1049.

Berman, P. W., & Pedersen, F. A. (eds.) (1987). *Men's transitions to parenthood: Longitudinal studies of early family experience.* Hillsdale, NJ: Erlbaum.

Bieri, J. (1960). Parental identification, acceptance of authority, and within-sex differences in cognitive behavior. *Journal of Abnormal and Social Psychology, 60*(1), 76–79.

Biller, H. (1971). *Father, child, and sex role: Paternal determinants of personality development.* Lexington, MA: Lexington Books.

———— (1974). *Paternal deprivation: Family, school, sexuality, and society.* Lexington, MA: Heath.

———— (1981). The father and sex role development. In M. Lamb (ed.), *The role of the father in child development* (2nd ed., pp. 319–358). New York: Wiley.

Biller, H., & Meredith, D. (1974). *Father power.* New York: David McKay.

Biller, H., & Solomon, R. (1986). *Child maltreatment and paternal deprivation: A manifesto for research, prevention, and treatment.* Lexington, MA: Heath.

Bing, E. (1963). The effect of child-rearing practices on the development of differential cognitive abilities. *Child Development, 34,* 631–648.

Block, J. (1971). *Lives through time.* Berkeley: Bancroft.

Block, J. H., Block, J., & Gjerde, P. (1986). The personality of children prior to divorce: A prospective study. *Child Development, 57,* 827–840.

Bloom-Feshbach, J. (1979). "The beginnings of fatherhood." Ph.D. diss., Yale University, New Haven.

Booth, A. (ed.) (1991). *Contemporary families: Looking forward, looking back.* Minneapolis: National Council on Family Relations.

Boyd, R. D. (1966). "Self-description questionnaire." Unpublished. University of Wisconsin, Madison.

———— (1974). "A report of the methodology for the study of ego identity." Unpublished. University of Wisconsin, Madison.

Bozett, F. W. (1985). Male development and fathering throughout the life cycle. *American Behavioral Scientist, 29,* 41–54.

Bradley, R. (1985). Fathers and the school-age child. In S. M. H. Hanson and F. W. Bozett (eds.). *Dimensions of fatherhood* (pp. 141–169). Beverly Hills: Sage.

Brim, O. G., & Kagan, J. (1980). *Constancy and change in human development.* Cambridge, MA: Harvard University Press.

Brint, S., & Karabel, J. (1989). *The diverted dream: Community colleges and the promise of educational opportunity in America, 1900–1985.* New York: Oxford University Press.

Brody, G., Pillegrini, A., & Sigel, I. (1986). Marital quality and mother-child and father-child interactions with school-aged children. *Developmental Psychology, 22*(3), 291–296.

Bronfenbrenner, U. (1961). Some familial antecedents of responsibility and leadership in adolescents. In B. Bass & L. Petrullo (eds.), *Leadership and interpersonal behavior* (pp. 239–271). New York: Holt, Rinehart & Winston.

Bronfenbrenner, U., & Crouter, A. (1982). Work and family through time and space. In S. B. Kamerman & C. D. Hayes (eds.), *Families that work: Children in a changing world* (pp. 39–83). Washington, D.C.: National Academy Press.

Bronstein, P. (1988a). Father-child interaction: Implications for gender-role socialization. In P. Bronstein & C. P. Cowan (eds.), *Fatherhood today: Men's changing role in the family* (pp. 107–124). New York: Wiley.

Bronstein, P. (1988b). Marital and parenting roles in transition: An overview. In P. Bronstein & C. P. Cowan (eds.), *Fatherhood today: Men's changing role in the family* (pp. 3–10). New York: Wiley.

Brooks-Gunn, J., & Furstenberg, F. (1989). Long-term implications of fertility-related behavior and family formation on adolescent mothers and their children. In K. Kreppner & R. Lerner (eds.), *Family systems and life-span development* (pp. 319–339). Hillsdale, NJ: Erlbaum.

Browning, D. S. (1973). *Generative man: Psychoanalytic perspectives.* Philadelphia: Westminster Press.

Browning, D. S., & Browning, C. (1991, August 7–14). The church and the family crisis: A new love ethic. *The Christian Century,* pp. 746–749.

Bureau of the Census (August 1984). Educational attainment in the United States: March 1981 and 1980. *Current Population Reports,* Series P-20, No. 390.

———— (July 1990). Child care arrangements: Who's minding the kids? Child care arrangements: Winter, 1986–1987. *Current Population Reports,* Series P-70, No. 20.

———— (December 1990). Household and family characteristics: March 1990 and 1989. *Current Population Reports,* Series P-20, No. 447.

Camilli, G., & Hopkins, K. (1978). Applicability of chi-square to two-by-two contingency tables with small expected cell frequencies. *Psychological Bulletin, 85*(1), 163–167.

Capps, D. (1983). *Life cycle theory and pastoral care.* Philadelphia: Fortress Press.

———— (1984). Erikson's life-cycle theory. *Religious Studies Review, 10* (2), 120–127.

Carter, H., & Glick, P. (1970). *Marriage and divorce: A social and economic study.* Cambridge, MA: Harvard University Press.

Cath, S. (1986). Fathering from infancy to old age: A selective overview of recent psychoanalytic contributions. *The Psychoanalytic Review, 73,* 469–479.

Cath, S., Gurwitt, A. R., & Gunsberg, L. (eds.) (1989). *Fathers and their families.* Hillsdale, NJ: Analytic Press.

Cavan, R., & Ranck, K. (1938). *The family and the Depression.* Chicago: University of Chicago Press.

Chapman, F. S. (1987, February 16). Executive guilt: Who's taking care of the children? *Fortune, 115*(4), pp. 30–37.

Christensen, K. (1989). *Flexible staffing and scheduling in U.S. corporations* (Research bulletin no. 240). New York: The Conference Board.

Chodorow, N. (1978). *The reproduction of mothering.* Berkeley: University of California Press.

———— (1981). Oedipal asymmetries and heterosexual knots. In S. Cox (ed.), *Female psychology: The emerging self* (2nd ed., pp. 228–247). New York: St. Martin's Press.

Clarke-Stewart, K. A. (1980). The father's contribution to children's cognitive and social development in early childhood. In F. A. Pederson (ed.), *The father-infant relationship* (pp. 111–146). New York: Praeger.

———— (1988). Parents' effects on children's development: A decade of progress. *Journal of Applied Developmental Psychology, 9,* 41–84.

Cochran, W. G. (1952). The chi-square test of goodness of fit. *Annals of Mathematical Statistics, 23,* 315–345.

Cohen, J. (1965). Some statistical issues in psychological research. In B. B. Wolman (ed.), *Handbook of clinical psychology* (pp. 95–121). New York: McGraw-Hill.

———— (1977). *Statistical power analysis for the behavioral sciences.* New York: Academic Press.

Cohen, R., & Weissman, S. (1984). The parenting alliance. In R. Cohen, B. Cohler, & S. Weissman (eds.), *Parenthood* (pp. 39–49). New York: Guilford.

Colby, A., Kohlberg, L., Gibbs, J., & Lieberman, M. (1983). A longitudinal study of moral judgment. *Monographs of the Society for Research on Child Development, 48* (1–2), 1–124.

Commons, M. L., Armon, C., Richards, F., & Schrader, D. (1989). A multidomain study of adult development. In M. Commons, J. Sinnott, F. Richards, & C. Armon (eds.), *Adult development*. Vol. 1: *Comparisons and applications of developmental models* (pp. 33–56). New York: Praeger.

Conger, R. D., Elder, G. H., Lorenz, F. O., Conger, K. J., Simons, R. L., Whitbeck, L. B., Huck, S., & Melby, J. N. (1990). Linking economic hardship to marital quality and instability. *Journal of Marriage and the Family, 52,* 643–656.

Couture, P. D. (1991). *Blessed are the poor?* Nashville: Abingdon.

Côté, J. E., & Levine, C. (1988). The relationship between ego identity status and Erikson's notions of institutionalized moratoria, value orientation stage, and ego dominance. *Journal of Youth and Adolescence, 17,* 81–99.

Coverman, S. (1985). Explaining husband's participation in domestic labor. *The Sociological Quarterly, 26,* 81–97.

Coverman, S., & Sheley, J. H. (1986). Change in men's housework and child-care time, 1965–1975. *Journal of Marriage and the Family, 48,* 413–422.

Cowan, P. A. (1988). Becoming a father: A time of change, and opportunity for development. In P. Bronstein & C. P. Cowan (eds.), *Fatherhood today: Men's changing role in the family* (pp. 13–35). New York: Wiley.

Cowan, C. P., & Bronstein, P. (1988). Fathers' roles in the family: Implications for research, intervention, and change. In P. Bronstein & C. P. Cowan (eds.), *Fatherhood today: Men's changing role in the family* (pp. 341–347). New York: Wiley.

Cowan, C. P., & Cowan, P. A. (1987). Men's involvement in parenthood: Identifying the antecedents and understanding the barriers. In P. W. Berman and F. A. Pedersen (eds.), *Men's transitions to parenthood: Longitudinal studies of early family experience* (pp. 145–174). Hillsdale, NJ: Erlbaum.

—— (1988). Who does what when partners become parents: Implications for men, women, and marriage. *Marriage and Family Review, 12,* 105–131.

Cox, M., Owen, M., Lewis, J., & Henderson, V. K. (1989). Marriage, adult adjustment, and early parenting. *Child Development, 60,* 1015–1024.

Craig, M. M., & Glick, S. J. (1964). *A manual of procedures for application of the Glueck Prediction Table.* New York: New York City Youth Board.

Crosby, F. J. (1991). *Juggling: The unexpected advantages of balancing career and home for women and their families.* New York: Free Press.

Crouter, A. C., & Crowley, M. S. (1990). School-age children's time alone with fathers in single- and dual-earner families: Implications for the father-child relationship. *Journal of Early Adolescence, 10,* 296–312.

Crouter, A. C., MacDermid, S., McHale, S. M., & Perry-Jenkins, M. (1990).

Parental monitoring and perceptions of children's school performance and conduct in dual- and single-earner families. *Developmental Psychology, 26,* 649–657.

Crouter, A. C., Perry-Jenkins, M., Huston, T., & McHale, S. (1987). Processes underlying father involvement in dual-earner and single-earner families. *Developmental Psychology, 23,* 431–440.

Curran, A. (1989, January). Why men don't take paternity leaves. *Health, 21*(2), 49, 86.

DeAngelis, T. (1990, February). Clinicians can aid infertile couples. *APA Monitor, 21*(2), 24–25.

DeFrain, J. (1979). Androgynous parents tell who they are and what they need. *Family Coordinator, 28,* 237–243.

Demos, J. (1970). *A little commonwealth: Family life in Plymouth Colony.* New York: Oxford University Press.

Deutsch, H. (1944). *The psychology of women* (vol. I). New York: Grune & Stratton.

Deutschman, A. (May 20, 1991). Pioneers of the new balance. *Fortune,* pp. 60–68.

Dickie, J. (1987). Interrelationships within the mother-father-infant triad. In P. W. Berman & F. A. Pedersen (eds.), *Men's transitions to parenthood* (pp. 113–144). Hillsdale, NJ: Erlbaum.

Dickstein, S., & Parke, R. D. (1988). Social referencing in infancy: A glance at fathers and marriage. *Child Development, 59,* 506–511.

Dielman, T., Barton, K., & Cattell, R. (1977). Relationships among family attitudes and child rearing practices. *Journal of Genetic Psychology, 130,* 105–112.

DiMaggio, P., & Mohr, J. (1985). Cultural capital, educational attainment, and marital selection. *American Journal of Sociology, 90*(6), 1231–1261.

Djerassi, C. (June 1, 1990). Fertility awareness: Jet-age rhythm method? *Science, 248,* 1061–1062.

Dorland's Medical Dictionary (1988). 27th ed. Philadelphia: W. B. Saunders.

Dornbusch, S., Ritter, P., Leiderman, P., Roberts, D., & Fraleigh, M. (1987). The relation of parenting style to adolescent school performance. *Child Development, 58,* 1244–1257.

Douvan, E. (1963). Employment and the adolescent. In F. I. Nye & L. W. Hoffman (eds.), *The employed mother in America* (pp. 142–164). Chicago: Rand McNally.

Doyle, D. (1985). "Theories and concepts of parenting." Unpublished. Boston University, Boston.

Dublin, L., & Amelar, R. (1972). Sexual causes of male infertility. *Fertility and Sterility, 23,* 579.

Easterbrooks, M. A., & Goldberg, W. A. (1984). Toddler development in the family: Impact of father involvement and parenting characteristics. *Child Development, 55,* 740–752.

————— (1985). Effects of early maternal employment on toddlers, mothers, and fathers. *Developmental Psychology, 21*(5), 774–783.

Edwards, C. N. (1973). Interactive styles and social adaptation. *Genetic Psychology Monographs, 87,* 123–174.

Ehrhardt, A., Ince, S., & Meyer-Bahlburg, F. L. (1981). Career aspiration and gender role development in young girls. *Archives of Sexual Behavior, 10,* 281–298.

Eiduson, B., & Alexander, J. (1978). The role of children in alternative family styles. *Social Issues, 34,* 149–167.

Elder, G. H. (1969). Occupational mobility, life patterns, and personality. *Journal of Health and Social Behavior, 10,* 308–323.

————— (1974). *Children of the Great Depression.* Chicago: University of Chicago Press.

————— (1975). Age differentiation and the life course. *Annual Review of Sociology, 1,* 165–190.

————— (1979). Historical change in life patterns and personality. In P. B. Baltes & O. G. Brim (eds.), *Life-span development and behavior* (vol. 2, pp. 117–159). New York: Academic Press.

Elder, G. H., & Caspi, A. (1988). Economic stress in lives: Developmental perspectives. *Journal of Social Issues, 44,* 25–45.

Elder, G. H., Liker, J. K., & Cross, C. (1984). Parent-child behavior in the Great Depression: Life course and intergenerational influences. In P. B. Baltes & O. G. Brim, Jr. (eds.), *Life-span development and behavior* (vol. 6, pp. 109–157). New York: Academic Press.

Elmer-Dewitt, P. (September 30, 1991). Making babies [review of infertility treatments]. *Time,* pp. 11–16.

Erikson, E. H. (1950). *Childhood and society.* New York: Norton.

————— (1958). *Young man Luther.* New York: Norton.

————— (1959). *Identity and the life cycle.* New York: Norton.

————— (1964). *Insight and responsibility: Lectures on the ethical implications of psychoanalytic insight.* New York: Norton.

————— (1967). Memorandum on youth. *Daedalus, 3,* 860–870. Reprinted in D. Bell (ed.) (1968), *Toward the year 2000* (pp. 228–238). Boston: Houghton Mifflin.

————— (1968). *Identity, youth and crisis.* New York: Norton.

————— (1969a). Adult stage: Generativity versus stagnation. In R. Evans (ed.), *Dialogue with Erik Erikson* (pp. 50–53). New York: Dutton.

————— (1969b). *Gandhi's truth: On the origins of militant nonviolence.* New York: Norton.

————— (1969c). On student unrest: Remarks on receiving the Foneme Prize. Second International Convention on Human Formation from Adoles-

cence to Maturity, Foneme Institute, Milan. Reprinted in S. Schlein
(ed.) (1987), *A way of looking at things: Selected papers of Erik H.
Erikson, 1930–1980* (pp. 685–698). New York: Norton.

———— (1970). Reflections on the dissent of contemporary youth. *Daedalus,*
97(1), 154–176. Reprinted (1970) in *International Journal of Psycho-
analysis, 51*(1), 11–21.

———— (1974). *Dimensions of a new identity.* New York: Norton.

———— (1975). *Life history and the historical moment.* New York: Norton.

———— (1976). Reflections on Dr. Borg's life cycle. *Daedalus, 105*(2), 1–28.

———— (ed.) (1978). *Adulthood.* New York: Norton.

———— (1980a). Elements of a psychoanalytic theory of psychosocial develop
ment. In S. Greenspan & G. Pollack (eds.), *The course of life: Psychoanalytic contributions toward understanding personality development* (vol. 1,
pp. 11–61). Washington, DC: NIMH, U.S. Government Printing Office.

———— (1980b). On the generational cycle. *International Journal of Psycho-
analysis, 61,* 213–223.

———— (1982). *The life cycle completed.* New York: Norton.

Erikson, E. H., & Erikson, J. M. (1981). On generativity and identity. *Harvard
Educational Review, 51*(2), 249–269.

Erikson, E. H., Erikson, J. M., & Kivnick, H. (1986). *Vital involvement in
old age: The experience of old age in our time.* New York: Norton.

Erikson, J. M. (1988). *Wisdom and the senses: The way of creativity.* New
York: Norton.

Evans, R. I. (1969). *Dialogue with Erik Erikson.* New York: E. P. Dutton.

Everett, W. (1977). Vocation and location: An exploration in the ethics of
ethics. *Journal of Religious Ethics, 5,* 91–114.

Farkas, G. (1976). Education, wage rates, and the division of labor between
husband and wife. *Journal of Marriage and the Family, 39,* 473–483.

Farrell, M. P., & Rosenberg, S. D. (1981). *Men at midlife.* Boston: Auburn
House.

Featherman, D. L. (1980). Schooling and occupational careers: Constancy
and change in worldly success. In O. G. Brim & J. Kagan (eds.), *Constancy and change in human development* (pp. 675–738). Cambridge,
MA: Harvard University Press.

Feldman, S. S., & Gehring, T. M. (1988). Changing perceptions of family
cohesion and power across adolescence. *Child Development, 59,*
1034–1045.

Feldman, S. S., Nash, S. C., & Aschenbrenner, B. G. (1983). Antecedents
of fathering. *Child Development, 54,* 1628–1636.

Feldman, S. S., & Wentzel, K. R. (1990). The relationship between parenting
styles, sons' self-restraint, and peer relations in early adolescence. *Journal of Early Adolescence, 10,* 439–454.

Feldman, S. S., Wentzel, K. R., & Gehring, T. M. (1988). A comparison of the views of mothers, fathers, and preadolescents about family cohesion and power. *Journal of Family Psychology, 3,* 33–52.

Ferree, M. M. (1980). Working class feminism: A consideration of the consequences of employment. *Sociology Quarterly, 21,* 173–184.

Feuer, G. (1983). "The psychological impact of infertility on the lives of men." Ph.D. dissertation, University of Pennsylvania, Philadelphia.

Field, T. (1978). Interaction behaviors of primary versus secondary caretaker fathers. *Developmental Psychology, 14,* 183–184.

Finkelhor, D., Gelles, R. J., Hotaling, G. T., & Strauss, M. A. (eds.) (1983). *The dark side of families: Current family violence research.* Beverly Hills: Sage.

Fivush, R., Gray, J., Hamond, N., & Fromhoff, F. (1986). "Two studies of early autobiographical memory." Report 12, The Emory Cognition Project, Department of Psychology, Emory University, Atlanta.

Flanagan, C. A. (1990a). Change in family work status: Effects on parent-adolescent decision making. *Child Development, 61,* 163–177.

Flanagan, C. A. (1990b). Families and schools in hard times. *New Directions for Child Development, 46,* 7–26.

Frank, S., Hole, C. B., Jacobson, S., Justkowski, R., & Huyck, M. (1986). Psychological predictors of parents' sense of confidence and control and self- versus child-focused gratifications. *Developmental Psychology, 22,* 348–355.

Frank, S., Avery, C., & Laman, M. (1988). Young adults' perceptions of their relationships with their parents: Individual differences in connectedness, competence, and emotional autonomy. *Developmental Psychology, 24,* 729–737.

Franz, C. E., McClelland, D., Weinberger, J. (1991). Childhood antecedents of conventional social accomplishment in midlife adults: A 36-year prospective study. *Journal of Personality and Social Psychology, 60,* 586–595.

Freud, A. (1952). The role of the teacher. *Harvard Educational Review, 22,* 229–234.

Friedenberg, E. (1969). Current patterns of generational conflict. *Journal of Social Issues, 25*(2), 21–38.

Friedman, H. J. (1982). The challenge of divorce to adequate fathering: The peripheral father in marriage and divorce. *Psychiatric Clinics of North America, 5*(3), 565–580.

Furstenberg, F. F. (1985). Sociological ventures in child development. *Child Development, 56,* 281–288.

Galinsky, E., Hughes, D., & David, J. (1990). Trends in corporate family-supportive policies. *Marriage and Family Review, 15*(3–4), 75–94.

Gallup, G. (1983). *Opinions about motherhood: A Gallup/Levi's maternity wear national poll.* San Francisco: Levi Strauss.

——— (1991). *The Gallup Poll: Public opinion 1990*. Wilmington, DE: Scholarly Resources.

Gardner, P. (1975). Scales and statistics. *Review of Educational Research, 45,* 43–57.

Gedo, J. E., & Goldberg, A. (1973). *Models of the mind: A psychoanalytic theory*. Chicago: University of Chicago Press.

Gerson, K. (1985). *Hard choices: How women decide about work, career, and motherhood*. Berkeley: University of California Press.

Gilligan, C. (1982). *In a different voice*. Cambridge, MA: Harvard University Press.

Gilligan, C., Ward, J. V., & Taylor, J. (1988). *Mapping the moral domain: A contribution of women's thinking to psychological theory and education*. Cambridge, MA: Harvard University Press.

Glazer, E. S. (1990). *The long-awaited stork: A guide to parenting after infertility*. Lexington, MA: Lexington Books.

Glueck, E. (1966). Distinguishing delinquents from pseudodelinquents. *Harvard Educational Review, 36,* 119–130.

Glueck, S., & Glueck, E. (1950). *Unravelling juvenile delinquency*. New York: Commonwealth Fund.

——— (1962). *Family environment and delinquency*. London: Routledge & Kegan Paul.

——— (1964). *Ventures in criminology: Selected papers*. Cambridge, MA: Harvard University Press.

——— (1968). *Delinquents and nondelinquents in perspective*. Cambridge, MA: Harvard University Press.

Goldberg, W. A., & Easterbrooks, M. A. (1984). The role of marital quality in toddler development. *Developmental Psychology, 20,* 504–514.

Goldstein, H. S. (1982). Fathers' absence and cognitive development of 12- to 17-year-olds. *Psychological Reports, 51,* 843–848.

Goodman, L. A., & Kruskal, W. H. (1954). Measures of association for cross-classification. *Journal of the American Statistical Association, 49,* 732–764.

——— (1972). Measures of association for cross classification: 4. Simplification of asymptotic variances. *Journal of the American Statistical Association, 67,* 415–421.

Gottfried, A. E., & Gottfried, A. W. (eds.) (1988). *Maternal employment and children's development: Longitudinal research*. New York: Plenum.

Greenberg, M., & Morris, N. (1974/1982). Engrossment: The newborn's impact upon the father. In S. Cath, A. Gurwitt, & J. M. Ross (eds.), *Father and child: Clinical and developmental considerations* (pp. 87–100). Boston: Little, Brown.

Greenberger, E. & O'Neil, R. (1990). Parents' concerns about their child's development: Implications for fathers' and mothers' well-being and attitudes toward work. *Journal of Marriage and the Family, 52,* 621–635.

Gronseth, E. (1978). Work sharing: A Norwegian example. In R. Rapoport and R. N. Rapoport (eds.), *Working couples* (pp. 108–121). St. Lucia, Australia: University of Queensland Press.

Grossman, F. K. (1987). Separate and together: Men's autonomy and affiliation in the transition to parenthood. In P. W. Berman & F. A. Pedersen (eds.), *Men's transitions to parenthood: Longitudinal studies of early family experience* (pp. 89–112). Hillside, NJ: Erlbaum.

Grossman, F. K. (1988). Strain in the transition to parenthood. *Marriage and Family Review, 12*(3–4), 85–104.

Grossman, F. K., Eichler, L., & Winickoff, S. (1980). *Pregnancy, birth, and parenthood.* San Francisco: Jossey-Bass.

Grossman, F. K., Pollack, W. S., & Golding, E. (1988). Fathers and children: Predicting the quality and quantity of fathering. *Developmental Psychology, 24,* 82–91.

Grotevant, H., & Cooper, C. (1986). Individuation in family relationships: A perspective on individual differences in the development of identity and role-taking skill in adolescence. *Human Development, 29,* 82–100.

Gurwitt, A. R. (1982). Aspects of prospective fatherhood. In S. Cath, A. R. Gurwitt, & J. Ross (eds.), *Father and child: Developmental and clinical perspectives* (pp. 275–299). Boston: Little, Brown.

Gutmann, D. L. (1975). Parenthood: Key to the comparative psychology of the life cycle? In N. Datan & L. Ginsberg (eds.), *Life span developmental psychology* (pp. 167–184). New York: Academic Press.

Hansen, G. L. (1991). Balancing work and family: A literature and resource review. *Family Relations, 40,* 348–353.

Hanson, S. M. H. (1986). Parent-child relationships in single-father families. In R. A. Lewis & R. E. Salt (eds.), *Men in families* (pp. 181–195). Beverly Hills: Sage.

Hanson, S. M. H., & Bozett, F. W. (1987). Fatherhood: A review and resources. *Family Relations, 36,* 333–340.

Haug, M. (1972). Social-class measurement: A methodological critique. In G. Thielbar & S. Feldman (eds.), *Issues in social inequality* (pp. 429–451). Boston: Little, Brown.

Hauser, S., Jacobson, A., Noam, G., & Powers, S. (1983). Ego development and self-image complexity in early adolescence. *Archives of General Psychiatry, 40,* 325–332.

Hawley, G. (1984). *Construction and validation of an Eriksonian measure of psychosocial development.* Ph.D. diss. University of North Carolina, Chapel Hill.

———— (1988). *Measures of psychosocial development.* Odessa, FL: Psychological Assessment Resources.

Hayghe, H. (February 1986). Rise in mothers' labor force activity includes those with infants. *Monthly Labor Review,* pp. 43–45.

Hazan, C., & Shaver, P. (1990). Love and work: An attachment-theoretical perspective. *Journal of Personality and Social Psychology, 59,* 270–280.

Heath, D. H. (1976). Competent fathers: Their personalities and marriages. *Human Development, 19,* 26–39.

———— (1977). Academic predictors of adult maturity and competence. *Journal of Higher Education, 48,* 613–632.

———— (1978). What meaning and effects does fatherhood have for the maturing of professional men? *Merrill-Palmer Quarterly, 24*(4), 265–278.

———— (May 1989). "Review of Research on Psychological Maturity and Competence." Paper presented at the Visiting Scholars Conference of the College of Education and Psychology, North Carolina State University, Raleigh, NC.

Heath, D. H., with Heath, H. E. (1991). *Fulfilling lives: Paths to maturity and success.* San Francisco: Jossey-Bass.

Heilbrun, A. B., Harrell, S. N., & Gillard, B. (1967). Perceived childrearing attitudes of fathers and cognitive control in daughters. *Journal of Genetic Psychology, 111,* 29–40.

Hennig, M., & Jardim, A. (1977). *The managerial woman.* Garden City, NY: Anchor.

Hetherington, E. M. (1972). Effects of father absence on personality development in adolescent daughters. *Developmental Psychology, 7,* 313–326.

Hetherington, E. M., & Frankie, G. (1967). Effects of parental dominance, warmth, and conflict on imitation in children. *Journal of Personality and Social Psychology, 6,* 119–125.

Hock, E. (1980). Working and nonworking mothers and their infants: A comparative study of maternal caregiving characteristics and infant social behavior. *Merrill-Palmer Quarterly, 26,* 79–101.

Hoffman, L. W. (1983). Increased fathering: Effects on the mother. In M. Lamb (ed.), *Fatherhood and family policy* (pp. 167–190). Hillsdale, NJ: Erlbaum.

———— (1984). Work, family, and the socialization of the child. In R. D. Parke (ed.), *Review of child development research: The family* (Vol. 7, pp. 223–282). Chicago: University of Chicago Press.

Hoffman, M. L. (1970). Moral development. In P. H. Mussen (ed.), *Carmichael's manual of child psychology* (3rd ed., vol. 2, pp. 261–359). New York: Wiley.

———— (1975). Altruistic behavior and the parent-child relationship. *Journal of Personality and Social Psychology, 31,* 937–943.

———— (1981). The role of the father in moral internalization. In M. Lamb (ed.), *The role of the father in child development* (pp. 359–378). New York: Wiley.

Hogan, D. P. (1987). Demographic trends in human fertility, and parenting across the life span. In J. Lancaster, J. Altmann, A. Rossi, & L. R. Sherrod (eds.), *Parenting across the life span: Biosocial dimensions* (pp. 315–349). New York: Aldine.

Hollingshead, A. B. (1959). "Two-factor index of social position." Working paper, Department of Sociology, Yale University, New Haven.

—— (1975). "Four-factor index of social status." Working paper, Department of Sociology, Yale University, New Haven.

Hollingshead, A. B., & Redlich, F. C. (1958). *Social class and mental illness.* New York: Wiley.

Honzik, M. (1967). Environmental correlates of mental growth: Prediction from the family setting at 21 months. *Child Development, 38,* 337–364.

Hoover-Dempsey, K. V., Bassler, O. C., & Brissie, J. S. (1987). Parent involvement: Contributions of teacher school socio-economic status, and other school characteristics. *American Educational Research Journal, 24,* 417–435.

Houser, R., & Seligman, M. (1991). Differences in coping strategies used by fathers of adolescents with disabilities and fathers of adolescents without disabilities. *Journal of Applied Rehabilitation Counseling, 22*(1), 7–10.

Humphrey, M. (1977). Sex differences in attitude to parenthood. *Human Relations, 30,* 737–749.

Huston-Stein, A., & Higgins-Trenk, A. (1978). Development of females from childhood through adulthood: Career and feminine role orientations. In P. Baltes (ed.), *Life-span development and behavior* (Vol. 1, pp. 257–296). New York: Academic.

Hyde, J. S., & Essex, M. J. (eds.) (1991). *Parental leave and child care: Setting a research and policy agenda.* Philadelphia: Temple University Press.

Irvine, J. J. (1990). *Black students and school failure: Policies, practices, and prescriptions.* New York: Praeger.

Jacobson, G., & Ryder, R. G. (1969). Parental loss and some characteristics of the early marriage relationship. *American Journal of Orthopsychiatry, 39,* 779–787.

Jencks, C., Smith, M., Acland, H., Bane, M. J., Cohen, D., Gintis, H., Heyns, B., & Michelson, S. (1972). *Inequality: A reassessment of the family and schooling in America.* New York: Basic Books.

Johnson, M. (1975). Fathers, mothers, and sex typing. *Sociological Inquiry, 45,* 15–26.

Johnson, S., & Lobitz, G. (1974). The personal and marital adjustment of parents as related to observed child deviance and parenting behaviors. *Journal of Abnormal Child Psychology, 2,* 193–207.

Jones, L. Y. (1980). *Great expectations: America and the baby boom generation.* New York: Coward, McCann & Geoghegan.

Juster, F. T. (1985). A note on recent changes in time use. In F. T. Juster & F. P. Stafford (eds.), *Time, goods, and well-being* (pp. 313–332). Ann Arbor: Institute for Social Research.

Juster, F. T., Courant, P., Duncan, G., Robinson, J., & Stafford, F. (1978). *Time use in economic and social accounts.* Ann Arbor: Inter-University Consortium for Political and Social Research.

Kagan, J. (1958). The concept of identification. *Psychological Review, 65,* 296–305.

Kanter, R. M. (1977). *Work and family life in the United States: A critical review and agenda for research and policy.* New York: Russell Sage Foundation.

Kemper, T., Reichler, M. (1976). Marital satisfaction and conjugal power as determinants of intensity and frequency of rewards and punishments administered by parents. *Journal of Genetic Psychology, 129,* 221–234.

Kerlinger, F., & Pedhazur, E. (1973). *Multiple regression in behavioral research.* New York: Holt, Rinehart & Winston.

Kirk, H. D. (1985). *Adoptive kinship: A modern institution in need of reform.* Port Angeles, WA: Ben-Simon Publications.

Kleinbaum, D., & Kupper, L. (1978). *Applied regression analysis and other multivariable methods.* North Scituate, MA: Duxbury Press.

Koestner, R., Franz, C. E., & Weinberger, J. (1990). The family origins of empathic concern: A 26-year longitudinal study. *Journal of Personality and Social Psychology, 58(4),* 709–717.

Kogos, J. (1991). *The impact of family structure on moral reasoning: A correlational study.* B.A. honors thesis, Department of Psychology, Emory University, Atlanta.

Kohlberg, L. (1963). Moral development and identification. In H. W. Stevenson (ed.), *Child psychology: 62nd yearbook of the National Society for the Study of Education* (pp. 277–332). Chicago: University of Chicago Press.

Kohlberg, L., & Ryncarz, R. (1990). Beyond justice reasoning: Moral development and consideration of a seventh stage. In C. N. Alexander & E. J. Langer (eds.), *Higher stages of human development: Perspectives on adult growth* (pp. 191–207). New York: Oxford University Press.

Kohlberg, L., Ricks, D., & Snarey, J. (1984). Childhood development as a predictor of adaptation in adulthood. *Genetic Psychology Monographs, 110,* 91–172.

Kohn, M. (1977). *Class and conformity: A study in values.* Chicago: University of Chicago Press.

——— (1980). Job complexity and adult personality. In N. Smelser & E. H. Erikson (eds.), *Themes of work and love in adulthood* (pp. 193–210). Cambridge, MA: Harvard University Press.

Komarovsky, M. (1940). *The unemployed man and his family.* New York: Columbia University Press.

Kotre, J. (December 20, 1975). Generative humanity. *America,* pp. 434–437.

——— (1984) *Outliving the self: Generativity and the interpretation of lives.* Baltimore: Johns Hopkins University Press.

Kotre, J. & Hall, E. (1990). *Seasons of life: Our dramatic journey from birth to death.* Boston: Little, Brown.

Kotelchuck, M. (1976). The infant's relationship to the father: Experimental evidence. In M. E. Lamb (ed.), *The role of the father in child development* (1st ed., pp. 329–344). New York: Wiley.

Kraft, A. D., Palombo, J., Mitchell, D., Dean, C., Meyers, S., & Schmidt, A. (1980). The psychological dimensions of infertility. *American Journal of Orthopsychiatry, 50*(4), 618–622.

Lamb, E. J., & Leurgans, S. (1979). Does adoption affect subsequent fertility? *Transactions of Pacific Coast Obstetrics and Gynecology, 46,* 37–43.

Lamb, M. E. (1977). Father-infant and mother-infant interaction in the first year of life. *Child Development, 48,* 167–181.

——— (ed.) (1981). *The role of the father in child development* (2nd ed.). New York: Wiley.

——— (ed.) (1982). *Nontraditional families: Parenting and child development.* Hillsdale, NJ: Erlbaum.

——— (ed.) (1986). *The father's role: Applied perspectives.* New York: Wiley-Interscience.

Lamb, M. E., & Easterbrooks, M. A. (1981). Individual differences in parental sensitivity: Origins, components, and consequences. In M. E. Lamb and L. R. Sherrod (eds.), *Infant social cognition: Empirical and theoretical considerations* (pp. 127–153). Hillsdale, NJ: Erlbaum.

Lamb, M. E., & Elster, A. B. (1985). Adolescent mother-infant-father relationships. *Developmental Psychology, 21*(5), 768–773.

Lamb, M. E., Hwang, C., Broberg, A., Brookstein, F., et al. (1988). The determinants of parental involvement in primiparous Swedish families. *International Journal of Behavioral Development, 11,* 433–449.

Lamb, M. E., & Oppenheim, D. (1989). Fatherhood and father-child relationships: Five years of research. In S. Cath, A. R. Gurwitt, & L. Gunsberg (eds.), *Fathers and their families* (pp. 11–26). Hillsdale, NJ: Analytic Press.

Lamb, M. E., Owen, M. T., & Chase-Lansdale, L. (1979). The father-daughter relationship: Past, present, future. In C. B. Kopp & M. Kirkpatrick (eds.), *Becoming female* (pp. 89–112). New York: Plenum.

Lamb, M. E., & Sagi, A. (eds.) (1983). *Fatherhood and family policy.* Hillsdale, NJ: Erlbaum.

Lamb, M. E., Pleck, J., Charnov, E., & Levine, J. (1987). A biosocial perspective on paternal behavior and involvement. In J. Lancaster, J. Altmann, A. Rossi, & L. R. Sherrod (eds.), *Parenting across the life span: Biosocial dimensions* (pp. 111–142). New York: Aldine De Gruyter.

Lamb, M. E., Pleck, J., & Levine, J. (1985). The role of the father in child development: The effects of increased paternal involvement. In B. S. Lahey & A. E. Kazdin (eds.), *Advances in clinical child psychology* (vol. 8, pp. 229–266). New York: Plenum.

Landecker, W. (1960). Class boundaries. *American Sociological Review, 25,* 868–877.

Landy, F., Rosenberg, B. G., & Sutton-Smith, B. (1969). The effect of limited father absence on cognitive development. *Child Development, 40,* 941–944.

LaRossa, R. (1983). The transition to parenthood and the social reality of time. *Journal of Marriage and the Family, 45*(3), 579–589.

LaRossa, R. & LaRossa, M. M. (1981). *Transition to parenthood: How infants change families.* Beverly Hills: Sage.

Lasser, V. (1986). "The relationship between ego development and perceptions of parent behavior in adolescent girls." Ph.D. diss., Northwestern University, Evanston, IL.

Lasser, V., & Snarey, J. (1989). Ego development and perceptions of parent behavior in adolescent girls: A qualitative study of the transition from high school to college. *Journal of Adolescent Research, 4*(3), 319–355.

Laub, J. H., & Sampson, R. J. (1988). Unraveling families and delinquency: A reanalysis of the Gluecks' data. *Criminology, 26*(3), 355–380.

Lee, C. (1991). Parenting as discipleship. *Journal of Psychology and Theology, 19*(3), 268–277.

Lee, L., & Snarey, J. (1988). The relationship between ego and moral development: A theoretical review and empirical analysis. In D. Lapsley & C. F. Power (eds.), *Self, ego, and identity: Integrative perspectives* (pp. 130–150). New York: Springer-Verlag.

Lein, L. (1979). Male participation in home life: Impact of social supports and breadwinner responsibility on the allocation of tasks. *The Family Coordinator, 29,* 489–496.

Leone, C. & Richards, M. (1989). Classwork and homework in early adolescence: The ecology of achievement. *Journal of Youth and Adolescence, 18,* 531–548.

Levant, R., & Kelly, J. (1989). *Between father and child: How to become the kind of father you want to be.* New York: Penguin Books.

LeVine, R. A. (1988). Human parental care: Universal goals, cultural strategies, individual behavior. In R. A. LeVine, P. M. Miller, & M. Maxwell West (eds.). *Parental behavior in diverse societies* (pp. 3–12). San Francisco: Jossey-Bass.

LeVine, R. A., & White, M. (1987). Parenthood in social transformation. In J. Lancaster, J. Altmann, A. Rossi, & L. Sherrod (eds.), *Parenting across the life span: Biosocial dimensions* (pp. 271–293). New York: Aldine de Gruyter.

Levinson, D. J. (1978). *The seasons of a man's life.* New York: Ballantine.

——— (1986). A conception of adult development. *American Psychologist, 41*(1), 3–13.

Levy, F. (1987). *Dollars and dreams: The changing American income distribution.* New York: Russell Sage.

Levy-Shiff, R., & Israelashvili, R. (1988). Antecedents of fathering: Some further exploration. *Developmental Psychology, 24*(3), 434–440.

Levy-Shiff, R., Goldshmidt, I., & Har-Even, D. (1991). Transition to parenthood in adoptive families. *Developmental Psychology, 27,* 131–140.

Lewis, O. (1959). *Five families.* New York: Basic Books.

——— (1964). *Pedro Martinez: A Mexican peasant and his family.* New York: Vintage.

——— (1969). *A death in the Sanchez family.* New York: Vintage.

Lewis, M., & Rosenblum, L. A. (1974). *The effect of the infant on its caregiver.* New York: Wiley.

Lewis, R. S. (1990). Mercury program. *Academic American Encyclopedia* (vol. 13, pp. 307–308). Danbury, CT: Collier.

Lickona, T. (1983). *Raising good children.* New York: Bantam Books.

Liker, J. K., & Elder, G. H. (1983). Economic hardship and marital relations in the 1930s. *American Sociological Review, 48,* 343–359.

Linden, E. (August 15, 1988). While back in Boston. *Time,* pp. 16–17.

Logan, R. (May 1987). "Parenthood and the development of intimacy and generativity." Unpublished. Northwestern University, Evanston, IL.

Longman, P. (June 1985). Justice between generations. *The Atlantic Monthly,* pp. 73–81.

Lorenz, F. O., Conger, R. D., Simons, R. L., Whitbeck, L. B., & Elder, G. H. (1991). Economic pressure and marital quality: An illustration of the method variance problem in the causal modeling of family processes. *Journal of Marriage and the Family, 53,* 375–388.

Lozoff, M. (1974). Fathers and autonomy in women. In R. Knudsen (ed.), *Women and success* (pp. 103–109). New York: Morrow.

McBride, B. A. (1989). Stress and fathers' parental competence: Implications for family life and parent educators. *Family Relations, 38,* 385–389.

——— (1990). The effects of parent education/play group program on father involvement in child rearing. *Family Relations, 39,* 250–256.

McCall, R. B. (1977a). Challenges to a science of developmental psychology. *Child Development, 48,* 333–344.

——— (1977b). Childhood IQ's as predictors of adult educational and occupational status. *Science, 197,* July 29, 482–483.

—— (1984). Developmental changes in mental performance: The effect of the birth of a sibling. *Child Development, 55,* 1317–1321.

Maccoby, E. (1990). Gender and relationships: A developmental account. *American Psychologist, 45,* 513–520.

Maccoby, E., & Martin, J. A. (1983). Socialization in the context of the family: Parent-child interaction. In E. M. Hetherington (ed.), *Handbook of child psychology: Socialization, personality and social development* (vol. 4, pp. 1–102). New York: Wiley.

McDermott, J. (January 3, 1990). Juggling job, family, leads to frustration; looking for a better balance at work (Griggs-Anderson poll). *Oregonian,* (4th ed., Living Section), p. F01.

MacDermid, S. M., Huston, T., & McHale, S. (1990). Changes in marriage associated with the transition to parenthood: Individual differences as a function of sex-role attitudes and changes in the division of household labor. *Journal of Marriage and the Family, 52,* 475–486.

MacDonald, K., & Parke, R. D. (1984). Bridging the gap: Parent-child play interaction and peer interactive competence. *Child Development, 55,* 1265–1277.

—— (1986). Parent-child physical play: The effects of sex and age of children and parents. *Sex Roles, 15*(7–8), 367–378.

Mackey, W. C. (1985). *Fathering behaviors: The dynamics of the man-child bond.* New York: Plenum.

MacKinnon, L. P. (1991). Love and labor: Balancing work and family. *Ridgeview Insight, 12*(2), 4–11.

McLoyd, V. C. (1989). Socialization and development in a changing economy: The effects of paternal job and income loss on children. *American Psychologist, 44,* 293–302.

—— (1990). The impact of economic hardship on Black families and children: Psychological distress, parenting, and socioemotional development. *Child Development, 61,* 311–346.

MacNab, T. (1985). "Infertility and men: A study of change and adaptive choices in the lives of involuntarily childless men." Ph.D. dissertation, The Fielding Institute, Santa Barbara, CA.

Mahlstedt, P. (1985). The psychological component of infertility. *Fertility and Sterility, 43,* 335–346.

Mai, F. (1973). Conception after adoption: Myth or fact? *Medical Aspects of Human Sexuality, 7*(8), 162–168.

Maier, H. M. (1976). Human functioning as an interpersonal whole: The dimensions of affect, behavior, and cognition. In R. Lodge (ed.), *Teaching for competence in the delivery of direct services* (pp. 60–71). New York: Council on Social Work Education.

Manion, J. (1977). A study of fathers and infant caretaking. *Birth and the Family Journal, 4,* 174–179.

Marsh, H. (1991). Employment during high school: Character building or a subversion of academic goals. *Sociology of Education, 64,* 172–189.

Martin, C. D. (1980). *Beating the adoption game.* La Jolla, CA: Oak Tree Publications.

Matthews, R., & Matthews, A. (1986). Infertility and involuntary childlessness: The transition to nonparenthood. *Journal of Marriage and the Family, 48,* 641–649.

Mazor, M. (February 1979). Barren couples. *Psychology Today,* pp. 101–108.

———— (1980). Psychosexual problems of the infertile couple. *Medical Aspects of Human Sexuality, 15,* 32–49.

———— (1984). Emotional reactions to infertility. In M. Mazor and H. Simons (eds.), *Infertility: Medical, emotional, and social considerations* (pp. 23–35). New York: Human Sciences Press.

Mazor, M., & Simons, H. (eds.) (1984). *Infertility: Medical, emotional, and social considerations.* New York: Human Sciences Press.

Messina, K. E. (1984). "Erikson's last four stages of psychosocial development as perceived by young adults, middle-aged adults, and older adults." Ph.D. dissertation, George Washington University, Washington, DC.

Medical Research International (1990). In vitro fertilization-embryo transfer in the United States. *Fertility and Sterility, 53*(1), 13–20.

Menning, B. (1975). The infertile couple: A plea for advocacy. *Child Welfare, 54,* 454–460.

———— (1977). *Infertility: A guide for the childless couple.* New York: Prentice-Hall.

———— (1979). Counselling the infertile couple. *Contemporary OB/GYN, 13*(2), 1–8.

———— (1980). The emotional needs of the infertile couple. *Fertility and Sterility, 34,* 313–317.

Miller, B. C., & Sollie, D. L. (1980). Normal stresses during the transition to parenthood. *Family Relations, 29,* 459–465.

Miller-McLemore, B. J. (1989). Produce or perish: A feminist critique of generativity. *Union Seminary Quarterly Review, 43,* 201–221.

Minuchin, P. (1985). Families and individual development: Provocations from the field of family therapy. *Child Development, 56,* 289–302.

Mitchell, R., & Trickett, E. (1980). Task force reports: Social networks as mediators of social support. *Community Mental Health Journal, 16,* 27–44.

Moen, P., Kain, E., & Elder, G. (1983). Economic conditions and family life: Contemporary and historical perspectives. In R. Nelson & F. Skidmore (eds.), *American families and the economy: The high costs of living* (pp. 213–259). Washington, DC: National Academy Press.

Monsaas, J. A., & Engelhard, G. (1990). Home environment and the competitiveness of highly accomplished individuals in four talent fields. *Developmental Psychology, 26,* 264–268.

Montemayor, R., & Brownlee, J. R. (1987). Fathers, mothers, and adolescents: Gender-based differences in parental roles during adolescence. *Journal of Youth and Adolescence, 16,* 281–291.

Mortimer, J., Finch, M., Shanahan, M., & Ryu, S. (1992). Work experience, mental health, and behavioral adjustment in adolescence. *Journal of Research on Adolescence, 2,* 25–57.

Mosher, W. D., & Pratt, W. F. (1990). Fecundity and infertility in the United States, 1965–88. *Advance Data from Vital and Health Statistics of the National Center for Health Statistics, 192,* December 4, 1–7.

Moss, H. A., & Susman, E. J. (1980). Longitudinal study of personality development. In O. G. Brim & J. Kagan (eds.), *Constancy and change in human development* (pp. 530–595). Cambridge, MA: Harvard University Press.

Mussen, P. H. (1969). Early sex-role development. In D. A. Goslin (ed.), *Handbook of socialization theory and research* (pp. 707–731). New York: Rand McNally.

Mussen, P. H., & Distler, L. (1959). Masculinity, identification, and father-son relationships. *Journal of Abnormal and Social Psychology, 59,* 350–356.

——— (1960). Childrearing antecedents of masculine identification in kindergarten boys. *Child Development, 31,* 89–100.

Myers, J. K., & Straus, R. (1989). A sociological profile of August B. Hollingshead. *Sociological Inquiry, 59,* 1–6.

National Center for Health Statistics. (1982). Reproductive impairments among married couples: United States. *National Survey of Family Growth Series, 23*(11), December. Hyattsville, MD: U.S. Department of Health and Human Services.

——— (1987). Fecundity, infertility, and reproductive health in the United States, 1982. *National Survey of Family Growth Series, 23*(14), May. Hyattsville, MD: U.S. Department of Health and Human Services.

——— (1990a). Advance report of final marriage statistics, 1987. *Monthly Vital Statistics Report, 38*(12), suppl. 1, April 3, 1–23.

——— (1990b). Advance report of final divorce statistics, 1987. *Monthly Vital Statistics Report, 38*(12), suppl. 2, May 15, 1–19.

——— (1990c). Advance report of final natality statistics, 1988. *Monthly Vital Statistics Report, 39*(4), August 15, 1–48.

——— (1990d). Births, marriages, divorces, and deaths for 1989. *Monthly Vital Statistics Report, 38*(12), April 4, 1–20.

——— (1991a). Annual summary of births, marriages, divorces, and deaths:

United States, 1990. *Monthly Vital Statistics Report, 39*(13), August 28, 1–28.

———— (1991b). Advance report of final divorce statistics, 1988. *Monthly Vital Statistics Report, 39*(12), May 21, 1–20.

———— (1991c). Advance report of final marriage statistics, 1988. *Monthly Vital Statistics Report, 40*(4), August 26, 1–24.

———— (1991d). Births, marriages, divorces, and deaths for 1990. *Monthly Vital Statistics Report, 39*(12), April 8, 1–20.

Neisser, U. (1967). *Cognitive psychology.* New York: Appleton Century Crofts.

Neugarten, B. (1969). Continuities and discontinuities of psychological issues into adult life. *Human Development, 12,* 121–130.

———— (1979). Time, age, and the life cycle. *American Journal of Psychiatry, 136*(7), 887–893.

Norton, A., & Glick, P. (1986). One parent families: A social and economic profile. *Family Relations, 35*(1), 9–17.

Noyes, R., & Chapnick, E. (1964). Literature on psychology and infertility, *Fertility and Sterility, 15*(5), 543–558.

Oberg, J. E. (1990). Space exploration. *Academic American Encyclopedia* (vol. 18, pp. 120–121). Danbury, CT: Collier.

Okin, S. M. (1989). *Justice, gender, and the family.* New York: Basic Books.

Osherson, S. (1986). *Finding our fathers.* New York: Free Press.

Osofsky, H., & Culp, R. (1989). Risk factors in the transition to fatherhood. In S. Cath, A. R. Gurwitt, & L. Gunsberg (eds.), *Fathers and their families* (pp. 145–165). Hillsdale, NJ: Analytic Press.

Osofsky, J., & Osofsky, H. (1984). Psychological and developmental perspectives on expectant and new parenthood. In Ross D. Parke (ed.), *Review of child development research: The family* (vol. 7, pp. 372–397). Chicago: University of Chicago Press.

Parke, R. D. (1981). *Fathers.* Cambridge, MA: Harvard University Press.

Parke, R. D., & Beitel, A. (1988). Disappointment: When things go wrong in the transition to parenthood. *Marriage and Family Review, 12*(3–4), 221–265.

Parke, R. D., MacDonald, K., Burks, V. M., Bhavnagri, N., Barth, J., & Beitel, A. (1989). Family and peer systems: In search of the linkages. In K. Kreppner & R. M. Lerner (eds.), *Family systems and life-span development* (pp. 65–92). Hillsdale, NJ: Erlbaum.

Parke, R. D., & Tinsley, B. R. (1981). The father's role in infancy: Determinants of involvement in caregiving and play. In M. E. Lamb (ed.), *The role of the father in child development* (pp. 429–457). New York: Wiley.

Paul, E. (1991). *Adoption choices: A guide to national and international adoption resources.* Detroit: Visible Ink Press.

Pedersen, F. A. (1976). Does research on children reared in father-absent families yield information on father influences? *The Family Coordinator,* 25, 459–464.

———— (1980). Overview: Answers and reformulated questions. In F. A. Pedersen (ed.), *The father-infant relationship* (pp. 147–163). New York: Praeger.

———— (1987). Introduction: A perspective on research concerning fatherhood. In P. W. Berman & F. A. Pedersen (eds.), *Men's transitions to parenthood: Longitudinal studies of early family experience* (pp. 1–12). Hillsdale, NJ: Erlbaum.

Pedersen, F. A., Suwalsky, J., Cain, R. L., Zaslow, M. J., & Rabinovich, B. A. (1987). Paternal care of infants during maternal separations: Associations with father-infant interaction at one year. *Psychiatry, 50,* 193–205.

Peterson, B. E., & Stewart, A. J. (1990). Using personal and fictional documents to assess psychosocial development: A case study of Vera Brittain's generativity. *Psychology and Aging, 5*(3), 400–411.

Piediscalzi, N. (1973). Erik H. Erikson's contribution to ethics. *Journal of Religion and Health, 12*(2), 169–180.

Pita, D. (1986). "Identity, intimacy, and parents' agency and communion as predictors of parental generativity." Ph.D. diss., Boston University, Boston.

Piaget, J. (1967). *Six psychological studies.* New York: Vintage Books.

Platt, J. (1973). Infertile couples: Personality traits and self-ideal concept discrepancies. *Fertility and Sterility, 24,* 972.

Pleck, J. (1981). *The myth of masculinity.* Cambridge, MA: MIT Press.

———— (1983). Husbands' paid work and family roles: Current research issues. In H. Lopata and J. Pleck (eds.), *Research in the interweave of social roles.* Vol. 3: *Families and jobs* (pp. 251–333). Greenwich, CT: JAI Press.

———— (1985). *Working wives, working husbands.* Beverly Hills: Sage.

———— (1986). Employment and fatherhood: Issues and innovative policies. In M. E. Lamb (ed.), *The father's role: Applied perspectives* (pp. 385–412). New York: Wiley.

———— (1987). Dual-career families: A comment. *The Counseling Psychologist, 15,* 131–133.

———— (1988). Fathers and infant care leave. In E. F. Zigler & M. Frank (eds.), *The Parent Leave Crisis.* New Haven: Yale University Press.

———— (August 1990). "Family-supportive employer policies: Are they relevant to men?" Paper presented at the 98th Annual Convention of the American Psychological Association, Boston.

Porter, N. L., & Christopher, F. S. (1984). Infertility: Towards an awareness of a need among family life practitioners. *Family Relations, 33,* 309–316.

Potter, R. G., & Parker, M. P. (1964). Predicting the time required to conceive. *Population Studies, 18,* 99–116.

Powell, D. R. (1980). Personal social networks as a focus for primary prevention of child maltreatment. *Infant Mental Health Journal, 1,* 232–239.

Power, F. C., Power, A., & Snarey, J. (1988). Integrity and aging: Ethical, religious, and psychosocial perspectives. In D. Lapsley & F. C. Power (eds.), *Self, ego, and identity: Integrative approaches* (pp. 130–150). New York: Springer-Verlag.

Power, T. G., & Parke, R. D. (1984). Social network factors and the transition to parenthood. *Sex Roles, 10,* 949–972.

Power, T. G., & Shanks, J. A. (1989). Parents as socializers: Maternal and paternal views. *Journal of Youth and Adolescence, 18,* 203–220.

Powers, S., Hauser, S., Schwartz, J., Noam, G., & Jacobson, A. (1983). Adolescent ego development and family interaction: A structural developmental perspective. *New Directions for Child Development, 22,* 5–25.

Presser, H. B. (1988). Shift work and child care among young dual-earner American parents. *Journal of Marriage and the Family, 50,* 3–14.

——— (1989). Can we make time for children? The economy, work schedules, and child care. *Demography, 26,* 523–543.

Propper, A. M. (1972). The relationship of maternal employment to adolescent roles, activities, and parental relationships. *Journal of Marriage and the Family, 34,* 417–421.

Pruett, K. D. (1989). The nurturing male: A longitudinal study of primary nurturing fathers. In S. Cath, A. R. Gurwitt, & L. Gunsberg (eds.), *Fathers and their families* (pp. 389–405). Hillsdale, NJ: Analytic Press.

Quinton, D., & Rutter, M. (1985). Parenting behavior of mothers raised "in care." In A. R. Nicol (ed.), *Longitudinal studies in child psychology and psychiatry* (pp. 157–201). New York: Wiley.

Radin, N. (1972). Father-child interaction and the intellectual functioning of four-year-old boys. *Developmental Psychology, 6,* 353–361.

——— (1981a). Childrearing fathers in intact families, I: Some antecedents and consequences. *Merrill-Palmer Quarterly, 27*(4), 489–513.

——— (1981b). The role of the father in cognitive, academic, and intellectual development. In M. Lamb (ed.), *The role of the father in child development* (pp. 379–428). New York: Wiley.

——— (1982). Primary caregiving and role-sharing fathers. In M. Lamb (ed.), *Nontraditional families: Parenting and child development* (pp. 173–203). Hillsdale, NJ: Erlbaum.

——— (1986). The influence of fathers on their sons and daughters. *Social Work in Education, 8,* 77–91.

——— (1988). Primary caregiving fathers of long duration. In P. Bronstein &

C. P. Cowan (eds.), *Fatherhood today: Men's changing role in the family* (pp. 127–143). New York: Wiley.

—— (1991). Research findings concerning the influence of fathers on children: Statement given to the Select Committee on Children, Youth, and Families, House of Representatives, 102 Congress. In *Babies and briefcases: Creating a family-friendly workplace for fathers* (pp. 76–85). Washington, DC: U.S. Government Printing Office.

Radin, N. & Goldsmith, R. (1985). Caregiving fathers of preschoolers: Four years later. *Merrill-Palmer Quarterly, 31,* 375–383.

Radin, N. & Russell, G. (1983). Increased father participation and child development outcomes. In M. E. Lamb & A. Sagi (eds.), *Fatherhood and family policy* (pp. 191–218). Hillsdale, NJ: Erlbaum.

Radin, N., & Sagi, A. (1982). Childrearing fathers in intact families in Israel and the USA. *Merrill-Palmer Quarterly, 28*(1), 111–136.

Rapoport, R., & Rapoport, R. N. (1965). Work and family in contemporary society. *American Sociological Review, 30,* 381–394.

Ray, S. A., & McLoyd, V. C. (1986). Fathers in hard times: The impact of unemployment and poverty on paternal and marital relations. In M. Lamb (ed.), *The father's role: Applied perspectives* (pp. 339–383). New York: Wiley.

Rebelsky, F., & Hanks, C. (1971). Father's verbal interaction with infants in the first three months of life. *Child Development, 42,* 63–68.

Reuter, M. W., & Biller, H. B. (1973). Perceived paternal nurturance-availability and personality adjustment among college males. *Journal of Consulting and Clinical Psychology, 40,* 339–342.

Reynolds, H. T. (1977). *Analysis of nominal data.* Beverly Hills: Sage.

Ricks, S. (1985). Father-infant interactions: A review of empirical research. *Family Relations, 34,* 505–511.

Roazen, P. (1976). *Erik H. Erikson: The power and limits of a vision.* New York: Free Press.

Roberts, C. L., & Zuengler, K. L. (1985). The postparental transition and beyond. In S. M. H. Hanson & F. W. Bozett (eds.), *Dimensions of fatherhood* (pp. 196–216). Beverly Hills: Sage.

Robinson, J. P. (1977). *How Americans use time: A social-psychological analysis of everyday behavior.* New York: Praeger.

Roland, M. (1968). *Management of the infertile couple.* Springfield, IL: Thomas.

Rosenthal, R. (1990). How are we doing in soft psychology? *American Psychologist, 45,* 775–777.

Rosenthal, R., & Rosnow, R. (1984). Binomial effect-size display. In R. Rosenthal & R. Rosnow, *Essentials of behavioral research: Methods and data analysis* (pp. 208–211). New York: McGraw-Hill.

Rosenthal, R., & Rubin, D. (1979). A note on percent of variance explained in a measure of the importance of effects. *Journal of Applied Social Psychology, 9,* 395–396.

———— (1982). A simple general purpose display of magnitude of experimental effect. *Journal of Educational Psychology, 74*(2), 166–169.

Rosnow, R., & Rosenthal, R. (1988). Focused tests of significance and effect size estimation in counseling psychology. *Journal of Counseling Psychology, 35*(2), 203–208.

———— (1989). Statistical procedures and the justification of knowledge in psychological science. *American Psychologist, 44*(10), 1276–1284.

Ross, H., & Taylor, H. (1989). Do boys prefer daddy or his physical style of play? *Sex Roles, 20,* 23–33.

Ross, J. (1982). Mentorship in middle childhood. In S. Cath, A. R. Gurwitt, & J. Ross (eds.), *Father and child: Developmental and clinical perspectives* (pp. 243–252). Boston: Little, Brown.

Rossi, A. (1984). Gender and parenthood. *American Sociological Review, 49,* 1–19.

———— (1989). A life-course approach to gender, aging, and intergenerational relations. In K. W. Schaie & C. Schooler (eds.), *Social structure and aging: Psychological processes* (pp. 207–236). Hillsdale, NJ: Erlbaum.

Rubin, Z. (1982, June). Fathers and sons: The search for reunion. *Psychology Today,* pp. 23–33.

Russell, C. (1987). *100 predictions for the baby boom: The next 50 years.* New York: Plenum.

Russell, G. (1982a). *The changing role of fathers.* St. Lucia, Australia: University of Queensland Press.

———— (1982b). Highly participant Australian fathers: Some preliminary findings. *Merrill-Palmer Quarterly, 28*(1), 137–156.

———— (1982c). Shared-caregiving families: An Australian study. In M. Lamb (ed)., *Nontraditional families: Parenting and child development* (pp. 139–171). Hillsdale, NJ: Erlbaum.

———— (1985). Grandfathers: Making up for lost opportunities. In R. A. Lewis & R. E. Salt (eds.), *Men in families* (pp. 233–259). Beverly Hills: Sage.

———— (1986). Primary caretaking and role-sharing fathers. In M. Lamb (ed.), *The father's role: Applied perspectives* (pp. 29–57). New York: Wiley.

———— (1989). Work-family patterns and couple relationships in shared caregiving families. *Social Behaviour, 4,* 265–283.

Russell, G., & Radin, N. (1983). Increased paternal participation: The fathers' perspective. In M. E. Lamb & A. Sagi (eds.), *Fatherhood and family policy* (pp. 139–165). Hillsdale, NJ: Erlbaum.

Russell, G., & Russell, A. (1987). Mother-child and father-child relationships in middle childhood. *Child Development, 58,* 1573–1585.

Rutter, M. (1980). *Changing youth in a changing society.* Cambridge, MA: Harvard University Press.

Ryff, C., & Heincke, S. G. (1983). Subjective organization of personality in adulthood and aging. *Journal of Personality and Social Psychology, 44,* 807–816.

Ryff, C., & Migdal, S. (1984). Intimacy and generativity: Self-perceived transitions. *Signs, 9*(3), 470–481.

Sachs, B. E. (1983). "Paternal generativity: The influence of the transition into fatherhood on first-time fathers' relationships with their own fathers and their definitions of their generative identities." Ph.D. diss., University of Maryland, College Park.

Sagi, A. (1982). Antecedents and consequences of various degrees of paternal involvement in child-rearing: The Israeli Project. In M. Lamb (ed.), *Nontraditional families: Parenting and child development* (pp. 205–232). Hillsdale, NJ: Erlbaum.

Salt, R. (1982). "Perception of paternal and maternal touch and self-esteem in pre-adolescents." M.A. thesis, University of Maine, Orono.

——— (1991). Affectionate touch between fathers and preadolescent sons. *Journal of Marriage and the Family, 53,* 545–554.

Sandberg, D., Ehrhardt, A., Mellins, C., Ince, S., & Meyer-Bahlburg, H. (1987). The influence of individual and family characteristics upon career aspirations of girls during childhood and adolescence. *Sex Roles, 16,* 649–668.

Santrock, J. W. (1970). Influence of onset and type of paternal absence on the first four Eriksonian developmental crises. *Developmental Psychology, 3,* 273–274.

Scarr, S., Phillips, D., & McCartney, K. (1989). Working mothers and their families. *American Psychologist, 44,* 1402–1409.

Schroeder, P. (1989). Toward a national family policy. *American Psychologist, 44,* 1410–1413.

Schubert, J. B., Bradley-Johnson, S., & Nuttal, J. (1980). Mother-infant communication and maternal employment. *Child Development, 51,* 246–249.

Sears, R. R. (1970). Relation of early socialization experiences to self-concepts and gender role in middle childhood. *Child Development, 41,* 267–289.

Sears, R. R., Maccoby, E., & Levin, H. (1957). *Patterns of childrearing.* Evanston, IL: Row, Peterson.

Seginer, R. (1983). Parents' educational expectations and children's academic achievement: A literature review. *Merrill-Palmer Quarterly, 29,* 1–23.

Select Committee on Children, Youth, and Families (September 1989). *U.S. children and their families: Current conditions and recent trends, 1989.* Washington, D.C.: U.S. Government Printing Office.

———— (February 1990). *Children's well-being: An international comparison.* Washington, D.C.: U.S. Government Printing Office.

Sennett, R., & Cobb, J. (1972). *The hidden injuries of class.* New York: Random House.

Shep, M., & Ridley, J. (1965). *Public health and population change.* Pittsburgh, PA: University of Pittsburgh Press.

Silberman, M. A. (1989). "Family influences in the development of moral reasoning." Ph.D. diss., Northwestern University, Evanston, IL.

Silver, H. (1991). Fair Labor Standards Act. *Collier's encyclopedia* (vol. 9, pp. 528–530). New York: Macmillan.

Silverberg, S., & Steinberg, L. (1990). Psychological well-being of parents with early adolescent children. *Developmental Psychology, 26,* 658–666.

Simons, H. (1982). "Infertility as an emerging social concern." Ph.D. qualifying thesis, Heller Graduate School of Social Welfare, Brandeis University, Waltham, MA.

Simons, R. L., Whitbeck, L. B., Conger, R. D., & Melby, J. N. (1990). Husband and wife differences in determinants of parenting: A social learning and exchange model of parental behavior. *Journal of Marriage and the Family, 52,* 375–392.

Slade, M. (May 21, 1984). Looking at religion and babies. *New York Times,* p. B6.

Smelser, N., & Erikson, E. H. (1980). *Themes of work and love in adulthood.* Cambridge, MA: Harvard University Press.

Smith, L., & Sipchen, B. (August 12, 1990). Two-career families face dilemma in balancing work, home life: Telephone poll results. *Los Angeles Times,* pp. A1, A26, A28.

Smith, T. E. (1989). Mother-father differences in parental influence on school grades and educational goals. *Sociological Inquiry, 59,* 88–98.

Snarey, J. (1987). The vital aging of Eriksonian theory and of Erik H. Erikson [Review of *Vital involvements in old age* by Erik Erikson, Joan Erikson, and Helen Kivnick]. *Contemporary Psychology, 32*(11), 928–930.

———— (March 1988). Men without children. *Psychology Today,* pp. 61–62.

———— (1991). "Erikson, Erik H." In *St. James guide to biography* (p. 261). Chicago: St. James Press.

Snarey, J., Friedman, K., & Blasi, J. (1986). Sex role strain among kibbutz adolescents and adults: A developmental perspective. *Journal of Youth and Adolescence, 15,* 221–239.

Snarey, J., Kohlberg, L., & Noam, G. (1983). Ego development in perspective:

Structural stage, functional phase and cultural age-period models. *Developmental Review, 3,* 303–338.

Snarey, J., & Lydens, L. (1990). Worker equality and adult development: The kibbutz as a developmental model. *Psychology and Aging,* 5(1), 86–93.

Snarey, J., Son, L., Kuehne, V., Hauser, S., & Vaillant, G. (1987). The role of parenting in men's psychosocial development: A longitudinal study of early adulthood infertility and midlife generativity. *Developmental Psychology,* 23(3), 593–603.

Snarey, J. & Vaillant, G. E. (1985). How lower and working class youth become middle class adults: The association between ego mechanisms of defense and upward social mobility. *Child Development, 56,* 899–910.

Sollie, D. L., & B. C. Miller (1980). The transition to parenthood as a critical time for building family strengths. In N. Stinnett, B. Chesser, J. DeFrain, & P. Knaub (eds.), *Family strengths: Positive models for family life.* Omaha: University of Nebraska Press.

Speicher-Dubin, B. (1982). Relationships between parent moral judgment, child moral judgment and family interaction: A correlational study. *Dissertation Abstracts International, 43,* 1600B. (University Microfilms International Order no. 8223231)

Spencer, M. B., & Markstrom-Adams, C. (1990). Identity processes among racial and ethnic minority children in America. *Child Development, 61,* 290–310.

Stangel, J. (1979). *Fertility and conception.* New York: New American Library.

Steffensmeier, R. H. (1982). A role model of the transition to parenthood. *Journal of Marriage and the Family, 44,* 319–334.

Steinberg, L., & Dornbusch, S. (1991). Negative correlates of part-time employment during adolescence: Replication and elaboration. *Developmental Psychology, 27,* 304–313.

Steinberg, L., Elmen, J. D., & Mounts, N. (1989). Authoritative parenting, psychosocial maturity, and academic success among adolescents. *Child Development, 60,* 1424–1436.

Stierlin, H. (1974). *Separating parents and adolescents.* New York: Quadrangle.

Stipek, D., & McCroskey, J. (1989). Investing in children: Government and workplace policies for parents. *American Psychologist, 44,* 416–423.

Strauss, M. A. & Gelles, R. J. (1986). Societal change and change in family violence from 1975 to 1985 as revealed in two national surveys. *Journal of Marriage and the Family, 48,* 465–479.

Strauss, M. A., Gelles, R. J., & Steinmetz, S. K. (1980). *Behind closed doors: Violence in the American family.* Beverly Hills: Sage.

Strauss, W., & Howe, N. (1991). *Generations: The history of America's future, 1584 to 2069*. New York: William Morrow.

Sutton-Smith, B., & Rosenberg, B. G. (1970). *The sibling*. New York: Holt, Rinehart, & Winston.

Taymor, M. L. (1969). *The management of infertility*. Chicago: Thomas.

——— (1978). *Infertility*. New York: Grune & Stratton.

Tessman, L. (1982). A note of father's contribution to his daughter's way of loving and working. In S. Cath, A. R. Gurwitt, & J. Ross (eds.), *Father and child: Developmental and clinical perspectives* (pp. 219–238). Boston: Little, Brown.

——— (1989). Fathers and daughters: Early tones, later echoes. In S. Cath, A. R. Gurwitt & L. Gunsberg (eds.), *Fathers and their families* (pp. 197–223). Hillsdale, NJ: Analytic Press.

Thomas, E. (May 19, 1986). Growing pains at 40. *Time*, pp. 22–41.

Thomas, D. L., & Cornwall, M. (1991). Religion and family in the 1980s. In A. Booth (ed.), *Contemporary families* (pp. 265–274). Minneapolis: National Council on Family Relations.

Thompson, J. E. (1931/1946). *Algebra for the practical man*. New York: Van Nostrand.

——— (1931/1947). *Trigonometry for the practical man*. New York: Van Nostrand.

Tierney, J. (1983). The myth of the firstborn. *Science, 169,* 16.

Tinsley, B. R., & Parke, R. D. (1988). The role of grandfathers in the context of the family. In P. Bronstein & C. P. Cowan (eds.), *Fatherhood today: Men's changing role in the family* (pp. 236–250). New York: Wiley.

Tinsley, H. E., & Weiss, D. J. (1975). Interrater reliability and agreement of subjective judgments. *Journal of Counseling Psychology, 22*(4), 358–376.

Tipton, S. (1982). *Getting saved from the sixties: Moral meaning in conversion and cultural change*. Berkeley: University of California Press.

——— (September 20, 1985). Psychology of adulthood. [Review of *Outliving the self* by J. Kotre.] *Commonweal*, pp. 504–505.

Troyat, H. (ed.) (1967). *Tolstoy*. New York: Doubleday.

Turek, S. (1977). *Orthopaedics: Principles and their applications*. Philadelphia: Lippincott.

Vaillant, G. E. (1974). The natural history of male psychological health, II: Some antecedents of healthy adult adjustment. *Archives of General Psychiatry, 31,* 15–22.

——— (1977). *Adaptation to life*. Boston: Little, Brown.

——— (1978). Natural history of male psychological health: VI. Correlates of successful marriages and fatherhood. *American Journal of Psychiatry, 135,* 653–659.

Vaillant, G. E., & Milofsky, E. S. (1980). Natural history of male psychological health: IX. Empirical evidence for Erikson's model of the life cycle. *American Journal of Psychiatry, 137*(11), 1348–1359.

Vaillant, G. E., & Vaillant, C. 0. (1981). Natural history of male psychological health: X. Work as a predictor of positive mental health. *American Journal of Psychiatry, 138*(11), 1433–1440.

Vanek, J. (1974). Time spent in housework. *Scientific American, 231,* 116–120.

Volling, B., & Belsky, J. (1991). Multiple determinants of father involvement during infancy in dual-earner and single-earner families. *Journal of Marriage and the Family, 53,* 461–474.

Voydanoff, P. (1990). Economic distress and family relations: A review of the eighties. *Journal of Marriage and the Family, 52,* 1099–1115.

Waldrop, J. (October 1989). The adoption option [in 1986]. *American Demographics,* p. 11.

Warner, G. S. (1934). *"Pop" Warner's Book for Boys.* New York: Robert M. McBride.

Weiss, R. (1990). *Staying the course: The emotional and social lives of men who do well at work.* New York: Free Press.

Weller, S. (1991). "Growth of Little League baseball." Unpublished report. Williamsport, PA: Little League Baseball.

Whelpton, P., Campbell, A., & Patterson, T. (1966). *Fertility and family planning in the United States.* Princeton: Princeton University Press.

White, L., & Booth, A. (1985). The transition to parenthood and marital quality. *Journal of Family Issues, 6,* 435–449.

Whiting, B. B., & Whiting, J. W. M. (1975). *Children of six cultures: A psycho-cultural analysis.* Cambridge, MA: Harvard University Press.

Wicks, S. (1977). "The effects of non-conclusive infertility diagnosis on married couples: An exploratory study." M.A. thesis, Boston University School of Social Work, Boston.

Will, G. (October 30, 1991). Democrats may be asking: Are you better off today? [1990 Census Bureau data]. *Atlanta Journal,* p. A9.

Williams, E., Radin, N., & Allegro, T. (1992). Sex-role attitudes of adolescents reared primarily by their fathers: An 11-year follow-up. *Merrill-Palmer Quarterly, 38*(4).

Woods, M. B. (1972). The unsupervised child of the working mother. *Developmental Psychology, 6,* 14–25.

Worthington, E., & Buston, B. (1986). The marriage relationship during the transition to parenthood. *Journal of Family Issues, 7,* 443–473.

Wright, J. E. (1982). *Erikson: Identity and religion.* New York: Seabury.

Wright, J., Allard, M., Lecours, A., & Sabourin, S. (1989). Psychosocial distress and infertility: A review of controlled research. *International Journal of Fertility, 34*(2), 126–142.

Youniss, J., & Smollar, J. (1985). *Adolescent relations with mothers, fathers, and friends*. Chicago: University of Chicago Press.

Zajonc, R., & Markus, G. (1975). Birth order and intellectual development. *Psychological Review, 82,* 74–88.

Zaslow, M., Pedersen, F. A., Suwalsky, J., Rabinovich, B., & Cain, R. L. (1986). Fathering during the infancy period: Implications of the mother's employment role. *Infant Mental Health Journal, 7*(3), 225–233.

Zedeck, S., & Mosier, K. (1990). Work in the family and employing organization. *American Psychologist, 45,* 240–251.

Zigler, E. F., & Frank, M. (1988). *The parental leave crisis: Toward a national policy*. New Haven: Yale University Press.

Index

Note: Page numbers in italics indicate tables.